D1617063

SOCIAL RESEARCH AND SOCIAL REFORM

A. H. Halsey
Photo: Jeremy Grayson, © *Radio Times*, 1978.

SOCIAL RESEARCH AND SOCIAL REFORM

Essays in Honour of A. H. Halsey

Edited by

COLIN CROUCH AND ANTHONY HEATH

CLARENDON PRESS · OXFORD
1992

Oxford University Press, Walton Street, Oxford OX2 6DP
Oxford New York Toronto
Delhi Bombay Calcutta Madras Karachi
Petaling Jaya Singapore Hong Kong Tokyo
Nairobi Dar es Salaam Cape Town
Melbourne Auckland
and associated companies in
Berlin Ibadan

Oxford is a trade mark of Oxford University Press

Published in the United States
by Oxford University Press, New York

British Library Cataloguing in Publication Data
Data available

Library of Congress Cataloging in Publication Data
Social research and social reform: essays in honour of A.H. Halsey/
edited by Colin Crouch and Anthony Heath.
Includes bibliographical references and index.
1. Sociology—Research. 2. Social problems. 3. Social service.
4. Halsey, A. H. I. Halsey, A. H. II. Crouch, Colin. III. Heath,
A. F. (Anthony Francis)
HM48.S566 1992 301'.072—dc20 92–5581
ISBN 0–19–827854–3

Typeset by Hope Services (Abingdon) Ltd.
Printed and bound in
Great Britain by Bookcraft (Bath) Ltd,
Midsomer Norton, Avon

PREFACE

While it is often a mistake to interpret a scholar's work in terms of his personal biography, in the case of A. H. (Chelly) Halsey the mistake would be to ignore the meaning of his own background for his intellectual contribution. The clear profile of his life is stamped on the equally sharp profile of his academic work. It might seem strange for this to be true of someone, one of whose main aims has been to render sociology more scientific, empirical, quantitative. But that paradox is all part of the relationship between the man and his work.

His early experience of a strong, Christian family, membership of the skilled manual working class, opportunities for upward social mobility through grammar school education, and initial career as a public health inspector contain the kernel of much of what was to follow. This can be seen merely from the titles of some of his major works: *Social Class and Educational Opportunity* (1956); *Educational Priority* (1972); *Heredity and Environment* (1977); *Origins and Destinations* (1980); *English Ethical Socialism* (1988)—but from the detailed content of many more, especially his Reith Lecture series of 1977, *Change in British Society*, the book form of which has so far run to three editions.

Halsey is both English and Anglican, drawing his values not from abstract principles but from the lived experience of family, community, faith, and nation: it was a specifically *English* ethical socialism that he described in his recently published book; and *Change in British Society* is rooted in cultural understanding as well as empirical demography. At the same time, however, two other essential Halsey components are a passionate commitment to the cause of racial equality and an intellectual commitment to comparative study.

It was the offer of further educational opportunities to men in the armed services towards the end of the Second World War that gave Halsey his own unexpected opportunity to acquire a university education, as one of that remarkable generation of post-war adult students at the London School of Economics and Political Science. Thereafter, to his surprise, Halsey's life was lived in universities: London, Liverpool, Birmingham, and, since 1962, Oxford. They became his new community and he became their active citizen, participating intensively in university governance and devoting two of his major works to their affairs: *The British Academics* (1971) and *The Decline of Donnish Dominion* (1992).

Although Halsey has long been a 'sociologist's sociologist', defining and proselytizing for the discipline as such, and defending it against the prejudice and ignorance of its enemies, the experience of the old B.Sc. (Econ.) degree at the LSE gave him an appreciation of the social sciences as a totality, and of sociology's place within a wider world of economics, political science, and philosophy—and of statistics. It was at the School that Halsey acquired the respect for evidence, for 'political arithmetic' as he likes to term it, that has informed all his subsequent work and which has led him to urge often reluctant younger generations of sociologists to explore increasingly sophisticated quantitative methodologies.

Loyal to the values of both his community of origin and that of his LSE contemporaries, he is deeply committed to the political cause of democratic socialism. In some respects, then, Halsey has shared the conviction of the LSE's founders, Beatrice and Sidney Webb, that the socialist case will be 'proved' by empirical research, that laying bare the facts will demonstrate the extent of an inequality or an injustice so that the British people will be moved to act. This is perhaps one of the ways in which the passion for reform is reconciled with respect for research and evidence. But there is another side to Halsey that renders his politics very different from 'scientific socialism', whether of the Fabian or Marxist variety. Just as his Christian convictions embody a strong hint of the willing acceptance of discomfort of the English Puritan tradition, so he has always been willing to accept uncomfortable evidence.

For example, he was among the few sociologists on the political left prepared to accept the possibility of evidence of a genetic component in intelligence, a possibility that might seem to have challenged his egalitarian concerns. He neither allowed his convictions the luxury of turning their back on the evidence, nor did he fall into the simple positivist trap. Evidence that some people (even some ethnic groups) might be genetically less capable of high achievement than others was for him in no way evidence that there should therefore be less redistributive social and educational policy. What do we do if a member of our family has a handicap?, he asked. Do we therefore do less for them? No. We devote extra resources to bring them up to the standard of the rest; and that is what should therefore happen within the national or indeed international family. In this way the socialism born of lived experience in family and community can accept and coexist with a genuine openness to disappointing evidence in a manner difficult for that which derives itself from abstract principles or which claims itself to be a science.

The combination of social concern, practicality, and pursuit of advanced statistical methods has made Halsey a natural choice when there is a need for someone with a policy commitment but a proper understanding of advanced and sophisticated research. Of primary importance here was the directorship of the Oxford Department of Social and Administrative Studies, which he held from 1962 until the retirement in 1990 to which this book is a memento. He here pursued his three central preoccupations: the advancement of social policy (through policy-oriented research and the training of social workers); the furtherance of the study of sociology within the University of Oxford; and the increasing sophistication of empirical research. He was always working against the Oxford grain: a university that does not automatically accept such things as social work training as part of its educational mission; the British university that has done least to integrate sociology within its undergraduate provision; and which is among the least willing to accept modern quantitative methods within the social sciences.

Outside Oxford, British governments have benefited from, though not necessarily welcomed, his advice. He was a natural choice as adviser to Anthony Crosland when the latter was Secretary of State for Education and Science during the creative years of the move to comprehensive education, 1965–8—a cause of which Halsey had been among the first post-war advocates. He was responsible for the research on patterns of recruitment into the civil service that was an important component of the Fulton Report of 1968.

Also during those years he directed experimental government

projects on community development and educational priority areas. This was quintessential Halsey: a concern for educational opportunity in deprived areas rooted, not in centrally imposed social engineering but in 'bottom-up' activity based on the human resources of local communities; and all within a framework of action research. The social scientific evaluation of the projects ran alongside and interacted with their practical development. (Most of the results are summarized in *Educational Priority* (1972).)

More surprising was for Halsey to be presenting advice to Mrs Margaret Thatcher when she held the education portfolio in the early 1970s. The theme was far more Halsey than Thatcher: nursery education. Again there was the aim of improving educational chances within the context of the local community. The Halsey vision of pre-school education was not the child-dumping form of that institution that the recipient of his advice has chosen in recent years to stigmatize, but a site for encouraging the active engagement of parents in their children's education within a school that is a resource for their community, not an alien force that tries to influence their little barbarians for a few hours each day while they themselves are kept beyond the school gate.

There was little call for advice embodying Halsey's values from governments in the Britain of the 1980s; but some other groups saw a growing need for it. Halsey was among the major contributors to the Archbishop of Canterbury's report *Faith in the City* (1985), which was both one of the most notable commentaries on social policy of that decade and one of the main indicators of a revival of Christian social concern, a movement with which Halsey had been associated long before it became popular again.

Halsey's policy involvements have also been international—evidence of the cosmopolitanism of this most consciously English of sociologists. In the late 1960s he chaired CERI, the education research centre of the Organisation for Economic Co-operation and Development. He has also worked on comparisons between British and US education systems, and he has now embarked on a new major research project devoted to the comparative study of education systems. And here one stops, without a conclusion and with the mention of an ongoing research project. The œuvre of A. H. Halsey is work in progress.

The contents of this book try to mirror most of these essential Halsey concerns. First, there is a *conception of social reform*, grounded in the nineteenth-century ethical socialist tradition embodied in such institutions as Toynbee Hall and the work of Canon Barnett after whom Barnett House, the headquarters of the DSAS, was named. These important roots are discussed by Julia Parker. Juliet Cheetham considers the continuity of these ethical traditions, alongside modern technique and the fruits of social research, in the social work training for which the Department has been so important. The importance of community, participation, and the rights of citizenship—as opposed to bureaucratic central direction—in Halsey's conception of the welfare state is pursued by Colin Crouch.

Second, there is the *evaluation of social reform* that Halsey's concern for evidence leads him to rank alongside advocacy in the policy process. We therefore present chapters reviewing experience in a number of policy areas with which he has been associated: poverty, in an appropriately comparative perspective (Graham Room); the effectiveness of schooling (Andrew McPherson and J. Douglas Willms); The universities, again comparatively (Martin Trow and Sheldon Rothblatt); the role of social movements (Rory Williams); and the pursuit of equality of educational opportunity (Anthony Heath, Colin Mills, and Jane Roberts).

Finally, Halsey's consistent linkage of the pursuit of reform to the need for sound and innovative research methods is captured in discussions of *social research and social reform*. These include action research, of the kind he pioneered in the Community Development Projects with George and Teresa Smith; his early encouragement of concern for questions of gender (Ann Oakley); the role of research in campaigns for the reform of education for 16–18 year-olds (David Raffe); and evaluation research applied to labour-market policy (Harold Wilensky).

Wilensky's chapter is pessimistic about the role of research of this kind in furthering the policy process, and certainly during the 1980s there was official scepticism about the role of social science research, in favour of 'conviction' alone, as a guide to policy. It is also true that in terms of substantive values and policies too, during that decade Halsey's seemed to be a voice from the past, stressing equality, community, and the public good at a time when it was the opposites of these values that were being strenuously celebrated.

However, matters look different from the perspective of the early 1990s. The collective interdependence of mankind has been borne in upon us by ecological disaster—not an explicit Halsey theme, but one well reconciled with his concerns for material restraint and for acceptance of human interdependence. More directly, persons from all parts of the political spectrum now call in aid family, community, and religion. Halsey has consistently done so, however unfashionably. As this brief record of his continuing contribution shows, he has never been among the advocates of a centralized and ideological social engineering. As both they and, more recently, the proponents of possessive, anti-egalitarian individualism see their projects fail, the voice of practical, community-rooted co-operation assumes its place at the centre of political and social debate.

C.C.
A.H.

Oxford
1991

CONTENTS

FIGURES

TABLES

NOTES ON CONTRIBUTORS

Juliet Cheetham is Professor and Director of the Social Work Research Centre in the University of Stirling. Previously she was lecturer in Applied Social Studies and Fellow of Green College at Oxford University. She has been a member of a number of public bodies including the Commission for Racial Equality and the Social Security Advisory Committee. Her main research interests are social work effectiveness and race relations. Her publications include *Social Work with Black Children and their Families* (with S. Ahmed and J. Small, 1986) and *The Evaluation of Social Work Effectiveness* (forthcoming).

Colin Crouch is Fellow and Tutor in Politics at Trinity College, Oxford, and a past Chairman of the Sub-Faculty of Sociology in the University of Oxford. He has written extensively on the politics of industrial relations in western European countries. He is joint editor of *The Political Quarterly*. His works include *The Student Revolt* (1970), *Class Conflict and the Industrial Relations Crisis* (1977), *The Politics of Industrial Relations* (1979 and 1982), *Trade Unions: The Logic of Collective Action* (1982), and *Industrial Relations and European State Traditions* (forthcoming).

Anthony Heath is an Official Fellow in Sociology at Nuffield College, Oxford. He worked with Professor Halsey and John Ridge on *Origins and Destinations: Family, Class and Education in Modern Britain* (1980). He has also published *Rational Choice and Social Exchange* (1976), *Social Mobility* (1981), *How Britain Votes* (with Roger Jowell and John Curtice, 1985), and *Understanding Political Change* (1991).

Andrew McPherson, a student of Professor Halsey's in 1964–5, is currently Co-Director of the Centre for Educational Sociology at the University of Edinburgh, where he holds a personal chair in Sociology. He is the author of a number of papers and books in the history and sociology of education including *Reconstructions of Secondary Education* (with John Gray and David Raffe, 1983) and *Governing Education: A Sociology of Policy since 1945* (with C. D. Raab, 1988).

Colin Mills is currently a lecturer in sociology at the University of Surrey. Prior to that he was a prize research fellow at Nuffield College, Oxford.

Ann Oakley is Director of the Social Science Research Unit in the Department of Policy Studies at the Institute of Education, University of London. She is author of many books and articles in the field of gender, family sociology, and the sociology of health and reproduction, including *The Sociology of Housework* (1974), *Subject Women* (1980), *The Captured Womb: A History of Antenatal Care* (1984), and (with S. Houd of the World Health Organization) *Helpers at Childbirth: Midwifery Today* (1990).

Julia Parker is a University Lecturer in Social Administration in the Department of Applied Social Studies and Social Research, Oxford University. She has written on many aspects of social policy and administration. Her publications include *Social Policy and Citizenship* (1975), and *Women and Welfare: Ten Victorian Women in Public Social Service* (1989).

David Raffe studied PPE and then Sociology at Oxford University, where he was supervised by Professor Halsey. He is Reader and Co-Director (with Andrew McPherson) of the Centre for Educational Sociology at the University of Edinburgh. He has worked at the CES since 1975, contributing to the design, conduct, and analysis of the Scottish Young People's Survey. His publications include *Reconstructions of Secondary Education* (with John Gray and Andrew McPherson, 1983), *Fourteen to Eighteen* (1984), and *Education and the Youth Labour Market* (1988). His current research interests include secondary and post-secondary education, the youth labour market, and policy for the 14–18 age group.

Jane Roberts is Data Services Officer in Nuffield College. She was joint author (with Mike Noble, George Smith, and Joan Payne) of *The Other Oxford* (1987), an investigation into the effects of changes in the provision of welfare benefits. She is currently working with Professor Halsey on the third of his Surveys of Teachers in Higher Education, and providing further analyses of the earlier surveys in this series.

Graham Room is Reader in Social Policy at the University of Bath. He is editor of the journal *European Social Policy* and a regular consultant to the EC Commission in the development and evaluation of its social programmes. His publications include *The Sociology of Welfare* (1979), *Europe Against Poverty* (with Dennett *et al.*, 1982), *Health and Welfare States of Britain* (with Williamson, 1984), *Cross-National Innovation in Social Policy* (1986), and *New Poverty in the European Community* (1990).

Sheldon Rothblatt is Professor of History and Director of the Center for Studies in Higher Education at the University of California, Berkeley. His publications include *The Revolution of the Dons: Cambridge and Society in the Nineteenth Century* (1968 and 1981), *Tradition and Change in English Liberal Education: An Essay in History and Culture* (1976). He is currently preparing a book on the comparative history of British and American higher education since 1800 with Martin Trow.

George Smith was a graduate student of Professor Halsey in the 1960s and then worked as research officer on the Educational Priority Area and Community Development Projects. After a period as lecturer in applied social studies at Oxford, he is currently a part-time research consultant to Her Majesty's Inspectorate at the Department of Education and Science. He also continues part-time research at the Oxford Department of Applied Social Studies and Social Research. His main publications are in the fields of educational disadvantage, community development and inner city policy, and low income/welfare benefits.

Teresa Smith is a lecturer in applied social studies at the University of Oxford, and a councillor on Oxfordshire County Council. She was a graduate student in Professor Halsey's department in Oxford. She subsequently worked in the West Riding Educational Priority Area Project, and later with Professor Bruner in the Oxford Pre-school Research Group. Her main publications are in community work and pre-school policy; her current research for the Department of Health is on family centres.

Martin Trow took his Ph.D. in Sociology at Columbia University in 1956. He joined the Sociology Department at Berkeley, moving to the Graduate School of Public Policy at Berkeley in 1969 and is currently working on a study of British and American higher education with Sheldon Rothblatt. He is also serving a two-year term as Vice-Chairman and then Chairman of the University of California State-Wide Academic Senate and faculty representative to the Board of Regents. He is co-author of a number of books including *Union Democracy* (with S. M. Lipset and James Coleman, 1956), *Students and Colleges* (with B. R. Clark, *et al.*, 1972), *Right-Wing Radicalism* (1980), and, of course, *The British Academics* (with A. H. Halsey, 1971).

Harold L. Wilensky is Professor of Political Science in the Department of Political Science and Research Sociologist, Institute of Industrial Relations and Institute of International Studies, University of California, Berkeley. His many books include *The Welfare State and Equality* (1975); *Organizational Intelligence* (1967); and *Industrial Society and Social Welfare* (1965). His chapter in this volume is part of his forthcoming book, *Tax and Spend: The Political Economy and Performance of Rich Democracies.*

Rory Williams studied Greats at Corpus Christi and did postgraduate research in sociology of the family at Nuffield College, Oxford. In 1977 he joined the Medical Research Council's Medical Sociology Unit, then attached to Aberdeen University, and now holds a senior research post at the unit, which has moved to Glasgow. He is the author of *A Protestant Legacy: Attitudes to Death and Illness among Older Aberdonians* (1990).

J. Douglas Willms is Associate Professor in the Faculty of Education in the University of British Columbia, and also a Research Fellow at the Centre for Educational Sociology in the University of Edinburgh, where he has written widely on issues in school effectiveness and in 1991 with Stephen W. Raudenbush he edited *Schools, Classrooms and Pupils: International Studies of Schooling from a Multilevel Perspective*. Due to appear shortly is his *Monitoring School Performance: A Non-Technical Guide for Teachers and Administrators.*

1

Canon Barnett: Ethical Socialist

JULIA PARKER

Samuel Barnett has a special claim to a place in the tradition of British ethical socialism, not so much as a thinker nor as a writer nor as a teacher but as a man who lived out his 'practicable socialism' in the East End of London during the last thirty years of the nineteenth century. A university man, though without a notably distinguished academic career; a writer and preacher without marked originality or eloquence, it was the force of his moral conviction and his particular vision of the good society and the means of reaching it that made him an inspiring influence on those who knew him and an important, if idiosyncratic, figure in the late Victorian movement for social reform.

He is best remembered as founder and warden of Toynbee Hall, the first university settlement, set up in 1884 and dedicated to the memory of Arnold Toynbee and to the ideals of social service and social obligation associated with his name. Barnett's own memorials are in Westminster Abbey, where he was installed Canon in 1906, and in Oxford at Barnett House, established in 1914 to carry on the work of social investigation and the education of young men and women in social research and social and economic problems which had started when undergraduates from Oxford and Cambridge went to settle in Whitechapel nearly half a century earlier.

Ethical socialism has been analysed by Dennis and Halsey as a persistent thread in English political thought running from Thomas More to Tawney. It finds varying expression with different individuals and in different historical and political circumstances. But whatever the emphasis on the diverse strands in the tradition, certain beliefs are fundamental. It involves a commitment to liberty, equality, and fraternity, however interpreted, in the ordering of social relationships. It rejects determinist accounts of historical development and underlines the significance of individual responsibility and moral choice in shaping the character of social institutions: and linked to this faith in the power of human will and action is the conviction that social progress must, in the end, depend on the strength of individual men and women; on the receiving of the rights and the acceptance of the duties of citizenship (Dennis and Halsey 1988). For Barnett, too, material prosperity could never in itself be a sufficient measure of social advance. For him, the problem confronting society at the end of the nineteenth century was much the same as that identified by Dahrendorf a hundred years later, of finding ways to extend to everyone the 'entitlements' to a common culture and a shared way of life.

> The liberal agenda is in the first instance about citizenship. This is in part a classical subject of liberal policy. Sex and gender questions are still not resolved. Civil rights are always under threat. Human rights need active defence everywhere . . . The new entitlement questions are however above all social. They have to do with the tendency to define people out of the social universe of the majority, with persistent unemployment, inner city blight, regional disparities and the underclass. (Dahrendorf 1988: 175–6)

Two aspects of Canon Barnett's personality give him a distinctive position among ethical socialists. First was his religion. His conception of the ideal society where men sought freedom and equality and the common good was derived from his Christianity and it was the spreading of the Christian faith that offered the best hope of its achievement. In her biography of her husband Henrietta Barnett remarks that he was remembered more for his efforts at social reform in Whitechapel than for his religious work but that religion 'held the main place in his heart's core' (H. O. Barnett 1918). Second, Canon Barnett was a pragmatist and a man of action who insisted that theory and doctrine, however hallowed by secular or sacred traditions of thought or faith, must adapt to changing knowledge and circumstances. Thus, the liturgy and ritual of the Anglican Church were incomprehensible to many of the people of East London and advances in the new biblical criticism and in science required a new interpretation and presentation of Christian dogma. And thus, Barnett employed his most powerful prose to denounce some of the most cherished principles of the Charity Organization Society, especially its opposition to state poor relief which he considered irrelevant and harmful in the 1890s. His words have a startling contemporary relevance in the controversies over the resurgence of political and economic liberalism in the 1980s.

> It (the council of the C.O.S.) has not said a word to lift up the heads of those who are in despair, to train the imagination of the sanguine, or to put into words unspoken hopes. Like Lot's wife, its eyes are turned back to the past, and it is every day farther in the rear of the crowd who rush wildly away from the fires of poverty . . . The council is not in sympathy with the forces which are shaping the time . . . (S. A. Barnett 1897: 341)

The rejection of Charity Organization Society doctrine and the traditions of individualism and economic liberalism from which it grew was by no means total, however. Barnett refused to accept that state help was necessarily demoralizing but he believed that dependency was undesirable, that co-operation in charity was necessary and that individual dealing in relief giving was essential. Equally, Barnett took from the socialists those elements of collectivism that he judged necessary to forward his objectives, but refused to allow the power and authority to government that might threaten the freedom and autonomy of individual men and women. He was a man who firmly took the middle way and in so doing brought together some of the fundamental tenets of liberal and socialist political thought. The issues he confronted were the central questions of the responsibilities of government and people in advancing well-being and distributing the common wealth. This essay will examine his objectives, his understanding of the world about him, how he believed it might be changed, and his contribution to social reform.

THE IDEAL CITY

If Canon Barnett was a man of action rather than of ideas this did not mean that he lacked his Utopian dreams. But whereas

More's Utopia was an island inhabited by people whose social relationships and behaviour, values and customs were defined and analysed in elaborate sociological detail, Barnett's brief sketch of the ideal city presented a set of values assumed to be beyond question in representing the goal of human endeavour. It offered a guide to good conduct rather than an opportunity for its creator to explore the complexities of the social relationships and politics of the good society. The very simplicity of Barnett's conception lends it a universal appeal.

> In the ideal city none will be very rich and none will be very poor. Knowledge and good will join together to give to every child the best education, and to secure its use of the gift; to render every house and street as healthy as the healthiest hillside in the world; to provide the best doctor and the most comfortable hospital for everyone who is sick; and to have at hand a friend for everyone in trouble.
>
> In our ideal city Art will grow out of common life, undisturbed by contrasts of wealth and poverty. The people will have pleasure in their work, and leisure to admire whatever is beautiful. (S. A. Barnett 1913: 149)

Nor indeed was the ideal city vulnerable to criticism for unlike that of More, the product of rational calculation of men's best interests without necessary reference to any faith, Barnett's Utopia was a matter of revealed religion.

> His will is that each capacity, each taste, each quality, should be developed; that each individual should rise to the height of his being, should do his best and enjoy his most. He would have in his kingdom no lower class. (S. A. Barnett 1897: 54–5)

The lack of a lower class, however, did not mean that in the ideal city all men and women would be equal. Barnett attached more importance to good fellowship and fraternity than to equality. 'Many classes', he wrote, 'make the strength of society . . . give charm to intercourse and stability to government . . . by their variety make unity.' There was nothing wrong in the existence of classes but there was the greatest wrong in their antagonism (ibid.: 99). The idea of fraternity as the basis for social order, has never found its way to the centre of political debate, though Halsey insists that it takes sociological priority over both equality and liberty in that it is the principle that defines the group within which social values are to be applied

(1986: 17). The problem, then, for Barnett remains today; it was to find ways of encouraging a city of many classes to work not for one of its parts but for the whole; rich and poor to consider one another and work for common ends, for pride in the city to take the place of pride in the dominance of one class (Barnett and Barnett 1909: 29).

This commitment to the common good runs through all of Barnett's writing. In 1905 he set out far-reaching proposals for dealing with the unemployed, but reforms would only reach their end, he warned, as members of a community realized their mutual responsibility to ensure that the capacities and talents of each were raised to the highest level (ibid.: 86). One element in the elevation of collective well-being above the interests of individuals or classes was the idea of 'service'. Men and women, Barnett claimed, were sent into the world to be one another's servants (ibid.: 10). There was no satisfaction in health and wealth unless used for the common good, and indeed they imposed heavy responsibilities on their possessors. Individuals had the duty of self-examination. They must enquire whether expenditure on travel, pictures, or food made them more fit to serve others, whether they employed servants to enable them to be more useful or to show off their wealth and whether the aim of possessions was to exalt self or to demonstrate a way of life which all should enjoy (S. A. Barnett 1911: 67). For Barnett in a Christian society the ideal life would lie in 'being' not 'having'. Members of society should accept no luxury which did not make them more interesting or more serviceable to their neighbours, enjoy no luxury unless it could be shared and seek to possess nothing which they could not desire that everyone should possess in a perfect state (S. A. Barnett 1913: 172). 'God said of old; "Thou shalt do no murder". God says now; "Make common what is best. Give by sharing"' (ibid.: 84).

The giving by sharing, however, did not imply equality of material possessions as much as equal opportunities for all to enjoy the best in education, in art, and in religion:

> The poor need the best . . . Not just comfortable dwellings but those architecturally most beautiful; not just open spaces but spaces made as interesting as a nobleman's park; not just broad, clean, light streets,

but streets as varied, as suggestive as a page of history; not just books but the best books; not just pictures to amuse, but pictures to awake sleeping imagination and kindle embers of fancy; not just churches which are weather-proof, but churches rich in colour, form, and sound; not just missionaries able to tell the Gospel story but teachers cultivated in all knowledge—the most refined members of our great universities, men and women of the poet mind. (S. A. Barnett 1897: 281–2)

The acute destitution that Barnett found in Whitechapel must go, because it threatened civilized human relationships and individual freedom. But the less extreme social and economic differences would be readily bridged by mutual respect, a sense of service, and commitment to the common good.

Freedom was the second great ideal to be enshrined in Barnett's Utopia. Not the meagre freedom from want that is acknowledged by the most doctrinaire of nineteenth-century economic liberals, and regarded by Hayek as a proper objective for a welfare state (1960: 29), but the much grander concept of freedom for all to develop their abilities to the utmost, to escape 'the limits put upon the growth of men's souls' (S. A. Barnett 1911: 41) by both pauperism and luxury alike. Freedom depended on the power to take advantage of its possibilities. It implied a moral claim to health, knowledge, sanitary dwellings, open spaces, schools, universities, and to all the means of life making for true enjoyment (S. A. Barnett 1913: 141). This is pointing to a set of citizenship rights or entitlements as conceived by T. H. Marshall. The question remains unanswered as to how far such rights can be fully realized in a market economy, albeit one relatively civilized by the development of a welfare sector (T. H. Marshall 1981: 135).

But freedom, for Barnett, also meant living under authority. The later part of the nineteenth century he saw as a time of 'masterless' men. Old forms of authority had succumbed to the increase in individualism. Among the rich were many who owed no duty to tenants nor to work people and who suffered the 'weariness of doing as they like' (S. A. Barnett 1897: 272). A masterless class of workpeople was restless and unreliable and without the power of association, and consciousness of danger provoked a desire for strong government. Ecclesiastics offered some peace through submission to doctrine, but no place for free thought. Socialists offered an ideal society but a materialist conception that was fatal to freedom, endangered the family, and enslaved the individual (ibid.: 275–6). Freedom in Barnett's Utopia rested on the authority of the Christian religion.

THE SOCIAL PROBLEM: IN DARKEST ENGLAND

The England in which Barnett lived presented a stark contrast with the society he wished to see. Industrialization and the growth of towns had separated rich and poor and broken the bonds of mutual respect and obligation which in the past, Barnett assumed, had softened the distinctions of rank and status and afforded some security and dignity to the poor. The two nations were represented most vividly in the East and West of London where the wretchedness and brutality of life in the streets around Toynbee Hall were for Barnett a continuing indictment of the 'careless luxury' further west. The gross inequalities were an affront to fairness and justice in their denial of the means to civilized life to a large proportion of working people but they also impoverished the cultural life of the whole community and were a potential threat to civil order.

This was the 'social problem' that was arousing increasing interest in the universities, among politicians, and throughout the professional classes in the 1860s and 1870s. It inspired some men and women to the reform of the nation's poor laws and of charitable effort and others to wider collective measures to establish a better quality of life and increase social and economic opportunities for all. Canon Barnett moved during his years in Toynbee Hall from a belief in the power of organized charity to deal with social distress to a conviction that statutory intervention was also an essential element in social reform; a shifting emphasis on different means to a constant end, that reflected increasing experience and understanding of social conditions in Whitechapel.

It was degradation of character rather than material deprivation that most disturbed the Barnetts in the earlier years. As time passed, however, Barnett became more aware of the power of men's surroundings to shape their moral and spiritual lives. Gross social inequalities corrupted both rich and poor and they also opened a gulf between the classes that prevented the growth of a sense of fellowship and common purpose. In Whitechapel, Barnett noted, one-fifth of the people suffered from lack of food and 'hasty charity' led only to 'waywardness of mind and bitterness of spirit' (S. A. Barnett 1897: 80). While 100,000 East Londoners dwelt in single rooms, their childhood spent in the streets, their old age in the workhouse, the people in West London, knowing this, carelessly spent their money in 'profitless vanities' (ibid.: 102). Increasingly separated in the cities as the rich moved further west the two classes, as Barnett defined them, developed in their different habitats and under the influence of their neighbourhoods, their different tastes and pleasures, manners, speech, dress, and ethical standards (Barnett and Barnett 1909: 26–7).

Moreover while the classes were increasingly divided in wealth, leisure, and culture, the poor were beginning to receive the education to arouse both aspirations and resentment at their lack of opportunity. The problem of reconciling social antagonisms thus assumed fundamental importance. And it was exacerbated by the 'insolent and degrading' use of wealth by a less-educated propertied class. Luxury, Barnett claimed, was a greater social danger than drunkenness in fostering social divisions and he denounced it in Veblenesque terms: 'the West End shops with their many objects, costly and useless . . . the fruits highly priced only because they are out of season, the dresses whose outrageous extravagance seems designed to show that their wearers cannot be workers, the barbaric show of jewels and precious stones' (S. A. Barnett 1911: 57). But not only was the conspicuous display of wealth an affront to the wretchedness of the poor, it also corroded the character of the rich. Luxury was as fatal to freedom, understood as the power of an individual to develop to the limit of his abilities, as pauperism. It stifled the finer qualities in human nature and induced men and women capable of sacrifice to pursue their own ease and pleasure. This had wider social implications. It destroyed powers of judgement, for those who made their own enjoyment a law unto themselves could not be keen to secure justice for the drunkard and the vicious. Absence of moral indignation over crime was due not to charity but to the self-indulgence of those who made public opinion.

Luxury was also socially wasteful for it called for the employment of labour which might have been used to increase national resources, while the law of diminishing satisfactions meant a rich man gained less from the extra pounds he spent than would a poor man. And, finally, luxury exalted false values. The example of the rich was a direct cause of the poverty of the poor for if a chief good were an abundance of possessions other values were crushed.

If the excesses of the rich were damaging both to themselves and to society, so the privation of the poor also represented a limitation of men's freedom and a source of social unrest and discontent. Barnett distinguished a particular personality that he attributed to working people; they were strenuous, modest, unaffected, generous, and with good sense, but they lacked a wide outlook, were indifferent to knowledge and beauty and their pleasures were restricted. Workmen were 'scant' of life, of the interests and visions and hopes that came of knowledge and they tried to supply the lack through drink and gambling. 'They do not rejoice in their own being or in the use of their minds so their hopes are set on "having" rather than "being" . . . They are dull on holidays unless they find some outside excitement, and they shrink from solitude' (Barnett and Barnett 1909: 216).

This conception of the character of the working class led Barnett to fear that the Labour Party in power would be as narrowly committed to the pursuit of material advantage as was the propertied class to the defence of its own interests. There would be change without progress, the same carelessness of things for common joy, the same indifference to beauty and the same exaltation of rights above duties.

But it was pauperism that was the fatal disease to which the working class was vulnerable. In a lecture in 1911 Barnett pointed to the symptoms—listlessness, discontent, vindictiveness, and servility. The pauper was not a free man, nor desirous to be, he was content to eat and not to work, to take gifts and be ungrateful. Without the capacities to take part in the government of his country, without and not wishing the privileges of citizenship, the pauper added nothing to the common wealth and had no ambition to do so. The sudden death of all paupers, terrible though it might be to say, would be a great economic gain and hardly a social loss (S. A. Barnett

1911). The responsibility, however, lay firmly with the state. The nation by its laws had created pauperism. In failing to enable the poor to develop their capacities it had treated them as animals to be driven or led. It had substituted punishment for education.

Such views, as we shall see, led Barnett eventually to wholesale condemnation of government housing and education policies, of the poor laws and of organized charity. But he also maintained a persistent optimism about the extent and indeed the growth of private benevolence and sympathy for the poor. In 1897 he wrote that some antagonism did exist between the classes but that it was often misrepresented by 'socialists and cynics'. There was much kindly interest among the rich in the poor, though also a sense of superiority. Relief was too often seen as a favour rather than a right and hostility developed if the poor appeared ungrateful. Even so, the chief cause of antagonism was ignorance. 'If rich and poor could see one another as God sees each; if they could get rid of the ignorance which hides from each the real goodness of the other there would be on earth peace, and good will among men' (S. A. Barnett 1897: 103). The times, Barnett insisted, were full of promise. People were more aware of the need for reform and never before was there such sympathy with suffering. Great physical improvements had occurred in Whitechapel with decent houses, public libraries, and concert halls. The poor law guardians were men and women of good will, anxious to refuse careless relief and to give instead the means to independence. Class barriers were falling before the 'still small voice of friendship'.

Alongside this cheerful assertion of increasing benevolence, however, lay a contradictory view of social relationships and of a society fatally divided by conflicting class interests. East London was very inadequately paid for what it did for the West in hard, dull, unbroken toil in East End factories. 'All have received from the poor but few acknowledge the debt' (S. A. Barnett 1897: 255). Writing a few years later in 1904 Barnett put more emphasis on the conflict between the classes. The rich were chiefly concerned with defending property, the poor, represented by the Labour Party, concerned for the interests of labour. Each class struggled for its own rights in parliament and in local authorities. One's gain was held to be another's loss and weak compromises emerged. Class pulled against class. 'Each has its eye on an ideal in which its own members are dominant, not one in which all the citizens get equal benefit' (Barnett and Barnett 1909: 28).

AND THE WAY OUT

The question then was how the two nations so 'woefully divided' of late Victorian England might join together in a commonwealth of free men and women united by mutual respect and service and where the best things were shared. Barnett's efforts to find an answer to the question can be traced in his life in Whitechapel as vicar of St Jude's and warden of Toynbee Hall. It was not a simple answer, for it reflected the deep ambivalence in Barnett's analysis of social and class relationships. Were the resentments and antagonisms between the classes due to the ignorance and misunderstanding of essentially benevolent and well-intentioned people or to the unavoidable opposition of conflicting class interests?

In the earlier years it was the voluntary effort of benevolent people that Barnett saw as the most important means to social reform. But his experience in the East End convinced him that neither individual good will nor organized charity alone could deal with the material and spiritual poverty of the London working class. The state was also needed to provide a better physical environment and wider educational and cultural opportunities. But if voluntary effort was insufficient to meet prevailing destitution, the state too had its limitations. Legislation could not make moral men and women. Progress towards the ideal city could only come as men and women accepted their responsibilities for one another, and this for Barnett meant accepting the teaching of the Christian church just as for Titmuss in a more secular age it meant accepting the ethic of altruism and practising the 'gift relationship'. These three main strands in Barnett's approach to social reform appear in his work in Toynbee Hall, in his later rejection of Charity Organization Society principles in favour of a more interventionist state, and in his teaching as an Anglican minister whose Christian beliefs informed everything he did.

THE VOLUNTEERS

Samuel and Henrietta Barnett went to St Jude's in 1873, to a church 'empty and unused' and a poverty-stricken parish 'inhabited mainly by a criminal population much corrupted by doles'.[1] The first task, and one that absorbed Barnett throughout his life, was to make the church more relevant to the experiences and needs of Whitechapel people, an ambition echoed in the Archbishop of Canterbury's enquiry into urban priority areas in 1985 (Church of England Commission 1985). The religious life of the inner city remains an unsolved problem for the Anglican church in the late twentieth century. But the emphasis in *Faith in the City* is more clearly secular. At St Jude's the services were modified and pictures and music brought into the church. But making religion 'a more vital matter for the man in the street' (H. O. Barnett 1918: 110) was not the only object. The community and citizenship for which Barnett strove must be founded on faith but also required a widening of all kinds of cultural and social opportunities so that people might have the education that would give them freedom and the enjoyment of beauty. This led the Barnetts into campaigning for local amenities, for libraries, playgrounds, open spaces, wash houses, dispensaries, and for the removal of slaughter houses. Following Octavia Hill's example they bought an old building to convert to model dwellings with the help of lady rent collectors who would befriend the tenants and ensure self-improvement and social harmony. The pursuit of citizenship also meant service on local voluntary and statutory bodies as poor law guardians or school managers and the establishing of a Country Holiday Fund for Whitechapel children. And it also meant setting up a church library, arranging art exhibitions, lectures, discussion groups, and organizing men's and boys' clubs. This is a kind of activity that continues in the many community development projects that have emerged over the last twenty years. At Toynbee Hall Barnett was endeavouring to arouse a sense of social responsibility among rich and poor in the absence of any significant government interest in welfare. The renewed emphasis on community action in the 1980s reflected disillusion over the power and will of the state to supply welfare after a period when it had been tried and found wanting. (See, for example, Bulmer *et al.* 1989.)

Central to the parish work of St Jude's was the conviction that social improvement rested on friendly intercourse between the classes. Henrietta Barnett records her resolve to invite to Whitechapel all the most intellectual people they met so that her husband's work might become better known (H. O. Barnett 1918: 145). Barnett himself counted it a religious duty to give parties, and guests were carefully invited from different classes so that common talk might break down the barriers built by mutual ignorance. But it was not only distinguished visitors who came to the East End. Increasingly Barnett was attracting undergraduates to spend their vacations in Whitechapel joining the more permanent settlers, a movement that received formal recognition in the establishing of Toynbee Hall in 1884 following meetings at Oxford and Cambridge.

The settlement movement exemplified Barnett's belief in the power of knowledge and social intercourse to dispel class antagonisms and of personal friendship to unite rich and poor in face of huge cultural and material inequalities. There was a need for educated, leisured, and public-spirited men in East London to revive the local institutions, the vestries, the poor law, and charitable bodies all enfeebled by the lack of people to man their committees. It was the duty of the rich to labour for the welfare of those whose labour created their own wealth. These might have been Barnett's words but they were spoken by Philip Lyttleton Gell at a Cambridge meeting in 1884 when it was resolved to co-operate with Oxford in settlement work. Neglect of the labouring poor, Gell continued, would lead to social chaos which might be avoided either by 'socialistic officialdom' with a band of officials maintained at public expense or by calling back to their civic responsibilities the 'wealthy middle-class deserters from the common wealth . . . to . . . take up the burden of their forgotten duty to their neighbours' (Gell 1884: 8–9). Meanwhile university men were to 'fill the breach', moved by love for their fellow men, sorrow for suffering and sin, 'and faith in the power of the friendship which you offer him to enrich both yourself and him. Personal contact and personal friendship inspired by such feelings is the medicine needed for every social difficulty' (ibid.: 11).

At the same Cambridge meeting Professor Michael Foster, not a friend, he said, to philanthropy emphasized rather the need to remove obstructions to individual progress through education, and education not only of the poor but of those who tried to help them. Work had the quality of mercy, it was twice blessed and especially among the poor. Out of the settlements enlightenment would come to aid the solution of social problems. More immediately, urged Professor Westcott, the west would be saved by destroying the east. The blessings associated with leisure, refinement, and culture—the delicacy of home life—could and must be made universal and that end university men in East London might help to attain.

> I have always believed that what is wanted . . . is not so much the power and means of happiness as a clear vision of the aim of life, a firm apprehension of the motive of action, and the ready offering of guidance. And surely that is what those who have the privilege of learning and working here ought to be able to give. (Gell 1884: 21)

These then were the ideas to which Barnett attempted to give practical form at Toynbee Hall. There university men would gather to offer friendship, service, and education to the poor and themselves learn about social problems and how they might be overcome. Although in later years Barnett increasingly emphasized the importance of social enquiry and was more ready to support state intervention, in the earlier period philanthropy and personal service was the major activity of the settlement.

> Friendship is the channel by which the knowledge—the joys—the faith—the hope which belong to one class may pass to all classes. It is distance that makes friendship between classes almost impossible, and therefore, residence among the poor is suggested as a simple way in which Oxford men may serve their generation. (S. A. Barnett 1888)

But while friendship and personal service were indispensable in attempting to deal with the 'great social questions of the day', indiscriminate doles for the poor created, in Barnett's view, infinite damage. Influenced by Octavia Hill and Charles Loch and the doctrines of the Charity Organization Society, he fully accepted that charitable relief should be given only after careful enquiry into individual circumstances, and subscribed to the policies of the Local Government Board in the 1880s to cut back outdoor relief. Universal provision by either state or voluntary effort without investigation of individual cases was demoralizing to the recipient and destroyed thrift and independence and family relationships. This was the conventional wisdom of the COS in the later nineteenth century. By the end of the 1890s, however, Barnett had explicitly rejected some of the society's most fundamental principles. It is his growing willingness to accept the state as an agent for welfare that represents the second strand in his approach to social reform.

Barnett's criticism of COS principles was directed at those doctrines that stood in the way of more collective provision for the poor. 'Independence of state relief' and 'saving' had, he claimed, become idols, defended by the COS as an idol defended by its priest (S. A. Barnett 1897: 337). Thus the Society opposed state pensions as involving the dependence of the poor on rates and taxes and objected to municipal experiments in finding work for the unemployed as 'increasing the habitual dependence of the poor', but made no attempt to discover whether all forms of state relief induced demoralizing dependence, nor whether a pension from the state was more degrading than one from a neighbour. Nor were there any suggestions of better ways of dealing with the unemployed. The COS also opposed municipal control of London hospitals but without any argument to show why a man should be degraded by being cured in a poor law infirmary but not if he were treated in Guy's. 'There appears to be no evidence of enquiry as to the respective results of state or voluntary relief, and the Council seem to think the proposal for municipal control is sufficiently crushed when it is condemned as a form of state socialism' (ibid.: 339).

Barnett then turned his attention to the importance the COS placed on saving as a means to independence. It was by no way clear, he said, that a man earning less than £1 a week, of whom there were many in London, should save his money rather than spend it on the 'development of the bodies, brains and souls of his children'. The Council gave no adequate consideration to any of these things but exalted saving to the glory of a principle. 'The Council, in regard for its idol, "thrift", makes a new

Beatitude—"Blessed is he who has remembered himself"' (ibid.: 340).

Barnett's paper marked his impatience with what he considered the rigid dogmas that had replaced the earlier inspired teaching of the Charity Organization Society. It had no proposals for dealing with the old or the sick or the unemployed. It had lost touch with the problems of the times.

> Abuses increase, beggars parade the streets, indiscriminate giving demoralizes whole neighbourhoods, and the Society's voice is hardly heard. Working men can find no work, striving homes are broken by want, and the Society suggests no remedy. Good natured people advocate ways of relief which experience has a thousand times condemned. Relief is so given and the Society has no power to check or to guide. (S. A. Barnett 1897: 343)

Disillusion with charitable work had been growing for some time. In 1880 Barnett had warned of the dangers of rigid classification of deserving and undeserving poor and several years later wrote to his brother of the need for the COS to develop a better appreciation of its possible work (H. O. Barnett 1918: 655–7). What this meant for Barnett was greater readiness to recognize the need for the state to play a part in social reform. But this the COS refused to do, 'they were just impossible—refusing to do anything except to clothe themselves in the dirty rags of their own righteousness'.[2]

THE STATE

However Barnett might differ from the COS in his view of the role of the state in social affairs, his own approach to public authorities and the machinery of government was cautious. Social advance depended on raising cultural, spiritual, and moral values. Philanthropy was unhelpful and aroused resentment because the rich even if willing to be generous yet gave charity which offended self-respect, built orphanages where individuality was crushed, and offered entertainments where 'higher aspirations for beauty' were forgotten. How then might progress come about? Even in 1904 Barnett's answer to this question makes no direct reference to public services. He suggested three different solutions. First, rich and poor should live close together and this would arouse mutual sympathy and willingness to work for the common good. Second, there should be simpler living for the rich and higher thinking for the poor. Luxury increased social divisions and was a greater social danger than drunkenness. Workmen wanted education only for higher wages and increased comforts but needed education to enlarge their imagination, enrich their leisure, and help them to respect their opponents. The best in knowledge and beauty must be within the reach of all, for there could be no unity if people were prevented from admiring the same things, taking pride in their fathers' great deeds, and sharing the same great literature. Third, Christian teaching must be related to contemporary social problems and experience.

The three solutions did not imply any aversion to statutory action, but rather Barnett's conviction that benevolent legislation could only develop if men and women were tolerant and educated and Christian. When rich and poor thought morally many causes of poverty would be removed. Religion was the fuel that constrained the nation to direct its laws against the ignorance which prevented so many citizens 'enjoying their best and doing their utmost' (S. A. Barnett 1911: 140).

If laws were necessary, however, they must be most carefully scrutinized. The test of legislation was whether it would increase morality in the nation and it was in this spirit that Barnett considered statutory responsibility for pensions, for the unemployed, for the feeding of hungry children, and for poor relief generally. Pensions should be universal, a form of deferred wages offering freedom from anxiety in old age and recognition that everyone had directly or indirectly contributed to the national wealth. In this way they would strengthen a sense of national obligation. The exclusion under the 1908 Act of those who had habitually refused work and of those possessing ten shilling a week should cease. Such provisions required intrusive enquiries that would provoke resentment. They would also discourage thrift and lead to deceit—to pretences of transferring money to children and to 'dodges to keep income low'. The requirement would, in other words, encourage immoral acts. A similar concern with the morality of the nation and with Victorian values has been invoked by government in the 1980s in defence of welfare policies which are the reverse of those proposed by Barnett. Thus thrift, independence, and hard work are to be encouraged by less generous and more selective social security arrangements rather than the universal benefits that Barnett wished to see.

Unemployment and the pauperism associated with it assumed major importance in the 1880s and 1890s as a problem that defied the attempts to deal with it of either organized charity or the poor law authorities. By 1909 Beveridge had firmly identified it as a problem of industrial organization, but the 1834 Poor Law had been posited on the assumption that able-bodied unemployment was voluntary and best tackled by a deterrent system of statutory relief, with charity providing for the deserving. The obvious social distress through lack of work at the end of the century aroused mingled sympathy and alarm but deterrent poor law policies continued and the twinges of public conscience were assuaged, at any rate in part, through voluntary doles for the poor, the diverse charitable activity increasingly ineffectually co-ordinated by the Charity Organization Society and subscriptions to the intermittent Mansion House funds for distribution to the unemployed.

The refusal of the COS to contemplate new policies for working men who could find no work had been one of Barnett's main criticisms in 1895. And by 1903 he had elaborated his own plan for action, a co-operative effort of state and voluntary bodies (Barnett and Barnett 1909: 67). First the unemployed must be distinguished from the unemployable. The former should be left to their friends and the trade unions whose funds should be subsidized by the state. The latter society must support otherwise the social costs of disease and delinquency would be too great. Deterrence was fashionable, but deterrence would not make people work. So Barnett proposed a mixture of education, training, and discipline. Men incapable of independent work would live in 'communities', updated workhouses where they might contribute something to their own support. These 'labour schools' would be in the country and would require men to live apart from their families—a deterrent element necessary to prevent abuse. But unlike workhouses they should be modelled on schools not prisons and would open to everyone a 'door of hope', removing from the labour market a group who depressed wage levels but whose labour could now be for the common good. Moreover the scheme would offer opportunities for befriending and visiting, vital for Barnett as it was only 'one by one' that the mass of human beings could be raised. Vagrants should be detained, though without degrading treatment, and workhouses and inebriate homes transformed into sheltered communities where people should be encouraged to be useful. For no remedy would be effective that did not strengthen the will and raise aspirations. Compulsory detention would be required for habitual beggars:

> The community would, in fact, say to its prodigals, 'we cannot afford to let you waste yourselves and our substance; you must be restrained, but you shall not be degraded or shut out from hope. . . . You shall have work worthy a man's doing; you shall have necessary recreation and interests; you shall be able to earn and save money; you shall have the chance which you missed of fitting yourself for citizenship. You shall have everything except liberty, and that you may win. If, however, you misuse this chance, then you must be relegated to prison and prison fare'. (Barnett and Barnett 1909: 95)

Barnett also insisted, however, on the necessity for other forms of statutory intervention beyond retraining and labour exchanges. Men were out of work not only because they were unfit (born of feeble parents and untrained) but because industry was badly organized. There must be adequate unemployment insurance, government schemes of public works, and above all better education, with young workers under sixteen required to attend three evening classes a week.

The public feeding of school children raised more awkward dilemmas. On the one hand children were undernourished and unable to learn, but communal feeding would remove one of the bonds of family life. The family meal, Barnett bellieved, fed the memories as well as the bodies of children. 'It stores in their minds the thought of their parents' care, it brings out their sympathy with one another's needs, it teaches manners, provokes common conversation, impresses the use of order' (ibid.: 108). The best way to ensure that children were properly fed, he thought, would be to 'enlist Christian charity' to discover the reason for underfeeding and then to deal with the ignorance, carelessness, disease, or poverty. It would be far better for children to eat in families than at a 'barracks mess'. But Christian charity had failed and children were starving and the problem was to devise ways of feeding them without damaging self-respect and weakening family responsibility. Whether the money came from charity or from public funds was immaterial so far as the effect on family life was concerned. What was important was to avoid any attempt to distinguish the deserving from the undeserving, any marking off of a pauper class which might 'increase in the nation habits of suspicion or of cringing' (ibid.: 114). The compromise that Barnett proposed was a porridge breakfast for all, a nutritious diet but one unlikely to remove the sense of duty either of parents to provide for their children or of society to enquire into the causes of poverty.

The narrowness of state welfare provision was attracting increasing criticism by the end of the nineteenth century. It was a criticism that Barnett joined and that led him to argue for the reform of poor law policy and administration as well as for the development of wider public services. The workhouse, a central feature of the Poor Law, was unsuitable for old people and for children, and more use should be made of other resources. Barnett calculated in 1902 that boarding out ten adults and ten children could help a rural economy to the tune of £400 a year. Parish councils would supervise boarding out arrangements and be 'dignified by the trust'. Moreover there might be reciprocal services. An old man or woman could be worth two or three shillings a week in child-minding, fruit picking, sewing, and so on. 'As to those boarded out', Barnett concluded, 'it goes without saying they would be happier and more fit for life' (ibid.: 122). The workhouse stood for the punishment of poverty and was out of place in modern society where poverty was not the fault of individuals. The punishment of misfortune was unjust. Children, indeed, should not be under the Poor Law at all but removed to the education authority which should provide for each according to his needs, offering the same opportunities and attention that other children received.

It was not surprising that Barnett welcomed the recommendations of the Poor Law Commission of 1905–9, though he attended more to the proposals on which the Commissioners agreed than to the matters that divided them. The most important new principle, he thought, was that relief should involve treatment to restore the individual to his place in society recognizing that none was beyond the reach of education. A second vital principle was that prevention was better than relief. The Commissioners had pointed to the disorganization of industry and the misuse of boy labour. Barnett wanted full-time employment of young people forbidden and attendance at continuation classes required and he endorsed the proposals for labour exchanges and insurance protection for the unemployed (S. A. Barnett 1911: 51).

The problem of poverty for Barnett, however, was inextricably bound up with the problem of wealth and here too was cause for state action. Not only might wealth destroy the moral character of its possessors in leading to extravagance and luxury, it also represented the waste of resources that might have been used to help the poor. It was the duty of the nation to limit luxury and to check accumulations that were not the result of the owner's work; to prevent the loss of freedom through wealth as well as the loss of freedom through poverty. In considering this question Barnett advocated the version of the theory of surplus value developed by L. T. Hobhouse, J. A. Hobson, and the New Liberals.[3] No individual had the right to control 'millions of money'. He should restore to the community whatever he possessed 'beyond what he required to develop his own being, or beyond what he could personally direct for his neighbour's use' (S. A. Barnett 1913: 108).

There was also room for more vigorous statutory measures to tackle the specific evils of drunkenness, vice, and ignorance. Drink destroyed freedom and the capacity for life. The nation should control the drink traffic but also protect people against it through regulating overcrowded dwellings and unhealthy work and through opening up the means to a fuller life. There should be more education and more leisure and public museums, galleries, libraries, music, and gardens with which to enjoy it.

> The nation cannot indeed make people sober by act of parliament, but it has the power to do what no individual and no voluntary society can do; it can train the children to seek for truth and to admire beauty, and bring within everyone's reach things which are true and beautiful. (S. A. Barnett 1911: 95)

By 1911 Barnett believed that although the spread of education had increased respectability and 'sober enjoyment' there remained a want of knowledge that left men and women a prey to sensational newspapers, restricted individual freedom, and prevented the majority from exercising the judgement that would guide the nation to peace and greatness. 'Their political action is vacillating, their philosophy of life limited, and their pleasures such as are not humanizing' (S. A. Barnett 1911: 122). The dangers of ignorance required university education to be widely available and free. Elementary and secondary education were not enough. Men must be able to reason as well as accumulate information.

Barnett's advocacy of more collective responsibility was never an advocacy of a mere extension of statutory bodies and statutory power. The test of legislation was its power to stimulate effort, to make it more difficult for 'idlers and loafers' among the poor to live on relief and also to stir 'rich idlers into some form of fruitful energy' for as a stimulus to effort 'an open way down is as important as an open way up' (S. A. Barnett 1907: 29). But stimulus to effort could only come through personal relationships. The progress of social reform depended on legislation but also on voluntary service. Thus, in education the officials possessed knowledge and experience but administration could easily become mechanical and rigid. It was the lot of volunteers as school managers to inspire and also to control the experts. In poor relief there was need for centralized administration by officials to avoid confusion and variety of practice, and officials brought both knowledge and devotion. But administration tended to become mechanical, to alienate 'public interest from public duty', and the safeguard was that officials be responsible to a body of 'ordinary citizens' (Barnett and Barnett 1909: 53–9). The question of the balance of power and responsibility between government and people is an ancient one. For Barnett it arose in the conflict between officials and volunteers and was to be resolved by the latter acting as guardians of the public interest. In the contemporary debates it is often the people themselves who are accorded rights to participate in the planning and administration of public services.

The need for both official and voluntary effort is a continuing theme in Barnett's writing, but also one of the justifications of his work at Toynbee Hall. Settlers, he believed, could mitigate class suspicion and increase goodwill and they could also inspire local government with a 'higher spirit'. It was a true instinct to distrust 'machinery' but social improvement required organization and officials. Settlements brought into poor neighbourhoods people whose training made them sensible to abuses and whose humanity made them conscious of others' needs, and they brought into local government people who could 'formulate its mission' (ibid.: 265–9).

In the end, however, neither voluntary action nor legislation were reliable means to the society Barnett wished to see. Social progress called for redistribution of resources, personal service, and individual effort that would be painful and difficult for all classes. Only religion could give the impetus and provide the sustaining force for the legislation and the personal endeavour that would be necessary.

THE CHURCH

The religion wanted and 'by which most might be done', was not that 'that ranged men in sects' to discuss doctrine nor even to go to church. It was, as Barnett put it, 'that through which men become conscious of an immanent God' (Barnett 1897: 105). This meant 'moral thoughtfulness'. Social reform depended on individual reform. 'When we are changed, God through us will change the world' (ibid.: 261). How, Barnett demanded, if an employer prayed could he countenance a 'law of trade' that fixed wages below subsistence, defend offices and workshops that destroyed health, or permit a man who had worked for him for forty years to become a pauper in old age. If a workman prayed what would he think of the work he scamped and the minutes he idled. The employer might not at once raise wages, Barnett conceded, but he would not be a hard master and the more thoughtful workman would recognize the employer's goodwill.

The power of religion to bring about social harmony, however, was not at all the same thing as the power of the Anglican Church. On the contrary, church leaders had failed to deal with current issues, to relate Christianity to the economic and scientific movements and thought of the last fifty years, or to find ways of resolving the antagonism between rich and poor.

> They go on using a phraseology which is not understood, preaching sermons about dead controversies and condemning controversies long forgotten. They teach, but the people, tried and troubled by the thoughts of duty to the rich or duty to the poor, find no help in their teaching. Their sermons have become almost a byword for dullness and inaptness. (S. A. Barnett 1897: 320)

It was in an effort to shake off the dull weight of the past that Barnett set out to revive the services of St Jude's. The church was not his, he wrote, but the parishioners'. They could hope for more adequate forms of service in the future but in the mean time that of the Church of England seemed to Barnett the best available, though it needed widening and enriching with history and literature, music, and art.

> It is by knowing grand lives . . . that men now living will themselves strive to live holy lives . . . It is . . . by the sight of grand pictures . . . that men are able to understand what lies behind the life of every day . . . Lastly, it is in grand music that men find the truest expression for thoughts and prayers which voices cannot utter. (S. A. Barnett 1913: 92–3)

Music and art, Barnett saw as a religious effort to spread goodwill and good fellowship and they should therefore be available on Sundays, but this was a view that he had to defend to the Bishop of London who had written in disapproval of Sunday exhibitions. Barnett maintained that his duty as a minister of the Church was to bring people to the knowledge of God. The preaching a puritan Sunday would only convince people that the clergy were interfering with innocent pleasures. If the Bishop knew the lives of the people of Whitechapel he would not regret action which showed the Church had a higher aim and Christianity a wider basis than the sanctity of a day. 'I cannot think that you would say it is better, for the value of old Sunday associations, to keep the people amid the paralysing and degrading sights of our streets than to bring them within view of the good and perfect gifts of God.'[4]

More generally, Barnett saw the contribution of religious teachers to the solution of economic and social problems in arousing 'moral thoughtfulness' and offering a modern conception of a Christian society. As it was there was little regard for the misfortunes of the weak. Competitive trade required a supply of ready labour but when their labour was no longer needed men and women were thrown aside as 'old machines on a scrap heap'. Sanitary laws were enforced but these were as necessary for cattle as for men and women and there was little care that workers should have pleasant homes and inspiring recreations. New laws and new methods of relief would be vain without a greater sense of Duty and a greater devotion to Right. It was this that the Church must teach. It is ironical that during the 1980s relations between organized religion and government have grown increasingly acrimonious as church leaders become more outspoken in their criticism of inadequate social policies and the widening social inequalities they create.[5]

CANON BARNETT AND HIS WORK

Where then does Barnett stand in the social and religious movements of the late nineteenth century? In his relation with the Church as with his attitudes to the state he clearly belongs to the Christian Socialists, a group of men more or less Christian and more or less socialist among whom Norman includes Ruskin, not a churchman, beset by religious doubts, not interested in politics, seeking extensive social change though without belief in the political apparatus required to bring it about (Norman 1987: 121–5). For all the Christian Socialists the response to social evils was religious rather than political so that secular socialists regarded them with scepticism. Their importance in social reform lay not in their socialism but in their view of humanity, they were shocked not so much by the low wages and insanitary dwellings as by the debased leisure and alienation from church of the poor. While Chartism was a social and religious movement with a political programme, Christian Socialism was a religious and moral movement intended to make political activity unnecessary (ibid.: 6–10).

Similarly Barnett's priorities were moral and religious rather than economic and political. The machinery of government he distrusted; administration was only as good as the people who carried it out, officials were prone to rigidity and must be answerable to volunteers who would keep them in touch with the wishes of the people. Barnett was optimistic that 'the real interest of society' in the condition of the poor would one day find expression. 'Wisdom will unite with love, and then the life of people will be more regarded than the profits of trade' (Barnett 1913: 162). But it would be dangerous to act too quickly. Invoking law and institutions might dwarf character and develop animosities.

T. H. Huxley had worked as a parish doctor in the East End and later travelled round the world seeing 'all conceivable conditions of savage degradation' but had found nothing more degrading than East End life. He nevertheless insisted that the elevation of the individual was the only way to permanent improvement—and more important than providing better houses and drains (W. F. Aitken 1902: 115). So too for Barnett, improvement must come 'by growth from within, and not by accretions from without' (quoted ibid.: 44). During his visit to America in 1867 he noted the difference between himself and a radical American lawyer, the American believing that every man had a right to vote, Barnett believing that it was first every man's duty to make himself fit to vote (Abel 1969: 11).

Thus Barnett stood aside from the socialist reformers whom he saw as indignant advocates of a reconstruction of society, and also from those whom he called individualists who wished to develop a system of rewards and punishment for the deserving and undeserving poor. As a Christian he emphasized neither unfairness, as did the socialists, nor suffering, as did the individualists, but rather 'the limits put upon the growth of men's souls' (S. A. Barnett 1911: 41). Tawney put it slightly differently when he wrote that one wing of social reformers had gone astray, being preoccupied with relieving distress and patching up failures. This was good and necessary but it was not the social problem, nor a policy that would ever commend itself to the working classes. What they wanted was security and opportunity, not assistance in exceptional misfortunes but a chance of leading an independent and fairly prosperous life (Winter and Joskin 1972: 13). But for Barnett and Tawney as for all ethical socialists material progress was fraught with moral danger in so far as it brought an increasing demand for discreditable pleasures. The hopes of social advance therefore rested on education and the spreading of Christian values so that new opportunities might be rightly used. Education was the first and greatest need of the industrial classes, then shorter hours of labour, and then the free provision of the best forms of pleasure.

It was the priority that Barnett gave to attending to men's minds and souls rather than their material circumstances that led him to refuse an invitation to serve on the Royal Commission on the Poor Laws in 1905, preferring, as his wife records, to devote himself to 'the direct teaching of his faith'. (H. O. Barnett 1918: 677). Earlier, before leaving the East End for Bristol in 1892, he had written that if everyone were Christian there would be no need for socialism and that until everyone was Christian, socialism was impossible. The practical thing therefore was for everyone to cultivate personal friendship with his neighbours (quoted ibid.: 664).

The cultivation of personal friendship with neighbours was, of course, one of the primary aims of Toynbee Hall but perhaps also the least successful part of Barnett's work in the East End. It was also an aspect of the settlement's activities to which he himself attached less importance in later years; not that he ceased to think attention to individual relationships necessary, only that it was not sufficient to ensure reform. Under Barnett's guidance the emphasis of Toynbee work shifted from local philanthropy to more far-reaching research.

Canon Barnett's response to poverty in the East End was echoed in the Archbishop of Canterbury's report on urban priority areas a hundred years later; a call for action by both church and state to enable the poor and the powerless to rejoin the life of the nation and create a society in which benefits and burdens were more equally shared. In similar vein the Catholic Archbishop of Liverpool has argued that the church and voluntary effort are no longer able to provide the social services to which people are entitled and which they have come to expect.[6] Not surprisingly, in a country where wealth has multiplied fourfold and a tradition of state welfare gradually developed, government transfers and government policies come to represent a more convincing answer to urban deprivation than the lonely efforts of charitable individuals.

The early ideal of a settlement where rich and poor could meet in friendship, sharing common interests and a common culture so that working men might experience the best in art and music and literature, a means to life rather than to a livelihood, was perhaps doomed from the beginning. One of the early settlers, A. P. Laurie, suggests Toynbee Hall was in the wrong place. Whitechapel's population, he says, was a mixture of immigrant Jews and semi-criminals and the settlement was irrelevant to both. It would have ben better placed further east among the artisans and labourers working in innumerable industries but with no public institutions, no education facilities, no public opinion, and incompetent and corrupt local government. Laurie and several others moved out of Toynbee Hall wanting closer contact with the people of East London, especially with the Labour leaders, and to escape 'an atmosphere about Toynbee Hall which irritated us', though for which Barnett was not responsible. The settlers were supposed, Laurie remarks, to be noble young men doing good to the poor, 'but we didn't feel noble and had no desire to do good to anybody'. Slumming had become a fashionable amusement and Toynbee Hall was very much in the limelight. 'After a good dinner a crowd of men and women in evening dress would be personally conducted through the worst slums known, prying into people's homes and behaving in an intolerable manner. We wanted to get away from all this' (Laurie 1934: 73). Barnett himself was well aware of such dangers. After ten years at St Jude's he wrote of the increasing public interest in the poor and of the attendant dangers. Interest feeds on vice and there was a temptation to seek out the painful as a stimulant to effort. 'It is a fearful thing to find a half pleasurable interest in the sight of human degradation' (quoted in N. F. Aitken 1902: 106).

That Toynbee Hall was in the wrong place may well have been true. Few of the Whitechapel poor attended the lectures, classes, and entertainments intended to spread 'the best' and open wider opportunities among them. Audiences were drawn from the middle classes, from board school teachers and from the better off working men, many of whom came from other parts of London. And the classes in commercial subjects directly linked to job opportunities were the more popular among East Enders. Abel claims that many settlement activities, like the travellers' club that tended to exclude working men because it was too expensive, had little impact on the mass of the poor; they drew out of society only those already deviant, Matthew Arnold's 'aliens' (Abel 1969: 240).

There is little doubt, however, that the more modest ventures into practical philanthropy had some effect on the local community. Settlers ran clubs for children and for working men as well as for board school teachers; they served on school boards, poor law boards, and sanitary aid committees; later they organized a poor man's lawyer service and tenants' protection societies and later still they served on the care committees set up to administer the 1906 Education Act and the juvenile advisory committees attached to the Stepney Labour Exchange after 1909. Moreover, the Barnetts' social entertainments, art exhibitions, and musical evenings can have done little harm and may have given some pleasure, as one settler remarked. Above all, perhaps, Whitechapel children were sent for two weeks' holiday into the country. The first nine left St Jude's in 1877 but in 1913 45,000 went for a fortnight into the surrounding countryside. In all, a million children had spent two weeks away from the East End by 1916.

In later years, however, and particularly after 1900, Toynbee Hall grew increasingly important as a centre for social investigation and a training place for public service. In 1903 Beveridge became sub warden and wrote to his father that he for one did not believe that colossal evils could be remedied by small doses of culture and charity and amiability. The real use he wished to make of Toynbee and similar institutions was as centres for the development of authoritative opinion on the problems of city life (Beveridge 1953: 17). And many others, A. P. Laurie, R. H. Tawney, C. R. Ashbee, T. E. Harvey, and indeed Barnett himself shifted the emphasis of settlement work away from practical benevolence to social investigation, recognizing that the problems of the East End would never be solved in Whitechapel.

It was this aspect of Toynbee Hall that aroused the wrath of George Lansbury, an early and implacable opponent of the attempts of Canon Barnett and the Whitechapel guardians to cut back outdoor poor relief at the end of the nineteenth century. The one solid achievement of Toynbee Hall and of the mixing policy of the Barnetts, Lansbury declared, had been the filling of posts in government and administration by men and women who went to East London full of enthusiasm for the welfare of the masses, only to discover that their own interests and those of the poor were best served by leaving East London to become members of parliament, cabinet ministers, and civil servants, discovering that problems of life and poverty were too complex to solve, that the poor were bad and reform must be gradual and that nothing must be done to hurt the rich who kept such places as Toynbee Hall going (Lansbury 1928: 130).

Others took a more charitable view. Beveridge spoke of the value of settlements as a protest against taking the structure of society for granted. Frederick Rogers in 1913 saw Toynbee Hall under Canon Barnett as a place 'that radiated influences that touched the universities, the press, and politics for more than a generation and created ideas and enthusiasms which still live and work among us' (1913: 321). Mansbridge noted that Barnett drew great men from near and far to Toynbee (1948: 62). Harold Spender, who went to live in East London led by a 'prophet', Barnett, in 1890, remarked with some dismay that the newer settlers who came after him tended to join the ranks of labour and became more socialist than the British working man. 'That was not our idea of our task. We were there . . . to bridge the gulf between Disraeli's "two nations": not merely to cross the gulf and pitch our tents on the other side' (1926: 71).

Perhaps one of those most anxious to cross the gulf was Tawney who went to Toynbee in 1903 seeing settlements as centres for gathering information that might one day lead to collective action, places where rich and poor could meet to discuss matters of common concern to every citizen. But Tawney was uneasy with that aspect of the work of Toynbee Hall that involved the imposing of one culture and set of values on another—in spreading 'the best' among a deprived and degraded population. The purpose of Toynbee Hall should be to provide a neutral platform where working men and women would be encouraged to contribute their own ideas (Meacham 1987: 158). But the settlement did not enable Tawney to meet working people on terms of equality in the way he wished.

Literature relating to the Children's Country Holiday Fund which he directed he found 'monotonously benevolent'. After three years he left Toynbee, with Barnett's encouragement, to devote himself to teaching and particularly to the Workers' Educational Association.

At the centre of Toynbee Hall, moulding its character and guiding its direction, encouraging and responding to the changing emphasis of its work through the last twenty years of the nineteenth century and into the twentieth, was Canon Barnett. Somewhat unprepossessing in physical appearance, presiding over an institution which Tawney at any rate saw as based on outmoded assumptions of cultural superiority, his power lay in his dedication to the work of reform as he conceived it, his readiness to pursue new ideas, and his ability through his own convictions and ideals to inspire other men. For some, Barnett's lack of dogmatism and his willingness to shift his views in the light of increasing knowledge or changing circumstances represented a grave fault. C. S. Loch treated Barnett's criticism of the COS in 1895 with derision. 'With Mr. Barnett progress is a series of reactions. He must be in harmony with the current philanthropic opinion of the moment or perhaps just a few seconds ahead of it. Then having laid great stress on a new point, he would "turn his back on himself" and lay equal stress on the point that he had before insisted on' (1895).

Others, however, saw Barnett's willingness to alter his opinions as his greatest strength. The heart of his power, according to Nevinson, was his spiritual insight that enabled him to perceive the moment when change must come or life be lost. In this way he fulfilled the most difficult duty of leadership, 'he so hated idols that he was always ready to lead a revolution against himself' (Nevinson 1923: 91).

Nevertheless Barnett's refusal to commit himself to particular political or religious doctrines or dogma offended some who went to Toynbee Hall. Ashbee parodies him in the Revd Simeon Flux, conducting a latitudinarian mission, attempting to square a vague theory of Christianity with modern scientific knowledge in an earnest if empirical attempt to solve economic difficulties. But he 'could not take the cold plunge of the twentieth-century Socialism, the ripple of which he touched with a shivering toe. Perhaps it was more honest of him even not to do this, not to be definite, dogmatic; but it lost him the love of the younger generation, who looked to him for leadership' (Ashbee 1910: 175).

Most of those who knew him, however, were more impressed by the liberality and tolerance of Barnett's character. In Laurie's view he was too sound a thinker to adopt cut and dried ideas about what the future commonwealth should be or how it might be attained. He took no part in party politics and left the organization of Toynbee Hall 'very elastic', avoiding the trap of narrow doctrinaire socialism. 'I doubt if he ever expected it to have much influence on East London. He regarded it rather as a postgraduate university for young men from Oxford and Cambridge who might ultimately become Members of Parliament or civil servants (1934: 72). Nor did Barnett believe that settlements were the only means to social advance. 'I do not preach the duty of settling among the poor' he told residents at Toynbee Hall. 'I simply repeat the commandment, Love God' (quoted in Nevinson 1923: 91). Beveridge saw Barnett as infinitely wise with a strong temper controlled and directed by love of God and love of man. The strength of the house he founded was its ability to use many different sorts of people (1953: 38). This judgement is echoed by Albert Mansbridge who attributed some of the most successful achievements of the WEA to Barnett's advice and help. Toynbee Hall was his most obvious creative effort, but 'his power to create ideas in the minds of others and to inspire their hearts was his outstanding characteristic' (1948: 60).

For Spender, Barnett was a prophet. 'He stimulated without eclipsing. He guided without crushing. He conveyed a spirit' (1926: 70). Described by Beatrice Webb as a man of 'fathomless sympathy' and a 'nineteenth-century saint', his prophetic vision was of a state built on social justice where the interests of each individual were fused with the well-being of the whole community. Perhaps, as Mrs Webb suggests, Barnett was too intent on the end or purpose of human life, and 'a noble state of mind in each individual and in the community as a whole', to concentrate on the means by which it might be reached (B. Webb: n.d.: 19). If so this only attaches him all the more firmly to the Christian and ethical socialist tradition, among men and women who believe with Tawney that 'happiness and contentment are to be found not in the power of man to satisfy wants, but in the power of man to regard his position in society and that of his fellows with moral approval or satisfaction' (Winter and Joskin 1972: 19).

NOTES

1. Letter from the Bishop of London to Samuel Barnett on his move to St Jude's. Quoted in H. O. Barnett 1918: 69.
2. Canon Barnett to F. G. Barnett. Quoted ibid.: 657.
3. See Dennis and Halsey (1988) on L. T. Hobhouse.
4. Barnett to Bishop Temple, Apr. 1882. Quoted in H. O. Barnett 1918: 545.
5. *Faith in the City* was and is considered deeply hostile to Thatcherite social policy, and was condemned by a prominent conservative as 'Marxist theology'.
6. *The Elect and the Elected*, Transcript of BBC Radio 3 broadcast, 22 Oct. 1985.

2

Conceptions of Social Work[1]

JULIET CHEETHAM

We recommend a new local authority department, providing a community based and family oriented service, which will be available to all. This new department will, we believe, reach far beyond the discovery and rescue of social casualties; it will enable the greatest possible number of people to act reciprocally, giving and receiving service for the well-being of the whole community . . . (these departments) will . . . in a disproportionate degree, prevent human deterioration, improve the lives of the most vulnerable in our population and mobilise goodwill and voluntary effort within the community.

Report of the Community on Local Authority and Allied Personal Social Services (London: HMSO, 1968), paras. 2 and 706.

Community Care has been talked of for thirty years and in few areas can the gap between political rhetoric and policy on the one hand and between policy and reality on the other hand have been so great. To talk of policy in matters of care except in the context of available resources and timescales for action owes more to theology than to the purposeful delivery of a caring service.

Community Care: Agenda for Action (London: HMSO, 1988), para. 9.

For the last twenty years the story of social work and the personal social service with which it is inextricably linked has been one of extraordinary contrasts. These two quotations seem to come from two different worlds: one full of optimism and aspiration, grand and at times grandiose design; the other somewhat weary from experience, more cautious, more precise, requiring words to be linked to resources and action. Both reports express visions of policies developed independently and seemingly ignorant of sociological knowledge and enquiry.

The late 1960s and early 1970s were characterized by heady, perhaps foolhardy optimism, about the responsibility and capacity of social services and social work to deliver a better society for all, but especially for the most vulnerable. And this was not simply the language of excited committees; it could also find its way into legislation, with the Social Work (Scotland) Act 1968 stating 'It shall be the duty of every local authority to promote social welfare by making available advice, guidance and assistance on such a scale as may be appropriate for their area' (s. 12 (i)). The need for more resources was certainly noted but, in a climate of general political and public consensus about welfare, with no solid information about the extent of the needs to be met, was treated lightly save for the cautions and critiques of a few academics (Sinfield 1969; Townsend 1970). The Seebohm Committee was confident that the resources of the new social services departments, which were to usher in a new era of personal welfare and reciprocity, 'measured in manpower, buildings, training, intelligence and research . . . will still not be large in relation to local authority budgets' (para. 706). By implication, a major attraction of this new dawn was its relative cheapness.

THE PERSONAL SOCIAL SERVICES: VISION AND DISILLUSION

For a few years blithe confidence about what could be achieved was boosted by central government's encouragement to social services departments to think in terms of a steady rate of growth of 10 per cent per annum in real terms. The Labour government also enthusiastically pursued better health and social policies for disadvantaged people, driven forward by the passionate zeal and vision of ministers such as Barbara Castle and Richard Crossman. A plethora of service reviews and proposed policies for mentally ill, handicapped, and disabled people flowed from government committees, their major thrust being the development of community-based services for those already in or at risk of residential or institutional care (HMSO 1971; 1975).

The enthusiasm for the political commitment to end at least the worst horrors of institutional care, graphically portrayed by the Royal Commission on Law Relating to Mental Illness and Mental Deficiency (1957) and by Townsend (1962) in *The Last Refuge*, diverted attention from the considerable conceptual confusion about the nature, capacities, and responsibilities of 'the community'. For young people at odds with the law new and ambitious community-based preventive services were outlined in the Children in Trouble White Paper (1968) and in part enacted and implemented in the Children and Young Persons Act 1969. The local authorities' powers to pursue prevention which the Ingleby Committee had endorsed and the 1963 Children and Young Persons Act had allowed now became mandatory. The proactive role of local authorities was also stimulated by the 1970 Chronically Sick and Disabled Persons Act which required them to identify younger disabled people in their areas and make known their services, thus stimulating demand. In all these new visions social workers were to play key roles in assessing need, arranging or providing services, prompting Titmuss to remark in 1970 (unpublished) that 'whenever a new social problem is identified there is a call for more and more social workers'. They saw themselves, and were seen, as important contributors to social reform.

It was not long before the tide began to turn. With the economy thoroughly shaken by the oil crisis only the most modest growth in the health and social services was permitted. Need-led planning was replaced by scarcity-led planning, and there was disappointment that the development of community care services was not fulfilling the promises of White Papers and legislation. Social services managers' despondency at the gap between social work aspiration and resource reality was underlined by Utting (1977: 25), the Chief Social Work Officer in the Department of Health and Social Security. Recognizing that the proportion of national wealth devoted to the personal social services would not increase significantly he did not now expected major progress for 'the customer'. The improvements in the personal social services as 'second best substitutes' for family care would flow from better organization and closer integration with health services. At the same time public expectations and demand were growing, particularly from those over 75, whose numbers increased in England and Wales by over a million between 1971 and 1985, and from the ever growing number of people living in poverty. In 1975 just over twelve and half million people had incomes at or below 140 per cent of the supplementary benefit level; by 1983 there were over nineteen million (Parker and Mirrlees 1988: 512–14).

With austerity came demands for greater efficiency and, towards the end of our period, extreme alarm at rapidly rising social security expenditure on residential care for elderly people some of whom, it was argued, would be better and more economically cared for in the community. These social security payments were more than doubling annually, rising from less than £50 million in 1982 to £500m in 1986. A series of tough reports from the Audit Commission (1985; 1986) scathingly criticized the poor co-ordination of health and social services and conflicting social security and community care policies. In 1986 the Commission warned that, without radical action, there would be 'continued waste of scarce resources and, worse still, care and support that is either lacking entirely, or inappropriate to the needs of some of the most disadvantaged members of society and the relatives who seek to care for them' (1986: 6).

The commitment to social reform which was to be enacted through expanded health and social services was further shaken by doubts about both its sense and legitimacy. On the left social scientists, politicians, and service providers could agree that since the needs of so many of the clients of the personal social services are manifestations and by-products of poverty they could and should be 'resolved in other ways than by massaging them with the scarce liniments of social work and social care' (Webb and Wistow 1987: 70). Consistent with this analysis staving off the crises of poor people and rescuing social casualties were thus the inevitable frustrating daily experience of service providers who, as Sir Roy Griffiths poignantly remarked, had come to feel that 'the Israelites faced with the requirement to make bricks without straw had a comparatively routine and possible task' (Griffiths 1988: para. 7). All this seemed far removed from the vision of the Seebohm Committee, a vision which anyway was to have no place in the philosophy of a strong Conservative government with its outright disbelief in an enlarged role for the state.

In this unstable world the cool pragmatism of Sir Roy Griffiths' slim report on the future of community care was welcome relief with its imperative that 'policy and resources should come into reasonable relationship' (para. 9) and its clear message that lyrical rehearsals of ends without sober attention to means are pointless and irresponsible. The stage was thus firmly set for defining and ensuring the machinery and resources to implement such policies as may be determined by government and to insist on value for money. Fears that the play to be performed on this stage would not meet these ideals were expressed but largely disregarded.

SOCIAL WORK: CRITICISM AND EXPANSION

Social work inevitably reflects the fortunes and fancies of the personal social services and throughout the period there was a huge expansion in the numbers of social workers trained and in work and frenzied attempts to increase these numbers even more. In 1969 9,573 social workers were employed in local authority departments in England and Wales; in 1983, fourteen years later, this number had more than trebled to 29,605, including 3,535 welfare assistants (Parker and Mirrless 1988: 485), and in 1987 to 33,400. In Scotland there were similar spectacular increases. But there is also a paradox. Throughout the same twenty years this growing number of social workers were also subjected to relentless and ferocious criticism.

An early blast had come from Wootton who in 1958 (1958: 871) wrote witheringly of the 'fantastically pretentious facade' social workers erected to diguise simple activities; of their claims to powers verging on omniscience and omnipotence; and of 'their habit of confusing economic difficulties with personal failure or misconduct' (ibid.: 291). Brewer and Lait (1980), with less authority but in a much quoted text, doubted whether social work could or should survive, stressing its unproven assumptions, muddled objectives, and lack of outcomes. Also attacked were the worthy attempts of the Barclay Committee set up in 1980, in part to quell such attacks, to clarify and legitimize social work, and to bring some sense and consensus into a theory and practice which would encompass individuals and their communities. Pinker, for example, in his minority report, saw even the modest goals and activities of community social work as hopelessly unrealistic and inappropriate.

> It conjures up the vision of the captainless crew under a patchwork ensign stitched together from remnants of the Red Flag and the Jolly Roger—all with a licence and some with a disposition to mutiny—heading in the gusty winds of populist rhetoric, with presumption as their figurehead and inexperience as their compass, straight for the reefs of public incredulity. (Pinker 1982: 261–2)

The most damning criticisms of all were of social work practice in actual cases exposed to exhaustive analysis in the reports of the public enquiries following the deaths of children for whom social services departments had had responsibility. The first of these enquiries, into the death of Maria Colwell, took place in 1974 and attracted enormous hostile publicity for social work which was to be repeated almost annually, with the reports on the deaths of Jasmine Beckford (London Borough of Brent 1985) and Kimberley Carlisle (London Borough of Greenwich 1987) being particularly traumatic. Social workers (and far less often doctors and health workers) were accused of failures to comprehend and implement the law; to co-ordinate with other services; of naïve understanding of children's needs; of indecision and hopeless optimism about their power to influence families' welfare; and of mistaken views about the relative rights of parents and children. In short, they were held to have failed in their basic duty to protect the lives and limbs of their most vulnerable clients; and the failing was not simply technical but moral.

For all these critics, however, social workers had potentially important roles. For Wootton in 1970 they (as probation officers) were to operate community service orders, seen by her Committee charged with devising non-custodial penalties for young adult offenders as their most imaginative recommendation. For Brewer and Lait social workers could have useful roles to play in general practice. For Pinker social workers have an important contribution to make in their skilled, specialized work with individuals and families. The reports of enquiries into child deaths have also concluded with recommendations for the improvement of social work practice and for better social work training, but not for the dissolution of the institution or the transfer of its powers.

While some of these criticisms could be dismissed or diminished as being founded on an imperfact understanding of the tasks and the responsibilities of social work there was more embarrassment to come from research which at least in part had studied social work in its own terms. Social workers pursued agenda beyond their clients' comprehension or agreement (Mayer and Timms 1970). Although they could be liked and respected by clients much work drifted towards uncertain ends, with no demonstrable results (Sainsbury *et al.* 1982). Intensive work with offenders on probation was no more successful than ordinary supervision (Folkard *et al.* 1976). Worse still, it might have unintended, negative outcomes (Fischer 1976). Preventive work with children in intermediate treatment and other groups might serve only to stigmatize them as actual or potential persistent offenders, for whom the courts would, prematurely, pass severe sentences on the assumption that social work intervention had done no good (Thorpe 1978).

Criticism from without did not unite the ranks of social work and the arguments raged about the extent to which social workers should try to relieve the poverty of the clients (Jordan 1974); about the relationship between social and community work and the responsibility to combat political and social inequality (Bailey and Brake 1975; Benington 1975; Craig *et al.* 1982); about probation officers' contribution to criminal justice (Bottoms and McWilliams 1979; Walker and Beaumont 1981); about the location and identification of their practice (Hadley and McGrath 1980; Beresford and Croft 1986). There was criticism too of a social work curriculum which in its indiscriminate plundering of the social sciences had become a kind of supermarket for teachers and students who selected what appealed to them without stringent analysis of contradictions between and within disciplines. Competing theories did not therefore compete (Sheldon 1978). For those within social work all this could seem at the time as evidence either of vitality and a lively grasp of the complexities of policy and practice, or of total confusion. Those outside probably saw only confusion.

SOCIAL WORK'S SURVIVAL AND RECOVERY

Despite this critical hurly-burly and internal dispute social workers neither scattered nor were scattered. Perversely, or bravely, their practice and numbers have continued to grow, with the most recent demands for the employment of many more social workers coming in the report of the Wagner Committee (1988) which reviewed residential care where very few staff have social work qualifications. If the Committee's proposal that all senior posts should be filled by a qualified social worker were accepted some 33,000 more would be required.

This survival and expansion is in part the consequence of the state's inescapable (albeit perhaps reluctantly acknowledged) need for social workers to contain troublesome behaviour and to ration resources in responding to needs so acute or so onerous as to be beyond the management of the suffering individuals or their kin. It reflects too the progress social work has made in defining its ends and means and demonstrating its worth. On all these fronts there are opportunities and hazards.

Containment and Control

Although they are the source of considerable unease for many social workers their control and disciplinary functions should not be underestimated. These are a means by which the state attempts to contain, in their communities and without drastic intervention, citizens widely regarded as deviant, troublesome, or disturbing. Here social work is part of 'a more general movement away from the traditional laying down of *laws* towards an increasing resort to the mobilisation of norms . . . The norm which comes to supplement the law in cases of juveniles, children, the feeble minded . . . bases itself upon expert decision (certified by doctors, psychologists, social workers, etc.) regarding the normality of pathology of "characters", "mental or moral states", and "modes of life". These decisions, which need not be publicly explained, are based upon an expertise in the "human sciences" that is not widely shared nor easily challenged' (Garland 1985: 235–6).

Social workers are central to the operation of legislation designed to protect and support people with serious mental health problems; to supervise and influence the behaviour of offenders when the courts regard monetary penalties or custodial sentences as inappropriate; to monitor the care of allegedly incompetent parents and to remove to places of safety those children whose welfare is judged to be seriously at risk. Every year in England there are now some 40,000 children on Child Protection Registers. In the 1980s the reduced role of psychiatric hospitals and public alarm at prisons' escalating costs and disruption have further underlined the control and protection functions of social work. Changes in legislation may affect the operation of these functions but not their existence; and as we shall see, in these roles, from which there can be no escape, social workers will always be especially exposed to public criticism.

Needs and Rationing

When vulnerable populations become large and their needs acute, as with very elderly people, the state has to respond. Good sense, humanity, and political fashion combine to require proper assessment of often highly complex needs and, in the jargon of the White Paper on Community Care, 'packages of care in line with individual needs and preferences' (para. 1: 11). It is no simple task to elicit the wishes of the ambivalent, to grasp the capacities of the frail, and to judge, with them and their kin, what may be best for individual and collective welfare. But this already highly complex task does not of course, end there. Finite resources and ideologies about family responsibilities mean that assessing and responding to need is inexitricably tangled with assessing priorities, with the efficient targeting of services; in short, with rationing. These combined tasks which demand skill and provoke antagonism have long been the responsibilities of social workers and their forebears.

In contrast to the Seebohm report, in which social workers were much discussed and much demanded, Sir Roy Griffiths does not mention them by name and in the White Paper their function is largely implicit. Perhaps the recent history of social work has made it an occupational group unlikely to be regarded as an asset by the government in its public launching of a community care programme designed to deliver more sensitive, flexible, efficient personal social services to elderly, ill, and disabled people from all social classes. Perhaps, as Pinker has pointed out (1989: 85), this reflects the fact that while social security, health care, education, and to a lesser extent public housing, have become an integral part of the nation's political economy social work, being almost exclusively concerned with the most dependent and least economically successful minority groups has become steadily more isolated.

Nevertheless, by whatever name (and care manager is now a favoured term), the old familiar social work tasks of assessment, gatekeeping, service provision, advice, and counselling are firmly on the agenda of community care. And while multi-disciplinary contributions are extolled and needed there are as yet no serious alternative contenders for social work's leading role in the management of community care. Social workers also remain the principal actors in the implementation of the Children Act, 1989. Why is this so?

The Effectiveness of Social Work

The tenacity of established tradition, legislation, and administrative frameworks provides part of the answer. More positively there is recognition (albeit sometimes grudging) of the interests and ability of social workers to deal both with practical and emotional problems, an essential prerequisite of a sensible response to the often complicated sufferings of individuals and families which flow from age, disability, poverty, misfortune, and ineptitude. Particularly influential too, in the context of community care, has been the analysis of a variety of innovative care-in-the-community projects which has demonstrated the success of social work management and practice in maintaining in their own homes extremely vulnerable people, to their own and their carers' satisfaction, often at less cost than institutional care, and with enhanced quality of life (Davies and Knapp 1988; Ferlie, Challis, and Davies 1989). Hospital social workers can increase the rate with which elderly patients can be successfully discharged from hospital, thus relieving valuable health resources (Tibbitt and Connor 1988). Social workers can also find and sustain foster homes for extremely difficult and disturbed children who would otherwise be in expensive residential care (Aldgate, Maluccio, and Reeves 1989). They can also provide effective supervision for young and adult offenders who might otherwise be caught up in a needless escalation of court appearance and custodial sentences (Blagg and Smith 1989; McIvor 1989; 1990). To use the language of the market-place, which they had long despised but would now frequent, social workers could in the late 1980s claim to be cost effective. What has contributed to this little-sung triumph? Will it bring a well-grounded, brighter future for social work?

A GOOD OUTCOME FOR SOCIAL WORK?

A simple response to the first question about social work's emerging effectiveness would concentrate on its retreat, in the space of a few years, from optimistic aspirations for human welfare to more modest focused objectives; from flirtation with grand ends to preoccupation with practical means, including their management and cost. A simple response to the second question about the vitality and integrity of social work's future would emphasize the clear benefits of such evident rationality; but as we shall see, there are also grounds for caution.

Reassessing the Ends and Means of Social Work: The Retreat from Prevention

Public criticism and ridicule, research on the effectiveness of practice, and resources not equal to demand all prompted an intellectual reassessment of the feasible ends and means of social work. Practitioners were encouraged to settle, with their clients, for tackling, as far and as speedily as practicable, immediate pressing needs. This approach did not come easily because it appeared to challenge social workers' increasingly complex understanding of the multiple and interactive nature of their clients' problems; of the importance of focusing on their social and community context. The logic of such an analysis encouraged social workers to prevent at best occurrence but at least the deterioration of individuals' problems, an aspiration reinforced by the Seebohm Committee and enshrined in legislation.

The Committee encouraged social workers to undertake ambitious preventive work. Arguing that 'an effective family service must be concerned with the prevention of social distress' (para. 427), having earlier defined the family as incorporating 'everybody' (para. 32), the Committee outlined programmes of general and specific prevention, following the arguments of the Newsom Report (1963) and the Plowden Report (1967) with 'the concentration of effort and resources on particular areas and a focus on individuals at key transitional stages in life: leaving school, early parenthood, retirement and bereavement' (para. 427). Social workers welcomed then, and would still, the Committee's conviction that 'only when the imperative demands made by the casualties are diminished can prevention become possible; but the number of casualties can only be reduced by preventive action. It is critical therefore that this vicious circle is broken by a forceful and widespread commitment to prevention' (para. 454). What form this endeavour might take the Committee acknowledged was unclear. It was to be an experiment from which to learn on which systematic research was urgently needed.

In social work prevention was to take many forms: family advice centres; intermediate treatment groups; counselling and advice for the relatives of people killed in major accidents; the statutory authority to give help in cash or kind to prevent reception into care and, in Scotland, 'to promote social welfare'. Evaluating the outcomes of such preventive work presented major problems when goals were diffuse; for example, the prevention of stress or breakdown. The evidence relating to more specific goals, prevention of children's reception into care or juvenile court appearances, brought mixed messages for social work. Although significant reductions were achieved in the reception into care there was some evidence that preventive work with young law breakers did not influence their behaviour but did identify them when they finally appeared in court as problem children who had already failed to benefit from the attentions of social work. Higher tariff penalties might then be imposed, thus hastening the young person's journey through the criminal justice system to the severest sentences of detention, borstal, or youth custody. Disillusion began to overtake the initial promise of preventive social work.

There were also unanticipated problems in social workers' access to money to be used for preventive purposes. These budgets, which varied greatly throughout the country, were both valued and derided. They were valued as a means of making practical, timely responses to urgent needs, the meeting of which could enhance individuals' capacity to cope and underline the social workers' capacity and willingness to help. They were derided as a means by which the social security system could be both subsidized and relieved of its responsibilities to meet both urgent and chronic need (Hill and Laing 1978; Jackson and Valencia 1978; Jordan 1974). Social security claimants needing immediate help with food, household, and fuel expenses could simply be referred to social work or social service departments. This cash could also, it was argued, reinforce social workers' unwillingness to tangle with the complexities of the social security system and their dislike of substantial amounts of work securing welfare benefits (Stevenson and Parsloe 1978). Understandably, social workers and their departments resented being used as second-line social security offices and the indignity and distress of referring back often desperate people. They feared too the charges of inequitable financial help for clients whose circumstances appeared similar but for whom the social work response differed, either because budgets were exhausted or because of differing social work assessments.

Some way out of this tangle of dilemmas was provided by research which demonstrated that brief focused work with explicit goals, agreed with clients, is more effective than long-term work and is preferred by both clients and social workers. (Reid and Epstein 1972; 1977). Such thinking, often in vulgarized form, was influential in the expansion of intake teams and their attempts to sift short- and long-term problems, and in the adoption of case review systems and more frequent closing of cases (Goldberg and Warburton 1979). Of significance too, although still not properly recognized, was the accumulating evidence of the effectiveness of social work when it clearly identifies target problems, works extensively with them, applies task-centred or behavioural approaches, co-ordinates with other services with an agreed and definite policy, adopts a contractual style with clients, and rehearses rather than simply discusses possible solutions to problems (Reid and Hanrahan 1982; Sheldon 1986; 1987). Thus departments coped with mounting numbers of referrals, the consequence of an increasingly ageing, expectant, and vigilant population, although not without long waiting lists, great stress, and the virtual abandonment of preventive work, save that designed to deflect the worst disasters which might befall an individual.

COMING TO TERMS WITH SOCIOLOGICAL ANALYSIS

Social work was also strengthened through its growing relationship with sociological analysis which both enlarged its vision and narrowed its sights. The initial impact was to encourage a broader arena for its activities. The hazards of expecting social work, on its own, to play a major role in prevention were well recognized by the growing numbers of people who became committed to more radical preventive effort (although not usually labelled thus) through various forms of community work. This increasingly absorbed social work time and attention in the late 1960s and 1970s, much strengthened by the government's Community Development Programme. Improvements in housing, education, employment, recreation, and the environment became major targets for community work, the logic being that this amelioration would prevent much of the personal and social distress of those clients, or casualties, who frequented social work agencies. Respect for the citizenship of people living in disadvantaged areas accompanied encouragement for participation in the identification of needs, in self-help, and in the political process. The enemy was variously defined as capitalism, the state, the Council, the developer. Intervention and opposition were tailored accordingly; and the battles were mostly lost.

Debate raged about the contributions of social and community work, about their appropriate training, responsibilities, activities, and tactics, all fuelled by arguments and anguish about their proper relationship with the state, and with Marxist and liberal democratic politics. Social workers were accused of ignoring the structural, economic, and political forces which shape their clients' lives, of being blind to race and gender inequalities, of encouraging acquiescence and complacency; in short, of being major mechanisms of oppression and the continued impoverishment of the desperately poor and powerless. In their turn community workers were accused of ignoring individual needs and preferences in pursuit of the alleged common good; of political arrogance and manipulation; of gross naïvety in their expectations of the impact of public protest, characterized in the oft-quoted and rarely enacted 'march upon the town hall' by the citizens of neglected housing estates and rotting inner urban areas.

The broadening horizons of social and community work did not simply reflect the lively debates of the Left, which dominated social policy until the return of the Conservative government in 1979. They were in part a natural consequence of the increasingly close links between the education of its recruits and the expanding disciplines of social policy and sociology. A comparison of booklists given to social workers in the 1960s to those commonly circulated today shows these to have grown in the last quarter century from some 40 to more than 500 references. Of particular significance was the introduction of sociology into social work courses core curricula which only occurred to any significant extent in the late 1960s. Although the writer remembers a somewhat incredulous and suspicious audience at the launching of a book intended to illuminate the mysteries of the relevance of sociology to social work (Leonard 1968) at least some social workers and their teachers were not slow to revel in the illumination of social problems which they found in sociology and criminology, or to grasp the deficiencies of welfare highlighted by an increasingly analytical and critical social policy. A call for more universal family and community services and a focus on the social and political context of deprivation were the practical responses of this intellectual heritage; and initial excitement inhibited more disciplined analysis of the capacity of intervention, focused largely on individuals, small groups, or areas to incorporate sociological theory as a practical basis for action. In community work, as in social work, the refinement of feasible goals came relatively quickly, bringing relief at the possibility of practical achievement and disillusion with such modest gains. At the location of the power and decisions which would affect the inner city became clear, far beyond the Council's boundaries or the reach of the awakened local citizenry (Benington 1975), community workers either disbanded or, more frequently, trimmed their aspirations and focused their efforts on the amelioration rather than the transformation of the environment and on the strengthening of community support and advocacy groups. Such enterprises, once regarded with suspicion as harbingers of radical threat and protest became and remain essential ingredients of orthodox welfare programmes.

The practical humanity and experiences of some of those who espoused radical politics and did not shirk the needs of the people with whom they worked also forged a practice which could live with the tensions of a political analysis and the need for immediate individual relief. The meshing (not merging) of the two in work with individuals was vigorously demanded and demonstrated by Cohen (S. Cohen 1975) and Leonard (1984) and further illustrated by feminist writers whose experience with women in need had convinced them of the imperative and potential of working with practical and emotional problems within a political context (Wilson 1975; Dominelli and McLeod 1989). Evidence for the intellectual justification for this 'practice wisdom' could also be found in Brown's (1987) research on seriously and chronically depressed women which showed, over two decades, an increasingly complex aetiology in which the consequences of social disadvantage and life events could be mediated by individual support from within and outside the family, not all of which are beyond the capacity of social work to encourage or provide. Once again C. Wright Mills' injunction was to serve social work well: 'know that many personal troubles cannot be solved merely as troubles, but must be understood in terms of public issues . . . Know that the human meaning of public issues must be revealed by relating them to personal troubles—and to the problems of the individual life' (C. W. Mills 1959: 248).

The impact on social work of sociological analysis was thus complex. While their first taste of its illumination of personal and social problems had swept social workers to promise more than could be delivered, through more critical analysis and the hard experience of lack of influence in the worlds of politics and redistribution, it became both sensible and honourable to grasp the sober fact that some problems are just beyond solution or major amelioration through social work: the isolation and disabilities of some very elderly people; the struggles of parents with extremely limited incomes, living in unsuitable housing and depressing environments; the disaffection of unemployed, ill-educated young people are but a few. Help was, nevertheless, still possible, and given legitimacy by its potential effectiveness and consistency with clients' definitions of their needs and wants. (Reid and Hanrahan 1982; Sheldon 1986; 1987). Furthermore, public regard for social work could be justified by the accumulating evidence of social work's cost-effective contribution to community care (Challis and Davies 1986; Davies and Knapp 1988).

SOCIAL WORK TO 2000: HAZARDS AND POSSIBILITIES

Although the proposed policies of the Griffiths report included such unfamiliar agenda as the expansion of private and voluntary sector provision and the consequent diminution of the public sector, the leaders of social work recognized an era of opportunity for social work and the personal social services and pressed and pleaded for the report's recommendations to be implemented. Almost without demur directors accepted a mixed economy of welfare in which local authorities would in future become the arrangers rather than the providers of services, enabling agencies charged with promoting 'the development of a flourishing independent sector alongside good quality public services'. Even in Scotland, sometimes seen as last bastion and preserve of the public sector, the president of the Association of Directors of Social Work could state with equanimity that the Association cared not whence care came provided its quality could be assured. The 1990s were thus to be the decade of strategic objectives and priorities, of realistic planning which sets specific targets to take account of the needs of people in long-stay institutions, of local needs and of the results of assessments in individual cases. Service arrangements were to 'respect and preserve individual independence, have adequate quality control systems, offer freedom of choice and provide services in a sensitive and responsive way'. Such intentions enhance the status of service users, an aspiration further endorsed by the Children Act 1989 in its promotion of partnership between families with children in need and service providers.

In theory, therefore, precision planning and responsiveness to need and choice are to absorb social work and the personal social services in a manner far removed from the vague rhetoric and optimism of the Seebohm Committee. The serious, perhaps fatal flaw in this endeavour is the lack of clarity about the resources to be available for community care and the government's decision not to 'ring fence' centrally allocated money for these purposes, both of which Sir Roy had firmly indicated as critical components of the rational and effective planning of community care. Equally unclear are the origins of the resources needed by local authorities to comply with the provisions of the Children Act 1986 which require them to prevent children within their areas suffering ill-treatment or neglect. Once again prevention has returned to inspire and to baffle social workers.

That resources or their lack will continue to be a major preoccupation and bone of contention is certain but what other challenges and hazards will confront social work until the turn of the century? The three areas which opened this chapter will remain critical: needs, resources, and rationing; containment and control; and effectiveness.

Universal Aspiration or Residual Reality?

The issue of needs and resources is highlighted by the extent to which close identification with the delivery of community care will involve social workers in services more universal in scope and use than had traditionally been the case in departments dominated by child-care responsibilities. The problems of very elderly people and the demands they make on a willing but diminishing pool of carers (Bulmer 1987; Finch 1989) will be experienced directly or indirectly by most families in Britain. These problems are particularly severe when accompanied by dementia, suffered by one in ten of the elderly population (E. Levin *et al.* 1989). Wealth can diminish but not remove these problems. As the proportion of very elderly people reaches its peak in the next decade and a labour-hungry market absorbs women and young people in lucrative alternatives to caring for granny contact with social work and social services agencies could be a familiar experience for individuals and families from all social classes. Even elaborate private health or social care insurance will not provide the range of necessary residential and domiciliary services. Thus would social work not simply be a residual service reserved for the poor: it could be demanded and challenged by the vociferous middle classes. Health and welfare in old age could be regarded a valued state responsibility in the same way as this is expected for children. Resources could be expanded and social services regarded not as a stigmatizing last resort but as an essential component of universal human welfare, high on every party's political agenda.

So far the omens for such a future are not encouraging. Faced with the choice of public expenditure to reduce the demands of the community charge and or to underwrite an expansion of community care the government chose the former. As a political expedient at a time of mounting public unrest this proved sensible. There seemed general public relief that the threatened community charge increases of £15–20 for 1991 could be saved by delaying community care. Hardly a voice was raised to protest that such a sum might be perceived and readily paid as a bargain price for the services envisaged in the White Paper, for the welfare of the relatives of so many. Why have citizens' demands been so muted?

The immediate inequalities and pressures of the community charge certainly diverted attention from longer-term visions of welfare but these visions had already been narrowed by contemporary anxieties about dependency. In the 1980s 'the dependency culture' became for the government a syndrome to be broken; but the dependency in question was dependency on the state in the form of benefits or care. Dependency on or within families was for the government a quite different and apparently wholly desirable concept. So, for example, while wishing to promote individual self-help and enterprise among young people by drastically reducing the social security benefits available to them the government has ensured that those without employment will be to a substantial extent dependent on their parents until they are twenty-five. Considerable commitment to caring for a relative may also entail dependency for a carer whose domestic responsibilities preclude paid employment. As Graham (H. Graham 1983: 24) has pointed out 'being dependent is synonymous not with receiving care but giving it'. If it is intended that the welfare services should continue to challenge an undesirable culture of dependency they will be provided as a last resort, because all else has failed. They will not be regarded and will not be the supports to be chosen and accepted without stigma which is an implicit message of the White Paper. They will not be seen as the desirable fruits of the community charge.

There is another vision in which dependency is not the enemy of the state, an unnecessary burden on local taxation, and the feared end of every individual. It is simply a well-recognized, necessary, and for most people transitory fact of life for the very young and the very old and for many people who face the acute crises of illness, bereavement, or unemployment. In such circumstances the state or the family or both may willingly respond, with no presumption that state support comes only when families have failed or do not exist, or for the very poor. Social work can uphold such a vision.

Although their practice will be severely constrained by available resources, as assessors of need social workers have the opportunity to take a more holistic view of the pains and pleasures of dependency in listening to and challenging the assumptions and prejudices of managers, politicians, applicants, and users they can maintain a clear view of the price to families and individuals of promoting family interdependence to save the direct costs to the state. The White Paper recognizes that most care of dependent people is provided informally by families, neighbours, and friends and the reasonable assumption is that this state of affairs should continued. Less explicit is the recognition that Britain like other societies, now has an unprecedented number and proportion of very elderly people, some of whom have no kin or friends to support them and some of whose needs and dependency threaten the viability of family support. Carers are, however, to be given help to sustain them in their role and the White Paper, unusually, states that their needs must be considered explicitly. It is certain that comprehensive needs assessment which is not purely resource driven and therefore a form of dishonesty will reveal a sea of troubles which cannot be resolved but which must be recorded as one indication of the potential target of community care; and this must be done without social workers falling into the old trap of promising more than can be delivered. Clients must not be misled about what is possible; nor governments about what is needed.

This role, as recorder of needs, will not endear social work to governments intent on fostering an image of societies which are flourishing because of their economic and social policies and on reducing public expenditure. In such a climate the identification of need is not highly favoured. The government was, for example, considerably embarrassed by the unexpectedly high levels of disability revealed by the OPCS Survey of Disabled People (1988) and the implications for social security benefits and support services. Equally challenging, or embarrassing, could be local authorities' required identification of 'children in need' whom the Children Act 1989 has defined as 'unlikely to achieve or maintain or *to have the opportunity* (author's emphasis) of achieving or maintaining, a reasonable standard of health or development without the provision to him of services by a local authority'. Such children include the disabled, the neglected or abused, and those with developmental difficulties, or suffering social and emotional deprivation.

Comprehensive assessment of people needing community care, an apparently clear requirement of the community care plans demanded by the White Paper and the National Health and Community Care Act 1990, could also be a rich reservoir of information potentially embarrassing for both local and central government because of the gap between need and response and the identification of local, regional, class, and other inequalities. The bold local authorities will be those who take at face value the White Paper's demand for comprehensive assessment of need. Most may well be deterred from such action by fears of escalating community charges and the retaliatory capping by Ministers. The long struggle between central and local government has substantially changed the latter's views of its services. Pride in the nature and extent of welfare for its citizens has been displaced by preoccupation with low expenditure and community charges; and the electorate's longer-term priorities are not yet clear. In such a political and financial climate social service and social work authorities share the problems outlined by Glennerster (1989: 126) for social policy: 'the question is whether it will be in the government's interest to permit us to expose social ills and the limits of individualism, the consequences of government in action as well as service inefficiency . . . In a political climate that favoured social action governments were not adverse to funding research that justified more intervention or improved the effectiveness of social institutions. Now we have seen governments . . . cutting back on social research, on regular monitoring of social conditions because they fear it will provoke calls for more public spending . . . Monitoring and performance indicators have been developed not to show us where unmet need or hidden demands exist but how to reduce unit costs'.

Even if comprehensive needs assessment is allowed social workers may well quail in the wake of its implications. Such an approach, explicitly encouraged by the White Paper on community care and the Children Act 1989, can give the impression of unlimited resources simply waiting to be linked in the most effective way to those in need. But such needs assessment is also intended to be the means of rational rationing (or targeting, to use a softer language) thus raising quite fundamental questions about rights to welfare and the kind of society to be pursued. Social workers will be amongst the first to confront the stark choices they pose. A clear example is the extent to which carers are means to an end—more community care—or ends in themselves with their own needs and right to welfare. Putting it simply, should a person who is just about coping, at considerably physical and emotional cost, be encouraged to continue or be helped to deal with guilt and anxiety of relinquishing care? Who is the social workers' priority client? The likelihood is that a combination of limited resources and moral and political assumptions about familial duty will render this always painful question purely theoretical. Furthermore, substantial devolution of budgets to individual social workers or their immediate managers will bring not simply the freedom to create specially devised packages of care but the responsibility and pain of rationing and the attendant hostility this inevitably provokes.

There are further hazards for social work amidst the apparent promises and hopes that the expanded private and voluntary sectors will enhance both resources and choice. While those whose means allow them the best of the market may thrive the fate of those who are excluded is likely to be very different. The more affluent will receive the cream of the services, disproportionate to their needs, to the detriment of the poor. These inequalities could be a feature of social work provision which remained largely in the public sector but are a more likely outcome if private agencies flourish and manage, through fee income and pressure on public services, to obtain disproportionate resources and to offer the highest quality services. These agencies would probably be staffed by the best qualified social workers drawn, as they have been in the USA, by the rewards of working with an apparently more responsive clientele, somewhat removed from the rigours of eking out the limited services available to the most disadvantaged for whom the public sector provides. The shadow of the poor law could return to these services.

A substantial expansion of the resources and power of the voluntary sector could result in a similar division of welfare if its tradition of providing innovative services for some of the most needy and difficult people has to be abandoned because of lack of public and private resources. Charitable giving, one linchpin in the Conservative government's welfare policy, has not materialized to the extent it had hoped and the fortunes of most voluntary agencies are quickly affected by government patronage (Charity Trends 1990).

We cannot know, in 1990, how social work will survive and tackle these dilemmas. The politics of welfare in the extent to which citizens' demands about the quality and quantity of social work resources become issues to be reckoned with are unpredictable. One unintended consequence of local authorities' obligation regularly to publish in plain English, clear, accessible plans for community care, to promote partnership with parents and to establish complaints procedures may well be heightened public awareness of service potential and deficiency and therefore increased demand. Thus user participation and empowerment, largely intended to keep social workers in line, could enhance their resources.

Given its dependency on these resources social work cannot have whole control of its future but one memory of the past twenty years provides a useful warning. Eagerness to please and grand aspirations, encouraged by fashion and legislation but ill supported by practical commitment, must not (as it did in the wake of the Seebohm Report) obscure the boundaries of social work. Here the lessons of sociology once again provide both disappointment and protection. They disappoint because in underlying the significance of kinship, community, and markets in people's lives they also underline the limitations of social work in the promotion of welfare. They protect if this clarity prevents social work from claiming, or having thrust upon it, unrealistic ends and roles.

Constraint and Control

The potential problems of the ends and means of social work are highlighted again by its powers to constrain and control. Given the scope for mistakes, misunderstanding, and misery social workers' statutory powers present would they be wise to eschew them? Although social workers regard these powers with great ambivalence most accept their place in their practice and responsibilities. A cynical explanation would be that, in this role at least, there is always employment for social workers; the real reasons for their acceptance of statutory powers are more subtle and profound. They are based on the recognition that social work intervention may be at least a gentler and less harmful form of control than many court disposals; at best it may provide worthwhile means of tackling personal and social problems. The most common arenas for the exercise of social workers' authority are crime and delinquency, severe mental illness, and child care.

In explaining behaviour to courts and identifying hoped-for capacities for change social workers may mitigate courts' decisions. Motives may be extremely practical: social work can provide a more useful and usually a cheaper option. They may also be moral and humanitarian; many people with whom social workers are concerned have suffered great disadvantages and injustices and for them social work supervision may provide a measure of protection against severe penalties while also providing sufficient protection for the public.

For people with mental health problems social workers' powers may enable people to remain out of hospital when relatives or doctors wish them to be compulsorily maintained. Such decisions are contentious but here social workers' statutory authority formally recognizes the social context and impact of mental illness and the requirement to provide help and treatment whenever possible with the patient's consent.

The statutory powers for child protection recognize that the best means for promoting a child's interests may be highly complex and are rarely best met by speedy removal from parents who are providing less than adequate care. Negotiation, mediation, practical help, judgement, discretion, and, on occasion, statutory supervision have to be the order of the day. Although well-publicized disasters provoke accusations that social work contributes to problems of child abuse, family break up, and general social degeneracy in calmer times, most of the time, it is well and widely recognized that it is simply not possible to solve such problems by authoritarian, imposed disciplinary interventions. An officialdom which required changes of behaviour via court orders, removing the incorrigible to institutions, would be a hugely costly alternative, financially and socially.

So apart from crucifixions by public enquiry, wherein lies the risk for social workers in their powers to constrain and control? First, as outlined earlier, social workers may unwittingly provide a premature and speedy route to harsh sentences. Too much can be made of this and much sport can be had from watching the liaison of the left and right against social work: the former seeing it as an insidious trap and the latter as dangerous liberalism. Through the careful identification of ends and means and the timing of intervention with offenders social workers can reduce the potential dangers of too early involvement; but they cannot control sentencers who may use enthusiastically but inappropriately a non-custodial sentence such as community service. The White Paper (1990) Crime, Justice and Protecting the Public recognizes these risks in its proposals to place some limited constraints on sentencers as part of its determined strategy to reduce custodial sentencing, in which the probation service is expected to play a larger part.

The government in 1990 is not squeamish about acknowledging the punitive components of the strict and directive forms of supervision proposed partly, it argues, to ensure their acceptability to courts and the public. This poses a second risk for social workers, including probation officers, because their attitudes to punishment are highly ambivalent, for reasons which are not always clear or logical. Some find it distasteful to be identified with social institutions which appear to exacerbate the inequalities of the already disadvantaged. A few, probably now only a very few, may perceive crime and deviant behaviour as a product of psychological and social problems which can only be alleviated by treatment. Many opposed punishment because they regard its forms as inappropriately harsh or damaging. They also fear, not surprisingly, that their identification with punishment will complicate and compromise their relationships with people whose trust and co-operation is essential to their successful intervention, monitoring, and supervision. There are also serious concerns about clothing a package of supervision which is intended primarily to be controlling and punishing in the guise of help. There are dangers too when a person who has committed a minor offence but has serious problems is constrained, directly or indirectly, to accept a strenuous, intrusive programme of help and supervision, the conditions of which cannot be justified by the seriousness of the offence. In both these cases the integrity of the help is in doubt and the supervisors and the supervised have to deal with complicated double agenda. Breaches of the conditions of restrictive orders may also result in the imposition of penalties not justified by the original offence. Failure to comply with a programme of help can then be treated in the same way as the commission of a further offence.

Despite these genuine difficulties, in practice, as opposed to public pronouncement, social workers show more acceptance of the place of punishment and of their role in control and supervision. Davies and Wright (1989) found that while probation officers vary greatly in the extent to which they hold anti-correctional attitudes the idea of steering a middle course, 'holding the balance' between service to the courts and service to clients remains the dominant motif of their work. This stance is endorsed by McIvor's (1989) research which has shown that offenders on community service can see their sentences as both punishing and positive, and that strict supervision is associated with the high completion rate of orders. In a small but intensive study the author found social workers, probation officers, and juvenile court magistrates all acknowledging, albeit guiltily and reluctantly, a place for punishment, seeing it as part of their thinking, language, and personal experience (Cheetham 1985). If this is not more openly acknowledged double talk and double think could ensue in which sanctions are imposed, apparently for therapeutic reasons but with punitive intent.

Research, experience, and politics therefore suggest that social workers need a clearer, more positive understanding of punishment and their association with it. Without this they will be out of step with the majority of citizens. The government will also be encouraged to believe that firmness, enforcement, and directive programmes for community-based sentences for serious criminals are an impossible arena for social workers. There are then two possible consequences. The government will try significantly to influence the training of people dealing with offenders and reduce, as far as possible, its alleged contamination by social work thinking and practice. Alternatively, if this proves a hopeless task (and Davies has shown that probation officers identify closely with social work) the supervision of offenders might be transferred to a new cadre of worker, for example security or prison officers. The future is now quite uncertain. In 1989 the responsible Home Office Minister declared a faith in the Probation Service (and implicitly in its social work functions) thus:

> many offenders lead chaotic and disorganized lives and are sometimes so lacking in understanding that they do not appreciate the consequences of their actions . . . the Probation Service had much experience in dealing with these difficult offenders and has acquired over the years useful skills and techniques mixing authority and control with persuasion and understanding which combined with the discipline of Court Orders, can help bring about a change in behaviour. (Patten 1989)

A few months later the Green Paper (1990) *Supervision and Punishment in the Community* proposed the abolition of the requirement that probation officers must have social work qualifications. This paper also displays confusing and ambivalent attitudes towards the place and relationship of control and help in the supervision of offenders. In fact these flow from the White Paper's (1990) at times contradictory proposals that 'just desert', punishment to fit the crime, vigilant and strenuous supervision, help and rehabilitation should together form the basis of its policy to reduce custodial sentencing.

The challenge for probation officers is thus to find an intellectually sound, morally acceptable, and practically feasible method of grasping and firmly controlling the supervision and punitive components of some of their work, thus ensuring that both those at odds with the law and the courts can retain the advantages of programmes which combine skilled help and a measure of control. As Tonry (1990) has argued, it is perfectly legitimate and sensible for the probation service to ensure its continued presence in the criminal justice system by reinforcing its credibility to courts provided it does not adopt styles of supervision which, in the longer term, will be counterproductive because they escalate the numbers of offenders sentenced to custody.

The same challenge exists in cases where statutory intervention may be less explicit, or only used as a last resort, in which social workers will represent some standard of acceptable conduct. This may for some clients be too demanding and for other members of the community far too lax. The social worker's task is to work for accommodation between expectations and feasible achievement, taking account of individuals' rights, abilities, wants, and freedoms. The 1989 Children Act in its emphasis on partnership between parents, social workers, local authorities, and courts attempts to provide a legislative and practical framework to advance such accommodation. Nevertheless, the social worker's role remains, in part, inescapably moral. This is both a burden in the opprobrium it can attract and a privilege in its potential to combine tolerance and protection.

Social Work Effectiveness: Reality and Illusion

It may seem bizarre to highlight the pursuit of social work effectiveness as a potential hazard when its benefits are so obvious for clients and for social workers. The dangers arise when effectiveness depends on such narrowing of targets that the great pains and miseries that bear on the lives of many clients are at first disregarded and then forgotten. It is perfectly proper to strive towards what can be achieved, and to define according to available provision the sensible goals of social work, provided this is not regarded as the limit of human need or welfare. It is important to identify the extent to which agencies meet their own objectives, but only as one stopping place in the longer journey to discover what impact this has on these agencies' clients. The definition of objectives is also not a simple task. There may be legitimate long-term goals where the evidence of achievement may be hard to find. Can good parenting be defined as the sum of such short-term, identifiable objectives such as more leisure time spent with children, more attention to their diet and health, and more consistent discipline? And in drawing up such an agenda whose criteria for 'good parenting' should be taken into account?

There are cases too in which conflicts of interest preclude a single definition of effectiveness. A child may thrive better if removed from her parents while the removal demoralizes and embitters them. These are the more dramatic circumstances in which social work effectiveness is judged, but much social work involves oversight of people whose circumstances or behaviour give cause for anxiety (Goldberg *et al.* 1977, 1978; Davies 1981; Barclay 1982). Maintaining such people in a reasonably steady state, preventing deterioration of their circumstances by advance and services, reassuring them, their relatives, the neighbours, and the local authority that more drastic intervention is not appropriate are social work goals which defy simply assessments of their achievement.

There are similar problems in assessing the effectiveness of residential care for people for whom it was a last and unwelcome resort in failing health, towards the end of their lives (Booth 1985). Identifying the quality of care provided is a worthwhile task but not to be confused with the quality of life which may ensue (Bland *et al.* forthcoming). And contrary to popular rhetoric, in the assessment of effectiveness the consumer's voice cannot be the only one. An elderly person desperate to remain with her relatives may be highly satisfied with such an outcome; her daughter, son-in-law, and grandchildren may have quite different views. The residents in a home which encourages them to express their feelings and ponder on their ill-fortune and fears may appear far less satisfied than those in an establishment which has little tolerance of individuality, loss, or aspiration, and where conformity and mute acceptance can be confused with satisfaction. As social work programmes help people discharged from psychiatric hospital acquire confidence and raise their aspirations so may these very people become more critical of the help they are being given; one criterion of its success can therefore be heightened dissatisfaction (Petch 1990; forthcoming).

Contemporary emphasis on value for money also means that analyses of the effectiveness of services cannot be dissociated from their costs, a point forcibly made (but widely ignored) by Titmuss in 1958 (R. Titmuss 1958: 23–4). It is reasonable to compare the costs of different forms of service provision provided their outcomes, and the associated costs, are also examined. Community care may be a good bargain for the state but an appalling price for families.

Identifying the effectiveness of social work thus presents formidable intellectual and technical challenges and demands not simply a focus on objectives and outcomes but a commentary on their worth; not simply an account on clients' views of services but an account of the impact these have had. Most difficult of all are the tasks of relating social work intervention with its outcomes; and of demonstrating what happens, for good or ill, when social work is not available.

Social work's statutory powers and its involvement with conflicts that are essentially moral also present formidable challenges for evaluation. Ensuring the safety of children may mean limiting the rights of their parents to care for them. There will be contentious constraints on the freedoms of offenders serving community-based sentences. The price of respecting the self-determination of elderly people may be allowing risks to their health and safety. Less dramatically and more frequently, as Jordan (1987: 207) has eloquently argued,

> people turn to social services not only for practical support; they also look for resolutions of clashes of interest, when their processes of negotiation have broken down; as well as getting extra resources, they may be looking for a renegotiation of roles or a redefinition of household rights and responsibilities . . . Thus social workers are often invited into the informal systems of families or wider kinship groups to mediate between individuals or groups about shares of welfare . . . but the social worker's role is not a comfortable one. To mediate over fairness and shares of wealth . . . is to engage in a moral dialogue of fundamental, even ultimate values.

In such matters there are legitimate differences of opinion about whom should be accorded the most protection and how. There is a deep-run distaste for state intervention in family life, well illustrated by the public outcry surrounding Cleveland Social Services Department's removal from their parents of children who were thought to have been sexually abused within their families. On the right Ferdinand Mount (1983) has railed against 'public visitors' who intervene in family life having 'at their ultimate disposal a Stalinist array of powers'. On the left Christopher Lasch (1977) has attacked the imposition of essentially middle class behaviour on the working-class family. And yet the reality most social workers experience is that far from wanting (let alone being able) to impose norms of behaviour they defend diverse life-styles and individuals' rights to pursue their interests as they see fit, unless harm will clearly ensue. They negotiate for: modifications of behaviour to stave off drastic interventions by public bodies; rent arrears' reduction to prevent eviction; greater parental supervision to reduce school truancy and risk of court intervention; greater attention to personal care, food, cleanliness, and warmth to reduce the risk to life and limb and entry to residential care. Middle men traditionally do not command esteem and in this role social work can always be blamed for doing too much and too little. The irrefutable evidence of dead infants and elderly ladies cannot be matched by evidence of those still alive and coping, supervised, monitored, or helped by social workers. Thus some part of social workers' lives must be lived on a dangerous edge where they will be both much needed and much abused.

THE REGENERATION OF SOCIAL WORKERS

It is right that the last dilemma for social work should be one with which Halsey has been associated for over a quarter of a century. During this period in universities and polytechnics social work education flourished, in part because of central and local government funding and also because there have been large numbers of applicants wanting to qualify as social workers, and ready employment for them. There have been significant achievements, particularly in the attempts to weld together at least a modest education in the social sciences and practical training in social work practice. There has been a commitment to forging a relationship between theory and practice, even though the shortcomings of both may have rendered this relationship elusive. The fieldwork experience of social work students, although variable, has been a highly valued component of a social work qualification.

There have also been tensions and in recent years demoralizing uncertainty about the future of social work education. First, while it seems clear that the many tasks and responsibilities in social work require different kinds of training, in practice it has proved hard to distinguish these, not least because of the difficulty of identifying tasks and skills which should be the property of particular grades of worker. Furthermore, a strongly egalitarian ideology has been hesitant to countenance such differentials and has emphasized the importance of minimizing differences of class and status between client and worker. Thus a broadly based entry into social work training has been a priority. Qualifying courses, in different institutions, have been open to people with few educational qualifications and to graduates, all of whom, after two years, are intended to achieve for qualification a comparable standard in social work theory and practice.

At the same time the requirements for social work qualification have grown ever longer, now numbering some 130 items ranging from 'knowledge of the range of human needs . . .

individual liberty, natural justice . . . and welfare rights' through 'recognition of personal, racial, social and culture offences' to an ability 'to appraise the presence of risk indicators and help, provide care for, counsel, supervise . . . individuals and families in difficulties' (Central Council for Education and Training in Social Work 1989). The attention that can be given to such a cornucopia in two years is minimal and there is little chance that, without a stringent and wide-ranging examination sytem, students can demonstrate their knowledge and competence across such a range, as they are officially required to do. Less than 5 per cent fail to qualify. Thus social work education is characterized by both wide entrances and wide exits. It is possible that the proposed professional social work council (Parker 1990) in setting down minimum standards of practice and qualification, a code of ethics, and a national register will deal with some major anomalies and deficiencies. Its major challenge, to which most professional associations have failed to rise, will be to give the highest priority to the protection of clients' rather than social workers' interests.

Social work education has been criticized for being insufficiently practical and, especially in the case of probation, so dominated by critical analysis of major social institutions that workers' credibility is undermined. It could also be criticized, although rarely is, perhaps for fear of charges of élitism, for being intellectually thin. It could hardly be otherwise in the time available but the government has refused to extend basic training to three years; and the future for post-qualifying education is uncertain. It can also be argued that too much attention has been given to the education of a minority of people involved in social work services, while the greatest urgency is to train residential and domiciliary workers, most of whom have no qualifications at all, as the people who have the most direct contact with clients and who provide some of the most personal services.

The present recipe, as yet hardly tried, is to ground social work education more firmly in agencies, especially local authorities, with the intention of enhancing its relevance, and with the risk that students may have little incentive to see beyond these agencies' boundaries. The price of greater adroitness in the management of local authority business might be limited critical analysis of social institutions and human behaviour and a narrow vision of welfare. Much work remains to be done in identifying what social workers should know, be able to do, and understand. Recent emphasis has been on the first two. This has been much needed but social workers cannot be simply social mechanics. This chapter has tried to demonstrate that both their practical tasks and their moral responsibilities demand an understanding shaped by the social sciences. There are more things in human need and welfare than are dreamed of in the philosophies of White Papers and agency policy.

A greater (and welcome) preoccupation with matching needs and resources, a contemporary priority, may require a focus on small achievable goals which can seem trivial in the context of the sufferings for which relief cannot be given. This must not restrict social workers' vision of the larger horizons of their clients' lives and their own roles. Although it is now fashionable to deride the Seebohm Committee's vision of a brave new world founded in the personal social services, its aspirations for individuals and society remain admirable. Social workers can keep alive these aspirations because the knowledge that comes from witnessing and tangling with the worst consequences of inadequate social policies and of individual selfishness, incompetence, and cruelty gives them an authority, rarely recognized but perceived by Halsey (1989*a*: 233), in his view of the place of social workers and social scientists, together, in the sociology of social reform, and of their tasks for the rest of the millenium and beyond. 'The challenge to replace antomistic anarchy, exploitation and inequality by a welfare society has presented itself in shifting guise in all the phases of industrial development. For the next generation of social scientists and social workers it is as morally urgent and intellectually difficult as it ever was for their predecessors'.

NOTES

1. I am grateful to Roger Fuller, Christine Hallett, Anthony Heath, Julia Parker, Adrian Sinfield, and George and Teresa Smith whose helpful comments have improved this chapter. Its deficiencies remain my own.

3

Citizenship and Community in British Political Debate[1]

COLIN CROUCH

Citizenship, usually in tandem with community, returned to political debate in Britain in the late 1980s in a remarkable way. A. H. Halsey had signalled the theme even before the decade began; his 1977 Reith Lectures concluded with a plea for 'a democracy of citizens' (1978: chap. 8). Matters went quiet with the initial triumph of the new right and its vision of privatized individualism. Then in 1985 Michael Mann argued, from a sociologically informed Labour point of view, that the concept of shared social citizenship in T. H. Marshall's (1950) sense provided the basis for a revival of socialism in the face of this new hegemony. Marshall had described three stages in the development of modern British citizenship in rather stylized form, from civil rights in the seventeenth and eighteenth centuries, through political rights in the nineteenth, to social rights in the twentieth-century welfare state.

By 1988 the theme had been taken up with enthusiasm by official Labour Party spokesmen. The Marshallian idea of citizenship entitlements to equality of access by right to certain kinds of social welfare provided a powerful defence of the welfare state against attack from advocates of the free market, though in practice Labour politicians were, in their defensive mood of the decade, more likely to speak, not of rights, but rather differently of the need for 'compassion' for those being left aside in the increasingly unequal society of the 1980s.

Also from the political left, but different in content, was a new concern for citizenship in the sense of formal civil and political rights. This became concentrated in the activities of the organization Charter '88 that from 1988 onwards campaigned actively for a codified Bill of Rights and a written constitution for the United Kingdom. This has embraced a wide range of opinion from Marxists to Social and Liberal Democrats, but curiously leaving out much of orthodox Labour opinion that remained wedded to the informality of the British constitution.

Some advocates of an 'entrenched rights' approach to citizenship were directly critical of Labour's 'community concern' model; most perceptively so Michael Ignatieff:

> The language of citizenship is not properly about compassion at all, since compassion is a private virtue which cannot be legislated or enforced. The practice of citizenship is about ensuring everyone the entitlements necessary to the exercise of their liberty. As a political question, welfare is about rights, not caring, and the history of citizenship has been the struggle to make freedom real, not to tie it all in the leading strings of therapeutic good intentions. (Ignatieff 1989: 72)

The Charter '88 campaign should not, however, be seen as marking a new 'fourth stage' in the Marshall theory, since most of the rights called for belonged to the second or even first stage of the Marshall model. The claim is that these rights have in Britain usually remained informal and customary, and that the customs were increasingly being broken by the Conservative government (see, for example, the cases studied in Graham and Prosser 1988). In other words, British rights were in large measure the product of a shared political community, not formal aspects of citizenship as such; since this community was now breaking down, citizenship rules were needed to fill a vacuum that might otherwise become dangerous.

But the most interesting development came when members of the Conservative government and their supporters took up the citizenship theme, also in 1988. Ministers advocated 'active citizenship' in the sense of active community involvement by citizens, and contrasted this with Labour's 'passive' citizenship as a set of demands for rights and entitlements from the state. Of course, citizenship and community are generally perceived as 'good things'; they can also be defined very vaguely. Not much notice should therefore necessarily be taken of politicians' desire occasionally to associate themselves with these phenomena. However, the collectivist and political implications of the terms made it a matter of some note that Conservatives wished to raise their profile. Indeed the outbreak of 'citizenship' speeches by Ministers followed just a few weeks after the then Prime Minister, Mrs Margaret Thatcher, had made her instantly infamous remark 'There is no such thing as society, only individuals and families'. However, when a policy for citizenship eventually emerged during 1991 in the form of the 'Citizen's Charter', it proved to be entirely individual and non-political: a series of devices whereby individual complainants could seek redress against public servants, not politicians, in cases of inadequate service delivery—a *public consumer*'s rather than a citizen's charter.

There are in fact good reasons why politicians of the left and right alike should worry about the health of citizenship and community—the left more desperately and urgently, the right more surprisingly. These reasons are worth exploring. However, one major conclusion that emerges is that the expectations they have from citizenship are far higher than the policy implications that they are prepared to accept in order to secure it. The crucial point is the citizen as an active participant in the public business of the wider community; and most practical interpretations fight very shy of that indeed.

CITIZENSHIP AND THE LABOUR COMMUNITY

Labour sees itself as the pre-eminent party of community, collectivism, and concern for shared public matters. Its need for a politics of citizenship and community is therefore clear. However, its own community base is under considerable threat in these last decades of the twentieth century. There are also important tensions between community (local, particularistic) and citizenship (universal, equal) that are rarely acknowledged.

The bedrock of both Labour's viability as a major party and its sense of collective concern has been the working-class community. For well-known reasons this is now in severe decline. The main cause is the change in occupational structure that is rapidly reducing the proportion of the population engaged in manual work, in particular those manual occupations with a strong sense of autonomy, identity, and community. It was these characteristics—rather than the abstract and somewhat arbitrarily classified fact of 'manualness' (Lipset 1983)—that lay behind the solidity of traditional working-class identities. Indeed, important in the construction of working-class communities were the ambiguous consequences of various grades of manual work constituting distinct, invidiously defined status groups. Identity was more often with one or other of these, interpreted as class, than with class in any true social structural sense.

As Frank Parkin wrote several years ago (1967), the ability of subordinate groups to generate their own challenge to the established values and practices of dominant classes is not to be taken for granted; it needs a supportive sub-culture. It is difficult to see what will generate anything similar among the growth points of the new groups taking the place of the old working class: junior administrative personnel, counter-hands in fast-food establishments, office cleaners, and caretakers. Some of these groups are important reservoirs of support for public services, but they rarely produce a distinctive, active politics. Members of the welfare state professions and other public-service employees are a different matter, but they also present a political problem, as their defence of services can be represented as special pleading for maintaining their own positions. The frequent Labour and union slogan during the 1980s campaigns against cuts in the welfare state of 'protect jobs and services' was unfortunately worded. Welfare state professionals will remain a central group in social democratic politics for many years, but it becomes dangerous for a labour movement to rely on them alone as its vanguard.

Perhaps even more important than these changes is the unprecedented opportunity that employers now have to shape the kind of working class they would like to have. The first waves of western industrialization provided little evidence of this; not much was known about the potentiality of working-class politics, most employers were too busily engaged in a desperate bid to put some kind of work-force together and get day-to-day control over it to worry about such niceties; and the occasional experiments in enlightened paternalism remained odd exceptions. Lacking autonomous models of authority relations, most capitalists relied on the transfer to a new context of a pre-capitalist, status-based master–servant relationship.

In Britain and the rest of Europe socialism thrived on both the sense of class identity that this provided and the resentments generated by its inappropriateness. American capitalism developed somewhat differently, lacking the post-feudal legacy, and socialism has always been concomitantly weaker there (Burnham 1974). Japanese capitalists, reconstructing their economy after both military defeat and their own victory over the communist labour movement, built more rigorously on American examples but in a distinctive way.

It is partly under their and a new American influence that capitalism is now undergoing its recent period of development. Some employers are learning how to build environments in which workers' focus of expectations is the company rather than either a smaller (autonomous work-group) or larger (national trade union; national polity) entity; in which personnel policy makes it extremely hard for unions to gain either employee support or employer recognition; and in which the informal style of personal relations and control systems masks the exercise of power (Purcell 1987). Communities of a kind may thereby be constructed; but they are not autonomous creations of working people themselves.

In addition, commercially owned networks of communication now shape the perceptions and perspectives of people in a way that was not possible during the period of the initial formation of the working class. When something autonomous does develop, it is quickly embraced and reinterpreted by these media. Youth culture was pushed into the extremes of punk rock in order to avoid this pervasiveness, and even that was captured in the end. The only groups to escape are ethnic minorities whose cultural separatism is strongly defined.

Of course, variety and heterogeneity remain in the national media—though this will decline as newspapers and, under the new deregulated regime, television stations fall into the hands of a small number of general industrial conglomerates. And most striking of all is the sheer difficulty confronting any attempt by the mass of ordinary working people to generate any major institutions that they can really call their own.

The fate of the most substantial working-class contribution to national culture—Association football—during the 1980s was a case in point. Wire cages, electrified fences, and police trained in sophisticated methods of crowd control coped with the appalling behaviour of some young people among the football crowds, until the Hillsborough disaster induced an as yet unresolved nemesis of both the game and of ways of controlling it. There was little left in which working people could take pride as their creation; and most important an eclipse of any notion of mutual self-regulation that is the essence of community. Like the culture of punk rock, the 'community' of football was in danger of becoming a non-community of the alienated and the destructively angry. The sensible, acceptable football supporter became someone who watched the big match at home on the television screen. Football support was ceasing to be an active celebration of local pride and becoming yet another example of imbibing what the national electronic media provided.

Cultural pursuits and such matters as community confidence and pride may seem trivial, but they are the stuff of which community identity is made. As Zygmunt Bauman has argued (1988), the end of the working-class community also means for many people an end to a publicly oriented life, and hence to politics in any strong sense.

Halsey, summarizing literature on working-class communities in the early years of this century, comments:

> Working-class districts, including those where incomes were very low, and housing and amenities poorly provided, were also areas of domestic peace and neighbourly trust of a standard which we do not know today. People never thought of locking their houses if they went out during the day, and theft would have been cause for amazement. The traditional problems of the slum have since been more widely spread through the towns and cities, with the result that old working-class areas have lost their capacity to police the activities of strangers with the almost total efficiency of the period before the First World War. (Halsey 1986: 56)

Community is a vital means of securing people's orientation to a public sphere. But its relation to citizenship in a stricter sense is not unproblematic. Historically, the shared resentments of inferior status within working-class communities generated a powerful political demand for equality of status, that is for citizenship. But the very community identities that fuelled the demand were the product of invidious definitions that would be undermined by the achievement of citizenship. Community is often closed, particularistic; citizenship claims universality. Halsey points out how the move from community to citizenship needed some rather exceptional help:

> The Labour movement at the beginning of the century was based on the solidarity of local class communities. Labour markets and kinship networks were bounded by walking distances. For the vast majority of ordinary people national concerns were remote from daily life. Only war made Britons out of people whose social horizons were normally enclosed by the street, the village, or the neighbourhood. (Halsey 1986: 63)

Working people were aware of their contribution to the war and thus became aware of their collective dignity and potentiality. They also became aware of their place within a temporarily real national community. The combination made for a strong sense of citizenship.

In this context one recalls the 1984–5 coal-mining strike. The British labour movement here chose as perhaps its last momentous industrial struggle in the old economy the assertion of the right of men's sons and grandsons to crawl underground mining coal from the same pits as their forebears. The National Union of Mineworkers' campaign to save 'jobs, pits and communities' was of course directed at the Conservative government's policy of major pit closures. But mining communities as traditionally defined as geographically separate, inter-generational, and male dominated, are also destroyed by policies of rehousing, enhanced educational opportunities, and equal rights for women. The way of life which has traditionally sustained socialism and its living concept of community and citizenship is also the way of life which socialism is pledged to end. Or community often depends on conditions such as poverty and war that one would like to see eliminated.

CITIZENSHIP AND THE WELFARE STATE

Socialism's answer to its dilemma has been to *transcend* the particularism of the working-class community with the universalized, citizenship model of mutual support and caring embodied in the welfare state (see Plant 1988: 2, 3). Marshall's third stage of citizenship can thus be seen as emerging from the chrysalis of working-class community. One of the most celebrated formulations of this essentially moral view of the welfare state was Richard Titmuss's 1971 study of the British blood transfusion service as the embodiment of altruism.

But the BTS, dependent on voluntary action, is not typical of the welfare state. In the great majority of social services community is not transcended by altruism but by paid professionals and bureaucrats. In very many cases the transcendance is successfully achieved and indeed improved upon in the quality of care and equalled in the quality of human kindness. But often absent from professional care—and central to the concepts of both community and of altruistic concern as in the BTS case—is personal, active concern by people in general. And it is this quality that politicians seek to reclaim when they call citizenship, community, and compassion in aid as means of revitalizing concern for the welfare state under the circumstances of renewed individualism of the late twentieth century.

Halsey, thinking of the labour movement's problematic role in this and referring to a similar complaint by Richard Crossman, speaks (1986: 167) of the way in which 'the movement which had invented the social forms of modern participatory democracy . . . was ironically fated to develop through its political party the threats of a bureaucratic state'. David Marquand (1988), similarly noting how the institutions established by grass-roots nineteenth-century radicalism had become 'centralist, mechanistic, manipulative', makes the further point that as a result there was little public concern when many of these institutions were swept away in the 1980s: 'when it came to the point, the great corporations of the social-democratic consensus turned out to have no troops'. His point is not valid if applied to the welfare state as such, support for which has remained very firm; but it does apply to the wider panoply of 'national interest' boards, committees, and councils.

Alongside this must also be set certain long-term advantages favouring the individualistic vision, whatever its intermittent travails. First, governments of the new right are in the enviable position of being able to create the conditions for their own success in welfare policy. If the public services are gradually run down while access to corresponding private provision is gradually made easier for many middle-income families, opposition to subsequent more ruthless reductions in state welfare can be pre-empted in classic Hirschmanian fashion (Hirschman 1970). There will come a point where public services have deteriorated so far and opportunities for private solutions have become sufficiently available that many of the articulate professional and middle-income groups who frequently spearhead the defence of the welfare state will find it more feasible to strive for improved access to private benefits than to campaign for public services, especially when one considers the 'collective goods' handicap (Olson 1965) that inhibits such campaigns. And the middle-class groups are central to Mann's (1985) idea of the *universal* nature of welfare state citizenship in which everyone has an interest as opposed to the 'poor relief' of aid targeted on the needy. In other words, while initially unpopular, a policy of running down the welfare state will at a certain point create the conditions for popularity of the new right's widest privatization ambitions.

Further, campaigns to 'defend jobs and services' can be used to accuse public-service workers of parasitism, of insisting on overmanning at the taxpayers' expense in order to secure their own positions. Matters are made worse by the virtual inevitability of socialists falling into the trap produced by the combination of these three facts. Unable to secure rapid improvements in public services and alarmed by the growth of the private sector and the decline in public-service employment, they are almost certain to respond by trying to ban private services, making themselves the negative force closing off people's options and reducing the total quantity of welfare available. To predict this is not merely theoretical reasoning, but in part a simple extrapolation of what has already happened in housing policy with respect to council-house sales.

The strength of the welfare state as a living feature of citizenship has always been that certain services to which most people accord a high priority are simply unattainable to the great majority without public provision. As this becomes less true, socialists are tempted artificially to maintain or reimpose that unattainability. The motives for doing so are good: a private market in education or health care would produce great inequalities, especially if we assume that, as has happened in housing and pensions, Conservative encouragement of private provision will include subsidies for those able to take advantage of it. But once it is more than a small minority that begins to contemplate private provision, such a policy is politically suicidal and destructive of real citizenship.

CITIZENSHIP AND CONSERVATIVE CONCERNS

All the above tendencies are favourable for the future of modern new-right Conservatism, defined as a 'post-citizenship' force. We see emerging a docile nation of consumers, gradually abandoning potentially dangerous autonomous community networks for the privacy of home and television, with the main places outside the home where ordinary people congregate being only the employer-controlled work-place and shopping centres patrolled by private security guards.

Not all Conservatives, however, are entirely complacent about these trends. Traditionally British Conservatism did not seek a society of atomized individuals, but a nation bonded together by rural communities, the Church, and respect for the monarch and other social superiors. Communities, rural and urban, are disappearing—though one should not ignore the ability of middle-class neighbourhoods to maintain much of their strength in the Conservative heartland.

The churches, within their general decline, have bifurcated their contribution. In the Conservative heartland the church often goes on as before, binding the community together in its traditional values (and also maintaining elements of social concern). Outside that world, however, the churches have become anxious, seeing a yawning chasm between their inevitable orientation towards community and inclusiveness and the increasing atomization of the society around them. In such works as *Faith in the City* (1985), the Church of England's most substantial report on this question, Christians have found themselves pushed increasingly towards a 'social gospel' rather resembling the preoccupations of the Labour Party discussed above. That party is, in turn, rediscovering as a major inspirational source something of the late nineteenth-century

Christian socialist tradition that had, twenty years ago, seemed a worn-out seam.

The monarchy retains its ascendancy and role in national integration, but in doing so it no longer helps support a general structure of social deference. Rather, it has adjusted itself to a post-deferential world, making use of modern public relations techniques and laying increasing stress on the 'modern' image of the Royal Family's younger adult members.

Social deference of the kind reflected in the Primrose League's use of aristocratic ranks for its levels of officers no longer helps build a Tory-led national community. Indeed throughout the post-war decades the Conservative Party came increasingly to depend on affluence to replace deference as its major source of support from outside its own class base (Nordlinger 1967; McKenzie and Silver 1968; Jessop 1974). By the 1970s this was becoming highly uncertain. These were the years when conservatives of all kinds began to worry about 'ungovernability' (Beer 1982; Brittan and Lilley 1978; Crozier *et al.* 1975). This was always exaggerated; even during major strikes mainland Britain has not shown symptoms of a true incapacity of government to maintain order, as, in their different ways, Northern Ireland, Sicily, or parts of the old Soviet Union have done.

However, the anxiety was not without cause. The maintenance of order in a post-deferential society without guaranteed annual increments in national prosperity is problematic. Conservatives tend to have a greater awareness of both the importance and the fragility of social order than radicals. They developed a two-pronged approach to the problem. Most obvious has been the tougher policing of a 'law and order' policy. But the increased stress on individual market choice can be seen as an attempt at redefining in safe, Conservative terms the aspiration for personal freedom and liberty from constraint produced by the culture of the 1960s. This is very skilful, but it is not without its risks. It means seeking to provide social order through a mechanism—the breakdown of collective allegiances—that is normally seen as destructive of order. The personal social and moral conservatism of Mrs Thatcher and her circle served as a useful cover for the systematic destruction of traditional sources of British social stability that had in practice taken place. The recent concern for citizenship among Conservative leaders can be seen as uneasiness at the dangerous potentialities of the situation.

Of course, the *family* is usually exempted from new-right strictures on collective entities, and can in turn be seen as the hub of a wider network of kinship and neighbourly relations that are of the essence of community. However, it is not clear that this deviation from individualism sits happily with the central logic of new-right arguments. It owes its place to two elements in Conservative thought. First, it is through family that property is inherited and thus kept in private hands across generations. Yet, fundamental a tenet of right-wing thought though this is, it cannot be reconciled with the right's stress on the need for people to 'stand on their own feet' and to battle their way in the market-place without assistance. These latter arguments are used to limit welfare state assistance to the mass of ordinary people, while the right to inheritance from past generations enables a very privileged minority to enjoy a considerable amount of private social support.

Second, with the exception of some libertarian fringes of the new right, strongly represented in California and some other parts of the USA but hardly at all in the UK, the economically neo-liberal right shares all the old right's concerns about order and authority and sees the family, in particular parental authority, as the basic element of social hierarchy. From this flows a whole series of policy needs to safeguard the model of conventional marital and parental relationships, each of which involves a departure from the pure logic of the free market. From this has come a number of contradictions. Thus, rules that debar unemployed young persons living away from home from claiming social security benefits contradict the policy that young people seeking employment should not expect to find it in their home town, but should move to those parts of the country where the market is creating jobs: 'Get on your bike!' Similarly, while the exposure of young women to danger while selling their bodies in the market-place through prostitution is accepted by the right as a legitimate social concern, the exposure of young people to danger through bad working conditions and long working hours is seen as part of the facts of life of the free market with which interfering socialists seek to meddle at the expense of economic efficiency.

Once these exceptions on grounds of property inheritance and the maintenance of authority are admitted as reasons why market logic cannot be extended fully to the family, it is difficult for the new right to maintain that other kinds of social concern should not also be admitted to the political debate over the scope of the free market. Except in those societies where only the privileged, whose sole collectivist concerns are for inheritance and order, have access to politics, the new right will never attain its vision of a society where the free market is accepted unchallenged. On the other hand, a good deal of progress can be made, given certain social and political conditions, towards that vision, and Britain took several steps towards it during the 1980s. It is therefore worth while speculating on the form of society it implies, given some extrapolation from current trends.

Social inequalities would continue and become intensified as different regions and economic sectors enjoyed starkly different fates; but these inequalities would not follow identifiable lines of experienced solidarity, and would therefore not generate solidarities among the under-privileged. Inefficient parts of the economy would collapse, but others would keep going and several enjoy distinct success. Thus only minorities would be trapped in the desolation and hopelessness likely to lead to social discontent. In any case, as argued above, few groups would have the sense of autonomous identity needed to turn feelings of wretchedness into militant political action. (In Britain, coal miners, blacks, and perhaps young people are among the few groups that come in this category. In the 1980s they provided evidence of their mettle, but also of the growing capacity of increasingly skilled police action to contain them. Further, they do not present the new right with a problem; rather the reverse. Just as a declining welfare state creates support for policies of private welfare, so civil discontent among clearly identifiable minorities generates support for tough policies of law and policing. Action by public service workers could be dealt with under both headings; their numbers could be reduced in order to demonstrate further the incompetence of their services, and their discontent dismissed as the protests of the taxpayers' parasites.)

Many people, perhaps most, would remain prosperous and

would continue to acquire goods and services which would make their homes desirable, attractive places to be in. Electrified perimeter fences, private security guards, and dogs would keep the housing estates of the more wealthy free from fear and independent of general norms of behaviour in the wider society. Many people would still make use of basic state welfare and other services, but increasingly they would take advantage of growing opportunities for 'topping up' with private provision, which they would use in a quite non-ideological way.

Much of the information people receive would be disseminated by a small number of commercially owned sources. This information and much of their entertainment would be received electronically and passively within their homes. With the exception of highly educated, professional groups who deliberately sought such contact, most people would have little incentive to associate with others for serious purposes likely to generate information fashioned by themselves. The need to go to work would be a major exception to this, though the working environment and social interaction at work would be far more—and far more skilfully—controlled by management than is now normal.

Outside the well-equipped home and the regulated but friendly work-place would be the streets. Because not much of life would be lived in public spaces, there would be no informal norms of human interaction to govern conduct in the streets and other non-private places, such as the football terraces. Such locations would become the resort of the dispossessed and unemployed, indulging in personal crime or, much more rarely, organized but fragmented political action. This would further reduce general use of public space, concomitantly reducing still further its integration into any form of community. People would move around, but it would increasingly be privately motorized movement. Public transport services would have been run down, local shops would have given way to out-of-town hypermarkets, and the dangers of the streets would reduce walking and cycling.

The political requirements and the concept of citizenship practised by most people in such a society would be small: various *ad hoc* subsidies to help with awkward corners of welfare provision (like mortgages, perhaps general practitioner services); traffic control and road building; and a heavy dose of policing. Such a polity would not be fascist; there is no need to fear the erosion of elected government; no need for the public to be welded to some great national task. Fascism was a response to the early stages of working-class mobilization in societies that had little knowledge of subtle techniques of social control and mass communication; in which the working class could be seen by threatened élites as an undifferentiated and potentially solidary mass; and in which capitalism was less internationalized and less able to impose a degree of uniformity on the conduct of individual governments.

Norman Macrae, then deputy editor of *The Economist* and a prominent new-right author, presented in 1983 a gleeful account of the scope advanced technology will present for virtually abolishing organized face-to-face social interaction and reducing as much of life as possible—including democracy itself—to passive, isolated consumer purchasing:

> Basically, I think that voting anyone to run anything in the twentieth century is like Monarchy in the nineteenth century. It is where the world is coming from; it is not where it is going towards. In this twentieth century the way in which the world is going is towards consumers' freedom. At the moment we have a marvellous choice of goods at the supermarkets but we have no choice at all of the lifestyles we each wish to follow . . .
>
> . . . It should eventually be as cheap to ring up from China to New York as from the office next door in New York. This means that people can live in Tahiti if they want to and telecommute each day to their office in Milan.
>
> Once that happens, all sorts of happy social revolutions can occur. For example, politics should become much less important because, instead of voting for people to rule us in a particular way, we can move to the societies where the ways of running things are the ways we like. (Macrae 1983: 199, 201)

Perhaps this is all overdrawn. But there are reasons for not discarding it as totally unrealistic. If these characteristics are already to be found anywhere it is in certain parts of the USA, which will remain the single most powerful and influential nation in the world for the foreseeable future.

Such a society is attractive in its own right to those sufficiently wealthy to be able to enjoy a privatized, low-taxed life cut off and protected from the masses like a castellated late medieval aristocracy. It would also win support, *faute de mieux*, from a far wider circle once the chances of a decent community-based life have been destroyed.

However, not many people involved in public life, including politicians of the right, can afford to view its arrival with equanimity. Public deterioration *has* to press on their agenda; the environmental dangers of a highly motorized society, both locally and globally, have began to wreak havoc of a kind that requires at least the public relations attention of even the most cynical politician. Politicians also need from time to time to call on patriotic values of devotion to country and are therefore aware, at least subconsciously, that a mass of individuals and families that do not form a society will also not form a nation. In one of the most trenchant recent discussions of the relationship between citizenship and community, Oldfield (1990b) has argued that the two cannot be separated. Except in its most vacuous sense, citizenship implies an orientation to some collectivity. Such orientations cannot be taken for granted in human beings but are the results of the inculcation of certain *mores* and beliefs. The atomized individual of the market economy is not equipped with material of this kind but is quite explicitly without it.

Conservative politicians also have the tricky responsibility of policing the dangerous streets. Two recent contributors to the new citizenship debate, R. P. Dore (1987) and Sir Ralf Dahrendorf (1988), while not themselves Conservatives, have pinpointed a source of Conservative anxiety: the new, high levels of inequality may produce an underclass that is not incorporated into society and becomes dangerously alienated, a constant policing problem. Their discontent has a relative component to it: it is not just that they are poor; they are constantly left behind in the competitive struggle for new and better goods and services.

Politicians also have to come to terms with the contradiction of a society that simultaneously rejects state action to relieve social problems and is too engrossed in selfish indulgence to accept a privately charitable alternative. The possessive individualism of nineteenth-century England was checked by a puritanism that, albeit in a mean way, also encouraged work for the 'public good', from the Charity Organization Society (COS) to statues in the public parks. Mrs Margaret Thatcher, the former prime minister, may have presented herself as an embodiment of these values, but there was little in the hedonistic, Yuppy culture over which she presided and on which she depended for support to provide convincing evidence of a late twentieth-century equivalent.

Therefore Ignatieff's assertion that consumerism had driven out citizenship (1989: 66) presents too simple a picture of the Conservative position. But note the forms taken by citizenship as the Conservative government tried to give it expression. Its purest embodiments were the concepts of Neighbourhood Watch and the Citizen's Charter. The former helps reduce police costs by keeping a suspicious eye from one's window on what strangers are up to in the streets outside. The Citizen's Charter, as already noted, enabled individuals to target public employees, rather than the political process or political priorities, for complaints about deteriorating public services. These are the obvious residual forms taken by citizenship in the world of privatized escape from the dangers in the streets and depoliticized consumerism that I have described above. But as a revival of concern for the public domain its poverty is staggering.

Other aspects of new Conservative citizenship policy are more familiar attempts to rediscover something of the COS spirit of community action to help the sick and unfortunate in order to reduce the need for state action. Conservatives have labelled this 'active' citizenship, since it involves doing things for people, in contrast with the social democratic Marshallian model of citizenship as entitlements to receive, which they label 'passive'. This debate raises anew some of the famous old struggles between the COS and the Webbs' Fabian vision of the modern welfare state, and there is substance in the charge. But the weakness of this Conservative model has to be recognized; as Marquand (1988) has pointed out, it is entirely empty of any concept of public participation in decision-making; empty of any notion, intrinsic to citizenship, of equal rights. It is instead a paternalist local businessman's citizenship. The recipients of the charity are not thereby conceived as citizens.

The welfare state rhetoric of the Labour Party in the early 1980s as an appeal to 'compassion', that is to doing things for people who are seen as recipients is not very different from this. However, welfare as rights rather than as product of charity does have at least some relation to citizenship. Dore (1987) stresses the importance of established rights to universal provision as a major guarantor of human *dignity*, a quality not at all enhanced in the receipt of charity. Plant (1988) speaks of the welfare state as providing people with the resources they need in order to be *active* members of society. This is not, he stresses, a case of the welfare state being totalitarian, prescribing values for people, but simply making available the facilities for them to make their own choices.

These are important points. Nevertheless, they are still not citizenship as action directed towards the political community, the *civitas* or *polis*, and are primarily aimed at individuals. The 'public' becomes a synonym for large masses of individual persons; it altogether loses its sense, as in *res publica*, of those things which we have in common as members of community and society, and over whose dispensation we share.

Even the critique that Ignatieff has articulated, and his and Charter '88's concern with rights, is passive and individualized. The *struggle* for rights is active enough, but once they have been achieved they are passively and privately enjoyed. There is substance in the Tory charge here, though their own concept is so weak in significance. Nearly all those involved in a call for intensified citizenship baulk at a truly active concept. They all expect citizenship to play a part in cementing society together, but few are willing to accept that this implies the provision of many new opportunities for ordinary citizens to participate actively in running the institutions that directly affect their lives.

MODELS OF CITIZENSHIP

The attractiveness and richness of the elusive original Greek concept of citizenship is the right and duty to participate in the collective, public decisions of one's community, within a group that is more or less face-to-face and where the institutions and meeting-places are physical and visible and rub noses with everyday life. For those little city states, surrounded by similar but often hostile other groups, this meaning of the political community reached right out to the conduct of foreign policy. And citizenship could be coterminous with the bounds of community. Of course that is unworkable in larger societies; unworkable in ancient Greece without large numbers of non-citizens of inferior status—including all women—living within the society, often as slaves. But how much of it really has to be jettisoned as the concept becomes diluted with extension and variation?

The Romans cheapened the idea in what was to become the classic mass-produced and inflationary way: more of you can have citizenship if it is worth less. As power moved from a wider community to an imperial oligarchy, so citizenship, drained of political potency, could be extended to vast numbers of barbarians. Its active, political and participatory content became attenuated and it became essentially passive: *civis Romanus sum* meant mainly entitlement to protection by the forces of the empire, protection from being thrown into slavery, the right to participate in the non-political activity of owning and directing property.

The concept picked up again in the Middle Ages in the cities of Flanders, Germany, and Italy, to an extent also England and France, where weak and primarily rural monarchies and feudal rulers left the towns fairly free to develop their own polities. Again, some of the familiar institutions appear: a clear physical embodiment of the public sphere of life in town halls and places of assembly; the exclusion of the majority of the people from participation; and a strong sense of who is a member and who a stranger. But a far wider range of people participated than in the feudal polity proper, or in the stricter monarchical and aristocratic societies that were to follow; and they were in their way welfare states. Medieval city government was, as Black (1984) reminds us, essentially rooted in the government of craft guilds, which were in turn themselves little community polities with a sense of a public sphere of action.

Unlike the Greeks and with the exception of some of the Italian city states, these little polities were usually unarmed and had little to do with foreign policy. Their mundane concerns with matters of trade and public welfare left them out of the high politics, and consequently virtually all the political theory, of the period (ibid.). They have therefore bequeathed little to us as living political traditions beyond the empty symbolism of civic regalia and Lord Mayors' parades—except perhaps in Italy and Germany where the late emergence of nation states prolonged the vitality of at least a few city states into the latter decades of the nineteenth-century.

Medieval models were particularly and significantly absent from the two great, daring experiments with citizenship that occurred in the late eighteenth century, in France and the United States of America. *Everyone* (well, at least every adult male; extension to women and relaxation of the definition of adult were to follow much later) could be a citizen in a sense of universal suffrage that the Romans could never countenance. No monarchical or aristocratic power could stand in the way of the sovereign claim of the individual to participate in political affairs.

In many respects the American and French traditions then went in very different directions. In France the *citoyen individu* had been born in the heat of revolutionary fervour, temporary community, and had been heavily Parisian and therefore local and particularist; but its ambitions were the opposite. A French *citoyen* was first and foremost a citizen of the strongly centralist and rationalist Republic, not of a provincial town or village, certainly not of a guild. The traditional communities that attracted their own loyalties were placed within the strait-jacket of the new *départements*; the guilds were rendered illegal. Although it was in many respects a chauvinistic, French affair, it saw itself as universal in its ambitions, reaching above all particularisms to such universals as *les droits de l'homme*. During the Napoleonic period it tried to extend its institutions to the Swiss, the Dutch, the Italians, and the Rhineland Germans.

The French monarchy had wanted from ordinary people merely obedience and taxes; the Church, which was in any case a universal church, could see to any further public needs. And so, centralizing and dictatorial though it was in all matters of policy, it could leave the people alone in the particularism of their village communities, even local languages, as they did not count. Revolutionary France, like all modern governments, needed its people and therefore paid them the tribute of regarding the details of their local and occupational life as not beneath contempt. As a result it tried, though never with complete success, to rob that life of its autonomy. From that time on French localism has been primarily a force for alienation, protest, *incivisme*: community as the enemy of citizenship.

American state-building took a very different direction. France, locked in the European cockpit of warring states, needed a population base for war if for nothing else, and needed unity in a country divided over monarchy and religion. The US, although eventually to become the most heterogeneous and internationally involved state in the world, started life with all such problems (apart from the Mexicans) ending once the British had withdrawn. Political genius was devoted, not to concentrating power as in France, but to splitting it up. The separation of formal powers and the division of geographical levels of action produced a system which in turn facilitated the wealth of pressure groups that already by the 1830s struck the French observer Alexis de Toqueville as such a contrast with his own land.

But this did not give US citizenship a Greek character. Except in areas of foreign policy, Americans have been reluctant to impart the status honour of a *res publica* to their public institutions, whether at federal, state, city, or local level. Public policy is normally viewed cynically as the pork barrel, distinguished from private, market activity only by the absence of market accountability. The rights about which Americans most care are those that protect them from political forces, not those that give scope for action within the polity.

Both French and US traditions have of course remained (and have bequeathed legacies to their many imitators) far more genuine in the level of citizenship they accord than the Roman one in that they have maintained a universal adult suffrage for the appointment of members of sovereign political authorities. They, however, share with Rome the characteristic of checking citizenship through the elaboration of extreme individualistic private property institutions.

It is Marshall's 'third stage' of citizenship, the achievement of social rights through the welfare state, that constitutes the compromise eventually reached over property. Property rights would be invaded by the state, via taxation, to the point where they provided for a certain level of individual security for all citizens and a certain level of provision of collective goods. Beyond that they would be left alone. For most of the twentieth century a central, if not the central, political conflict has been over exactly where that line should be drawn. In practice the degree of inroad into property by welfare claims has been very limited. Given basic acceptance of the system by both powerful élites and organizations representing the relatively propertyless, it has become a polite, restrained conflict carried on largely without violence. But the 'third stage' did little or nothing to rescue the idea of active participation, though it did lead to the creation of institutions that could do so.

CITIZENSHIP AS PARTICIPATION

Participation: a tired old late 1960s theme that took wing on the streets of Paris in May 1968; was taken up by students, trade unions, and all manner of radical groups in the 1970s; led to all kinds of experiments; withered under the cold hand of boredom and dull routine during the 1970s; was put out of its misery by the tougher, more realistic climate of the 1980s; and was finally more than adequately replaced by the triumph of market forces that gave individuals the power to choose rather than the obligation to sit on boring committees that never pleased anyone?

No. Participation has never in fact disappeared from the agenda, and is now set for a return. Among policy makers and practitioners, especially in local government services, work of a practical and often professional kind has continued to be carried out on community responsiveness, community involvement, community participation, much of it admittedly in the context of regional economic, and consequently community, decline (Abrams 1977 (pursued in Bulmer 1986); Blunkett and Green 1983; Lipsey 1988; T. Smith 1989). Commitments going beyond those of the transitory contract are needed to make a society out of an agglomeration of self-seeking individuals constrained by nothing either stronger than nor more lovable than market forces. Of course, a good deal can be done with advertising, smart public relations, and news management, but it remains a shaky edifice. The *loyalty* has to be engaged of a populace decreasingly likely to offer 'The love that asks no questions'.

Several of the recent contributions to the citizenship debate come close to recognizing this. Plant (1988) wants a citizenship that does not rely on bureaucracy and special interest groups; and he is aware of the difficulties and limitations of trying to create community. However, he tends to prefer means for empowering individuals (for example, the welfare state as money transfers rather than as direct services), but this still leaves him without an answer to providing the collective aspects of active citizenship.

More strongly, Marquand (1988), having demonstrated the hollow nature of the Establishment character of Fabian welfare state democracy, argues for a more directly participatory, less Westminster-dominated polity. Similarly, Oldfield (1990a) stresses the distinction between the liberal citizenship of individual rights and the much tougher classical or civic republican concept of a *duty* to participate. He suggests that, for current expectations from a revived citizenship to be realistic, they have to embrace the latter, for all the awkward problems it creates. Elsewhere (1990b), Oldfield goes on to point out that in modern society it will not be possible for people to locate themselves in just one political community as in the Greek and medieval cases; we live in a plurality of types and levels of community, with some of these being in conflict with each other. It is within that kind of matrix, provided it is participatory, that we will find our equivalents of the *polis*. Although Oldfield sees such a concept of community extending to national and similarly remote levels, it will clearly be most strongly based on localities, occupational groups, or other more immediately accessible categories.

There are many areas of social life where, except under most elaborately artificial arrangements, the market freedom of 'take it or go somewhere else' is not enough to satisfy demand for choice and voice. Even within the private sector of education one can hardly change one's children's school every time one is dissatisfied with a teacher; or change one's job every time that work seems to be badly organized; or move house every time an undesirable development plan is proposed for one's neighbourhood. Participatory mechanisms, even if used frequently by only a few and only occasionally by the many, are the only ways in which a more subtle influence can be secured over such matters.

What form should such mechanisms take? Participation that remains at the level of a right to complain and object does little—indeed makes a negative contribution—to foster integration. Participation proper means sharing in decision-making, including the acceptance of delegated responsibility. This is where 1960s' concepts, with their stress on protest and opposition, were often not helpful and produced further atomization. Since we no longer live in Greek city states, and since we must insist on democracy (meaning in this an absence of formal barriers to participation), this participation must take place in a range of very local or sectoral agencies (for example, in the work-place, at the local school, in the neighbourhood).

The historical model is not so much the Greek city state but that unsung, relatively untheorized medieval legacy of guilds and other, not necessarily occupational, communities which expected active participation from many of their members in delegated self-regulation. The occupation or work-place remains among the most powerful contexts for such activity, but the modern welfare state has produced many more: most obviously schools, but with some difficulty also health services, old people's homes, local planning, consumer and environmental protection. The idea of 'urban parish councils', much discussed in the 1970s and implemented in Scotland in the form of community councils, should return to debate.

Institutions must be created or revitalized. Participation did not disappear as a political preoccupation during the 1980s; its rhetoric changed and so did its power structure. For example, while the words 'industrial democracy' and 'worker participation' were banned from the Department of Employment after 1979, the Newspeak phrase 'employee involvement' enjoyed a quiet vogue. Indeed, under the Companies Act 1985 companies were required to include in their annual reports a statement of what they had done to encourage this commodity. More substantially and less to do with government, forms of personnel management fashionable among the most advanced companies and management consultants included schemes for worker consultation. Of course, these were usually employer-dominated and devoid of rights, but this is a reflection of the power balance of the period. The central idea that winning commitment is likely to involve participation and not just market opportunities is the central point.

Meanwhile, within trade unions the government has insisted on a much increased accountability of leaders and officials to membership vote. Again, the balance of political power has restricted this to trade unions; but a model and example of ordinary people's membership rights in organizations are thereby established which are capable of more general application.

Perhaps most important have been the changes to the government of schools introduced in the 1980s. Proposals for increased parental participation here had already been made, as part of the general participation climate of the 1970s, to the previous Labour government. It, however, shirked the task, as it involved loosening the grip of local political parties over school governorships. The Conservatives, being currently uninterested in their own local government apparatus, were more willing to seize the nettle and to introduce elected parental governors. In later legislation (the Education Reform Act 1988) the government went on to devolve much more of the budgetary management of schools to these restructured governing bodies.

Again, reflecting the current political balance, this structure embodied certain controversial items. The increase in financial responsibility to be borne by individual schools goes alongside a transfer to central government of much of the educational discretion they previously enjoyed. The power gained by governors has been entirely at the expense of local, not central, government. The formulae for delegated finance make it almost impossible for LEAs to give special help to schools with particular problems caused by deprived local backgrounds; financial help is to go to schools that are already popular, thereby making it more difficult for schools with difficulties to do anything to improve themselves. These are, however, all details of the particular scheme; they are not intrinsic to the idea of parental governance. In general the policy is a very genuine example of Conservative 'active citizenship'.

Problematic is the premium placed on the ability of a

neighbourhood to have available the reservoirs of talent (in particular managerial and accountancy skills) that school governance requires. This will favour areas already rich in educated people at the expense of schools already struggling against the local cultural grain.

This has long been a major general objection to widespread community participation: it favours the articulate, the confident, the educated, and the rich. This argument is used as a cop out by ambiguously benign Fabians and local political worthies. There is no need for this defeatism. The earlier wave of interest in community participation in the late 1960s and early 1970s was accompanied by several innovative experiments, based partly on US experience, in encouraging neighbourhood participation in precisely those districts where it is hard to achieve. The most important projects of this kind in Britain were carried out under A. H. Halsey's leadership as the Home Office's Community Development Project in the late 1960s (see, for example, Lees and Smith 1975).

The results were not dramatic; encouraging effective participation in day-to-day activity is very hard work; the tension between the particularism of community and the universal claims of citizenship raises constant problems (for example in ethnic relations); it is expensive in its need to employ professional staff working as *animateurs*. However, some projects of this kind continue. Some of the lessons from them, in particular those involving the mothers of young school-aged children, have informed mainstream practice. In a changed political climate, with interest again centred on using participation to reduce rather than intensify inequalities, work of this kind will have a renewed prominence alongside such ventures as local management of schools.

In recent years the products of initiatives of this kind have begun to inform the thinking of such legendary devotees of bureaucratic centralism as the Labour left (see, for example, the initiatives of the latter years of the Greater London Council (Mackintosh and Wainwright 1987)), the Fabians (see, for example, Donnison 1983) and welfare state professionals. The infamous lay–professional barrier often breaks down as state agencies work with voluntary groups, some of which become an important arm of local service delivery: meals on wheels, parental involvement in primary school reading schemes, youth and sports clubs, resettlement of mental patients in the community, victim support schemes, adoption and fostering, adult literacy projects (Bulmer 1986; T. Smith 1989: 140–3; Walker 1982).

The list is varied and exciting. There are dangers, of course, as when governments reduce public funding to a policy sector because voluntary action, intended to supplement public services, has become prominent. Also, many experiments have been carried out as rather manipulative top-down exercises in securing greater managerial flexibility rather than genuine participation (Aleszewski and Mathorpe 1988). But the model of partnership is here. Its extension, under a political climate not intrinsically hostile to public services, is set to transform many of the relations between professionals and communities and to make possible to a far wider range of people, both through schemes for participation in management and through opportunities for linked voluntary action, a living reality of the idea of active citizenship in a rich sense.

NOTE

1. I am extremely grateful to George and Teresa Smith for comments on an earlier version of this chapter.

4

Social Movements and Disordered Bodies: The Reform of Birth, Sex, Drink, and Death in Britain since 1850[1]

RORY WILLIAMS

For some time now, conceptions of social reform have centred on the opposed agencies of market and state. No doubt this partly reflects the polarization of contemporary British politics. The New Right pin their banners to the self-motivated individual, and deplore anything else as reliance on the 'nanny state'; and their opponents search for new kinds of collective provision, while continuing to deplore market solutions as attempts to 'blame the victim'. Meanwhile, the 'social market', as a cure for the evils on both sides, often sounds like the result of the eighteenth-century medical consultation where one doctor having pronounced 'Yes, a collection of water', and another 'Well, I think it is wind', the third announces 'I take it to be something between wind and water' (Porter and Porter 1989: 56).

Yet this political polarity is matched by a sociological polarity which is equally difficult to remedy. Studies in contemporary social policy still depend heavily on counterposing the individual and the collective, both methodologically and conceptually. Methodologically they proceed by organizing atomized data from random samples or randomized groups in terms of policy questions created by institutions. Conceptually they add together individual attributes and attitudes as descriptions of the 'population'; and the professions and the bureaucracy create the knowledge by which this population is to be understood. Naturally policies thus created tend to individualize those who are controlled, while at the same time co-ordinating ever more effectively the knowledge of the controllers (Armstrong 1983).

Nor does it help to move from projects for reform to projects for revolution, for the actors are still largely the same, although the lines are different. Market capitalism still generates classes defined by their market situation and the contemporary problem has continued to be centred on the reasons why disadvantaged classes do not act 'for themselves', through the unions, the party and, once again, the state.

In these circumstances, the despairing eye in search of other actors capable of helping to transform the scene has occasionally fastened again on social movements. The unanticipated events of the 1960s led many social analysts, whether reformist or revolutionary in temper, to speculate further on the hidden power of such movements, and on the new 'self-producing' society in which they appeared to be embedded (Banks 1972; Bottomore 1979; Weiner 1981). Yet even as they wrote, some of them were uneasily conscious that most of the movements they were interested in seemed to have been glorious failures, or at best accidental successes, profiting from other changes in society which were wholly unconnected. This was particularly true outside the Labour movement, where certainly some achievements could be demonstrated, though most of them were heavily dependent on state intervention. But as one moved away from the public to the private sphere, and from legislative change to moral transformations affecting individual lives at the most personal and intimate level, so the apparent impotence, and the 'epiphenomenal' character, of the social movements concerned often seemed increasingly unavoidable on the basis of the evidence.

Three examples of such movements in the private sphere will suffice to show the circumstances in which careful historical enquiry concluded with scepticism. Writing in the early 1960s about the feminist movement over the preceding century, Joseph and Olive Banks summed up their evidence by saying, 'It would seem that feminism has not succeeded in making great or wide-sweeping changes in the status of women. Reforms that we can primarily attribute to feminist efforts have been small in scope . . . The most significant change in the position of women during the past hundred years, the fall in the birth rate, was not produced by feminism at all' (Banks and Banks 1976: 690–1). Similarly, after the most thorough examination of Victorian temperance movements to date, Brian Harrison concluded, 'There seems to be no direct relation between the intensity of temperance agitation and the decline of the evil . . . During the first forty years of temperance agitation the statistics for *per capita* consumption—increasingly accurate by the 1860s—show an actual increase . . . Again, the temperance movement was in marked decline at the time when the most striking, and statistically verifiable, reduction in the level of drinking occurred: that is, after the D.O.R.A. regulations of the first world war' (Harrison 1971: 354–5). Finally, though birth, sex, and drink in Britain have had much more profound historical scrutiny than death, my own investigations into the euthanasia movement, and into claims that it has brought a new rationalism into popular attitudes to dying, concluded thus: 'Evidently this claim cannot stand in any straightforward sense. The American demand for full information has not followed straightforwardly from a popular endorsement of euthanasia; and the British endorsement of euthanasia has somehow succeeded in co-existing with a frequent disinclination for knowledge' (R. Williams 1989: 208). Altogether, there is much to justify the generalization of Joseph Banks: 'The evidence of the working of social movements suggests that changes of behaviour on a large scale are rarely, if ever, induced by self-help organisations winning over large sections of a population to their point of view' (J. A. Banks 1972: 48–9).

Such conclusions might seem to place a tombstone on the study of social movements as agents of social reform, at least in the 'private' or 'cultural' sphere. Yet whenever we turn to look at what has happened over the past century in the cultural areas just discussed—in birth, sex, drink, and death, four terms which could almost stand as a biography of many British citizens a hundred years ago—the sweep of the social reforms which have occurred never fails to astonish. The revolutionary fall in the number of children born to each mother since the 1860s, and the changes in marriage, sexuality, and the economy which have accompanied it, need no rehearsal. Less generally known, perhaps, is the scale of the fall between 1831 and 1931 in per capita consumption of alcohol—in the case of beer, to three-fifths of its previous level, and in the case of spirits to a mere one-fifth (Harrison 1971: 37). And we have come to recognize equally dramatic changes in the way we deal with death: around the deathbed the former regime of silence instituted in the mid-nineteenth century (Armstrong 1987) has given way to the point where, in the late 1970s, four-fifths or more of American cancer patients wished to be told in detail about their diagnosis and prognosis (R. Williams 1989).

What are we to make of these changes? Are all explicable by features of the market or the state, as the two institutions developed over this period? And is the association of these changes with the feminist, temperance, and life and death movements purely contingent? Indeed, must we be even more sceptical, and say that the changes actually produced the movements' aims, provoking an epiphenomenal recognition of things already accomplished, as the fall in the birthrate became recognized *a posteriori* as an aim of the feminist movement (Banks and Banks 1976: 689)? Or did the movements, in spite of the conclusions already cited, play some important causative role, in ways less obvious than we are accustomed to suppose?

These are the questions with which this essay is concerned. They are worked out using as examples the movements already discussed, all of which were concerned with the ordering of disorderly bodies, that is, with all that is most intimate and personal in individual lives. It may fairly easily be accepted that social movements can help to change the law, as they did with the repeal of the Corn Laws and the emancipation of the slaves, but to change values and behaviour as well, especially in personal, bodily matters, is much harder. I have chosen to look at values and behaviour connected with birth, sex, drink, and death. Other relevant topics would be food, recreation, illness behaviour, and violence, but so far the history of most of these is less well documented; and in the topics chosen at least there can be little question that, to use Banks's words, 'changes of behaviour on a large scale' have occurred, and 'large sections of a population' were won over to a new point of view. Thus the changes were particularly intense at the level of daily life, and of those cultural practices that in other times and places have been especially representative of 'la longue durée'.

At the same time, since the general trend of the social changes which have occurred since Victorian times is often interpreted as a liberation from repression, with the implication that they represent a spontaneous upsurge following the progressive removal of moral and legal shackles, I have endeavoured to balance a 'liberating' movement (feminism) with a 'repressive' movement (temperance), and to compare both with a movement, or cluster of movements, which are not easily classifiable either way (those concerned with dying well). These are superficial labels, as Foucault has demonstrated on the prototypical subject of sexual liberation (Foucault 1976); the new discourse has only liberated people to serve new sexual imperatives, which it has itself formed and articulated. But even if the contrasts of liberation and repression are only apparent, we can at least, by seeing the similarities between apparently contrasting types of movement, get an insight into the amount of social labour which is involved in changes that might otherwise appear 'natural' and taken for granted.

THE EFFECTIVENESS OF SOCIAL MOVEMENTS

I shall accept from the outset that the social movements concerned here did not, by and large, bring about their stated aims on a national scale. This assumption corresponds, more or less, to the general conclusion reached by Banks, and is borne out in the three examples I have selected. Of the chief large-scale changes in women's lives, the reduction of births was, as we have seen, ignored in the early aims of organized feminists, and contraception and sexual freedom were actually opposed by them (Banks and Banks 1976). Similarly the big increase in women's peacetime employment—certainly a stated aim from the outset—only began three decades after first-wave feminism had gone into partial eclipse, and one decade before the resurgence of the second wave (Bouchier 1983: chap. 1). As for the temperance movement, its first forty years were directed strictly to teetotalism; and Harrison estimates that at the peak of its influence in the 1860s adult teetotallers numbered around a million—an impressive figure by modern standards, but still less than a tenth of the adult population (Harrison 1971: 20, 317). The stated aims of the euthanasia movement, meanwhile, are less measurable behaviourally, since the movement has first to achieve legislation which will tolerate the behaviour it advocates; but the exceptionally long period of agitation in Britain—over fifty years now since the first bill in 1936—has produced no change in the law and, in the brief period around 1981 when do-it-yourself methods were advocated, a sharp alienation of public sympathy (Editorial 1981). It is possible that the agitation leading up to the 1936 bill succeeded in generating the high level of popular support for legislation, first found in opinion polls at the time. But it is more likely that the agitation merely traded upon a previously established pattern of values; and a review of the literature, and a contemporary ethnographic study, suggest that these values are seldom rationalistic, and contain striking contradictions which have much to do with the old pattern of silence and disregard in the face of dying (R. Williams 1989; 1990).

Clearly, therefore, if these movements have in any way influenced or initiated large-scale social change, it must have been in ways which were only indirectly connected with their stated aims. Nor should we be surprised by this: it does not take much reflection or experience to realize that in history few people achieve their stated aims, not least because, in a changing situation, and against competing arguments, specific aims soon become irrelevant. We are dealing, therefore, in unintended consequences, and in influences or interactions which pass beyond the identifiable recruits of the movements concerned and reach a more elusive but much larger audience or public. These two categories of effect are of course well recognized in studies of social movements, but for present purposes we need to insist on some further distinctions.

To begin with, some unintended consequences are interesting, but can hardly count as a sort of effectiveness. Temperance societies did much to bring different social classes together, but that was entirely incidental to their aims. Much more interesting, for present purposes, are those consequences which, while not part of the movement's stated aims, nevertheless can be given some broader value, positive or negative, in terms of the arguments which underlay those aims. Thus the campaign to provide clean drinking water should have had a positive value for the temperance movement, since beer was drunk partly because it was safer than water; and if temperance reformers had been active in the campaign—they were not—that would have been one example of the kind of indirect effectiveness we are looking for.

Again, if unintended consequences need definition in this way, so too does the 'public' that exists outside a movement's membership. Obviously, evidence on those who have heard or read the movement's arguments at first hand, at meetings or in magazines, is highly relevant, though often hard to obtain, and the term 'public' has traditionally been reserved for those who then show their interest by registering a collective opinion on the subject, as at the ballot box, or at a pinch in demonstrations, petitions, delegations, etc. (Turner and Killian 1957: chap. 11). Yet ideally we would want to know much more than this. We would like to hear second- and third-hand versions of these arguments being discussed among friends and at family breakfast tables, and we would like to observe accounts of these going down the gossip chain, and the signs of new choices being contemplated, or even made. Opponents would be just as interesting as advocates; for at times the actions of opponents may be the most significant testimony of influence. The appearance of an organized anti-suffrage movement in the 1900s gave the feminists a far higher profile and demonstrated the strength of their case by the weakness of its own (Harrison 1978). Similarly, the disowning of the temperance movement by the government in the preparation for the Defence of the Realm Act in 1914 only made the clothes stolen from the movement the more striking. Thus the public for a movement must ideally include all those interested, for or against, in the arguments which the movement puts, whether they hear the arguments at first or third hand, and whether they respond with some collective demonstration, or merely discuss or act on their views in their own circles. Sadly, such publics are mostly, for the historian, hidden from view, and we need to find ways of assessing their extent which are cautious and empirical, but do not too readily adopt a null hypothesis when the evidence is feeble.

With these preliminary comments on method, what historical effectiveness can we suggest for the movements discussed here?

THE FEMINIST MOVEMENT

I shall concentrate here on the fall in the number of children born to each mother as the chief thing to be explained, for this revolution, which soon became involved in questions of contraception, is a necessary condition both for the subsequent sexual revolution and for the rising demand for paid work among wives in the 1950s.

The nineteenth-century fall in the English birth-rate, and its relation to feminism, has been the subject of a fine series of historical studies by Joseph and Olive Banks. If I take issue with their negative conclusions here, it is only by using the materials which they have made available. The original conclusion of Joseph Banks was that the fall was made possible by the rising economic aspirations of the Victorian middle class meeting the cold air of economic depression in the 1870s. But it was only made possible—that is, the rising aspirations were 'one of the chief factors' (J. A. Banks 1954: 202), or a 'necessary but not sufficient condition' (J. A. Banks 1981: 8). Thereafter, in a lifelong search for the sufficient conditions, Banks first ruled out feminism (Banks and Banks 1972), then the decline of religion and rise of secularism, and lit eventually on the increasing necessity of finding money for public school fees so that sons could be fitted for careers which were becoming increasingly meritocratic in the third quarter of the nineteenth century (J. A. Banks 1981: 48–9, 62).

The problem with this explanation is that it cannot easily account for the spread of family limitation to parents who did not envisage meritocratic careers and public school education for their sons. After reviewing a number of alternatives to bridge this gap, Banks ends by suggesting that it was the future time perspective inculcated by the school examination system which induced the rest of the population to plan their families (ibid.: 132–7). But this seems a counsel of despair.

Banks's difficulty arises partly because, since *Prosperity and Parenthood*, the dating of the pioneer family limiters has been pushed back from the 1870s to before the 1860s (Matras 1966; Branca 1975; Stone 1979: 261–6; Hollingsworth 1969: 339–53). Rather than the more general effect of depression on rising aspirations, therefore, it is the rising costs of education during the mid-century boom which he has come to emphasize. And similarly, any alternative explanation must also look to the situation before 1860.

Now, as we have seen, the Bankses ruled out organized feminism because birth limitation was only adopted as an explicit feminist aim near the end of the century; but a number of authors have since argued, first, that birth limitation was linked to feminist ideas by secularist and utilitarian authors from the early 1800s (MacLaren 1978; Branca 1975), and second, that the nineteenth century saw a general increase in unorganized or 'domestic' feminism—initially and especially among middle-class women (Degler 1980: L. Gordon 1976; Scott Smith 1973).

It has to be admitted that in their present form these arguments are not conclusive. It can fairly be objected to the first of them that the anti-religious polemic and novel moralities in which early nineteenth-century proposals for contraception were embedded were more likely to alienate than to convince the landed and professional families who first limited births. Of course the leading families also valued intellectual curiosity and tolerated eccentricity; and it is quite likely that they accounted for a proportion of those who purchased the four editions of Richard Carlile's book published between 1825 and 1826, and the nine editions of George Drysdale's published between 1855 and 1871. But the great mass of them remained solidly attached to the church; and since they knew well that artificial methods of contraception had hitherto been associated with prostitution and sexual indulgence—an association only strengthened by the advocates of free love—their practical condemnation of these methods was assured. Otherwise the readers of Carlile and Drysdale were doubtless largely to be found in those artisan circles which debated radical and secularist topics; and the social equals of this latter group did not limit births to any significant extent until late in the century. Thus the secularists remained largely isolated from the real innovators in birth-control.

Similarly the case for suggesting a rise in domestic feminism in Britain in the period before 1860 is also open to objections, if by domestic feminism is meant an effort by women to gain control over their own bodies and their own health which was essentially unilateral. Most of the evidence relevant to this version of things has been assembled by historians of America; and most dates from after 1870 (L. Gordon 1976; Degler 1980; Scott Smith 1973). Of earlier material, there is certainly evidence of an American popular health movement well before the 1850s (Branca 1975; Shearer 1989; Ehrenreich and English 1973). As a popular movement this probably did rely extensively on women, and was certainly often concerned with women's complaints, but it was promulgated by both sexes and was not confined to women's health. In Britain, by contrast, proponents of domestic feminism have relied not on popular but on medical evidence of concern for women, and especially concern for the spacing of births (Branca 1975). Yet this does not mean that the initiative was necessarily being taken by women, and in addition, as Banks has shown, birth-limitation, when it came, proceeded not by spacing births but by halting them after a suitable number of births had been achieved (J. A. Banks 1981: 72–4).

How can we reassemble all these pieces? The line of reconstruction which I would like to suggest follows that of Stone, Shorter, and, to some extent, Degler, and begins not with a unilateral change in the attitude of women, but with a change in the attitude of both sexes—the ideology of companionate marriage, which was increasingly asserted among the gentry and upper bourgeoisie of eighteenth-century England (Stone 1979; Shorter 1975; Degler 1980).[2] Requiring, and reinforced by, increasing education for the women of these classes, it was advanced by both sexes, and there can be little doubt that it entailed a new concern for the welfare of wives which could only have been to their advantage, and was thus in that sense emancipatory. Companionate marriage was the ideal of Mary Wollstonecraft, where it was linked to birth-spacing (Banks and Banks 1964: 16–17), and it was then taken up at the beginning of the nineteenth century by the utilitarians, some of whom quickly linked it to equal rights for women and to advocacy for methods of contraception.

In terms of general bourgeois attitudes, however, this extension of companionate marriage to a notion of equal rights for women, including a right to prevent further conceptions by artificial methods, was a false dawn. For contraception was firmly linked in the public mind with prostitution, and the notion of wives using it met fierce reaction. This, together with the secularist background of these arguments, ensured their exclusion from public acceptance for some decades. For the time being, the only means of restricting births publicly advocated was late marriage, preceded by self-restraint—the Malthusian prescription, whose widespread adoption was celebrated in the fourth annual report of the Registrar-General in 1842 (Farr 1842*a*). The arguments here were not concerned with women's welfare but with domestic and national prosperity.

For birth-limitation in marriage to gain credence in bourgeois society, therefore—and specifically for it to take the form of limitation only after a sufficient number of births—some new factor was needed; and I suggest this factor is to be found in new knowledge of the increasing risks of birth with increasing maternal age.

This is not a subject which has so far emerged from trawls in the medical or autobiographical literature of the time, where discussions of childbirth were dominated by the risk of puerperal fever. Either people did not write about risks by age, or historians have not recognized what they were saying; and in either case that is probably because the effect of age was too obvious. Couples could see well enough, when it occurred, that as birth succeeded birth and year succeeded year, the wife's health and capacity for childbearing had collapsed (for later examples see Llewellyn Davies 1915). And it is significant that doctors routinely noted age even when pursuing other causes of death in childbirth (Farr 1842*b*). What was needed, though, was the intellectual shift from age and parity as a retrospective explanation of a particular ill-starred maternity, to a live appreciation of them as prospective, systematic, avoidable risks.

Significantly, the discovery of this systematic knowledge was itself linked with concern for the welfare of wives, and thus with the domestic ideal constructed by the eighteenth-century bourgeoisie. In Britain the story can be seen unfolding in the project of the first Statistical Superintendent of the Registrar-General's office, William Farr. In the same fourth report of 1842 referred to earlier, Farr notes the figures for maternal mortality which he has discovered, and the signs that in the few years of data collection so far they are actually increasing, and announces, 'The proportion of mothers who perish at this important period is unquestionably excessive'. It is the manifesto of companionate marriage. In the reports which follow, he begins to record causes of maternal death by age, and argues for improved midwifery. But something else is troubling him. In 1844, it emerges—it is that he has no data on the ages of mothers surviving childbirth with which to compare the ages of mothers who died. Interestingly, this year, 1844, is also the year in which an anonymous publication explicitly advocated contraception to save wives from further risk after a number of previous births: 'See your pale and emaciated female, surrounded by consumptive children. Is it not horrible that she should be bearing also an unborn babe to add to their number? What a brute and slaughtering foe to her is her "husband", if he be aware that a prudential check exists to prevent such a birth as awaits him, and such a death as his unchecked passion hastens to his wife' (Branca 1975: 137). The subject is evidently in the air. But for the time being Farr has to abandon the question, and sets off on a long foray into life tables. Finally in 1856 he returns. He still does not have the data he wants, but by applying Swedish figures for the numbers of women bearing children in each age group he has at last found a method of estimating maternal risk by age, and publishes, with all the authority of a government document, the first comprehensive figures for England. After noting the heightened risk of primiparae, and the relatively low risk between ages 25–35, he concludes that thereafter with rising age 'the calamitous death of mothers in childbirth is governed by a mathematical law' (Farr 1842*b*: 129; 1844: 284; 1856: 74).

It is difficult in our day to comprehend the scale of the risks women faced at this time. The figures published by Farr suggest that over an average lifetime of childbearing at the scale prevalent in Class II before 1851 (for which see Branca 1975: 137), the accumulated risk meant a 4–5 in 100 chance of death in childbirth—this before taking any account of individual health and predisposing factors. At this rate the great majority of women must have known personally one or more women who had died in this way. Not surprisingly, as Shorter has shown, pregnant women prepared themselves for this eventuality

(Shorter 1984: chap. 5). But now there was specific, nation-wide evidence linking the risk of maternal death not just with idiosyncratic factors but simply with age. And from this point in the 1850s onward, women are found to be limiting birth after a certain age, and the older they marry, the sooner is the limitation applied (Matras 1966: Table 1).

As all parties on this issue have pointed out, this step of translating knowledge into action is hidden in the silences or whispers of the Victorian bedroom. But the logic of the progression can be stated as a hypothesis, given the accepted circumstances of the time. Since Malthusian self-restraint was the approved method of matching fertility with prosperity before marriage, it can be assumed that it was initially the approved method as, after a certain age, the risks of wives dying in childbirth increased. Yet besides the approved method, societies also institutionalize 'second best' rules for those—usually men—who feel they cannot keep to it. Second best in Victorian Britain, as in Tolstoy's Russia,[3] was resort to prostitutes, or to young maidservants who, if luck went against them, might either be married off or themselves become prostitutes. The rise in prostitution in the mid-nineteenth century was fed, not only by frustrated bachelors, but, if the present hypothesis is right, by desperate older husbands who did not wish to injure their wives, or at any rate did not wish to force them when they were frightened and unwilling, and who remembered their bachelor solutions in their hour of need.

This may seem too kindly an estimate of the Victorian paterfamilias. I do not mean to imply that many husbands, even in the professional and landed classes, did not continue to disregard their wives' welfare, but only to suggest that the fall in the birth-rate, initiated in the late 1850s, was the work of couples who did care about the wife's welfare, and who shared the theory that moral restraint was proper and sufficient for the purpose. The breakdowns in this theory can be supposed to have been unplanned, unacknowledged, and a matter of shame to the husband.

It is in this context that the organized feminist agitation of the 1860s against the Contagious Diseases Act, and against the whole tolerance of prostitution, must be seen. The effect of the agitation against the 'double standard' was to force into the open the whole structure of prostitution as a safety net for those who could not manage moral restraint; and by foreclosing that escape route in the minds of conscientious men, it compelled couples into a search for a new and less destructive second best.

It was at this point that the contraceptive prescriptions of George Drysdale, Francis Place, Richard Carlile, and the young John Stuart Mill began to make tacit progress in the consciences of the bourgeoisie. It is important to note that in this role they implied no 'apostasy' (Banks 1981: chap. 7), any more than prostitution did. Contraception was, no doubt, still a second best, and, like prostitution still not a matter for public discussion; but it was better than resorting to prostitutes. It was this context of choosing the lesser evil when restraint failed that makes sense both of the later continuing demand from the reading public for books like Drysdale's (21,000 copies by 1876), and of the divided feelings and vein of hidden support evoked by the Bradlaugh–Besant trial of 1877, which concerned the publication of straightforward contraceptive advice.

From this point on the process of diffusion to be presupposed is much the same whether it passed to the working class through servants or, as in Shorter's view (Shorter 1975; 1973), as a function of the increase of premarital sex in the working class. Servants were, after all, closely involved in the premarital sex of the bourgeois male, whether as abettors or as sex objects, and the hypothesis put forward for the bourgeoisie likewise presupposes the transfer of premarital habits to postmarital birth-limitation, whether initially in the form of resort to maidservants or prostitutes, or subsequently in the form of the contraceptive practices which were formerly associated with these situations. The turnover of young servants was, it must be remembered, very high, for they soon got married, and many then entered, or married into, other occupations. And they were then as capable as their bourgeois mentors of applying their premarital lessons to the postmarital situation (for the fertility of servants see J. A. Banks 1981: table 8.6), and of passing on their solutions to others.

However, for this application to be made they had to carry with them the ethos of companionate marriage, with its concern for the health and welfare of the wife and mother. The diffusion of this concept was a slow process, and probably owed as much to Marie Stopes and others on the one hand, and to Hollywood on the other, as to first-hand tales of the quality. At any rate it was only in marriages contracted after 1920 that a majority of the population admitted to using birth-control, and only after 1950 that the majority became overwhelming (Leathard 1980: 75, 105). But companionate marriage won the day, and the withdrawal of Anglican disapproval by the Lambeth conference in 1930 was again based on the conscientious arguments for the health of the wife and mother within marriage that the companionate ideal had made obligatory (ibid.: 47).

To sum up then: the hypothesis put forward is that the ideal of companionate marriage, formed in the eighteenth-century gentry and bourgeoisie, was both the stimulus to researching maternal deaths, and the ground of attempts at sexual restraint when risks by rising maternal age were confirmed in the 1850s. Failures of male restraint followed established 'second best' rules in resorting to prostitution and semi-prostitution, until feminist agitation exposed this to censure as an unacceptable double standard in the 1860s. Thereafter a new 'second best' rule began to be adopted—the use of withdrawal and/or artificial contraception as the wife got older, and this spread to all classes, initially through servants, but latterly and chiefly through the same marriage ideal being promulgated both through the media, especially the cinema, and as an argument for birth-control by feminists and family planners. This revolutionary change, virtually completed by the 1950s, was a necessary condition both for wives seeking work (rather than being driven to it, as in earlier times, by poverty), and for women generally to adopt the premarital sexual freedom of the 1960s.

On this hypothesis organized feminism played a key role, though not an explicitly planned or intended one, in the 1860s, and a submerged but deliberate role, from the 1920s on, in the family-planning movement; but its public, and the matrix from which it came, was the large pre-existing constituency of unorganized middle-class idealists of both sexes who developed the concept of companionate marriage. Organized feminism unintentionally changed the course of a pre-existing domestic feminism; and it was the debate between these two constituencies which evolved and determined the path which was to end in the demographic revolution.

THE TEMPERANCE MOVEMENT

Brian Harrison's judgement on the temperance movement is related to the fact that his detailed account stops in 1872; but he recognizes two alternative hypotheses (or 'escape routes')—that without the movement consumption before 1872 would have been higher, and that reduced consumption after 1872 owed much to the movement's work before 1872. He comments succinctly, 'Both claims are unverifiable' (1971: 355).

But are they? On the first hypothesis, one can certainly argue that, other things being equal, per capita consumption *ought* to have risen between 1832 and 1872 because of the enormous influx of immiserated Irish fleeing from the famine of the 1840s, whose circumstances, compounded of natural disaster, disorganized emigration, social dislocation, extreme poverty, and hostility from the English, were more conducive to drink than even those of the poorest indigenous class. It cannot be accident, or police methods alone, which made arrests for drunkenness in Lancashire in the 1860s reach figures around ten times the levels for the midlands or home counties (ibid.: 315, 363). By 1851 Liverpool's adult population was 29 per cent Irish born, and Manchester's 17 per cent (Census 1851: p. clxxxiii), and the population of Irish refugees only reached its peak in 1861. In the North West, this situation laid the foundations for a drink problem of a quite exceptional order, and even in the country as a whole, the number of Irish-born adults by 1861 was beginning to approach the number of all adult teetotallers.

But this is only one among many factors, and it is Harrison's second escape route which is most interesting—the possibility that the temperance movement laid the foundations for change, not only before 1872, but also during the period when it ceased growing, but had not begun to decline, between the 1870s and the 1890s. Here I must add that, although my emphasis differs, I rely for much of my material on Harrison's own insights concerning this period.

In order to evaluate this question, we need evidence of what factors were actually involved in the decline of drinking and drink problems when it occurred; and here the most satisfying evidence is that from the First World War. The war acted like a within-subject experiment, showing a startling drop in per capita consumption of beer and spirits and in alcohol mortality alike, as war conditions took effect, and a temporary resurgence of consumption as they were lifted (Williams and Brake 1980: Tables I.1 and I.18). That this was not the result of war *per se* is made clear by the figures for the Second World War, when a small drop in consumption of spirits was simultaneously countered by a rise in that of beer. So we can suppose with some confidence that the reason lay in the measures taken at the introduction of the Defence of the Realm Act.

What were these measures? They fell into various categories: (1) restricting sale of liquor, especially the licensed hours, (2) establishing canteens which offered food and non-alcoholic drinks, and (3) a fresh effort to use the power of an abstinent example, by the King this time, called the King's Pledge (ibid.: chap. 4; G. B. Wilson 1940: 128, 272). Each of these approaches corresponded to typical forms of temperance activity during the previous eighty years, and during the subsequent fifteen or twenty years when consumption fell to its lowest; and each can thus help to explain both earlier and later falls in consumption. In addition (4) cuts in output of beer and spirits after April 1917, and increasing dilution, helped to reduce consumption over the next three or so years; but this factor was specific to these years and cannot explain earlier and later reductions.

Licensing laws to restrict the selling of drink were not an objective of the temperance movement, but the use of law to prohibit drink selling was, and it formed their distinctive contribution to the debate over the role of the state from the outset. That the need for legal control became accepted even among liberals by 1872 was their triumph. Certainly they threw away potential gains in legal control when the 1871 Licensing Bill was withdrawn for lack of support, and they alienated legislative allies at the turn of the century, all because of their insistence that nothing but uncompensated prohibition would do. In these respects they may even have delayed the resolution of the drink question, as compared with an ideal reform movement which did not exist, or not in any strength of numbers. But compared with having no temperance movement at all, which is the relevant alternative here, these blunders were superficial. Without temperance opponents to the drink interest, Bruce's 1871 Bill could not have been attempted nor his 1872 Act carried (Harrison 1971: 269, 274). And without their continuing agitation on the drink problem up to the First World War the licensing approach could not have been pursued and proved to be workable. It was the evidence that the 1872 Act had not led to riots, and had caused the number of on-licences per head to start falling steadily and that, perhaps partly because of this, per capita consumption had begun falling after 1877, that suggested the effectiveness and workability of the licensing approach (Wilson 1940: 107); just as in Scotland the analogous restrictions of the earlier Forbes Mackenzie Act of 1853 were seen to be followed by a similar decline in consumption after 1860 (Smout 1987: chap. 6). These demonstrations prepared the ground for the Licensing Act of 1904 and the regulations of the First World War, whose convincing success led in turn to their reconstitution in the Licensing Act of 1921. Licensing was the moderate's solution, requiring practicability and effectiveness, to the contradiction between temperance pressure for prohibition and the drink interest's pressure for maximum latitude.

Since then, of course, in the relatively moderate drinking climate of the present, it has been argued that in certain circumstances relaxation of licensing may in the short run actually be beneficial, but whatever the merits of this debated proposition (for which see especially Clayson 1973; Duffy and Plant 1986; Goddard 1986), it can scarcely stand as a counterweight to the evidence of massive change from Victorian levels of drinking which corresponds to increased licensing restrictions.

The second arm of First World War policy was the provision of counter-attractions. By this time the government was able to exploit a wide range of non-alcoholic drinks which had emerged during the nineteenth century. Tea, cocoa, cordials, and tap water, all rarely consumed in the early 1800s, were staples by the early 1900s. And while temperance reformers were laggardly, as I noted earlier, in helping to improve the water supply—perhaps foreseeing that water would never offer much attraction to Britons as a sociable drink—they were deeply involved in the phenomenal rise of tea to national status, marketing it (for example, Horniman), advocating it, arguing against fears of its effect on nerves or digestions, and creating the social occasions and gatherings with which it was to become permanently associated—the evening visit, the afternoon ritual, and the religious meeting. The same is true of cocoa, manufactured by Quaker families involved in temperance reform, such as the Frys, Cadburys, and Rowntrees, and much advertised in temperance literature. On cordials, admittedly, temperance support was patchy. Coffee consumption, too, never rivalled that of tea and soon fell into slow decline, but coffee-houses and eating houses developed steadily through the second half of the century. Temperance reformers fluctuated in their involvement in these, early initiating temperance hotels, then discouraging cafés in favour of home life, and finally, in the 1870s, promoting them zealously. Overall, though it can fairly be said that temperance idealists, not so much acting as instruments of the movement as taking initiatives consistent with its aims and often using its literature, did a great deal to create the counter-attractions which unquestionably worked and became integral to the British way of life, and which were used with decisive effect in the First World War.

The growth of these counter-attractions was probably even more influential than stricter licensing in bringing about the fall in per capita consumption after 1877; but neither is compatible with the final feeble surge in consumption, and the peak in alcohol mortality, that ushered in the new century before the final great decline of the drink problem. The reasons for this surge, which coincided with the Royal Commission of 1896–9, remain a matter of speculation. No doubt such factors as the growth of club premises, which fell outside existing licensing restrictions, may be indicted. But the 1890s were also a period in which temperance income declined, and temperance reformers came under an attack which was, for the first time, a moral attack. The socialist critique emerged at a time when the movement was to become locked in unedifying squabbles about the compensation of redundant publicans, and the moral vacuum thus created may explain the third feature of successful First World War policy—the King's Pledge.

The eagerness of the government in 1914 to distance itself from the temperance movement is striking—yet in doing so, it felt a need to reconstitute the pledge on non-sectarian lines. And this was not because it expected the British people to become teetotal during the war, for all its other actions were aimed at drinking in moderation. Rather, it was the element of sacrificial example, purged of authoritarianism, which was felt to be an effective aid to moderation in others. And this is testimony to the moral influence on others which teetotallers had exerted at their best.

Thus, in a word, temperance reformers compelled the licensing solution as a compromise between their prohibitionism and the drink interest, made tea a still more British drink than beer, and by abstinence set new standards for what others could count as moderate drinking. On this interpretation, it can be claimed that the movement was a necessary condition of the great twentieth-century decline in consumption and alcohol mortality; and a confirmation of this view can be seen in the fact that the fresh and continuing rise in consumption and alcohol mortality since the 1960s has, in the marked decline of the movement, evoked no national response adequate to halt, let alone reverse, the trend in the course of thirty years.[4]

These effects of the movement were all largely incidental to its official aims—the spread of teetotalism and the prohibition of purveyors of drink; but all were highly relevant to the rationale which generated those aims. Indicative is Sir William Lawson's remark on the licensing reformers: 'I wish them God speed. If they can find a way of carrying on the trade without doing harm, the Alliance will be dissolved tomorrow' (Williams and Brake 1980: 9). Furthermore in all these respects the crucial influence was exerted outside the ranks of the movement's members, amongst moderate drinkers and pragmatists who were often considerably irritated by the movement's absolutism. And while that absolutism often seems, from our vantage-point, to have been counter-productive, still without the movement it is very doubtful that the cultural and dietary practices of the mid-nineteenth century could have been so extensively changed.

MOVEMENTS CONCERNED WITH DEATH

As I have noted, these movements as yet lack a historian, and the present sketch is necessarily impressionistic.[5] The euthanasia movement was the earliest of the contemporary reforming movements concerned with death, becoming formally organized in 1935 in Britain and in 1938 in America. But in the 1960s it was overtaken by a number of other developments, some organized and some very diffuse. In Britain the chief development was the hospice movement; in America actual hospices were instituted only later and more slowly, but related ideas about open communication with, and alleviatory care of, the dying, and attempts to rethink the experience of bereavement, began to be discussed intensively in certain circles. Admittedly psychiatrists and psychotherapists had maintained a vein of interest in bereavement throughout the century, and anthropologists had written about death in other societies. But now theologians, philosophers, and sociologists took up these topics, and more to the point, professional and voluntary organizations concerned with medical, nursing, religious, and pastoral care became involved. Through the latter, and through the media, the laity, as patients, carers, and parishioners, became aware of a new discourse for dealing with death; and even teachers of high school psychology in the USA (Lofland 1978: 81–3) began to discuss it with their pupils. These routes of diffusion suggest that adoption of the new ideas would be swifter in the middle class, and there are indications that this was indeed the case (Gilhooly *et al.* 1988; R. Williams 1990: chap. 3). But by the late 1970s the shift in ideas had become so widespread that in certain areas and in certain respects, notably in the US on the subject of open communication, some of the new notions were virtually the rule.

There are of course qualifications to be made about the evidence of popular change on these topics. Much of the evidence is about reported attitudes, not about behaviour. There are major differences between Britain and America (R. Williams 1989), and in particular British attitudes have been fairly constant on euthanasia since the 1930s. There are also regional variations within each country, which in Britain may well be connected with the variable diffusion of hospices. Thus Aberdeen, at a time when it had no hospice, and in a geographical position in north-east Scotland which was relatively isolated, continued to conserve attitudes mostly typical of an earlier period of silence and avoidance, while in London, where the hospice movement had been under way for some years, a contemporary study showed that only a third of terminal cancer patients did not discuss the possibility of a fatal outcome (McIntosh 1977; Hinton 1974). This last instance is of course consistent with the processes of change I have suggested, and in spite of the qualifications I have given the examples of change are persuasive. It seems clear that in North America in the late 1970s cancer patients wanted to know much more specifically about their prognosis than they did around 1960, and public opinion showed much more acceptance than in the late 1940s of purely palliative treatment, short of outright suicide or killing (R. Williams 1989: 203, 205). Similarly in England the London cancer patients of the 1970s just cited compared with a Lancashire study of popular opinion in the early 1950s where only around half of those questioned wished even a diagnosis of cancer, let alone the prognosis, to be discussed (Paterson and Aitken-Swan 1954).

One may also ask, though, whether the change has really been effected through the movements, and through the routes of diffusion, discussed. Until the processes concerned have been more fully documented there will of course be room for doubt; but we can at least consider the principal alternative explanation—that changes in values have been a direct response to changes in the pattern of mortal illness.

Certainly the swift infections and epidemic killers which permit only a short forward prognosis have dwindled away to the point where death is now chiefly due to slow degenerative disease, typified by cancer, whose course can be foreseen well in advance (Lofland 1978). But the chronology of the change is instructive. In Britain the current death rate from cancer was in effect established, bar minor increments, in the course of the second decade of this century, after a rapid threefold rise over the second half of the last century as infections ceased to preempt it. And by the 1930s TB had waned so much that cancer had already become the principal long-term wasting disease

(Registrar-General 1944: Table 9; 1972: 11). Compared with deaths from consumption—often, from Florence Nightingale's observation, peaceful (1952: 110)—it is intelligible that many cancer deaths of the 1930s should have struck contemporaries as painful and grim, and this is probably quite sufficient to account for the rise of the euthanasia movement at that time, as a later advocate has also noted (G. Williams 1958: 293–4).

But all this was thirty years before the real burgeoning of movements concerned with death. What accounts for this interval, especially considering the immediate response of the euthanasia movement?

At present the best indications can be found in the life of Cicely Saunders—the first swallow of the 1960s summer, and the initiator of the hospice movement, whose ideas were echoed across the Atlantic even when hospices as such were not yet being built there (Kübler-Ross 1970; du Boulay 1984; chap. 15). Her originality, and its sources, emerge clearly when we compare the response of the medical profession to the emergence of cancer as a major killer. In 1951 the Marie Curie Memorial Foundation brought together a committee which included two high-ranking consultants who in 1940 had been working at the Royal Cancer Hospital and the Marie Curie Hospital (Joint National Cancer Survey Committee 1952). Their survey—the first of its kind—examined the distribution of services for cancer patients at home, but otherwise broke no new ground. Similarly in 1957–8, the Gulbenkian Foundation carried out a survey on care of the dying which actually reinforced the traditional view that 'normally the truth should be withheld' (Hughes 1960: 42). These reports did essential professional work in documenting failures in the distribution of existing services, but had none of the new features which were about to blossom into a coherent revaluation of death.

Against this continuing professional tradition Cicely Saunders mobilized two hitherto separate and then little-known sources of ideas about the dying—the method of alleviatory dosing evolved at St Luke's Hospital, and the religious tradition of tolerant openness and tactful spiritual preparation among the Irish Sisters of Charity at St Joseph's. Herself a devout Evangelical and a former nurse, she had had experience as an almoner in 1947 of talking to the dying in intense personal circumstances, and so in 1951 conceived the plan of reading medicine in order to unite all these elements in a single approach. By 1959, in her first major publication after two years of postgraduate research, the initial formulation was essentially complete (Saunders 1959).

However, it is clear from her story that this unification of religious and medical approaches to death involved an evolution in both which was not accomplished without considerable labour and discussion in a wide circle. Medicine had to confront therapeutic failure in a positive spirit which found room for development in alleviating techniques. And religion had to find an ecumenical understanding of beliefs and symbolic responses among patients which in many cases fell outside its own formularies. In America Kübler-Ross testifies to some of the initial hostility this process evoked from medicine (1970); and the difficulties of marrying religious conviction with ecumenical considerations is apparent in the planning of St Christopher's Hospice (du Boulay 1984; chap. 7). It is not surprising that much of the middle ground in both countries should have been supplied by medical and paramedical disciplines like psychiatry and medical sociology which were interested in religious and symbolic ideas without being committed to them.

If this account is broadly correct, therefore—and much historical detail remains to be filled in—responses to the changing pattern of mortal disease varied from the immediate to the delayed according to the amount of social and intellectual labour required in reformulating existing ideas. Several parallel movements resulted, sometimes competing, with duels between the euthanasia and the hospice movements being a long-running feature (for the beginnings of this see Saunders 1959; Editorial 1961; Colebrook 1961; Saunders 1961). Similarly these two movements are the only ones which can be said to have formulated clear aims—the one to change the criminal law, the other initially to spread independent hospices, but latterly to feed hospice ideas into medical practice. As I have noted, the euthanasia movement has not so far succeeded in its aims. The hospice movement has done well in Britain, with well over two hundred allied organizations across the country (Charity Choice 1990), but as yet it is difficult to know what proportion of the dying these organizations reach, and how faithfully they reflect the founding principles.[6] Yet as before, when one turns to effects which are indirect though relevant to these movements' aims, and to publics outside their membership, there is a case for saying that they may have been quite surprisingly effective in creating widespread changes in values.

THE ROLE OF MARKET, STATE, AND PROFESSIONS

In all the three examples of social movements which I have discussed, I have put a case for their indirect effect on, and interaction with, a public outside their membership and consequently for their agency in creating widespread cultural changes. Ideally such a case should be accompanied by studies of movements which had no such public, or which had, yet failed to create any such effect, but for that there is no space; and it is enough to recall that the mortality of social movements is high. Indeed those that survive and become effective show some of that 'sensitive dependence on initial conditions' which characterizes cycles of weather, animal populations, and other turbulent phenomena for which the paradigms of chaos theory have been devised (Gleick 1987).

However, as an account of where social movements themselves come from, such explanations are untidy, and they do not fit easily into the relatively static framework of theory about the market, the state, and the professions patronized by the state, on which most contemporary social explanation is founded. Can such institutions really not explain either these movements' existence, or their effectiveness? I conclude with a brief look at this question.

As regards the fall in the birth-rate, I have argued against the traditional view that the market provided the immediate necessary conditions for change. Clearly such a contention would need more space than I have been able to give it, and I would not wish to rule out attempts to produce a more integrated and complex picture. Companionate marriage preceded industrial capitalism, but may doubtless have been facilitated by commercial capitalism as well as by ownership of land. And the illicit sex of the late eighteenth century onward may doubtless have owed much to urbanization under commercial and then industrial capitalism, as well as to the reaction against Puritanism (Stone 1979: chaps. 6, 12; Shorter 1975; chap. 7). All this helped to set the scene. Then when the time came, the economic calculations involved in late marriage may well have become translated, after the practice of birth-control began, into considerations for engaging in the practice which were accessory to the wife's health. But I am suggesting that these influences merely formed part of the surrounding climate within which the central process of development took place.

The market played its most continuous role in the vicissitudes of the temperance movement, yet it was remarkably indeterminate. On the one hand was the drink interest; but on the other was the opportunity afforded to develop competing drinks and counter-attractions which was rapidly and effectively seized by reformers and industrialists. The market nurtured both offspring with its customary indifference, and left the way open to moralists and cynics alike, stipulating only that success would depend on their relative abilities to create cultural tastes.

In attitudes to death, finally, social change began with a shift in patterns of mortal disease which certainly owed much to the nutritional achievements of capitalism. But thereafter responses were diverse and even contradictory, and involved the working out of complex cultural processes according to their own laws.

Turning now from the market to the structure of social classes created by the market, there is obviously a tendency in these movements for membership and public to be disproportionately drawn from the middle class. This is true of early feminism and of the movements concerned with death. Yet the temperance movement was probably most deeply rooted in the respectable working class; and when the labour movement began to gather strength it was centred in this class, and rechannelled the main energies of both the feminist and the temperance tradition for several decades (Banks 1986: chaps. 4–5; Harrison 1971; chap. 17). There is thus no simple lesson of class allegiance to be drawn from these movements either.

But what of the state? Certainly the state provided an arena for the cultural debate about sexual behaviour in the agitation against the Contagious Diseases Act (leaving aside its central role in many feminist issues not discussed here); and it has played a similar role in enabling euthanasia to be debated at regular intervals. But this is not a strong organizing function. In present issues, the interventionist role of the state is most clearly seen in the temperance question; but the state was initially a most unwilling actor, and its coercive function in the licensing laws was forced upon it by a temperance movement bent on still more coercive measures. Finally, we can also say that the state has taken on the role of patron in the case of the hospice movement, at first by grants, and by contracting for a number of beds, and later by incorporating Continuing Care Units into the NHS; but volunteer finance was nevertheless the backbone of the early movement in the time when it was proving itself.

The last and greatest institutional structure dealing with disordered bodies is of course the medical profession—how far was it the puppeteer of these events? Remarkably, the nineteenth-century medical profession was generally opposed to birth-control and frequently in opposition to the temperance movement (MacLaren 1978: chap. 7; Harrison 1971: 307). And even if William Farr's work, as Foucault would have pointed out, provided some of the necessary tools of knowledge for the birth-controllers, we still have to ask what values led Farr to single out death in childbirth as especially unacceptable, and who used the knowledge he provided. In Foucault's later work on the history of sexuality he is much more conscious of lay groupings taking up these tools of knowledge to shape their own image of society (Foucault 1976: 143–4, 160–1), and though he encapsulates these as 'the bourgeoisie' they are in fact equally recognizable as a diffuse, unorganized social movement originating in, though not coextensive with, the bourgeoisie—the advocates of companionate marriage. And later, as I have said, feminists who actively preached the same notion made common cause with the labour movement.

As for the movements responding to cancer death, while the medical profession had done a good deal to produce the new pattern of mortality, it was profoundly divided about the right response to it. Doctors founded the Voluntary Euthanasia Society, and doctors opposed it and evolved the hospice alternative. Indeed it is also worth noting that the hospice concept was first formulated outside the medical profession, and just as the temperance reformers used commerce to further their ends, so Cicely Saunders actually entered the medical profession to further hers.

Market, state, and professions seem therefore to have been far from decisive in these great cultural changes; but are they a fundamentally necessary condition for the emergence of social movements in the first place? It has been suggested that Protestantism and capitalism created the conditions for this kind of 'self-producing' society (Banks 1972: 19–23). Yet it seems that this hypothesis depends heavily on studies of failure in precapitalist millennial movements. A very different conclusion would have to be drawn from studies of the rise of the monastic orders, to name one example. These only later became institutional structures—but that in itself indicates their success as social movements.

Indeed if there is any general hypothesis to be drawn from the study of the social movements considered here, it is perhaps that the religious imagination, in a broad sense that would include evangelizing secularist cosmologies, may be a necessary condition at their inception. By this I do not mean the conformism in church-going and conventional morals so prominent in the Victorian period, but the strongly held cosmological beliefs and personal ethical convictions, whether orthodox or otherwise, which are so often evident. Companionate marriage was related both to the religious ideas of the Puritans (Stone 1979: 176–80) and to those of the earlier Christian tradition (Goody 1983: 151–6). Many early feminists were earnest Evangelicals, while others owed much to secularist and communitarian thought (Banks 1986: 14–15; L. Gordon 1976: chaps. 4–5). The early temperance movement was closely linked to public profession of nonconformism (Harrison 1971: chap. 8). And the movements concerned with death are currently populated respectively by secularists, Catholics, Evangelicals, and more ecumenical varieties of believer.[7] Naturally the specific influence of this factor is as varied as the beliefs concerned, and there were, as I have noted earlier, other necessary conditions too for the genesis of the social movements considered here. But the religious aspect merits further enquiry. It is perhaps one of the lesser known aspects of the birth-control movement, for example, that Marie Stopes had a message from God before she founded her first clinic (Briant 1962: chap. 11). But that too is a subject which there is no space to pursue.

NOTES

1. I am very grateful to Ken Mullen and Helen Roberts for giving me a number of leads on unfamiliar aspects of the topics covered in this chapter, and to Mick Bloor and other colleagues at the Medical Sociology Unit who commented on the text. In addition, Brian Harrison has been especially generous with his characteristically invigorating criticism. Naturally none of them can be held responsible for the line I have taken. Nor can Chelly Halsey, other than by starting me as a student on an abiding interest in the sources of nineteenth- and twentieth-century social change.
2. See also Mount 1983. The present argument is unaffected by Mount's criticism of Stone and Shorter. He suggests that the evidence can as well be read to show marital affection as a constant which is merely liable to periodic censorship and suppression by church, state, and Utopian zealots. But if the eighteenth-century bourgeoisie eulogized marital affection partly because they had escaped 'enthusiasm' and state despotism that is good enough for my purpose.
3. Tolstoy provides a good example of such a 'second best' rule: in the 1870s he defended the necessity of prostitution in a letter, saying that it preserved other families' wives and daughters from dissatisfied bachelors and husbands, and that 'it would be impious and unintelligent to pretend that God was wrong to tolerate this state of affairs' (Troyat 1967: 326).
4. For the figures see Plant 1982; for some conclusions comparing countries without temperance movements see P. Davies 1983; and for the view that a recent downturn in American consumption is due to a new temperance movement see D. B. Heath 1989.
5. On the euthanasia movement see G. Williams 1958, and the publications of the Voluntary Euthanasia Society. On the 1960s hospice movement and revaluation of death details can be gleaned from a number of sources: primary is du Boulay 1984; but see also Corless 1983; Hillier 1983; Kübler-Ross 1970; Lofland 1978; Lunceford 1981; Manning 1984; Saunders 1984; Torrens 1981; Wilkes 1981.
6. In 1981 Wilkes estimated that only 10% of local cancer deaths occurred in the Sheffield Unit, and thought the national average must be less than half that figure (Wilkes 1981); see also the call for better information to evaluate success in Torrens 1981.

7. Secularists in the rationalist part of the euthanasia movement; Catholics in the anti-abortion movement; Evangelicals and ecumenists, see above on the hospice movement and also Lofland 1978: pt. 3.

5

Government against Poverty in the European Community

GRAHAM ROOM

INTRODUCTION

From the mid-1960s to the mid-1970s, A. H. Halsey devoted a great deal of his attention to the American and British anti-poverty programmes which had been launched under the auspices of Democratic and Labour Governments respectively. He was active in the development of the British Community Development Project (CDP) and he was national director of EPA, the Educational Priority Area initiative, both of which built consciously on their American forerunners (Halsey 1972).

Writing in the early 1970s, he surveyed the experience of these programmes on both sides of the Atlantic: first, the efforts by social scientists, in part at the instigation of government, to understand the persistence of poverty and deprivation in the midst of plenty; secondly, the renewed debate about the scope for government intervention in our liberal-capitalist societies, to combat this poverty; finally, the development of action-research programmes as a form of experimentation in a political context, involving new types of relationship between social research and social reform (Halsey 1974). But even while expressing his enthusiasm for these programmes, Halsey warned that they were posited on the questionable assumption that 'the welfare society may be attained through the legitimate use of the existing political structure' (ibid.: 125).

Halsey had taken an active role in the transatlantic flow of ideas on action to combat poverty out of which the British programmes grew. However, the diffusion did not end there. In the early 1970s, the Irish coalition government drew, in turn, upon the British and American experiences when designing its own programme for anti-poverty action; and Ireland's entry into the European Community in 1973 gave it the opportunity to transform its domestic programme into a European initiative. By this somewhat circuitous route, many of the ideas and slogans of those earlier programmes in the English-speaking world—'participation', 'action-research', etc.—were taken over into the first anti-poverty programme undertaken by the European Community, in the period 1975–80.

These European programmes have continued, if only on a small scale, through the 1980s and into the 1990s. And the issues on which Halsey focused, in his survey of the Anglo-American experience, recur within the European experience also.

ON UNDERSTANDING POVERTY: TRENDS AND DEBATES

During the 1980s, poverty moved sharply up the agenda of political debate in many European countries, as it had done in the Anglo-Saxon countries in the 1960s. Social scientists in these countries, in many cases at the instigation of the European Community, showed increasing interest in trying to measure and to understand this poverty.

Of course, any attempt at measurement depends crucially upon the choice of definitions. The European Commission has itself favoured a definition according to which the poor are those households where the disposable income is less than 50% of the average disposable income in the country concerned (European Commission 1981; 1988*b*). On this definition, one recent study indicates that for the twelve countries of the Community, the number of people in poverty increased slightly from about 38.6 million around 1975 to 39.5 million around 1980, but then jumped to approximately 43.9 million in 1985 (O'Higgins and Jenkins 1989). Over the ten years, this involved a rise in the poverty rate from 12.8 per cent to 13.9 per cent.

During the same period, increasing numbers of people were receiving social assistance. In many countries of the Community, the number has doubled since the beginning of the 1970s. It can, of course, be misleading to claim that the population of social assistance recipients corresponds to the population of the poor, not least because an improvement in benefit levels would then have the perverse effect of making it appear that the population of the poor has grown. Moreover, there is a significant population of the 'hidden poor', who although eligible do not apply for social assistance, because of ignorance or fear of stigma, and who are therefore not included in the population of social assistance recipients. Nevertheless, trends in the numbers of recipients can, at least, indicate the scale on which the public authorities are supporting households on low incomes: and the dramatic increase in these numbers during recent years gives reason for concern.

During the 1980s there were three major changes in the composition of the poor population in the twelve countries of the European Community (Room, Lawson, and Laczko 1989). The *first* is that the unemployed now constitute a much larger proportion of the poor than they did in the 1970s. This is, most obviously, because social insurance benefits have failed in most Community countries to protect the majority of the unemployed. This failure arose, first, from the rapid growth of recurrent as well as long-term unemployment, and the high rate of unemployment among young people and women who have not been able to build up insurance rights. No less important have been the restrictions which are inherent in unemployment compensation policies. These link entitlements to previous contribution and employment records; they include disqualifications from benefit where unemployment is deemed 'voluntary'; and, most important of all, they impose limits on the duration of payments. Some governments have made efforts to develop, within their social insurance systems, non-contributory elements which aim to avoid the shame which is generally associated with social assistance. Others have sought to develop schemes of guaranteed minimum income. Nevertheless, with high levels of long-term unemployment, increasing numbers of the able-bodied have been left to rely on means-tested assistance or on support from families and voluntary agencies.

High unemployment and changes in the labour market have affected weaker groups in particular. This includes disabled people and women bringing up children on their own. However, it is most strikingly illustrated by the fate of ethnic minority groups, who in countries like the United Kingdom experience a disproportionate share of the deprivation of the older urban-industrial areas into which they are concentrated. Young people are also at particular risk. Many are now chronically dependent on social assistance and basic welfare. This reflects their confinement within, at most, the precarious section of the labour market, and their poor chances of building up any entitlement to unemployment insurance benefits.

The *second* major change in the population of the poor is that although, in many countries, elderly people are still at considerable risk of being in poverty, this is considerably less than was the case ten or fifteen years ago, largely because of improvements in pensions schemes. The declining significance of elderly people among the population of the poor is the more remarkable, when we recall that in most countries they make up an increasing proportion of the population as a whole. Nevertheless, in a number of Community countries, old people, while constituting a smaller proportion of the poor than in the past, are still substantially at risk of poverty. More generally, there are signs that the general improvement of living standards among the elderly hides widening disparities of incomes and welfare between the 'young old' and the very old. A much larger proportion of the very old are women, who have traditionally gained lower pensions and benefits than men. Equally serious is the prospect for today's long-term unemployed when they eventually retire. Their interrupted work and contribution records are likely to mean that the unemployment which separated them from the bulk of the working population during their working lives will during the coming decades turn them into the 'new poor' of the elderly population.

The *third* set of changes in the population of the poor is connected with changes in family structure. In some of the more rural countries, such as Italy and Portugal, the percentage of the poor who belong to large families seems to be declining. This is, to a considerable extent, because throughout the Community, couples are choosing to have smaller families: Ireland has been slowest to adopt this change. The other major change in family structure, evident in all the countries of the Community, is the growth in the number of single-parent families. In general, the circumstances of single-parent families have worsened over the last decade, at least as judged by their more widespread dependence on social assistance. In many countries, their employment opportunities have been greatly restricted by cuts in child-care facilities; and in the UK, for example, a smaller proportion of single mothers work part-time than mothers living with their husbands. At the same time, attempts in some countries, such as France, to provide alternative social protection for single parents have been surrounded by controversy, because of fears that they will create disincentives to work or to marriage.

Reflecting on the theories of poverty which were current during the 1960s, Halsey pointed out in his 1974 essay that the anti-poverty projects of the British programmes, at least, assumed that what the American social science literature called 'down-town poverty' could be taken as the focus of their attention. On this view, modern urban conditions tended to concentrate social deprivation into the decaying inner ring of conurbations; and—whether as cause or consequence—all local institutions tended to be defective—the family, the school, social welfare agencies, the job market. Moreover, according to this literature a mixture of situational and sub-cultural factors meant that those who were living in such deprived areas would tend to stay there. Intervention which focused on 'communities' or local administrative units held the promise of breaking this cycle.

In Europe during the 1980s, the growing concern about poverty which is evident in national and Community debates has tended, instead, to focus upon the 'new poor': groups of the population who are newly at risk of poverty because of various society-wide processes of change (Room *et al.* 1990). In the United States, in contrast, the recent debate has continued to focus upon an alleged 'underclass', spatially segregated and defective in its social institutions as well as materially deprived and overwhelmingly non-white, despite the fact that many of the broader changes in the composition of the poor population, summarized above for the European countries, have had close counterparts in the United States (W. J. Wilson 1985; Ruggels and Marton 1986). This tends to suggest the importance of ideological and institutional factors in structuring public and scientific perceptions of poverty trends: with the 'residual' welfare state of the United States (and, to a lesser extent, of the United Kingdom) directing the practical interest of decision-makers and the theoretical interest of social researchers towards the recipients of means-tested benefits, increasingly composed of non-white single mothers; while in Continental Europe, it is the failure of the 'institutional' systems of unemployment compensation to protect those who were until recently supposed to be part of the working population that is central to the practical concerns of trade unions, political parties, and other commentators active in the recent debates (Room *et al.* 1990, chaps. 2–3).

ON FIGHTING POVERTY

A second theme of Halsey's 1974 essay was the scope for government intervention in our liberal-capitalist societies, in order to combat poverty. In Europe, despite the increased concern about poverty during the 1980s, resistance to any expanded government role has come from at least two directions. Conservative governments have sought to reduce or deny their obligations to relieve need and mitigate the insecurities of a market society. Instead, their energies have been directed towards liberalizing and deregulating their economies, in the belief that the expected improvement in economic performance will in due course benefit all sections of the population. Employers' organizations have been among those supporting this deregulation. In the Netherlands, for example, they have favoured ending the links between wages, legal minimum wages, and social security benefits; and lowering the level of minimum wages and social benefits, in the expectation of positive effects on employment. They have also been advocating greater differentiation in social security with respect to family size: with the existing social minimum reserved for a 'complete' family with two children and the social minimum for one parent families being set lower.

Resistance has come from a second direction also. Particularly in the countries of southern Europe, poverty has long tended to be seen as an object of *charitable* action by agencies operating under the inspiration of the church, rather than *political* action by government. These agencies have not been uniformly enthusiastic to support any expanded government programmes directed at combating poverty. This resistance is not peculiar to the southern countries, however. In Germany, for example, Catholic social teaching—which has long had a significant influence on the social legislation of the state—expresses the principle of 'subsidiarity', under which the family, the local community, and the church, rather than regional or national government, have the first responsibility for undertaking social care. In Belgium, government initiatives have played a much larger role in efforts to combat poverty in Socialist Wallonia than in Catholic Flanders (Vandenbroucke 1987: 71). It is true that in these various countries church organizations have been obliged to leave social security—cash benefits—to the state, and that in terms of resources, the state sector of social protection is much the larger. It is also true that the financial resources for their services come largely from public sources. Nevertheless, the capacity of these charitable organizations to appropriate public funds confirms their power, rather than putting it in question; and their influence on the agenda of public debate, particularly in regards to social welfare, is not in doubt.

The scope for action to be taken by the European institutions has been just as fiercely contested. For the European Commission, the Social Action Programme launched at the 1972 Paris Summit, of which the first poverty programme of 1975–80 eventually formed a part, was a means of extending and legitimizing the powers of the European institutions in the social field: a field where the Treaty of Rome is at best ambiguous and at worst hostile towards their intrusion. For this very reason, several of the Member States, and most notably the Germans, opposed these new social programmes because of the dangerous precedent which they set. Only as a result of pressure from the other governments did the Germans reluctantly acquiesce in the launching of the first anti-poverty programme in 1975 and its subsequent extension in 1977. However, being so contentious, this poverty programme of 1975–80 was limited to a budget of approximately £13.5 million over five years, with additional sums from national sources for the action projects (financed as these were on a 50 : 50 basis between Brussels and the Member States). The second programme, approved by the Council of Ministers in 1984, attracted less opposition; but harsher economic times meant that in real terms it was even smaller than its predecessor.

However, the decision by the Community countries to create by 1992 a single 'economic space', within a more closely integrated political community, has dramatically changed the terms of this debate. The Cecchini report (1988) argues that the completion of the Single Market can substantially increase the Community's rate of economic growth, with an extra two million jobs in the short term and five million in the medium term. However, the European Commission has warned that, initially at least, the creation of the Single Market will bring significant social and economic dislocations. These are expected to have 'very severe negative effects' for certain regions and certain categories of people. The Commission warns of 'social exclusion and marginalisation and the . . . appearance of new forms of poverty'; and it fears that this will also bring 'pathological social behaviour' (European Commission 1988*a*). The Commission also fears that the increasingly competitive environment of 1992 will cause working conditions generally to deteriorate, with specific legislation being desirable in relation to irregular and precarious employment (ibid.: paras. 48, 78). These fears, acknowledged by the national governments of the Community with varying degrees of enthusiasm, are serving to legitimate new and extended forms of intervention by the European institutions in the social field.

The European Commission is concentrating its remedial efforts on its structural funds, which support training and infrastructure investment in structurally backward regions and regions suffering industrial decline. Recent Community legislation envisages, moreover, that the Commission will be much more actively engaged in negotiating European-funded programmes with local and regional government and with other partners active at that level, rather than working only through the national authorities. In other words, the legislation acknowledges that the institutions of the European Community should be actively involved in the negotiation of working agreements and programmes of work which make use of European funding. To some extent, therefore, the European Community institutions, having set in motion the disruptive forces of the Single Market, are acknowledged as having a central responsibility for building a new 'settlement' between the various social actors concerned with the distribution of work and welfare in the countries of the Community.

At the same time, however, it is likely that the European authorities' scope for effective action in these fields will remain limited. In the papers which the Commission has presented to the Council of Ministers, it emphasizes the supposedly brief 'transition' period, during which adjustments to the new world of the Single Market will need to be assisted by special social measures. The Commission appears to take the view that the negative effects of the Single Market will be primarily short-term and can be fairly readily alleviated or compensated, until the long-term gains overwhelm them. This represents a political compromise by the Commission with liberal doctrines that the market will, except in abnormal times, tend towards equilibrium and towards the socially optimal utilization of physical and human resources. As yet, little respect is paid to the view that the market system is inherently self-destabilizing and liable to produce an economically and socially non-optimal use of resources (Goldthorpe 1978).

The European Commission, with the support of most Member State governments, also wants to develop at a European level what can be broadly described as rights of 'industrial citizenship' (Marshall 1950): the worker's right to dispose of his or her labour power untrammelled by restrictions of nationality; to take part, through Community-wide systems of collective bargaining, in the decision-making processes by which the work-place is governed; and to enjoy certain basic minimum standards of health and safety in the working environment. Beyond this, the Commission is beginning to map out a still broader set of European social rights, not only for those in work but also for those who are outside the labour market (European Commission 1989).

It remains to be seen how far this social dimension of the European Community will develop, and the extent to which it will address the new patterns of poverty which have emerged in the 1990s. Of course, at first glance, it may seem as though some aspects of this poverty—for example, those which are associated with changing patterns of family formation—is unlikely to be directly affected, for better or worse, by the development of the Single Market. To this extent, the Community is unlikely to argue for specific programmes of intervention at European level in order to prevent or combat such forms of marginalization. However, even patterns of family formation and breakdown are shaped in part by changes in employment opportunities; and at least in the short term, the Single Market is likely, as already seen, to bring increased unemployment to some regions and population groups. In addition, the programmes of structural transformation and economic development which the Commission expects to promote, particularly in the southern countries, may bring further disruptions to the traditional family structure. These social costs of the Single Market, although less obvious, could mean that the Commission will be called upon to pay increasing attention to community development and family support, not just to economic development and training. But these are areas of policy into which the Community institutions have, as yet, hardly ventured.

EXPERIMENTAL SOCIAL ADMINISTRATION

Halsey (1974) took stock, finally, of the development of action-research programmes as a form of experimentation in a political context, involving new types of relationship between social research and social reform. The American, British, and European programmes have all involved small-scale projects intended to explore new methods of social provision, which if successful could then be applied more generally (Marris and Rein 1974; Halsey 1972; Lees and Smith 1975; Dennett *et al.* 1982). These programmes have obvious political attractions because they demand only a limited commitment from government. The projects are launched for only a limited duration; the resources they involve are small; and governments are careful not to commit themselves in advance to implementing the recommendations that emerge. Moreover, in the European case at least, the quasi-scientific aura of the 'pilot experiment' has been intended to protect such initiatives from national governments' jealous preservation of their own powers, in a field where the European Commission had only a very restricted mandate for intervention. Yet if anything, this merely underlines the relevance of the American experience: for there, too, the Federal government had resorted to 'pilot experiments' in part in order to fend off the hostility of local power structures.

Nevertheless, even before the first of the European programmes was launched, in the mid-1970s, disillusionment and cynicism had set in. Action-research had not, it seemed, lived up to its promise; and the collaboration between research, action, and policy-making had been less than wholly successful (Town 1973; Lees and Smith 1975). Marris and Rein, in their study of the early American experiments (1974) provided the classical analysis of the dilemmas and tensions which this collaboration encountered. They pointed out that the action-research projects launched in the anti-poverty field were addressed to—and demanded collaboration and legitimation from—three different audiences: the social scientific community, policy-makers at local and national levels, and, finally, the disadvantaged communities themselves and their indigenous organizations. The action-research projects had then simultaneously to confront—in many cases unsuccessfully—three 'dilemmas of social reform'. First, the scientific demands of rigorous evaluation were frequently in tension with the changing political and practical demands imposed on the action-research by its masters and clients. Secondly, although it was politically necessary for the action-researchers to retain a broad-based commitment from policy-makers, the action-research frequently affected these policy-makers' practical interests in very different ways, putting in question the conventional lines of demarcation between them and the terms of reference within which they initially sought to constrain the projects. Finally, action-researchers needed to maintain and develop involvement by the local communities with whom they were working; but this, too, was a delicate and politically contentious task, when most of the key decisions which affect the lives of these people remained outside the projects' remit and control.

These same dilemmas have pervaded the experience of the European programmes, albeit taking forms specific to that political and institutional context. To take the last-mentioned first, the European programmes have at least paid lip service to 'participation' by the poor communities themselves in the design and implementation of the action projects. Interpreted as self-help and voluntary effort, 'participation' was attractive to Member States with liberal and conservative governments; interpreted as community action and solidarity, it helped to make the programmes palatable to governments of the Left. Yet the gap between what seemed to be promised and what was pratically feasible has been a recurring irritation in the European programmes, sapping the morale of project workers and project users. For many of the latter, 'participation' seemed to offer a new deal: with the project setting out to engage their interest, to win their trust, and to provide them with opportunities to become full participants in society. It made the programme a moral enterprise as well as a scientific one. The termination of the projects at the end of each programme, without an assured preservation of these new opportunities, commonly aroused the moral indignation and shock not only of the project workers but also of the 'target group' concerned: emotions that were variously directed at project workers, evaluators, and Commission officials. Because of the small scale of the projects, this frustration has seldom if ever boiled over into the expressions of community discontent which Marris and Rein (1974) recorded in their account of the American experience; but its intensity has been none the less.

The second dilemma which Marris and Rein highlighted was concerned with the task of enlisting and maintaining the support of key policy-makers and power-holders; and, indeed, of ensuring that the 'lessons' of the action-research would be 'multiplied' by these decision-makers and applied more generally. In the European programmes, what has been striking is, first, the significant variations between countries in the expectations held of the programme by national governments, the key decision-makers who might have been expected to multiply the fruits of the programmes. Equally significant has been the 'mismatch' between the government departments (national and European) which have had responsibility for selecting projects and for managing the programme and the policy areas highlighted by the action-research as most relevant to combating poverty.

Thus, the interests of the principal government departments concerned varied considerably between countries, reflecting on the one hand the policy preoccupations in national debate and, on the other, the eagerness or otherwise of the more and less powerful departments to take on what was variously perceived as a burden or an opportunity. In France, for example, the principal government department concerned was also responsible for the government's programme of emergency relief: involving emergency accommodation and nutrition, training and rehabilitation. The projects which France submitted to the Commission in 1985 bore the marks of this national programme; other significant public programmes, also concerned with poverty and the social development of urban neighbourhoods, were omitted.

In the UK, the responsible department is concerned with personal social services and, not surprisingly, so are many of the projects which were submitted and approved for the UK. This departmental responsibility has also structured the expectations of the UK government with regards to the benefits of this programme. Officials and their political advisers have been interested, first and foremost, to know whether the programme and its evaluators have demonstrated more cost-effective and efficient methods of supplying social services, using objective and quantifiable measures. Such officials have also been looking for arguments in favour of shifting services away from local authority control and into the voluntary sector; methods for evaluating the qualitative element in policies; and evidence to help them resolve current policy debates, for example, on community care. However, at a time when poverty is, in an increasing number of cases, associated with changes in the labour market and economic restructuring, it may be inappropriate to judge an anti-poverty programme primarily in terms of the lessons which it generates for personal social services.

At the level of the European institutions, what has been striking is the relative isolation of the poverty section of the Social Affairs directorate from other arms of the Commission, concerned for example with employment and training policies, regional development, and equal opportunities. Only towards the end of the second programme, in the late 1980s, did the officials concerned develop these links in any deliberate way. And the political weakness of the Commission throughout this period meant that as far as national policy-makers were concerned, the Commission was always reluctant to press on them any of the clear policy lessons emerging from the poverty programmes. Equally, at the level of the individual projects, it has been rare for the Commission actively to champion their achievements in the projects' negotiations with local decision-makers.

Finally, what of the dilemmas of rigorous evaluation, faced with the changing political and practical demands imposed by political masters (in particular the European Commission) and clients (most obviously the projects)? Although this dynamic political environment may mean that the evaluation of action-research must forgo the conventional canons of 'scientific' evaluation, it does not follow that all claims to rigour must be abandoned (Room 1986: chap. 3). Nevertheless, few of the action-research programmes, at national or European level, have avoided their evaluators suffering considerable anguish in their efforts to maintain their professional self-respect, at the same time as they demonstrate their practical 'usefulness' to both projects and policy-makers. And in the European programmes, as in some of their national predecessors, these strains have at times resulted in high levels of internal conflict and threatened the programme concerned with major political disruption.

As this European experience therefore reveals, confirming that of the earlier programmes in the Anglo-Saxon world, the objectives, organization, and implementation of 'experimental social administration' do not go uncontested. They are shaped by the wider struggle for power between different social groups, engaged in promoting or resisting particular plans for social change. Thus, to the organizer of these European programmes, 'cross-fertilization' between projects working in different countries may have appeared as a means of testing out particular methods of social provision in different contexts, with a view to assessing their more general relevance and limitations. Project workers themselves have often taken a very different view. For many of them, 'cross-fertilization' is of value principally to the extent that it allows them to build up political alliances and campaigns on a cross-national basis. Working methods developed elsewhere may be of some interest, particularly if they can be cited as precedents for reform when projects confront decision-makers in their own countries; but projects are unlikely to give high priority to testing out, on their home ground, innovations developed elsewhere, in the service of scientific rigour and national policy-making. The challenge which faces those who are responsible for European programmes of cross-national innovation is, therefore, how to mobilize broader movements and lobbies of this sort, as part of the process of stimulating institutional reform, rather than regarding them as a distraction from an experiment.

To the programme organizer, similarly, 'evaluation' may appear primarily as a means of rationally assessing the costs and benefits associated with new methods of social provision. In recent years, it is the cost to the public purse that has been of principal concern to national policy-makers: a programme of pilot projects is of interest if it can demonstrate ways of cutting those costs. Project workers, in contrast, are often more interested in exposing needs that are *not* being met by existing services and whose 'costs' therefore lie where they fall, rather than being a charge on the public purse. The evaluation exercise, rather than providing dispassionate evidence on which new policy initiatives can be based, may instead expose the competing assumptions which these different actors hold about the scope and responsibilities of public policies. Here the challenge which faces those who are responsible for European programmes is that of constructing, from the social policy scenarios which emerge from this pooling of different national experiences, not only scientifically rigorous assessments of project effectiveness, but also politically feasible arguments for institutional reform, capable of mobilizing a constituency of support across the Community. These programmes may then, as Halsey hoped in his concluding words on the British and American programmes of the 1960s, 'generate unplanned political movements towards large-scale . . . reform of the distribution of resources and opportunities in a rich but unequal society' (Halsey 1974: 138).

6

School History and School Effectiveness in Scotland[1]

ANDREW MCPHERSON and J. DOUGLAS WILLMS

INTRODUCTION

Sociology and social policy have commonly framed the problem of school effectiveness as follows: can public education be provided in ways that mitigate social disadvantages which themselves have educational causes and consequences (Halsey, Floud, and Anderson 1961; Karabel and Halsey 1977; Halsey, Heath, and Ridge 1980)? Our chapter discusses two contrasting approaches to this question and applies them to secondary schooling in twentieth-century Scotland.

The first approach is based on an input/process/output model of schooling. This model regards schools as quasi-experimental treatments of pupils whose characteristics on entering secondary school are statistically constrained to be similar. It then infers the effects of schools from between-school variations in pupils' outcomes. One assumption of the model is that it is valid to treat pupils, schools, and all other entities in the model atomistically; that each entity can be validly described without reference to other entities. The atomistic assumption is challenged by the second, relational, approach to schooling. This approach focuses on the role of state education in mediating competition and conflict between social groups. The relational assumption is that schools, pupils, and other entities are validly described only when their relations with each other are included in the description.

We draw on both approaches to explain differences between secondary schools in their impact on pupils' outcomes. In particular we show how the social settings or 'contexts' which helped individual schools achieve these effects were themselves shaped by intergroup conflicts and reconciliations that have characterized the provision of public education for well over a century. By itself, however, neither approach adequately captures this process of reproduction and change. Only by drawing on both approaches can the central question of school effectiveness be satisfactorily addressed.

In the next section (Problem and Theory) we discuss the two approaches in more detail. The following four sections set out the historical background and research questions (Background and Questions), describe the data and statistical models (Methods), and present the findings of an analysis of school effectiveness at the end of the 1970s (Results) and (Summary). In the final section (Discussion), we discuss how one might locate an account of school effectiveness between the untenable extremes of the atomistic and the relational so that a better understanding of the potential of schooling can emerge.

PROBLEM AND THEORY

The input/process/output model derives in part from the status-attainment literature (Glass 1954; Blau and Duncan 1967; Kerckhoff 1974; Sewell and Hauser 1975; Hope 1984), and in part from the idea of schools as quasi-experimental treatments of pupils. In reality, of course, such 'treatments' are not fully controlled, nor are pupils assigned randomly to them. The task is therefore to model the random assignment of pupils to schools in order to isolate variation in schooling outcomes that is associated with attendance at particular schools and, beyond that, with what might be inferred to be happening in those schools. This rationale has been criticized on the grounds that it does not directly observe school practices ('treatments'), and that school life is more complex than true experiments. For example, pupils may constitute 'treatments' both for each other, and for their teachers. However, developments in the past decade have gone some way towards accommodating such difficulties. Attempts have been made to take account of the different experiences of different types of pupils, such as ethnic or social-class groups, or less able pupils (Burstein 1980). This in turn has allowed for a consideration of relationships between pupil groups within schools, where these relationships are not mediated by teachers, or are mediated by them only indirectly. Distinctions have also been made within schools between different classroom groups and different curriculum tracks, and attempts have been made to incorporate directly observed 'practice' (Rutter *et al.* 1979; Mortimore *et al.* 1988; Smith and Tomlinson 1989). Also, schools themselves have been located in their varying ecological and administrative contexts (Purkey and Smith 1983). In sum, there is now a greater recognition that '[e]ducation is a multilevel enterprise . . . and [that] realistic models will have to reflect that structure' (Rachman-Moore and Wolfe 1984; see also Goldstein 1987; Raudenbush and Willms 1991).

Nevertheless, a fundamental difficulty remains because the approach does not cope well with the phenomena of change, conflict, and confusion that are as much a feature of social life as consensus, stasis, and order. The various 'levels' or constituent units of a multilevel model of schooling (for example, regions, neighbourhoods, schools, groups within schools, individuals) are defined atomistically with respect both to other units of the model and to other members of the same unit. This is done in order that reality can then be represented by means of 'variables'. A variable attributes the variable possession of a phenomenon to each member of a particular level or unit of the model. Thus race, gender, or socio-economic status (SES), say, are attributed in some degree to each individual member of the individual level, or to each school at the school level, and so on. Though 'variable' in the sense that possession of an attribute may differ in amount across members of a level or unit, the attributed phenomenon (SES, say) is given an invariant logical status across all members of the level. Having the status of an individual characteristic (as opposed to that of the epiphenomenon of relationships), the value of a variable for one member of the level in question (say the SES of an individual or a school) is assumed to be independent of the values for other members of the same level, and independent also of other levels. The individual's characteristic does not change in response to changes elsewhere. This is the atomistic assumption and it is central to the statistical modelling of the effects of schools on pupils.

Nevertheless, it is easily challenged. By example, part of the significance of my living in neighbourhood *X* is that others do not live there. Thus some 'attributes' of my neighbourhood are purely relational and could not be defined except by reference to other neighbourhoods (*X* is defined as not 'not *X*'), nor changed except by making changes in them too. Similar arguments can be made in relation to other attributes of members of a level (for example, attributes of SES, ethnicity, gender). Moreover, the argument can also be made across levels. Since no neighbourhood can be defined except by reference to other neighbourhoods, something external to the level of neighbourhood must be necessary to its definition. Hence it is not an independent level. Thus neither levels, nor the attributes of their constituents, can be adequately defined atomistically. The definitions must be derived from human relations and meanings, from the classifications people use.

But here we meet two problems. First, human relations are lived over time and, with time, things change. Change, of course, is ubiquitous and continuous, but whether or not it is recognized as significant is a procedural matter, a matter of convention and purpose. 'Did the son go to the same school as his mother?' can meaningfully be answered either 'yes' or 'no', even when he enrolled in an institution with the same name as hers, housed in the same building. The atomistic model is synchronic in so far as it assumes away the problem of change by treating its constituent units as the same from moment to moment. It always, therefore, does some violence to the definitions and meanings it derives from human relations lived over time. And it does this on a second count too. If conflict is a feature of human relations, a feature of human conflict is classificatory dispute concerning definitions of space, time, individuals, and classes. These are apparent in statements like 'It's not the school it used to be', 'Those pupils don't belong here' and 'She has failed to fulfil her potential'. Thus the atomistic model is at odds with reality to the extent that it assumes away the problems of conflict and classification.

Broadly speaking, the heroic assumptions of atomism constitute the subject-matter of the relational approach. The latter understands education in terms of unfolding conflict, competition, and compromise between groups, prominent among which are religious and ethnic groups and social classes. The growth of the educational state and the accompanying expansion of provision is a central preoccupation. In some, pluralist, variants there is no single explanation for expansion, nor single interest served by it (Kogan 1978; Archer 1979; 1982). Other variants, some with a functionalist emphasis, derive expansion from education's role in modernization (Floud and Halsey 1961; Marshall 1963; Boli, Ramirez, and Meyer 1985). Non-pluralist accounts, by contrast, assert that the nature and growth of public education systems are to be understood by the service they perform for dominant groups who have captured or influenced them. Attention is paid to the differentiation of material and cultural provision within the state system and to social groups' differential opportunities for access to such provision (Bourdieu and Passeron 1970; Meyer 1970; 1977; Byrne, Williamson, and Fletcher 1975). Definitions of schooling itself, its criteria of excellence, its length, phasing, and institutional form are also held to be culturally arbitrary and to favour some groups rather than others (Davie 1961; Bowles and Gintis 1976). In this context, the spread of certification has a particular significance (Apple 1979; Collins 1979).

In the second approach, then, the place called school is just one site of wider group conflict and compromise. Schools exist not atomistically, but relationally; relationally with respect to other schools in the system whose different functions or statuses help to define their own, and relationally with respect to wider institutional features. These features include the 'rules' governing entry to school such as informal residential segregation and formal selection tests, and those governing the levels of exit from school, such as public certification. From this perspective, schools do not have fixed and impermeable boundaries, nor total internal coherence. The school can no more be differentiated from the community it serves than can its individual pupils from the families from which they come. Teachers negotiate purposes and procedures with pupils, parents, and the wider community, and all collectively construct the experience of schooling. To all of this, the metaphor of schooling as experimental treatments of randomly allocated groups is inappropriate, as is the assumption that the analytical separation of levels (individuals, families, peer groups, schools, etc.) corresponds to reality.

There are, nevertheless, two major difficulties with this position as well. First, it is heavily constrained by the terms used to describe the initial groups—social classes, ethnic groups, or whatever. Precisely because these groups are conceptualized as relational phenomena, an adequate definition of them would include reference to all their levels and types of experience, including their experience of education, or exclusion from it. In its extreme form, the relational approach is holistic and faces an acute problem of circularity when it attempts to distinguish different groups, levels, or types of experience. The second problem is that, in the absence of such an attempt, the model becomes wholly deterministic and quite incapable of recognizing, let alone explaining, situations where some things change and others do not. It therefore cannot accommodate agency, whether the agency of individuals or of organizations such as schools or the state itself.

BACKGROUND AND QUESTIONS

Scotland had a relatively developed system of primary, secondary, and tertiary education before industrialization and modern urbanization began, and, compared with most European countries, there was less differentiation of provision along social-class lines (Osborne 1966; Scotland 1969; Anderson 1983*a*). However, the system could not cope with the growth and shift of population that resulted from industrialization. At the beginning of this century the state set itself to supplement the state secondary-school system, then consisting of more than 60 schools, by designating a 'second generation' of 'Higher Grade' schools, eventually numbering just under 200. Most of these schools were originally intended to provide, not a fully credentialled secondary education to 17 or 18 years, but a general education at most to 16 years. All were designated before the First World War and all that survived (which was the majority) later acquired full secondary status, mostly in 1923. A minority of the post-primary school population at this time attended secondary schools or Higher Grade schools, the remainder being educated in schools of lower, non-secondary status which terminated at 14 years (Wade 1939).

Between 1885, when the Scotch (later Scottish) Education Department (SED) was founded, and 1945 when secondary education in Scotland was made universal, officials of the SED promoted a distinctive conception of 'secondary' education that has important implications for our analysis. The policy they followed in consolidating and extending the secondary-school system was based on a number of principles: that the main aim of secondary education was to prepare pupils for university; that it should be undertaken only by pupils who planned to remain at school until at least 17 years, and preferably 18; that it should be provided economically; and therefore that it should be 'centralized' in single-purpose secondary schools that served localities where the demand for such education was high. This in turn implied a sharp differentiation of pupils at the age of 12 or thereabouts into 'secondary' and 'non-secondary' categories, and, if numbers allowed, into 'secondary' and 'non-secondary' schools (Anderson 1983*a*).

Several of these principles were new to Scotland and were bitterly opposed by contemporaries who valued the social accessibility of the older parish schools. These schools had typically offered all levels of schooling, including a preparation for entry to university, to all pupils in the neighbourhood. In effect, the SED policy was opposed because it threatened to erode one of the major respects in which Scottish public education differed from that in most other European countries, and in England in particular, namely its organization along lines that were less differentiated by function or social class. The main implication of this policy for our own argument is that the conception of 'secondary' education promoted by the SED had socially regressive implications: wealthier parents would have found it easier to support their children through the extended schooling entailed in the SED's policy; and schools in wealthier areas would have been more likely to receive the 'secondary' designation, and to be supported as such from central funds.

Meanwhile, a complicating factor was religion. The pre-industrial public education system was run by the Protestant Church of Scotland which, despite schism in 1843, remained a powerful though slowly declining influence. From mid-nineteenth century onwards, there was substantial Catholic-Irish immigration into the rapidly industrializing Clydeside conurbation in the west of Scotland. Poverty and discrimination combined to block the social mobility of many Irish immigrants. Nor did education offer a ladder to more than a few. Catholic schools were controlled by the Catholic Church, and provision was severely constrained by finance. But in 1918 or shortly thereafter, virtually all Catholic schools were taken over by the state, including the handful that by then had attained, or were shortly to reach, full secondary status (Treble 1979; Fitzpatrick 1986). Catholic schools have subsequently retained their religious identity within the state system. In the late 1970s 19 per cent of Scottish pupils attended them. However, the social disadvantage of Scottish Catholics continues (Payne and Ford 1977), though probably not to the same degree as in Northern Ireland (Cormack and Osborne 1983; Osborne 1985).

Universal secondary education was organized on a selective basis from 1945 to 1965 when the decisive move was made towards the abolition of selective transfer to secondary school. During this period roughly 200 to 230 secondary schools offered 'senior-secondary' courses leading to national certification at 17 or 18 years, and thence to university. These schools consisted almost entirely of the 60 or so pre-1902 secondary schools, almost all of which had survived, together with a larger number of schools that traced their origins to the second generation of Higher-Grade schools founded, or recognized as such, between 1902 and 1918. By the early 1960s, over a third of the population was admitted to senior-secondary courses. The remainder of the school population in the period 1945–65 went to short-course ('junior-secondary') schools that terminated at 15 or 16 years. These schools had lower prestige and did not offer national credentials. To many such schools comprehensive reorganization after 1965 added a full range of courses up to 18 years. Other short-course schools amalgamated with schools offering senior-secondary courses. The remainder were closed and replaced by new six-year comprehensive schools. By contrast, virtually none of the 200 or so schools in the higher-status, 'senior-secondary' sector 1945–65 was closed as a result of comprehensive reorganization. Instead, with the abolition of selective transfer, almost all of them became area comprehensives (a handful only leaving the state system for the private sector). A large minority of them had always admitted all local pupils on an area basis, but with rigid allocation on entry to certificate or non-certificate courses (McPherson and Willms 1987; McPherson and Raab 1988: chaps. 15 and 16).

Comprehensive though it was, the state school system at the end of the 1970s incorporated three distinct phases of historical development. In the data for this study, there was a first generation of 66 schools that had constituted the national secondary school system in the nineteenth century (pre-1902 schools). None of these schools was Catholic. Second, there were 126 of the second-generation schools founded or designated between 1902 and 1918, mostly by 1908 (1902–18 schools). Ten of these were Catholic. Then there was a third generation of a further 278 schools. Most of these had acquired secondary-school status only after 1945, but only about 20 had achieved full, credentialling six-year status by the early 1960s, before comprehensive reorganization. We call these 278 schools the 'post-1965' schools because most of them were founded or reconstituted as a result of comprehensive reorganization and owed their capacity to award the full range of credentials to that reform. Seventy-one of these schools were Catholic.

Contemporary Scottish comprehensive schools divide into a large minority that have served their communities at least since the First World War and, until 1965, with a monopoly of credential conferment; and a small majority that have only just completed their first 25 years as full secondary schools. Because of the incremental development of the secondary system, it may be that the older established schools still tend to serve neighbourhoods of higher socioeconomic status (SES). Area comprehensive schools inevitably have pupil intakes that reflect the residential segregation of the neighbourhoods they serve. This may in turn have implications for the reproduction of inequality through schooling. Longer-established schools may enjoy advantages of prestige, experience, and teacher quality. Also, previous research in Scotland and the United States has found that, for a pupil of given ability, attendance at a school with a high pupil SES has tended to be associated with higher examination attainment (Summers and Wolfe 1977;

Brookover *et al.* 1978; Willms 1985; 1986). Such an effect is commonly referred to as the effect of school 'context', or as a 'contextual' effect.

We may now state these conjectures formally in the form of four questions, each of which is asked separately for the Catholic and the non-denominational sectors.

1. How great is the between-school variation in the SES of the pupil intakes?
2. Is the SES of the pupil intake associated with the history of the school?
3. How great are between-school variations in nationally certified attainments overall, and at varying levels of school mean SES?
4. Do pupils in older schools on average attain higher results: (i) when pupils' individual characteristics are not controlled, (ii) when they are controlled at the individual level, and (iii) when the 'contextual effect' of pupil composition is also controlled? The concept of a contextual effect is further explained in the Methods section that follows.

METHODS

Data

The data for the 1981 Scottish School Leavers Survey (SSLS) were derived from postal questionnaires covering a wide range of questions about schooling, family background, and employment. Burnhill (1984) describes the design of the questionnaires, the sampling procedure, and the response rates at different stages of the survey. The questionnaires were mailed to pupils roughly nine months after they left school. The target population was all school leavers in Scotland in 1979/80 other than the fraction of 1 per cent in special schools. Pupils completed their schooling before the introduction of legislation on parental choice of schools. The sampling fraction was 37 per cent. The response rate for pupils who received the questionnaire was 89.6 per cent, resulting in an achieved sample of over 23,000 pupils.

Variables

The outcome measures are based on pupils' examination results in the Scottish Certificate of Education (SCE) examinations at the Ordinary Grade and the Higher Grade. At the end of their fourth and final compulsory year of secondary school, pupils deemed capable presented for one or more O-grade examinations. About 80 per cent of the 1981 SSLS pupils had presented for at least one O-grade examination in their fourth year. About half of the pupils remained in school for one or two additional years, during which time most presented for SCE Higher (H) grade examinations (Gray, McPherson, and Raffe 1983).

Two of our outcome measures are based on pupils' fourth-year O-grade results in English and arithmetic. O-grade examination awards are designated as one of six percentage categories: A: 70–100 per cent; B: 60–9; C: 50–9; D: 40–9; E: 30–9; and Fail: below 30 per cent. We also identified two additional categories of fourth-year attainment: sitting a preliminary O-grade examination administered within the school, but not sitting the SCE O-grade examination; and sitting neither a preliminary examination nor the O-grade examination.

We also use an overall measure of SCE examination attainment. It has 14 categories which combine information on both the number of O- and H-grade awards, if any, and the O-grade award grades. The 14 categories are designed to reflect benchmarks of attainment in popular use by pupils, teachers, and employers. Raffe (1984*c*) has shown that these attainment categories are related to pupils' employment prospects in the first year after leaving school.

Each outcome measure was scaled on a logit distribution using a technique for re-expressing grades described by Mosteller and Tukey (1977). Willms (1986) discusses the rationale for employing this technique and its underlying assumptions. With this standardization of the outcome measures, the major results can be expressed as 'effect sizes' (Glass, McGaw, and Smith 1981); they indicate a sector's performance in relation to the national average, expressed as a fraction of a standard deviation.

Four variables are employed as statistical controls for pupil intake in the main analyses: father's occupation, number of siblings, mother's education, and sex. These variables were selected after testing several combinations of variables, including the above four variables together with mother's occupation and father's education. For the entire sample of pupils the four variables selected are statistically significant predictors of all three outcome measures. Mother's occupation and father's education were tested in preliminary analyses but were dropped from the model because they did not contribute substantially to the explained variance of any outcome variable, after the other four variables were in the model.

The Registrar General's Classification of Occupations (OPCS 1970), which includes seven employment categories, was used to classify the occupations of the pupils' fathers. Using the 1977 SSLS data we scaled father's occupation for each individual using the Hope–Goldthorpe scale (Goldthorpe and Hope 1974). The average Hope–Goldthorpe value for all pupils within each of the Registrar General's employment categories constituted the scaled values for each category. Mother's education was coded as a dummy variable: 0 = education to less than 16 years, 1 = education to 16 years or more. Sex was coded 0 for boys, 1 for girls.

We also calculated a socio-economic-status variable, which is the first principal component (Harman 1976) of the three indicators of SES: father's occupation, mother's education, and number of siblings. At the individual level the SES variable captures most of the variance in pupil attainment attributable to father's occupation, mother's education, and number of siblings (R-squared of 0.224 compared with 0.238). However, the relationship between these variables and pupil outcomes may vary for different groups of pupils. Where appropriate, therefore, the regression analyses include the indicators of SES entered as separate covariates.

Table 1 shows the means, standard deviations, and correlation matrix for the three outcome variables and the control variables, for all pupils in the sample

Classification of Schools

The 1981 SSLS includes data for 23,151 pupils in 470 Scottish secondary schools. With the exception of special schools

TABLE 6.1. Means, Standard Deviations, and Pearson Product-Moment Correlation Matrix of Variables Describing Examination Results and Background Characteristics, for all Scottish School Leavers (1981 Survey)

	Mean	SD	SCE Attainment	English O grades	Arithmetic O grades	Sex	Father's Occupation	Mother's Education	Number of Siblings	SES
Mean	—	—								
SD	—	—								
SCE Attainment	0.000	1.000	—							
English O grades	0.000	1.000	0.800	—						
Arithmetic O grades	0.000	1.000	0.835	0.777	—					
Sex	0.487	0.500	0.028	0.128	−0.010	—				
Father's Occupation	42.536	11.847	0.425	0.341	0.361	0.005	—			
Mother's Education	0.234	0.423	0.294	0.236	0.242	0.004	0.293	—		
Number of Siblings	2.551	1.622	−0.242	−0.225	−0.232	0.016	−0.168	−0.109	—	
SES	0.000	1.000	0.473	0.391	0.408	−0.002	0.778	0.737	−0.533	—

Note: Analyses were based on the weighted sample of 23,151 pupils. Correlations were estimated using pairwise deletion of missing data.

serving handicapped pupils, the schools are the full population of state and private secondary schools in Scotland in 1981. In the light of the historical developments discussed in the previous section, we divided the 470 schools into five sectors: non-denominational pre-1902 (n = 66); non-denominational 1902–18 (n = 116); non-denominational post-1965 (n = 207); Catholic pre-1918 (n = 10); and Catholic post-1965 (n = 71). Recall that few contemporary schools had first become fully credentially six-year secondary schools between 1918 and 1965. It should also be noted that religious denomination is a classification of schools and not of pupils.

Models for Estimating Sector Effects

We employed two different models for estimating sector effects. The first is a straightforward pupil-level analysis of covariance (ANCOVA), which includes four dummy variables denoting enrolment in particular sectors, and the four pupil-level family background variables. The second model is a multilevel equation that accounts for both the individual and 'contextual' influences of family background on pupil outcomes. It extends the pupil-level model by adding the within-school means of each of the family background variables. The coefficients of the school mean variables indicate the strength of the contextual effects (see Alwin 1976; Alwin and Otto 1977; and Burstein 1980 for a discussion of these models).[2]

If there are significant contextual effects, and if the distribution of school mean SES varies across the five sectors, then the estimates of sector effects will differ for the two models. The estimated effects in the two models also have different substantive interpretations. In the pupil-level model, the estimate of the sector effect attempts to answer the queston: 'what would have been the expected outcome score for a pupil with nationally average background characteristics if he or she had enrolled in a particular sector?'. The model assumes that the 'nationally average' pupil could exist in all sectors, and that we can accurately fix expected outcome scores on the basis of our information about individual pupils. Like the pupil-level model the contextual-effects model takes account of the characteristics of individual pupils. In addition, however, it includes the characteristics of the pupil mix of each school. It asks the question, 'how would a nationally average pupil have done in a particular sector as a result of school factors that were not associated with its pupil mix?'.

RESULTS

Between-School Variation in SES (Question 1)

Figure 6.1 shows the relationship between school mean attainment and school mean SES for all Scottish secondary schools (excluding those that were represented in the data by fewer than 20 pupils). Each smaller circle represents a state school, and each smaller square represents an independent school. The vertical axis of the graph has two scales: the values on the left side correspond to the scaled attainment scores in standard deviation units; the values on the right side show the SCE attainment categories. The horizontal axis shows the school mean SES. Recall that for the entire SSIS sample, the SES measure and the overall attainment score have a pupil-level mean of zero, and a standard deviation of one. Considering just the variations along the horizontal axis, we see that the between-school variation in SES is substantial. Approximately 10 per cent of all Scottish secondary schools (35 of the schools shown on Figure 6.1) have an SES score that is at least one-half of a standard deviation below the pupil-level mean. Most of these very low SES schools are in the Strathclyde Region, and mainly in Glasgow, the area with the greatest between-school SES segregation. At the other extreme are the independent or private schools, which have a mean SES above 1.00 (the 16 smaller squares on Figure 6.1). These schools serve only about 3.5 per cent of all pupils in Scotland; however, they figure prominently in certain areas, especially the cities, where they cream some of the most able pupils from the state sector. But even within the state sector about 10 per cent of the pupils attend schools with a mean SES of 0.5 or greater (31 of the schools shown in Figure 6.1).

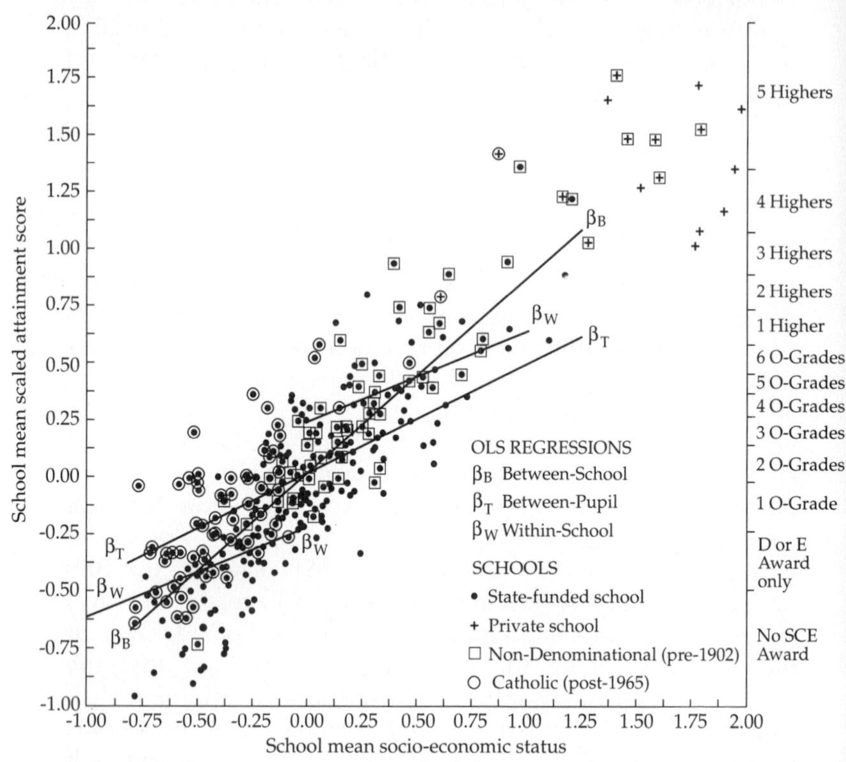

FIG. 6.1. Relationship between SCE Attainment and SES

Between-Sector Variation in SES (Question 2)

Table 6.2 shows the mean SES score, and the proportion of pupils with fathers in each OPCS category, for each of the five sectors. This table, together with Figure 6.1, shows that there are considerable differences between the sectors in the pupils they serve. The pre-1902 non-denominational schools, on average, enrol pupils from higher social-class backgrounds: their average SES score is 30 per cent of a standard deviation above the national average; 31.6 per cent of the pupils' fathers had 'professional' or 'intermediate' occupations (the two highest

TABLE 6.2. Number of Schools and Pupils in the 1981 Scottish School Leavers Survey, Mean and Standard Deviation of Socio-economic Status, and the Proportion of School Leavers' Fathers in each OPCS Social Class Category, by School Sector

School Sector	Number Schools	Number Pupils	SES		Proportion of School Leavers' Fathers							
			Mean	SD	I Professional	II Intermediate	IIINM Skilled Non-Manual	IIIM Skilled Manual	IV Partly Skilled	V Unskilled	VI Unclassified/ No Occupation	Total
Non-Denominational												
Pre-1902	66	3634	0.301	1.09	7.7	23.9	7.6	31.0	13.4	3.6	12.8	100.0
1902–1918	116	5720	0.066	0.98	3.6	19.7	7.7	35.9	14.1	3.8	15.1	99.9
Post-1965	207	9468	0.011	0.99	4.5	16.5	7.8	37.8	14.1	4.0	15.4	100.1
Catholic												
Pre-1918	10	461	−0.187	0.95	4.3	14.7	6.4	37.9	13.8	4.3	18.6	100.0
Post-1965	71	3868	−0.385	0.85	1.6	9.9	5.4	43.6	16.3	5.8	17.5	100.1
All Scottish Schools	470	23151	0.000	1.00	4.3	17.3	7.3	37.2	14.4	4.2	15.3	100.0

categories) compared with only 21.6 per cent for all schools in Scotland. Figure 6.1 shows the positions of the pre-1902 schools along the SES continuum, denoted with larger squares. The average SES for the 1902–18 non-denominational schools was seven per cent of a standard deviation above the national average, and the average for post-1965 non-denominational schools was one per cent above the national average. Catholic pupils, however, were from much lower social-class backgrounds. The average SES score for pupils in pre-1918 Catholic schools was −0.19, and only 19 per cent of the pupils were from the upper two social-class categories. Pupils in the post-1965 Catholic schools were from even lower social class backgrounds: their average SES score was −0.39, and only 11.5 per cent were from Social Class I and II backgrounds. Figure 6.1 shows the position of the Catholic schools on the SES continuum; they are indicated by larger circles.

To some extent these between-sector variations are a function of the uneven geographical distribution of older schools, which are disproportionately located outside industrial areas, especially those of the Clydeside conurbation and its hinterland in the west of Scotland. However, disaggregation of the data into the 28 communities served by more than one non-denominational school showed that within each community, older schools tended to have higher SES intakes than other schools.

Between-School Variations in SCE Attainment (Question 3)

Overall Variation, Unadjusted

The large variation in SES is associated with large variation both in overall SCE attainment and in O-grade examination results. At the school level, the correlation between overall attainment and SES is 0.81, between English O-grade results and SES is 0.75, and between arithmetic O-grade results and SES is 0.79. Forty-five of the schools shown in Figure 6.1 are at least one-half of a standard deviation above the national average in overall SCE attainment. The average pupil in these schools acquires at least six O-grades, and as many as five Highers passes. Three passes is informally considered a minimum requirement for entry to higher education in Scotland.

TABLE 6.3. Parameter Estimates (and Standard Errors) for the Regression of SCE Attainment, English O-Grade, and Arithmetic O-Grade Scores on Sector, Family Background Variables, Sex, and Contextual-Effects Variables

	SCE Attainment		English		Arithmetic	
	Pupil-Level Model	Contextual-Effects Model	Pupil-Level Model	Contextual-Effects Model	Pupil-Level Model	Contextual-Effects Model
Intercept	−0.114* (0.016)	−0.109* (0.010)	−0.107* (0.010)	−0.113* (0.010)	−0.090* (0.010)	−0.094* (0.010)
Non-Denominational pre-1902	0.239* (0.019)	0.141* (0.019)	0.136* (0.020)	0.074* (0.020)	0.184* (0.020)	0.105* (0.020)
Non-Denominational 1902–18	0.091* (0.016)	0.069* (0.016)	0.105* (0.017)	0.087* (0.017)	0.066* (0.017)	0.045* (0.017)
Catholic pre-1918	0.236* (0.045)	0.274* (0.046)	0.284* (0.047)	0.335* (0.048)	0.132* (0.047)	0.189* (0.048)
Catholic post-1965	0.101* (0.018)	0.217* (0.022)	0.173* (0.019)	0.303* (0.023)	0.088* (0.019)	0.224* (0.023)
Between Pupil						
Father's Occupation	0.029* (0.001)	0.024* (0.001)	0.023* (0.001)	0.020* (0.001)	0.024* (0.001)	0.020* (0.001)
Mother's Education	0.403* (0.016)	0.322* (0.016)	0.328* (0.016)	0.284* (0.017)	0.325* (0.016)	0.270* (0.017)
Number of Siblings	−0.101* (0.004)	−0.091* (0.004)	−0.107* (0.004)	−0.097* (0.004)	−0.105* (0.004)	−0.094* (0.087)
Sex	0.069* (0.013)	0.066* (0.013)	0.262* (0.013)	0.246* (0.013)	−0.005 (0.013)	−0.015 (0.013)
Between School						
Mean Father's Occupation		0.033* (0.003)		0.024* (0.003)		0.028* (0.003)
Mean Mother's Education		0.193* (0.080)		−0.148 (0.084)		−0.044 (0.084)
Mean Number of Siblings		−0.047* (0.019)		−0.103* (0.020)		−0.097* (0.020)
Percent Females		−0.021 (0.055)		0.223* (0.058)		0.106 (0.058)
	0.244	0.271	0.187	0.200	0.180	0.198

Note: Regression analyses employed listwise deletion of missing data. N = 18,949. Parameter estimates marked with an asterisk are greater than twice their standard errors.

There are 35 schools (9 per cent of those shown in Figure 6.1) where the average attainment score is at least one-half of a standard deviation below the national average. The average pupil in these schools leaves school without any SCE awards.

Overall Variation, Adjusted for SES

Figure 6.1 also shows that there is considerable variation in school mean SCE attainment at all levels of SES. At any particular level of SES, the range in mean school attainment scores is shown in Figure 6.1 by the vertical distance between the lowest and highest performing schools at that level of SES. The difference in attainment scores between schools at the tenth percentile and those at the ninetieth percentile in their SES-adjusted performance is about one-half of a standard deviation, and is fairly constant at all levels of SES. This difference is about the same in arithmetic (0.53) and slightly larger in English (0.60) (results not shown). These differences are also very large in substantive terms: one-half of a standard deviation can mean the difference between receiving five O-grade passes instead of only one, or between receiving a C in English or arithmetic, instead of no award.

Between-Sector Variations in SCE Attainment (Question 4)

Table 6.3 shows the parameter estimates (unstandardized) and standard errors for the regression of each outcome measure on school sector, family background variables, sex, and the contextual effects variables. Each of the variables was centred about its mean (but not standardized); therefore, the constant term represents the 'effect size' for an average pupil in the reference sector (non-denominational post-1965 schools); and the coefficients for the other four sectors represent the difference in expected outcome scores between a given sector and the reference sector. Before discussing effect sizes, however, we first discuss the magnitude and statistical significance of the effects of pupil characteristics and contextual effects.

Effects of Pupil Characteristics and of Contextual Effects

The between-pupil coefficients for all three SES measures—father's occupation, mother's education, and number of siblings—are statistically significant across all three outcome measures. As in many studies of school effectiveness, these variables together explain about 15 to 20 per cent of the variance in academic attainment (White 1982).

The between-pupil coefficients for sex are also statistically significant for overall SCE attainment and English: females score about 7 per cent of a standard deviation higher than males in overall SCE attainment, and about one-quarter of a standard deviation higher in English. Their arithmetic scores are about the same as their male counterparts.

The coefficients for the school-level aggregates of mean scores on the three SES variables are statistically significant across all three outcome measures, with the exception of mother's education, which is statistically significant only for overall SCE attainment. These coefficients, which indicate the magnitude of the contextual effect of school mean SES, are very large in substantive terms. The overall contextual effect may be expressed in standard deviation units for a child with 'nationally average' background characteristics. If the child had a choice between a school where the average pupil came from a family with three children and with the father in a partly skilled occupation, versus a school where the average pupil came from a family with only two children, and with the father in a white-collar occupation (OPCS category IIIN), then the child's expected attainment score would be about one-half of a standard deviation higher on all three outcome measures in the latter school. This means obtaining four O-grade passes instead of only one, or a C in English and arithmetic, instead of no award. Among pupils who choose to enter the labour market at the end of fourth year in 1982, about 70 per cent of those with four or more O-grade passes were in a job nine months later, compared to under half of those with three or less O-grade passes (Raffe 1984*a*). Thus attendance at a high SES school instead of a low SES school powerfully influences life-chances.

In making these comparisons of attainment we are assuming that all of the educogenic factors associated with family background are captured by the three SES measures. It is quite likely that the contextual effect would be much smaller if we had measures for such factors as pupils' and parents' aspirations, pupil motivation, and pupils' prior ability. Indeed, Hauser

(1970) has shown that, in some cases, contextual effects may be nothing more than artefacts of an underspecified model. In the monograph on which this chapter draws, we address this problem with subsidiary analyses.

Sector Effects

The evidence for a contextual effect of school mean SES on pupil outcomes emphasizes the importance of estimating sector effects both with and without controls for contextual influences. The pupil-level model attempts to estimate the relative advantage of attending schools in a particular sector, without control for contextual effects. The contextual-effects model attempts to compare the relative performance of schools in different sectors, given the population of pupils served by each school in each sector.

Among the three non-denominational sectors, the post-1965 schools have the lowest adjusted pupil outcomes. An average pupil attending a school in this sector would be expected to score about one-tenth of a standard deviation below the mean on all three outcome measures. (The expected scores for this sector are given by the constants in row 1 of Table 6.3.)

The pre-1902 schools have the highest adjusted scores. Compared with pupils' scores in post-1965 non-denominational schools, the expected score for an average pupil in one of the pre-1902 schools is 24 per cent of a standard deviation higher in SCE attainment, 14 per cent of a standard deviation higher in English, and 18 per cent of a standard deviation higher in arithmetic. The advantage acquired by membership of a 1902–18 non-denominational schools is not as great: 9 per cent of a standard deviation in SCE attainment, 11 per cent in English, and 7 per cent in arithmetic. Because the older non-denominational sectors serve higher SES populations (see Figure 6.1 and Table 6.2), and because we observed significant contextual effects, the results suggest that some of the advantage of the older schools is acquired through contextual effects. After controlling for contextual effects the advantage of attendance at a pre-1902 school instead of a post-1965 school is only 14 per cent of a standard deviation in SCE attainment, 7 per cent in English, and 11 per cent in arithmetic. The relative advantage of 1902–18 schools drops slightly, by about 2 per cent of a standard deviation, on each outcome measure, after controlling for contextual effects.

Pupils in Catholic schools also score higher than comparable pupils in the post-1965 non-denominational schools. The expected SCE attainment score for a nationally average pupil in a post-1965 Catholic school is higher than in a post-1965 non-denominational school by 10 per cent in SCE attainment, 17 per cent in English, and 9 per cent in arithmetic. The difference is even greater for pre-1918 Catholic schools: 24 per cent in SCE attainment, 28 per cent in English, and 13 per cent in arithmetic.

As we observed earlier, the Catholic schools serve a lower SES population than the non-denominational schools (see Figure 6.1). After controlling for contextual effects, the effect sizes are considerably larger: for the post-1965 Catholic schools, 22 per cent in SCE attainment, 30 per cent in English, and 22 per cent in arithmetic; and for the pre-1918 Catholic schools, 27 per cent in SCE attainment, 34 per cent in English, and 19 per cent in arithmetic. Thus Catholic schools on average give their pupils very substantial advantages.

SUMMARY

The data show considerable SES segregation between Scottish schools. This segregation is partly a function of between-community differences in average SES. But two within-community processes are also involved. In most Scottish communities served by more than one non-denominational school, higher SES groups are over-represented in the older school or schools. Second, higher SES groups have opted out of the state sector. Both processes operate also in the Catholic sectors of state and private schooling, but their net effects on SES segregation are less because there are proportionately fewer older schools and private schools in the Catholic sector. Catholic pupils as a whole are over-represented in the lower SES groups.

There were substantial between-school variations in pupils' examination outcomes. These between-school variations were present at all levels of school mean SES, with the highest performing schools scoring at least one-half of a standard deviation above the lowest performing schools. Differences in attainment were associated with the history and denomination of the school, and they can be statistically expressed in terms of the attainment score that could be expected of a pupil at the national average of SES in each of the school sectors. In pre-1902 non-denominational schools the nationally average pupil was 23 per cent of a standard deviation higher in overall certified attainment than his or her counterpart in post-1965 schools. Nationally average pupils in the 1902–1918 non-denominational schools also enjoyed an advantage over their counterparts in the younger school sector, but it was not as large, varying between 6 and 10 per cent of a standard deviation across the three outcome measures. Most pupils in the Catholic sector attended schools that attained six-year status after 1965. On average they did not fare worse than pupils in post-1965 non-denominational schools; if anything they did better. For the pupil at the national average of SES the expected overall attainment score was about 10 per cent of a standard deviation higher in a post-1965 Catholic school than it was in a post-1965 non-denominational school. In the pre-1918 Catholic schools the advantage was higher than it was either in the post-1965 Catholic schools, or in the non-denominational schools, young or old.

The differential advantage to the nationally average pupil of attendance at different schools could be partitioned into the advantage associated with the socio-economic composition of the school (the contextual effect) and that associated with its history and denomination. Controlling for the contextual effect reduced the benefit to the nationally average pupil of attendance at one of the pre-1902 non-denominational schools, from 23 per cent of a standard deviation to 13 per cent in overall SCE attainment. Controlling for the SES context of the school (the mean pupil SES) also reduced the advantage of attendance at a pre-1918 Catholic school, but the reduction was less because the SES composition of such schools was lower than that of the non-denominational schools.

The effects of controlling for school context were greatest for post-1965 Catholic schools, the sector in which the mean SES of schools tended to be lowest. With school context controlled, the advantage associated with attendance at young Catholic schools increased from 10 per cent to 22 per cent in overall SCE attainment. This advantage is worth all of one or two examination passes, and adds considerably to the young person's chances of finding a job on leaving school at 16 years, or of gaining admission to favoured post-school courses at 16, 17, or 18 years.

DISCUSSION

These conclusions derive from a statistical model that makes atomistic and synchronic assumptions. It treats even the history of schools as just another variable. But the ways in which we have classified periods and types of development were not, and could not be, derived from a synchronic and atomistic perspective. Rather, we made reference (in 'Background and Questions') to a relational and diachronic account of how the structure of Scottish schooling (for example, the location of schools, and the institutional relations between schools—credentialling/non-credentialling) came to incorporate aspects of group conflict as the twentieth-century system developed. Similar arguments apply to the status of SES in the model, and of the other variables too.

The virtue of the atomistic approach is that it takes a temporal cross-section of reality and, by observing the correlations contained therein, guides judgements about which relationships might be open to change. It offers a release from the spectre of a hegemonic or multi-collinear world in which nothing can be changed because everything is related to everything else. But the crucial point is that we necessarily borrow from the relational world to construct our meanings and models, and we necessarily deliver our conclusions, about what might or might not be changeable, back to the relational world. The validity of the assumptions we make in these exchanges is crucial to the validity of our conclusions, and also to their practical utility. If assumptions must be made, and they must, can we make them on a basis that is less arbitrary?

Multilevel models are a way forward because they allow one to represent relational aspects of the world. For example, the influence of an individual's SES on his or her achievement can be shown to operate both directly, and also through the part it plays in the overall SES composition of the school ('school context'). But there are practical and logical reasons why a multilevel approach cannot comprehend all relationships, and why it always therefore runs the risk of attributing false 'characteristics' (that is, synchronic and atomistic epiphenomena of relational realities) to the members of a level. For example, it may be that the positive effects of Catholic schools are achieved, not through any characteristic of schools as such, but from the purely relational fact of the minority status of the Catholic population. 'We must make our schools work or they will take them away from us' is a fear that some Catholics voice. Thus we might be wasting our time if we looked to Catholic schools for examples of good educational practice, or to Catholic families for evidence, say, of 'educogenic' values. Alternatively, it may be that examples of good practice and educogenic values are indeed to be found among Catholic teachers and parents, but that they owe their existence to the minority status of Catholic culture. If this were so, the good school practice could not be regarded as an attribute solely of the school, nor could the educogenic values of families be regarded solely as attributes of families. In effect the boundaries of the levels of the model would be mis-specified, and conclusions drawn from it might give a misleading view of the possibilities of improving education by means of changes in the practice of schools outside the Catholic sector.

The way forward, clearly, is to articulate better theory. But theories must be tested, so the practical problem remains as to how, in any particular application, to move beyond the limiting assumptions of one's model. Our analyses have indicated how one may make progress within a model based on synchronic and atomistic assumptions. The main point is that the attributional or relational status of a property (such as SES) can, within limits, be tested empirically. Thus the contextual effect can be represented by means of partitioning the attainment/SES association among pupils into relational and attributional components. Researchers have conjectured that contextual effects, operationalized in this way may stem from social interactions among peers (for example, Winkler 1975; Summers and Wolfe 1977; Henderson, Mieszkowski, and Savageau 1978; Clifford and Heath 1984). This may be the case, and Erbring and Young (1979) provide a model for examining the intervening mechanisms through which peer group effects might arise. However, school mean SES is probably correlated with several school-level factors which in one sense are part of a 'school effect'. These include the disciplinary climate, the course content, teaching styles, teachers' expectations, and the allocation of resources. Logically, however, one can never discount the possibility that observed associations are an artefact of a mis-specification of the boundaries of the school, and of a consequent mis-assignment of attributes between pupils, schools, and other levels, such as the local community.

This is the most acute methodological problem in models of the input/process/output type, because conclusions about the effects of the school hinge in part upon the correct identification of the educogenic characteristics of the pupil intake. The danger always is that we will wrongly 'freeze' aspects of the relations between parents, pupils, and schools that are lived in a community context over time, and attribute them to the atomistically conceived pupil.

Our immediate solution to this problem in the example discussed in this chapter had been to say that, the less one's confidence in one's intake measures, the more one should rely in one's assessment of school effectiveness on the vertical, or near-vertical, comparison between (in the example in Figure 6.1) schools of proximate SES. As one's confidence in one's intake measures increases, the more one may validly attempt comparisons in terms of the performance of a pupil of specified characteristics, such as 'nationally average SES'. (Note that only the second approach is logically capable of identifying contextual effects. The first approach, in effect, treats measures of the pupil composition of schools, such as mean school SES, as surrogates for aspects of SES that have been inadequately measured for individual pupils.)

This procedural precept is not wholly arbitrary in that there *are* reasons for supposing that, when we take two pupils with the same measured SES, one of whom is in a low mean SES school, and the other of whom is in a high mean SES school, the SES value which the two pupils have been given is less likely to capture (to proxy for) all of the differences between the two pupils in their educational potential. In practical terms, a pupil's being low SES in a homogeneously low SES community is likely to be different from his or her being low SES in a high SES community; and the parents also are likely to differ between the two communities in respect of characteristics that may have a bearing on the educational success of their children. In the Scottish case, parents of the low SES child in a high SES neighbourhood are more likely to live in an area with an established tradition of secondary education going back at least to the beginning of the century, than are the parents of a low SES child in a low SES neighbourhood. The significance of the former parents' SES may therefore differ from that of the parents in the low SES neighbourhood. Our historical analysis of the social construction of the school system has shown that, until 1965, low SES neighbourhoods were more likely to have been provided with low-status, non-credentialling schools. When comprehensive reorganization gave them schools that could offer the full range of national credentials, the schools were still doubly disadvantaged. There was no tradition of credentialled secondary education in the area, and the new comprehensive schools were usually themselves in competition with the older-established schools serving the same community but located in higher-SES neighbourhoods.

If we cannot distinguish the effects of schools from the effects of their pupil intakes we cannot answer the question that we posed at the opening of this chapter: can public education be provided in ways that mitigate social disadvantages which themselves have educational causes and consequences? Clearly, one way forward is to make the theory more explicit and to measure directly the attitudes and processes conjectured by that theory. Recent British examples are Mortimore *et al.* 1988 and Smith and Tomlinson 1989. These studies examine the impact of school practices on the development of pupils over time. But we also need models that are longitudinal for schools as well as for pupils, and that examine the impact of schools on successive cohorts of pupils. Such studies, which are both multilevel and longitudinal for each of their levels (say, pupils and schools) have greater explanatory power than models which 'freeze' school organization and practice at one point in time. This is because they allow one to observe continuity and change separately at each level of the model. For example, Willms and Raudenbush (1989) have shown that changes in schools' contexts (mean SES) over a four-year period in Scotland in the early 1980s did indeed lead to the changes in pupil attainment that would be predicted from the cross-sectional type of analysis undertaken in this chapter. The study strengthens McPherson and Willms's (1987) conclusion that the reduction of SES segregation between schools, following comprehensive reorganization in Scotland, led to a reduction in SES differences in pupil attainment between the mid-1970s and mid-1980s. Paterson (1991), however, has shown that the first half of the 1980s saw no change in the effects on attainment of older schools and of Catholic schools. Moreover, the older schools were those towards which parents tended to gravitate when exercising parental choice, and such choices were exercised more often by higher SES parents (Echols, McPherson, and Willms 1990).

A fundamental lesson to be taken from a relational approach to schooling is that pupils are not randomly allocated to schools, in part because schools were not randomly allocated to communities. The persistence of the association of social disadvantage with educational failure is itself testimony to the power of public education in earlier generations. School and community interact in ways that reflect decades of historical structuring. Longitudinal multilevel models allow us to capture that structuring with greater confidence. In applying them we learn that public education can change pupil outcomes in ways that can work either with or against the grain of inherited inequality.

NOTES

1. This is a revised and abridged version of a monograph published by the same authors under the title 'Certification, Class Conflict, Religion and Community: A Socio-historical Explanation of the Effectiveness of Contemporary Schools', in Alan C. Kerckhoff (ed.), *Research in Sociology of Education and Socialization*, vol. vi. (Greenwich, Conn.: JAI Press, 1986).
2. There have been several recent improvements in the estimation of mixed (e.g., pupil-level and school-level) multilevel models (Aitkin and Longford 1986; Raudenbush and Bryk 1986; Goldstein 1987;

Raudenbush 1988; Willms and Raudenbush 1989; Raudenbush and Willms 1991). Willms's (1990) reanalysis of the data for this chapter using the Raudenbush and Bryk (1986) HLM program does not, however, change the main findings reported here which are based on Ordinary Least Squares regression. Paterson (1991) confirmed their stability over four surveys 1981–7.

7

Government Policies and Higher Education: A Comparison of Britain and the United States, 1630–1860

SHELDON ROTHBLATT and MARTIN TROW

INTRODUCTION

Over the past three hundred and fifty years, American and British colleges and universities have been created and have operated in the context of policies set forth by their respective central governments, policies which have had decisive effects on the way these institutions have developed. In this essay we will explore some of the policies which shaped the diverging character of the two systems, looking for ways in which those governmental policies have interacted with other non-governmental forces to give the systems and their component institutions the sharply contrasting characteristics that have long distinguished them.

In a short essay it is only possible to open some questions and point in the direction in which answers might be found. Our approach depends heavily upon a close comparison of British and American experience at roughly the same time in the history of the two societies and their institutions of higher education. We will be looking at several key developments in the early history of the two countries in order to illustrate their different responses to roughly similar problems in the relations of state and college or university. Finally, we will reflect on whether these developments reveal any underlying patterns in the state–institution relations which are reflected in the basic characteristics of the national higher education systems in the two countries.

THE COLONIAL EXPERIENCE IN AMERICA

Despite all the changes and transformations of state, society, and economy in modern times, the American higher education system has its roots in the colonial period, when it developed characteristics distinguishable from all other systems of higher education in the world, notably: its governance patterns, marked by a strong president and lay governing board; its extraordinary diversity of forms and functions; and its marked responsiveness to forces in society as well as in state and church. In one other respect the colonial colleges are familiar to us, and that is in the importance attached to them by the societies and governments of the colonies. At a time when most or many European universities were not really central to the vitality of their societies, or were more or less preoccupied with the preparation of theologians and divines serving an established church, or with defining the virtues and polishing the accomplishments of a ruling élite, seventeenth- and eighteenth-century colonial colleges in America, especially those in New England, were regarded by their founders and supporters as forces for survival in a hostile environment. They were perceived as crucial, indeed indispensable instruments for staving off the threat of reversion to barbarism, the threatened decline into the savagery of the surrounding forest and Indian.[1] The colleges also played a familiar role for these early Calvinists of maintaining a learned ministry and a literate laity. Moreover, in the young colonies as on the later frontier, civilization and its institutions could never be assumed to be inherited. They had always to be created and re-created; and for this purpose, learning and learned persons and the institutions that engendered them were needed.

The colonial colleges were founded as public bodies. They were established and then chartered by a public authority and were supported in part by public funds, in part by private gifts and endowments, in part by student fees. The mixing of public and private support, functions, and authority has persisted as a central characteristic of American higher education to this day, blurring the distinction between public and private colleges and universities. Americans have tended to regard all their higher education institutions as having a public dimension, and they have also allowed for a private dimension in their public institutions. As Jurgen Herbst argues, one cannot see the colonial colleges as either 'public' or 'private' institutions but as 'provincial', stressing their function of service to their sponsoring and chartering colony, rather than to their source of support or authority (Whitehead and Herbst 1986). While the distinction between 'public' and 'private' emerged with a certain clarity in the nineteenth century, and especially after the Civil War, it is still more appropriate to see the broad spectrum of American colleges and universities as lying along a continuum from fully public to nearly purely private. Every 'private' institution in the United States is today in receipt of public support, both through the favourable tax treatment for gifts and endowments made to higher education, as well as through publicly provided student aid. Conversely, public colleges and universities raise private funds from student fees, gifts and endowments, business and industry; and their lay governing boards give a degree of autonomy to their institutions similar to that of the private institutions.

The geography of the Eastern Seaboard, and the accidents of settlement, created a series of distinct and largely self-governing colonies, each tied to metropolitan London through a charter and governor, yet separate from one another in character, social structure, and forms of governance. That, in turn, meant that when colonial colleges were established, they differed from one another in their origins, links to colonial government, and denominational ties (Herbst 1982). There was no central government on the American continent with broad jurisdiction over them all, and thus no governmental body that would accept responsibility for ordering and governing an emerging class of institutions in similar ways, in response to a common law or governmental policy. Indeed, even after a Federal government emerged, it explicitly renounced its authority over education, including higher education, delegating that power to the constituent states. That self-denying ordinance was reinforced during the early years of the Republic when an attempt to create a national university in the capital was defeated, thus preventing what might well have introduced formal and informal constraints on the promiscuous creation of new colleges and universities after the Revolution (Trow 1979). So the colonies had the experience, before the Revolution, of a multiplicity of colleges or 'university colleges', similar in certain respects but differing in others. They had also the experience of having created these institutions of higher education at the initiative or with the encouragement of public authorities and powerful private constituencies. This stands in marked contrast to the conspicuous lack of such encouragement, and indeed the stubborn resistance, or deeply divided responses, by political and ecclesiastical authorities in England to the creation of new institutions of higher education, especially and particularly those originating outside the Establishment, in the decades before about 1830. The many dissenting academies created in the second half of the eighteenth century never had the encouragement of central or local government, and their failure to be fully acknowledged or gain a charter and the right to grant degrees were among the factors leading them to short lives and a dead end. It does not appear that this early and at one time promising precedent and experience in college building was of real use or inspiration to those who created the new English colleges and universities that arose first in London and Durham and then in the provincial towns and cities of Victorian England. One might therefore say that for Americans the colonial experience was a training in the arts of establishing institutions of higher education. And the skills and attitudes necessary for the creation of new colleges that were gained in the colonial period, along with the models of governance provided by the older institutions, led directly to the proliferation of colleges and universities after the Revolution: sixteen more between 1776 and 1800 (Robson 1983), and literally hundreds over the next half century.

The eight colonial colleges differed widely among themselves. In a sense, these early and most prestigious American colleges, the nurseries of so many of the Revolutionary leaders, legitimated diversity. But similarities also existed. The colonial colleges had to be created in the absence of a body of learned men. In the new world no guild of scholars existed, no body of learned men who could take the government of a college into its own hands. The very survival of the new institutions in the absence of buildings, an assured income, or a guild of scholars required a higher and more continuing level of governmental interest and involvement for institutions that had become too important for the colonies to be allowed to wither or die. Moreover, a concern for doctrinal orthodoxy, especially in the seventeenth century, provided further grounds for public authorities to create governance machinery in which its own representatives were visible, or held a final veto and continuing 'visitorial' and supervisory powers (an inheritance from Britain, where bishops frequently performed the function of safeguarding the wishes of founders and benefactors). The medieval idea of a university as an autonomous corporation composed of masters and scholars was certainly present in the minds of the founders of colonial colleges, but the actual circumstances of colonial life forced a drastic modification in the application of this inheritance. At Harvard, for example, the charter of 1650

> exemplified a carefully wrought compromise between a medieval tradition of corporate autonomy and a modern concern for territorial authorities over all matters of state and religion. The former was preserved, even though weakly, in the Corporation; the latter was institutionalized in the Board of Overseers. (Herbst 1982: 16)

Other colonies as well, for reasons similar to those of Massachusetts, carefully circumscribed the powers of the corporate universities, each making sure that its governors and legislatures retained ultimate power over the college through the composition of its external Board or through the reserve powers of the colonial government as 'visitor'. Even in Connecticut, where Yale's trustees were all Congregational ministers, the charter that incorporated the trustees as the President and Fellows of Yale College preserved to the colonial Court the right '"as often as required" to inspect the college's laws, rules and ordinances, and to repeal or disallow them "when they shall think proper"' (Herbst 1982: 47). The charter, Herbst notes, 'thus upheld the ultimate authority of the Court over the college, but also guaranteed the school's autonomy within specific limits' (ibid.: 47).

Indeed, only Harvard and William and Mary, in Massachusetts and Virginia, the only two seventeenth-century foundations, were established with a two-board government, one representing the institution or corporation, the other the external trustees. And in both of these 'the governmental practice . . . soon lost its distinctiveness and came to resemble that of the one-board colleges. American colleges were to be ruled by powerful and respected citizens, who would govern them for their own and their children's benefit' (ibid.: 61). Ironically, the nearest American colleges and universities ever came to recreating the first, or corporate, board was when they finally were able to gather together a guild of learned men who could command respect and gain a measure of professional authority. It was not until after the turn of the twentieth century that academic senates became significant parts of the governance machinery of American colleges and universities, and then only in the most prestigious institutions employing scholars who were able to use the academic market-place to compel respect and attention from presidents and boards concerned with the status and distinction of their institutions. The relative weakness of the academic profession in the United States, as compared with its strength in the United Kingdom, especially in Oxbridge, has had large consequences for the diverging development of the two systems (Trow 1985).

With the exception of New Jersey which, because of religious diversity occurring at the end of the colonial period, chartered two colleges, each colony granted a monopoly position to its college. In this respect, each colony behaved towards its college as England behaved towards Oxford and Cambridge and Scotland towards its universities, granting their colleges the power to award degrees within their respective 'province'. American colonial governments were attempting to prevent or inhibit the appearance of rival and competitive institutions, in much the same way that the government in England had prevented the dissenting academies from widening the educational market in the eighteenth century. Consequently (and other factors were doubtless involved) the dissenting academies never emerged as serious competitive degree-granting institutions and were destined to failure and (with the special exception of the institution that became Manchester College, Oxford) to eventual extinction (Armytage 1955; see also the essays in B. Smith 1986). But their existence—and relevance—was noted in the colonies, and reference was made to them as better models than the ancient universities during a dispute at

Yale in the 1750s over sectarian issues (Herbst 1982).[2] As models they were even more relevant to the proliferation of American colleges on the frontier between the Revolution and the Civil War, with the significant difference that the American colleges were encouraged and sometimes even modestly supported by public authorities.

Charters expressly reserved for colonial governments a continuing role in the governance of colleges, placing colonial officers directly on boards of trustees, or assigning to the Courts and legislatures the power of review. For example, the 1766 charter of Queen's College (later to become Rutgers) included among its lay trustees the governor, council president, chief justice, and attorney general of the province of New Jersey (McAnear 1955). By its charter of 1748, the College of New Jersey (later Princeton) placed the governor of the colony on the board as its presiding officer (ibid.: 86–7). And in the turbulent sectarian climate of eighteenth-century America, those reserve powers were in fact employed from time to time.

All the colonial colleges were provided with public funds of various kinds, though in varying amounts and degree of consistency. Some received a flat sum or subsidy to make up an annual shortfall in operating expenses or salaries, others assistance in the construction and maintenance of buildings. The Assembly of Virginia provided the College of William and Mary with a percentage of the duties collected on furs, skins, and imported liquor (Robson 1985). These subventions reflected an organic connection between the colony and 'its' college, and the colonies were not reluctant to use the power of the purse as a constraint on colleges when they were supposed to have carried their autonomy too far. The Connecticut legislature in 1755 refused its annual grant of £100 to Yale because of a sectarian dispute with the College's president (Herbst 1982: 76). As Bernard Bailyn has stated the situation, 'The autonomy that comes from an independent, reliable, self-perpetuating income was everywhere lacking. The economic basis of self-direction in education failed to develop.'[3]

The power of colonial governments over their colleges, then, derived from three fundamental sources: the power to give or withhold a charter; the continuing powers reserved for government within the charter; and the power of the public purse.

THE AMERICAN REVOLUTION

Before 1776 the colonies displayed a stronger or at least as strong a connection between state and college as was apparent in the mother country, but the relationship changed drastically after the Declaration of Independence. In a formal sense, the Revolution transformed colonial governments into state governments and superimposed a national confederacy and then a Federal government on top of them. However, at the same time the Revolution weakened all agencies of government, by stressing the roots of the new nation in popular sovereignty, the subordination of the government to 'the people', and the primacy of individual and group freedom and initiative. 'The individual replaced the state as the unit of politics', writes one historian, 'and the Constitution and Bill of Rights confirmed this Copernican revolution in authority.' And 'unlike the 18th-century venture in building a society from the top down,' American society after the Revolution 'originated in a multitude of everyday needs that responded to the long lines of settlement and enterprise, not the imperatives of union' (Wiebe 1984: 353).

But at least as important as the new conception of the relation of the citizen to state that emerged from independence was the opening of the frontier beyond the Alleghenies, which gave many Americans a chance to walk away from the settled and 'European' states that succeeded the old colonies, requiring them to create, indeed invent, new forms of self-government on the frontier (Elkins and McKitrick 1968). Among the institutions of the frontier were new colleges, resembling the colonial colleges in some ways but differing in others and linking the recently opened territories to the original culture of the Atlantic. In the 25 years after the Declaration of Independence, 16 colleges were established (and have survived), thus tripling the total number in existence (Robson 1983: 323). Of these, no fewer than 14 were created on the frontier. After 1800 the floodgates of education opened, and hundreds of institutions were established in both old states and new territories. Most of them were small and malnourished, and many collapsed within a few years of their founding. The reason for this explosion of educational activity was a change in the three conditions that had hitherto characterized government-college relations in the colonial period, the three conditions of restrictive chartering, direct interest by government in the administration of colleges, and public support of higher education.

The new states, both those which succeeded the old colonies and those carved out of the new lands to the West, did not give a monopoly to any single state college or university, reflecting the quite different relationship of state and societal institutions that emerged from the Revolution. The states granted charters much more readily than had colonies before the Revolution, and on decidedly different terms. Herbst tells of efforts in 1762 by Congregationalists dissatisfied with the liberal Unitarian tendencies of Harvard to create a Queen's College in western Massachusetts. The nation's oldest college and its Overseers opposed the proposal and prevailed, using the argument that Harvard 'was a provincial monopoly, funded and supported by the General Court for reasons of state' and 'properly the College of the Government' (Herbst 1982: 136). The principle that preserved a monopoly to the 'College of the Government', with its attendant rights and privileges, had to be overthrown for American higher education to break out of the restrictive pattern of higher education that had been historical practice. What is astonishing is not that it was subsequently overthrown, but that it was done with such ease as to scarcely occasion comment. Harvard lost its monopoly in Massachusetts when Williams was founded in 1793, although Yale managed to preserve its special privilege in Connecticut to 1823.

The founding in 1815 of Allegheny College in western Pennsylvania near the Ohio border illustrates the changes that took place after the Revolution in yet another way (E. A. Smith 1916). A group of the leading men in a village of some 400 people came together to establish a college, as others were doing all over the western frontier. The initial group who met in the village of Meadville constituted themselves a board of trustees empowered to create an institution that would bring light and learning to their community. The education was to embody what was then a fairly standard curriculum centring upon the study of Latin, Greek, Hebrew, and classical authorities. Since there were few secondary schools in the region to prepare pupils for higher education, the new board decided to admit a class of 'probationers', boys and young men who, without being fully matriculated for the degree, would undergo instruction for a year or so. Having successfully completed their probationary period, they would be admitted to the college's first class.[4]

The self-appointed trustees of the newly created college applied to the state government of Pennsylvania for a charter. However, without waiting for one to be granted, they immediately appointed a president, who was a Congregational minister, a graduate of Harvard, a headmaster of an eastern secondary school, and a cousin of one of the founders of the college. The founders appear to have had no doubt about the charter, nor much doubt about the possibility that money would be granted by the state legislature, where local representatives would press their case. They appointed a second professor—a local clergyman—and subscribed to the endowment. On the very day of his appointment, the new president of the college was authorized to solicit gifts 'in such parts of the United States as may be deemed proper' (E. A. Smith 1916: 18). A fund-raising tour took him immediately eastward to New England and New York, where he raised some $2,000 in cash and books to add to the $4,000 subscribed by the founders and their friends. As expected, the state of Pennsylvania contributed an additional $2,000 on the occasion of the grant of a charter.

Nevertheless, Allegheny remained in perennial financial difficulty for decades, and its history is marked by constant and almost always unsuccessful appeals to the legislature for support, despite the fact that the charter placed the governor, the chief justice, and the attorney general of Pennsylvania on the board of trustees ex officio. The continuing poverty of almost all American colleges after the Revolution, and the lack of firm guarantees to their survival by public authorities, were crucial to their self-conception and to their relations with the surrounding society. The absence of assured support shaped their responsiveness to the interests of their internal and external constituencies, the numbers and social origins of their students, and the numbers and character of the faculty recruited to teach.[5] The president of Allegheny, in an effort to provide for endowed chairs, approached a local society of Masons, which he had helped found in 1817, and there was talk of establishing an Architectonic Mathematical Professorship. An attempt was made to induce the Germans of Pennsylvania and other parts of the United States to raise a fund 'for a learned professor, whose duty it shall be, not only to teach the comprehensive and energetic German language, but to exercise his talents in disseminating the light of German literature and science.' A gracious letter in German and English was circulated, and the president's plan was laid before the Lutheran and Reformed Synods, but the college was too distant from the German centres of population, and the plan failed (E. A. Smith 1916: 53–4). The college did not gain financial security until it accepted the patronage and authority of the Methodist Church in 1833.

It is perhaps worth noting that the founders of Allegheny College, though frontiersmen, were what the eighteenth century would have considered 'gentlemen', well-educated and not poor farmers. A leading figure had been an officer in the Continental Army. It is also worth noting that the new college president, his cousin on the board, and probably other board members as well, all had interests in a large tract of nearby land being sold by a land development company in parcels to new immigrants to the Northwest Territories. The president had earlier visited that area, and on his return to the East had written fliers and advertisements for the company. Land speculation was and remained a central element in American life, and was so not only in the foundation of Allegheny College, but also in the development of higher education throughout American history. Land speculators all through the western movement assumed that the creation of a college in a region would make property more attractive to immigrants, and thus more valuable. That attitude speaks to the commercial spirit of the society at large, the unembarrassed way in which that spirit could be linked to the establishment of cultural institutions, and the way in which both culture and commerce could be seen to be defences against the barbarism which threatened to overwhelm Americans as they moved yet farther away from the secure and hallowed centres of civilization in the East Coast and Europe.

The founders of Allegheny received their charter two years after the founding of the college, though by that time it was already in operation. And they received it, along with a small subvention from the legislature, with no questions asked about the institution's academic standards. It was enough that the first president was a Harvard man.

The ease with which new colleges were granted charters after the Revolution, and especially after the turn of the century, was itself both symbol and instrument in the triumph of society over the state after the Revolution. Despite the efforts of the Federalists, central government itself over time came to be not the dominant institution in society (alongside the churches), but merely one player in social life, and not a very important one at that. By the fifth decade of the nineteenth century, the national government was scarcely visible in American life: 'no [national] bank, no military worth mentioning, no taxes that a growing majority of citizens could remember paying its officials' (Wiebe 1984: 353). And even state governments, closer to the people and with constitutional responsibility for education, confined their role to serving as the instruments of groups and interests in the society at large, including those who wanted to create colleges for a whole variety of motives: cultural, religious, and mercenary.

TWO NOTABLE FAILURES

But that did not occur without two significant efforts by government, one by the Federal government and the other by a state, to play a more traditionally authoritative role in the world of higher education. The first of these, the proposal to create a national university at the seat of government in Washington, was an effort to give to the federal government an institution for nation-building which would discipline and co-ordinate all the other institutions of higher education in the country, a capstone university whose recognition (we would now say 'accreditation') would give direction and standards to the whole of American secondary and post-secondary education. The second was the effort by the State of New Hampshire to reorganize and reconstitute Dartmouth College as a state institution, something closer to a provincial college than Allegheny College or the many other 'private' foundations being created at about the same time. The first effort was defeated by the Congress, the second by the Supreme Court.

The idea of a national or 'Federal' university was apparently born around the campfires of the Continental Army, but first given expression by Dr Benjamin Rush, a prominent physician and patriot of Philadelphia (Madsen 1966). The idea gained its strongest supporter in George Washington, who urged it on the Congress in his first and last messages, and made a contribution towards it in his will. He argued that it would promote national unity, save young Americans the expense and bother of going abroad for their higher education, and provide the basis for one really first-class university in a country already possessing a goodly number of institutions, all too small and poor to be competitive with the leading European institutions. As he noted in his final message to Congress,

> Our Country, much to its honor, contains many Seminaries of learning highly respectable and useful; but the funds upon which they rest, are too narrow, to command the ablest Professors, in the different departments of liberal knowledge, for the Institution contemplated, though they would be excellent auxiliaries. (Hofstadter and Smith 1961: 158)

Correct in his diagnosis, Washington underestimated the hostility in Congress to any attempt to strengthen the power of Federal institutions, especially one which would have such clear implications for the creation and development of local, state, and regional colleges and universities. And despite efforts to bring the issue back to the Congress by his successors, a national university was never created. For while suggestions to create a University of the United States were not accompanied by proposals to give it a monopoly over higher degrees, it would surely have been, in colonial terms, 'the Government's university', and as such would have had profound effects on all of American higher education. Its standards of entry, curricula, educational philosophies, and forms of instruction would have provided models for every college or 'seminary' which aspired to send some of its graduates to the university in the Capitol. A University of the United States might well have established national academic standards for the bachelor's degree, for the qualifications of faculty, even conceivably for entry to colleges, and in these ways have greatly influenced the character and curriculum of secondary feeder schools. We might speculate that eventually a national university would have shaped and constrained the growth of graduate education and research universities. It would surely have been the central instrument of Federal government policy regarding higher education in the Union. Therefore the defeat of the idea of a University of the United States was arguably the most important policy decision affecting the role of central government in American higher education, determining or at least conditioning the character of all future Federal government interventions.

The spectacular defeat of the idea of a central university needs to be discussed in the same breath with a second event of momentous consequence, the decision by the Supreme Court in 1819 in the case of *The Trustees of Dartmouth College* v. *Woodward* (for the State of New Hampshire), for this too had a profound effect on the place of public authority in the development of an American higher education system (Herbst 1982; Whitehead 1973; Whitehead and Herbst 1986). The New Hampshire state government seized the occasion of a dispute between the President of Dartmouth and its Trustees to attempt to change the college charter in order to bring public representatives directly on to the board. Other changes affecting the governance of the college, its curriculum, and sectarian linkages were also in train. New Hampshire maintained that although Dartmouth may have been established in colonial times as a 'private' corporation, it was founded to benefit the people of the state. Consequently, the public, through the state's legislature, deserved and required a voice in the operation of the college. The State of New Hampshire intended to 'improve' Dartmouth as a place of learning by modernizing its administration and curriculum, creating the framework for a university, and encouraging a freer, non-sectarian atmosphere.

The Trustees, claiming that the State of New Hampshire was illegally modifying Dartmouth's original charter, took its defence to the US Supreme Court, where their position was upheld in a landmark decision written by Chief Justice John Marshall. He wrote that the college was a 'private' rather than a 'civil' corporation, and affirmed the sanctity of the contract (as embodied in its charter) between the state and Dartmouth. In attempting to change the charter, the legislature, he continued, was substituting its own intentions for those of the donors; and the consequence, in his opinion, was that the college would be turned into 'a machine entirely subservient to the will of government' (Hofstadter and Smith 1961: 219). Marshall expressly affirmed the rights of private property over the implicit links of a colonial establishment with its charter-granting government. In this judgment, Dartmouth was not the 'Government's College', as the original colonial colleges had so long been. On the contrary, it was the exclusive possession of its Trustees.

Historians have been debating the significance of the Dartmouth College decision. It has even been argued that the public–private distinction did not occasion much comment at the time and does not seem to have been as central an issue as the secular–sectarian dispute (Whitehead and Herbst 1986: 338). Bailyn, however, has noted that the character and limit of state authority, the definitions of a private right or privilege, were hot issues in the 1780s at the time the Constitution was being framed (Bailyn 1960: 47), and it is difficult to think that Enlightenment ideas about individual or corporate autonomy in the exercise of power were totally absent from the minds of parties to the Dartmouth question. However that may be, the long-run implications seem beyond dispute. The Supreme Court decision, preventing the State of New Hampshire from taking over the institution, or altering its charter, had the practical effect of safeguarding the founding of 'independent' colleges. Henceforth the founders and promoters of private educational ventures knew that once a state charter was obtained, they and their successors were secure in the future control of their investment. The legal basis for the extraordinary proliferation of privately founded and governed higher education institutions in the United States was now in place.

HIGHER EDUCATION POLICY IN BRITAIN AT THE END OF THE EIGHTEENTH CENTURY

At the time of the American Revolution, the interest of the British state in the structure and functioning of higher education was primarily limited to maintaining the religious and political orthodoxy of the nation's universities. Those members who criticized existing arrangements or challenged them in any fundamental way were ejected or neutralized. At Oxford or Cambridge, religious tests were required of undergraduates for admission or graduation; and while no such subscription was necessary in Scotland, a test, albeit unevenly enforced, was imposed on university faculty there. In England, therefore, non-Anglicans could attend the two senior universities only if they were willing to perjure themselves (and submit to obloquy), but in Scotland, where the Presbyterian Church was Established, students of Dissenting and Nonconformist backgrounds were welcome. At Edinburgh and Glasgow, non-Presbyterians held professorships (Anderson 1983*a*: 53). In Ireland, before the Act of Union in the early nineteenth century, an independent Irish Parliament had dispensed with religious tests for conferring degrees at Trinity College, Dublin; but while open to Roman Catholic undergraduates, the offices and emoluments of the college were nevertheless closed to them until the 1870s (Moody 1958).

Where they existed, the requirements for orthodoxy were consistent with a constitution of Church and state and therefore resembled, in certain respects, the higher education practices in effect in American colonies. In England, as in America, no specific government policies existed with respect to those issues now deemed indispensable to the operation of an effective higher education system: admissions and access, curriculum, cost effectiveness, and accountability. To be sure, in Scotland the state (to be precise, the Crown) had long taken a major role in higher education, supplying universities and colleges with a small annual grant. Nevertheless, in both kingdoms the financing of higher education was largely a mixture of market forces and charitable endowments.

Statutes and ordinances, approved over the centuries by the Crown in Council or Parliament, provided in some half a hundred versions the framework of governance in which the ancient collegiate societies of Oxford and Cambridge functioned. The numbers of fellowships and scholarships were specified, as was the internal distribution of appointments according to schools and colleges of origin. Otherwise, in varying degree, the collegiate societies functioned in an astonishingly unrestricted environment, free not only from direct government interference but from what would later be understood and referred to as the force of public opinion. Interference, when it occurred, usually came in the 'acceptable' statutory form of an official 'visit', customarily by a bishop, invited by the fellowship to adjudicate conflicting claims and disputes. Indeed, although it would be an anachronism to say so, the ancient colleges (though not the universities) behaved as if they were 'private' institutions; and perhaps it is not surprising to learn that when, in the 1830s, debates about the public and private roles of higher education institutions occurred, colleges were even legally referred to as 'private'[6] despite a long history of royal interference right into the earlier decades of the eighteenth century.

The Crown (and Parliament) had long demonstrated their authority to revise college statutes. Consequently it was not from such legal safeguards as college constitutions and the habit of self-government that Oxbridge foundations were independent. The colleges of Oxford and Cambridge derived their liberties from an incontestable social fact, namely that their membership shared the values and beliefs of those who sat in Parliament or advised the Crown. Despite low enrolments (a feature of most eighteenth-century European universities), Oxford and Cambridge colleges educated all of the Georgian prime ministers (with two exceptions) and about one-half of all members of Parliament between 1734 and 1812, giving the English governing élite an educational cohesion comparatively unique in Europe (Gascoigne 1989). Such a historical situation did not require an elaboration of the differences between private and public, for the two realms were intertwined. In this the colleges of England were not so dissimilar from their American colonial counterparts, which were also intimately connected to élite society and were responsible for educating the clerical and political leaders of that society, whose patronage and association brought them prestige and, for some, a reasonably comfortable income.

Non-Anglicans, which also means Roman Catholics and Jews, were not closely identified with aristocratic society, although it would be an error to suggest that significant political and economic ties were absent, at least to certain aristocratic segments. Nevertheless, it is correct to say that in general non-Anglicans were excluded from direct participation in government and administration by the operation of a code of electoral laws. Being effectively excluded from Oxford and Cambridge by the requirement of an oath of religious loyalty, and in general ignored by the state, Dissenters had created over the course of the 'long eighteenth century', an alternate educational system for themselves, one that was weakly financed and can be anachronistically but also usefully described as 'private'. The curriculum of the dissenting academies reflected many of the modernizing education tendencies of the time, being stronger in science, social science, and vernacular languages than English schools and colleges, and similar in this respect to some if not all of the Scottish universities.

Whether the academies can be described as a 'higher education system' is problematical. They attracted pupils of high school age (as did Scottish and American institutions), and many of their pedagogical concerns were the consequence of typical adolescent problems such as pupil discipline. Nor did the academies educate candidates for the learned professions, apart from the chapels from which they drew support. While Oxford and Cambridge were also by this point relatively disconnected from the education of potential lawyers and physicians, their undergraduates at least were older, in a range similar to what we might expect today.

DRIFTING TOWARDS A HIGHER EDUCATION POLICY: LONDON AND DURHAM

Of course, no Revolution occurred in Britain to change or alter the existing relationships between the state and its universities and colleges. No Dartmouth decision was needed to separate the sphere of private from public educational activity, and no central government scheme for a national university was considered necessary when in the eyes of many the hoary colleges of Oxford and Cambridge already fulfilled that purpose. The Crown in Parliament was sovereign, not an abstraction called 'the people', and no constitutional institution outside the Crown in Parliament (such as a Supreme Court) existed as a counterweight to the exercise of public authority. Alterations in the relations of the higher education sector to the central government, therefore, were not dependent upon the definition of such abstractions as 'people' or 'society' but on the more concrete details of possible shifts in the attitudes or the social composition of the kingdom's governing institutions, a possible reflection if not always a clear one of larger changes in the nation as a whole.

It is therefore appropriate to speak about changes in state–university relations as more the result of a drift towards public policy than as a sudden and dramatic reversal or alteration, *ad hoc* solutions rather than carefully meditated ministerial decisions. Such drifts in Britain are familiar from other areas of the kingdom's history, and as such reinforce the long-standing opinion of historians that change was essentially piecemeal and improvised, practical responses to specific social problems and rarely a complete overhaul of existing institutions. Compared to adjustments and changes in the system of higher education in the United States, those in nineteenth-century Britain were less haphazard and unpredictable, more consistent in the application of slowly evolving principles, and much less dependent upon a seemingly feckless market economy. Probably the distinctions should not be overdrawn. Both Victorian Britain and Victorian America were liberal cultures. Resemblances existed, especially in the area of private initiative and philanthropy and in the importance of urban localism and local institutions. Yet even so, underneath surface similarities were institutional, legal, and cultural solutions to common problems that indicated profoundly divergent or diverging views on the organization of higher education systems and their primary curricula.

The first signs of the development of a government policy towards higher education in England appeared in the 1820s and 1830s in the controversies surrounding the foundation of the University of London. These led to an independent decision, taken from below, to expand and diversify the provision for higher education in England, and to improve access by opening university education to those groups effectively barred from attending the ancient universities because of cost or religious stigma or both, and prevented from entering the Scottish universities because of distance in the days before railways.

The basic facts concerning the formation of what is now

called University College London but was initially known as the University of London are familiar enough not to require repetition here, yet several aspects of the historical situation deserve special emphasis and elaboration.

The creation of a new university took place at a time of major political change leading to the extension of the franchise, the removal of civil disabilities from Dissenters and Roman Catholics (but not Jews), and the growth of a liberal philosophy of private endeavour. Recent research has pretty well established that a surprising amount of educational initiative took place in the final decades of the eighteenth century and early decades of the new century in an active market economy, heavily weighted towards consumer choice and discipline and even involving brand-name recognition.[7] The University of London was founded hard on the heels of this expansion of consumer interest. It was also created at a time when the numbers of non-Anglicans had greatly increased, so that any notion of an Anglican Establishment based on the majority, as, for example, advanced by Bishop Warburton in the mid-eighteenth century, was coming under fire. The formation of the University of London can be seen in two ways, either as a departure from the older pattern of college-building or as the final instalment in the system of educational institutions created by Dissenters over a century earlier, except that the founders also included moderate Anglicans, Roman Catholics, Jews, and secular-minded urban intellectuals essentially of non-aristocratic origins.[8]

The title 'university' was chosen in preference to 'academy' or 'college' for both symbolic and practical considerations, as the association of the word with Oxford and Cambridge, the Scottish universities, and the new institutions being founded in Germany and the United States carried overtones of prestige.[9] Actually, before the degree battles of the 1830s, no legal or commonly agreed upon definition of a 'university' existed, either in Britain or the United States. The issue had simply not arisen before, and nothing could be more apparent than the confusion of contemporaries arguing the case for uncertain precedents and groping for historical antecedents. The differences between 'college' or 'university' appeared to be clearest in the case of Oxford and Cambridge because of the division of functions that had arisen since the Middle Ages; but several Scottish universities, notably Glasgow and St Andrews, also possessed colleges, and there the distinctions were unclear since the colleges were less boarding establishments for the wealthy than a device for supplementing the incomes of the teaching staff. North of the Tweed the words 'college' and 'university' were virtually synonymous (Malden 1835), a lexical habit that decisively influenced American usage.

The new university did not seek nor did it receive a royal charter of incorporation. At law, the university was established as a business corporation or joint stock company, financed from the sale of shares, but the potential return on investments was limited as an answer to public criticism that the new university was not an educational undertaking but a profit-oriented enterprise. This strategem—for such it appears to have been—was doubtless adopted in order to maintain the institution's independence and status as a private venture, for otherwise, as a chartered or endowed or charitable institution, it would have fallen by law under the jurisdiction of Church and state and their legal and administrative instruments, such as the newly founded body of charity commissioners.

The University of London had not insisted on the right to grant degrees. The strategy of the founders, we have suggested, was to avoid additional controversies (the University was non-denominational and secular) that might imperil its existence as a corporate body. A royal charter of incorporation carried certain risks: the threat of state interference, the opposition of the High Church Oxbridge lobby. The power to award degrees likewise offended Church and state, but would also provoke the hostility and promote the rivalry of the hospital-based medical profession, since the new University also included a medical 'department'. In the next decade, however, the University reversed itself, doubtless encouraged by the reform movements that allowed both Dissenters and Roman Catholics to take seats in the House of Commons, the vigorous attack on Anglican privileges, and controversies over passage of the Reform Bill. Yet it is appropriate to assume that the right to grant degrees had been more or less entertained from the start, for the suggestion had even once been made that some sort of degree-granting authority might be obtained from an increasingly reform-minded House of Commons if the royal assent was out of the question. In 1830 the degree hardly possessed the career value now attached to it, but it was of some use in medicine, and also represented the final stage in the long-standing efforts by the marginalized groups of English society to obtain something like educational parity. Or, as stated by the newly appointed Professor of Greek, academic degrees 'impart to those who bear them a literary rank, not only in their own country, but wherever learning is cultivated. It is this identity and universal acceptation . . . which has sustained their value,' despite, he added, with a nod to the controversies of the 1830s, 'the undue facility with which they are granted in some instances' (Malden 1838: 3).

The godless institution in Gower Street was organized on the plan of a Scottish unitary institution rather than an English collegiate university, but for all practical purposes it appeared to be only a university college. Could a college award degrees? Historically (or so it appears to us) the authority to award degrees was not essential to the definition of a university (Williams 1910: 14–15). The sixteenth-century foundation, Trinity College, Dublin, was empowered to grant degrees—given the distance of Dublin from the imperial capital and other institutions with which it might affiliate, a separate degree-granting authority made sense. Yet Trinity College, a university college in size, had been founded as the nucleus of a collegiate university but had never grown into one. The Irish case both conformed to and departed from English precedent. It conformed because it was collegiate, at least in theory or principle, and it departed because Ireland was self-governing before the nineteenth century.

The original University of London lost the battle to obtain a royal charter which authorized the institution to grant degrees. It is simple enough to identify the parties to the dispute but difficult to explain the outcome. The Church Party in the Lords opposed—the bishops especially were in an anti-reform mood—but not the Commons. The Privy Council was divided but perhaps inclined to approve, and probably the Cabinet too (their membership overlapped), but in the event what emerged from the deliberations and controversies was an odd compromise. A new and fundamentally different institution with no teaching responsibilities was chartered, receiving the right to grant degrees and to charge and collect examination and degree fees. Another charter without degree-giving authority was granted to the original University of London—a rival Anglican institution, King's College, already possessing a similar one—and both institutions were officially designated university colleges. The new University itself was a 'public' or state-supported institution, administered by a miniscule staff that was virtually a committee of the Treasury. A Senate was composed of academics (none of them drawn from the London colleges) and professional men who were nominees of the Privy Council. The government's Office of Works maintained the premises. Its exclusive function was the setting and administering of degree examinations. The two university colleges were 'private', possessing their own governing councils. They enjoyed the option of preparing students for the degree examinations; and until the next major reform at mid-century when examinations were thrown open to all who had passed a London matriculation examination irrespective of their prior education, it was very nearly an exclusive enjoyment.

This peculiar settlement, giving the state the special right to set examinations for a university system, has been so little studied in detail that its origins remain relatively obscure. It was the outcome of a protracted and bitter fight in which all the authorities of Church and state partook. The result was the exact opposite of the Dartmouth decision. At the end of it, the involvement of the state in higher education affairs was in principle greater. A more directive role from the centre was now possible under the terms of a liberal parliamentary constitution, and new mechanisms for regulating expansion, curricular change, access, and diversity were being gradually created. Most of the implications of the solution of 1836 lay in the future, but the shift was discernible. And behind this shift lay another one, also gradual but unmistakable, namely, the loss of parliamentary supremacy by a class of landed gentlemen whose identification with the ancient universities was on the whole so complete that interference in the running of the colleges was thought unnecessary. As Oxford and Cambridge 'separated' themselves from landed society, their relationship with the state assumed a new formality and structure. The University of London of 1836 foreshadowed this change.

The new University of London also established a far-reaching precedent for the formation of new higher education institutions in Britain and the Empire. Henceforth, any new English foundation was required to begin its corporate life as a university college if degrees were sought, and in Ireland, Wales, Canada, and elsewhere, federations on the London model were formed. Even in Scotland, with its own traditions, a new university college scheduled to open at Dundee in 1883 entered its students for the London examinations (Anderson 1983*a*: 82).[10]

Merely stating the bare facts leading to the birth of the examining University of London is in itself a significant illustration of many of the differences in university-building between Britain and the United States. In the new nation, established and competing governmental structures were relatively ineffective. State monopolies were being abandoned or were becoming weak, and entrenched educational interests were unable to resist market challenges. There was no movement comparable to the one in England to create precise legal and institutional definitions or establish a widely accepted degree standard of achievement.

The case of the foundation of Durham University is especially interesting, for its history also helps us understand the higher education issues of the critical decade of the 1830s. Various schools and colleges had at one time or another existed in Durham for centuries, and Cromwell and his Privy Council had actually founded a college in 1657, probably on the model of 'schools' like Eton or Winchester. But no plan really ever succeeded, and the establishment of Durham University in 1832 was a genuine innovation. Durham began as an endowed institution drawing its income from the ample revenues of the Dean and Chapter of Durham Cathedral with the assistance of the Bishop (who was also Dean). While supporters of a higher education foundation in the diocesan city spoke often of an emerging demand for general education in the north, it is more certain that their actions were 'a sort of panic' (Fowler 1904: 22), a response to bitter attacks on the Church's politics and extraordinary wealth, derived increasingly from the lucrative coalfields of the diocese. In the 1820s and 1830s the hammer of Durham was the radical party of Dissenters, supporters of popular education and parliamentary reformers who used every opportunity in a tempestuous period of political change to threaten the Church with disestablishment or to withdraw its tithes. Durham's response was to attempt to disarm the 'incendiaries' (as one member of the Church phrased it) by using 'surplus' income to establish a university. Besides, rivals loomed on the horizon. The Dissenters talked of establishing a university in the industrial communities of Newcastle or Liverpool (Tempest 1960) and Anglican rivals had their eye on York.

The earliest Durham documents refer to the desire to establish either a college or a university, the two words appearing interchangeably, some supporters actually favouring a theological seminary, for which the word 'college' would have sufficed, as a number of theological training colleges already existed. The more influential backers, however, promoted the idea of a degree-granting institution, for which the word 'university' seemed to them more appropriate, having always in mind the organization and model of Oxbridge. They argued that the gentry of the North would settle for nothing less (especially as bishops would refuse to ordain any but graduates). Nevertheless, Durham really began, as did King's and London, as a university college. The statutes of 1834 identified the 'Warden of the College' as also the Vice-Chancellor of the University (Fowler 1904: 26). At this point the founders may have been using the college idea to emphasize the private nature of their undertaking. Their specific educational model was actually Christ Church, Oxford, where a cathedral organization and higher education were intertwined, the Dean and members of the Chapter also occupying academic posts in the House.

But if Christ Church was the model for the governance structure of Durham, the University of Cambridge provided the example of a collegiate university which appeared to supply an answer to the thorny question of admitting Dissenters. For at Cambridge, graduation but not matriculation required subscription. The division was accordingly this: as a university, Durham was public, as the university at Cambridge was in some sense public, as the new University of London was public. As such Durham was an 'open' university, its lectures available to all comers on the payment of appropriate fees. However, its degrees were only available to those who were enrolled in privately-endowed colleges, subject to collegiate discipline, willing to attend chapel and free in conscience to subscribe to the doctrine of the United Church of England and Ireland.[11]

It is an ironic development that while the supporters of the first University of London in Gower Street feared—and rightly feared—the power of the Church, the founders of the University of Durham, at approximately the same time, feared the power of the state as it might be wielded by what they saw as a formidable radical alliance. The supporters of clerical London created an institution that taught religion and placed students under a conventional religious discipline. The friends of secular London fought this English conception of a university, insisting upon a type similar to those being founded abroad, such as the University of Berlin or Bonn or Virginia. They wanted a university that would admit non-Anglicans, a University of the North that had been discussed by them for about a decade, a university every bit as strong in historical conception as the Oxbridge idea defended by the partisans of the Established Church.[12]

While planning the new institution, Durham's founders attempted to keep their deliberations relatively private, suspecting that Dissenters and parliamentary radicals would use every opportunity to disrupt the scheme. It was hoped that a new institution could be founded without much fanfare, but two factors made relative silence impossible. The first was the desire to grant degrees. The second was the necessity to steer a bill through Parliament—in this case, a private bill—legally authorizing the Dean and Chapter to transfer Church property to a different foundation. Since the consent of Parliament was therefore unavoidable, it was planned to originate a bill in the Lords, as the Chamber friendlier to the Church (Whiting 1932: 39–40).

In 1832, an Act of Parliament was passed enabling 'the Dean and Chapter of Durham to appropriate part of the property of their Church to the establishment of a university in connection therewith' (ibid.: 42). Did the Act constituting the University also empower it to grant degrees? Apparently the question was not settled to the satisfaction of the Dean and Chapter, perhaps because, whatever the specific powers granted under the Act, the Chapter itself had not yet agreed upon the exact type of institution it wanted. The matter required further clarification, and the Chapter subsequently decided to seek a royal charter. Several years of delay followed because of the opposition of Dissenters and the entry of yet another player, a newly created body of Ecclesiastical Commissioners appointed by the Crown to deliberate upon the redistribution of Church emoluments generally. A charter finally passed the Great Seal on 1 June 1837. Acknowledging that the University of Durham had been in existence for some time—a reference to the Act of 1832—the charter went on to add 'that the said University would be better established, and its character and design more clearly and appropriately determined, if its members were incorporated by Our Royal Charter' (ibid.: 71–4). The degrees now clearly authorized were conferred seven days later.[13]

While in the US the distinction between 'school', 'college', and 'university' was nowhere clearly spelled out, the words retaining the ambiguities common to the English-speaking world before the nineteenth century, in Britain the degree issue of the 1830s produced a legal meaning with important ramifications for the future organization of higher education: universities conferred degrees, colleges did not. Furthermore, higher education institutions could now be divided into Church-related and secular institutions, each for the time being responding to a different aspect of state authority. The Church, because it was Established and thus part of the state, was allowed to retain its historical role in higher education for all institutions on the Oxbridge model. The new and emerging secular part of the higher education system was put under state direction in a different way: through control over degrees. The state had declared the question of educational qualifications to be a matter of the public interest, too important to be left to the separate institutions or their teachers. It had also shown itself to be suspicious of the operation of the highly active consumer market in education generally that had developed since the eighteenth century, since that market had produced a greatly diversified elementary and secondary school system whose standards of achievement or religious disposition could not be easily guaranteed, although there was certainly evidence to suggest that whatever else it might have achieved, market discipline had also encouraged positive efforts at improvement.

In the 1830s the state's new interest in higher education was as yet unclarified and certainly, in retrospect, incomplete. The financing of higher education in England was still regarded as much more of a private than a public matter. The structure of the University of London did not alarm a fiscally conservative Treasury, since fees scheduled to meet the costs of administering and marking examinations could more or less cover expenditures. Yet what had been established in 1836 by the chartering of the second University of London was in principle far-reaching, a recognition that standards set and administered at the top of a system could reverberate throughout, creating barriers and constraints. '[I]n the ordinary course of proceeding', wrote an interested contemporary, 'it is plain that the examinations of the University will regulate the instruction of the Colleges and the studies of their pupils' (Malden 1838: 5). Degree examinations influenced teaching, the curriculum, innovation, diversity, and 'articulation', the name given by Americans in the early twentieth century to that process by which one type of educational institution was linked to another, primary to secondary schools, secondary schools to colleges and universities, and one kind of college or university to another. As the degree increased in value in the course of the nineteenth century, in response to the expansion of the civil service and the service economy more generally, the importance of examinations in certifying competence and regulating entry into the occupational structure likewise increased, fulfilling the hopes of those who believed in the necessity for standards to be set at the top of the educational system rather than derived from below (Rothblatt 1987).

GOVERNMENT POLICY IN SCOTLAND

This sketch of the drift to a higher education policy in England, however, leaves something to be desired in explaining Scotland. In some respects, Victorian Britain had a federal constitution.

While Ireland and Scotland no longer had independent parliaments, both were governed from Westminster but often as if they were indeed separate nations, which in fact in so many ways they were. In higher education the universities of Scotland, like Oxford and Cambridge, were Church and state institutions, linked to the Crown and the Presbyterian settlement and through mythistory to the Scottish people themselves.[14] Arrangements dating back before the Union of 1707 had put the universities in receipt of annual subsidies from the revenues of the Sovereign, principally in support of professorial chairs, but assistance in the construction and maintenance of buildings had also been available. In the 1820 at least one-half of all chair appointments were therefore made by the Crown, which also enjoyed ancient powers of visitation. But not all Scottish universities were under the same funding arrangements. Edinburgh, for example, had long been considered a 'town university' since the burgh controlled professorial appointments and handled the university's financial administration, and used this authority to interfere in the regular running of the institution (Anderson 1983*a*).

Like Oxford and Cambridge, the governance of the Scottish universities was based on an immense tangle of inherited ordinances and statutes which hampered their ability to respond to nineteenth-century changes in the economy, society, and in the relation of cities to countryside. As in England and the United States, a further difficulty lay in the definition of what could be considered higher or lower education. That difficulty was being eased at Oxford or Cambridge by the arrival in the eighteenth century of an older student (perhaps bearing some relation to the creation of the Cambridge honours degree, the first written examination in Britain), although the dons were slow to adjust their systems of discipline accordingly (for examinations see Rothblatt 1974; 1982). However, since in Scotland undergraduates were most often if not invariably quite young, the absence of a well-defined secondary system of education made differentiating between a university or college or high school somewhat difficult. (Indeed, several supporters of the original University of London contemplated having a school on the model of the High School in Edinburgh.) Professors were consequently fully engaged in a form of remedial education known as the 'junior classes' (Anderson 1983*a*: 4), wherein under-prepared students were brought up to snuff. These were similar to, and probably the forebears of, the 'preparatory departments' of American colleges in the nineteenth century. As Scottish society changed, virtually every feature of university life was the subject of acrimonious dispute. Great divisions of feeling existed with regard to governance, financing, the curriculum and the founding of new chairs, the proper tone or character of a university education, graduation rates, degrees and examinations, access, and the social or 'gentlemanly' functions of education, the latter a typically English concern and as such reflecting the Anglicization of Scotland.

The combination of archaic regulations and the log-jam of constitutional and jurisdictional disputes, the division of authority between academic Senates, town councils and religious bodies, and professional associations, as well as the growing quarrels within the Kirk that finally, in 1842, produced the Disruption and the Free Churches—in fact, the extraordinarily complicated interdependence of the universities and virtually every aspect of Scottish life—brought the Crown into the story as the only available mechanism for resolving disputes. Beginning in 1826 and meeting almost continuously through the rest of the century, a series of royal and executive ('statutory' in England) commissions discussed, mediated, and sometimes acting through Parliament but at other times using their own legal authority to do so, legislated far-reaching changes for the Scottish universities. The Treasury also played a part, especially in the second half of the century. While changes were discussed and pressed from the top, important unlegislated changes were occurring from below, most notably in the development of an effective secondary educaton sector which in time boosted the age of entering cohorts and made possible a greater degree of curricular specialization and variation.

For present purposes it is not necessary to review the enormous number of alterations legislated or recommended for legislation by the commissions, or the internal reforms stimulated by them and by wider social changes generally to repeat the point so well argued by Robert Anderson that by law, history, and popular agreement, the power of the Crown to legislate for the Scottish universities was never really questioned until the Edwardian period. No more than in, let us say, nineteenth-century Sweden was the state in Scotland regarded as different and separate from society. So far was this point accepted, that it did not appear shocking that few if any professors were actually members of the many Scottish commissions of inquiry that met in the Victorian era. And indeed this same point was made even more forcefully in the early twentieth century by the Secretary of the Carnegie Trust, who thought that the Scottish higher education establishment was even more tightly controlled than the German one (Anderson 1983*a*: 291).

Among the welter of issues considered, the 'London' problem of assuring a high level of academic achievement stands out. This question, in fact, antedated London and drew the attention of the very first royal commission on universities to be appointed in the nineteenth century, the Scottish Royal Commission of 1826, and it continued to be addressed in one form or another by all subsequent commissioners. The 1826 Commission proposed the introduction of an honours degree, compulsory essays, and class prizes, drew attention to the need for a higher attendance record and a much greater devotion to the study of classical languages—all as ways of encouraging incentive, competition, and academic rigour. Hitherto, the Scottish curriculum had been characterized by a concern for breadth, represented by a special emphasis on metaphysics, which observers who were influenced by the type of honours examinations developed at Oxford and Cambridge considered too vague and general.[15] Other obstacles to higher standards were thought to be the system of parochial schools, which fed immature and under-age pupils into the universities, thus necessitating the system of junior classes, part-time students, and low graduation rates. A major issue for the century, therefore, was shaping up in the 1820s, and can at some risk of simplification be described as a contest between those who believed in the Scottish system of relatively open admissions and were therefore willing to accept high drop-out rates as a legitimate trade-off, and those who wished, although in accordance with other Scottish traditions, to drive the system towards an élite model by tightening standards throughout, making more effective use of degree examinations to accomplish this end. By and large, American practice has been closer to the first of these positions than to the second.

More than a quarter of a century later, several highly influential academics adopted a modification of the London idea in proposing a single board of degree examiners for all of Scotland. But such modification would have interfered with the respected professorial system of combining teaching and examining and was effectively beaten back. What ultimately emerged by the end of the nineteenth century was a compromise, with degree examinations and honours courses more broadly based than in the kingdom to the south, but with higher entrance standards, an older entering student, the disappearance of close ties between the parochial and largely rural schools and the universities, and the evanescence after about 1890 of the junior classes.

ROYAL COMMISSIONS OF INQUIRY AND HIGHER EDUCATION

For several decades now a controversy has taken place over whether the Scottish higher education system with its strongly independent history was forced to conform with English practice in the course of the nineteenth century, transforming an essentially 'democratic' curriculum and entry policy into an 'aristocratic' or élite system (Anderson 1983*a*; Davie 1961; 1986). The Scottish higher education curriculum system today is a mixture of Scottish and English features, but in such matters as financing and access it conforms to the general English model. In relation to the state, Anderson is very persuasive: the Scottish universities and colleges have never been truly independent. Instead, therefore, of thinking about the reforms in Scottish education as travelling up the high road from England, we can also think of important changes travelling in the opposite direction, and the history of royal commissions of inquiry certainly makes this point.

As we have seen, some twenty-five years before the decision was taken to appoint royal commissions in England to inquire into the financing, distribution of emoluments, governance, and admission policies of the ancient universities, and to create statutory commissions to assist Oxford and Cambridge colleges in revising their ancient statutes, a royal commission was at work in Scotland. The machinery of investigation that was being developed by the nineteenth-century state to collect information, investigate practices, and recommend legislation for a great many social issues, was also being used to redraw the contours of the higher education system. Over half a century of activity, the state and its representatives, temporary or permanent, acquired great experience conducting systematic investigations, learning to ask the operative questions, and pinpointing the necessary sources of information. The result was a habit of putting higher education on the national agenda. The role of higher education in society, the economy, and Empire therefore became a matter of wide-ranging interest and discussion, well-covered in the newspapers and burgeoning 'serious' journalism of the Victorian era.

But the creation of a state apparatus of reform was not an independent development. It was accompanied by, perhaps influenced by, and certainly related to changes in the character and composition of what we customarily denominate the 'state'. Historians have debated the nature and effect of such changes, attempting to assess the impact of franchise reform on the social composition of cabinets, parliaments, and the bureaucracy. Apparently no sweeping changes occurred—indeed, the social composition of Parliament did not appreciably change until the second half of the nineteenth century, and the Cabinet remained heavily aristocratic until even later (Aydelotte 1962; Guttsman 1963). The bureaucracy did change—at least segments of it—and in fact had been very gradually changing since the last years of the eighteenth century, the principle of employment by merit rather than patronage insinuating itself into ministries and departments, bringing into administration the 'statesmen in disguise' of which George Kitson Clark once spoke (Clark 1973; Wickwire 1965). These were by and large the new, highly educated Victorian mandarins, competent, influential, astonishingly well connected. The new blood was largely of reformed public boarding-school and Oxbridge origins, inheriting an aristocratic ethic of service and an evangelical ethic of responsibility, and represented as well the growth of the professional sector that was to play such a decisive role in the evolution of the British state (Annan 1955).[16] By contrast, the defeat of the University of the United States and the subsequent weakness of the Federal government in higher education ensured that the American governmental bureaucracy would be staffed more on the principle of patronage than on merit, a pattern only partly modified by civil service reformers of the twentieth century. Indeed, that may have been a motive of Congress in its defeat.

Whatever their specific views on the purposes of education, the new mandarins were more or less united by some version of the liberal political outlook so characteristic of nineteenth-century thought. As far as possible, reform from above was to be accomplished on the cheap. It was to be achieved through a redistribution of existing sources rather than, with some exceptions, a supply of new resources. When applied to the heavily endowed educational sector of Oxbridge colleges, this policy of living off one's own meant that a vast and baffling array of inherited special privileges, exemptions, and emoluments designated as 'founder's kin', most of which was embodied in statutes, wills, and trusts, was subject to review and alteration. Only the state could invade wills and trusts (although their provisions could be evaded in the absence of vigilant oversight). Interestingly enough, in this matter, as noted in the Dartmouth College case, the American legal system was more conservative, more respectful of the intentions of founders, though of course in the United States wills, trusts, and charters did not extend back before the seventeenth century. But in England pressure from above could not be easily contained, especially since privilege and exemption were inevitably linked to other functioning parts of the educational system; and in over half a century of state activity the universities of Britain in effect drew closer to the state.

They drew closer despite a governmental policy of financial stringency, and the state's role in reshaping the existing system of higher education and in establishing standards for the newer, secular university system cannot be underestimated. The Scottish universities, because they had long been in receipt of annual grants, were allowed to keep their subsidy, but with one major alteration in the source of financing. In 1832 the annual grant derived from the Crown's hereditary revenues was transferred to Parliament, the amount being determined either by Act or annual vote (Shinn 1986: 22). The Sovereign's interest was therefore transformed into a public interest, and both Parliament and the Treasury were reluctant to do more. In 1883, under pressure from the Scottish academic community to increase support to their universities, the government proposed a funding solution that appeared to imply a hands-off policy for the future. Indeed, in responding to the surprised Scots and their Westminster representatives, the Treasury replied that government policy was 'to start the Universities with a fair and efficient endowment from the state in addition to their other resources'. As far as possible, in the interests of their freedom, 'the Universities . . . should economize for themselves their resources and mould for themselves their forms of active life' (Anderson 1983*a*: 259).[17]

Newer, and as it invariably happened, under-endowed or under-capitalized institutions, were treated cautiously. A small annual subsidy to the University of London was made after it was chartered in 1836, the state in effect supporting its own creation, its own 'national' university. When Manchester (Owens College) asked for financial support in 1852, it was told that government policy forbade offering money to higher education. However, after Manchester was federated with the Victoria University, another examining body formed to regulate the curriculum of a group of northern university colleges, a small subvention was eventually if hesitatingly arranged. In 1872 Aberystwyth in Wales received the same message as Owens College, but a decade later the newly formed examining University of Wales received an *ad hoc* grant (Shinn 1986: 23). Finally in 1889 a scheme of assisting the newer civic universities was agreed upon in light of weak local support relative to the changing missions of higher education. The Treasury still assumed and hoped that government assistance would merely supplement rather than supplant private beneficence.[18] Indeed, local aid was made a precondition for state assistance (ibid.: 23, 28, 60), and the transition to a new form of university–state financial relationship may now be said to have truly commenced.

The case for state assistance to higher education in the nineteenth century was not put by the mandarins at Whitehall but by educational lobbies and pressure groups, scientists, and other groups of academicians and Victorian intellectuals. Their reasons were many. Some were concerned about 'culture', others about the possible effects of a consumer ethic on educational standards, still others about economic and military competition with Germany in an era of changing technology. The fundamental fear, however, was that the adoption of a research mission in conjunction with what historically had been a teaching mission would prove more costly than the market could or would support. This was an argument that the state found itself unable to resist in the long run. In the meantime it followed nineteenth-century precedents, proceeding cautiously by limiting financial support to higher education to relatively small amounts, often on an annual or *ad hoc* basis, thus respecting the wishes of the Victorian taxpayer.[19]

One recent writer, discussing the relationship of the British state to science, has called it a 'reluctant patron' (Alter 1987). The description is apt when describing systematic government policy with regard to research and development. In general nineteenth-century Westminster preferred to rely on private initiative and private sources of assistance to encourage science and technology, although the various ministries of government each compiled a different record in connection with support of various kinds of applied science activities. For the British state was not a monolithic body but a collection of ministries and practices representing different traditions of government involvement with society.[20] These had been formed during the long period of aristocratic domination, but from approximately the 1830s onwards encountered an advancing liberal philosophy of private initiative. The result was a society of two cultures, one representing the aristocratic, metropolitan centre, the other the decentralized periphery of the provincial business and professional communities.[21] The contradictions are probably best captured in the work of a new generation of mid-Victorian schools inspectors. Civil servants such as Daniel Robert Fearon admired local initiative. In his London rounds Fearon tried to encourage the best emerging practices, but in yet other ways he remained *dirigiste*, and inclined towards administrative rationalization (Bryant 1986: 278–84).

CONCLUSION

British higher education policies and practices before 1860 increasingly diverged from American ones, reflecting the greater interest of central government in higher education. The various anomalies and carry-overs that had long characterized the higher education system were gradually either eliminated or modified, and the system itself was greatly if not completely rationalized. Rationalization consisted of separating elements hitherto considered as one. For example, gradually but surely Church influence over higher education was either removed by the end of the nineteenth century or confined to the 'private' sector of colleges. As secular and lay influence grew, the state assumed a more dominant role in higher education, taking a special interest in establishing machinery to guarantee the protection of academic standards from market forces. The invention of the examining university was a further rationalization of the system, an ingenious solution to an impending difficulty, creating and preserving a distinction between 'college' and 'university' by taking advantage of the newly discovered interest in competitive and qualifying examinations and by using the growing desire for degrees to regulate entry into select occupations. As a further refinement, degrees were subdivided into honours and ordinary. The university 'idea' was imposed on the system from above as a 'higher' idea and became in time the mark of a superior institution (Rothblatt 1989*a*), universities being also 'public' or 'national', the repositories of a higher mission, colleges remaining 'private' and parochial, the repositories of special or limited missions. Given this new and emerging conception of a university, it was easier for the Treasury or Parliament to justify expenditure on universities than on university colleges, and the state consequently chartered and funded the new examining universities with less reluctance than in the case of civic and municipal colleges as a legitimate sphere of activity, as well as a cheap and effective instrument of quality control. In sum, higher education began to be treated as a 'system', reflecting the drift towards a government policy.

If such rationalization of the higher education system is

characteristic of nineteenth-century Britain, it is less characteristic of the American system before the Civil War. It was not until after the 1860s that rationalization of higher education became an appealing idea. Before then, the collapse of the colonial political structure led to an increasing diversity of institutional forms, resulting in the promiscuous chartering of colleges, the failure of the idea of a national university, and the outcome of the Dartmouth College case. The first 'university' was not created until after the Revolution (Harvard, in 1780), and in this instance the word designated or reflected the presence of one or more professional schools attached to a liberal arts college. Yet this operational definition of a university never became legal or in any way official, and the word retained the ambiguities it possessed in Britain before the 1830s. The words 'university' and 'college' remained synonymous in everyday usage. A university in the United States was no more or less authorized to grant degrees than a college, and aspiring universities did not have to begin life as university colleges affiliated with degree-granting, examination centres with *de facto* control over the teaching syllabus. The titles 'university' and 'college' conveyed no sense of 'private' or 'public'; and while the title 'university' might be coveted by 'any college that aspired to be grand, as did numerous institutions in the South and West' (Hofstadter and Metzger 1955: 369), elsewhere a 'college', especially an older one, was equally and often more prestigious. No higher 'idea' of a university successfully emerged, and all ideas of a university were in practice considered meritorious (Rothblatt 1989*a*).

It is true that the American Revolution separated Church and state; but religious associations continued to influence the expansion of higher education, as indeed they did in Britain up through the 1830s, with a brief spurt again just after mid-century when Keble College was founded at Oxford and Selwyn College at Cambridge. But American denominational colleges and universities were founded continuously and in substantial numbers throughout the nineteenth century in a religiously plural environment, the secular and religious spheres intermixed in a broadly ecumenical Protestant spirit (even in Roman Catholic institutions). Furthermore, while the Supreme Court 'legally' distinguished private from public and prevented states from automatically assuming control of independently created foundations, the distinctions continued to be confused or convergent in a nation which rendered both conceptions subservient to a notion of 'community' and in parallel fashion had replaced service to Church and state with service to 'society' (Whitehead and Herbst 1986). It is not even certain that at the time of the Dartmouth decision, the preservation of a hard and fast distinction between public and private was intended, though it contributed to its crystallization.

In any case, the vulnerable financial position of most new independent foundations settled the issue in a special way, as they turned for assistance to 'society' (which in America included the 'state'), that is to say, to the market. To a certain extent, the same development occurred in the free market society of nineteenth-century Britain where new, under-financed university colleges went in search of patrons. However, the ease with which degrees could be given in America and the absence of any such conception as an 'examining university' or a 'national' or 'imperial' university (although the London experience was known) left new institutions vulnerable to consumer influence on the curriculum and degree programmes, producing early (1820s) experiments in a modular course structure which today is still criticized for lacking coherence and integration (Rothblatt 1989*b*). Doubtless this necessity was reinforced by the governing structure of higher education institutions, by the combination of weak or non-existent regent houses or academic senates and strong lay boards incorporating a mix of social, political, and economic interests. The guild idea of self-government was attenuated, and academics did not have a logical, a 'natural' or historical centre to which they could automatically turn for financial or academic support.

In Britain, with its long history of centralized activity and royal and parliamentary authority, there was such a logical or natural centre. But ironically the Victorian state was reluctant to be an outright patron of universities. Once the state had put universities on its desired funding basis, principally to make them accessible to the broad and influential body of non-aristocratic rate-payers—the bald-headed men at the back of the omnibus, as Lord Macaulay once referred to English public opinion—it preferred to leave actual governance to the academy.

This action strengthened the traditional guild idea of university governance. The bi-cameral constitution of most universities placed governance in the hands of a body of graduates and a body of residents, and by the end of the nineteenth century or the beginning of the twentieth, the former had lost ground to the latter. The absence now of mediating bodies, the removal of the Church or alumni or the 'public' or 'society', placed university–state relations on a new and direct footing, setting in motion the negotiations that eventually led to the creation of a new 'mediator', the University Grants Committee, yet another legacy—it can be argued—of creative Victorian liberal statecraft.

In the United States the lines of governance continued to be seriously blurred. No body of learned men or women succeeded in separating control of higher education from the wide community of interested citizens who had enlisted universities and colleges in the battle for survival against barbarism and never ceased to leave them alone. So as British universities became more 'national' in the nineteenth century, American ones remained 'provincial', still served their states, regions, and localities, each attempting, as their numbers grew, to find a special niche in the market. Not until the twentieth century, and especially after the Second World War, did certain research universities or élite colleges aspire to a wider role, either through the adoption of national admissions policies or through the establishment and expansion of graduate research and professional education. These policies were not always appreciated by lay boards, alumni, or in the case of public universities, state legislatures, whose loyalties and affections lay with those communities whose essential support in the last century prevented the emergence of those 'clearer' lines of demarcation appearing in contemporary Britain.[22]

The system of higher education in place today in Britain and the United States emerged after 1860. But by that date, directions of the two systems were already visible. In the UK, a greater interest by Westminster in higher education was leading to rationalization, policy, and increasing central control. In the US the role of Washington was subordinate to state and private initiative. Federal policy, except in a negative sense, hardly existed; and when it did emerge after the Civil War, it was remarkably self-denying, tending to drive authority and decisions down and away from the Capitol toward statehouses, institutions, teachers, and students. The differences between the two countries in their policies toward their colleges and universities have continued to widen and deepen. It is an open question whether the British government reforms of the 1980s reversed those long trends.

NOTES

1. 'From the very beginnings, the expressed purpose of colonial education had been to preserve society against barbarism, and, so far as possible, against sin' writes Henry May (1978: 32–3). He also points out that the European Enlightenment was a movement of towns, and towns were not so central to early nineteenth-century America or to the colonial period. The importance of education was consequently magnified. 'Nothing in the colonies remotely resembled the serene stagnation of Gibbon's Oxford' (ibid.: 34). Recent work—see Dame Lucy Sutherland (1973)—has shown that Gibbon's Oxford had a 'hidden' educational economy of some vitality, but the spirit of the point holds.
2. Another historian observes that 'The founders [of the mid-eighteenth-century colonial colleges] . . . transplanted the essentials of the educational system of the English dissenting academies and saw the system take root' (McAnear 1955: 44).
3. For remarks on funding in relation to institutional independence, see Bailyn 1960.
4. This pattern of a preparatory year in lieu of secondary school was a common feature of American colleges and universities until the establishment of a broad system of public high schools around the end of the nineteenth century. It also helps explain the radical variability of academic standards in the American college and university, a variability which reflected the diversity of the student body. A similar pattern persists today. Indeed, the absence of a 'reliable' system of secondary schooling characterized both English and Scottish higher education until the last decades of the nineteenth century, producing dilemmas in the higher education system corresponding to those found in the United States. However, England and Scotland acted strongly to resolve those dilemmas by introducing high and roughly common standards of entry to universities, while the US has accepted and continues to live with them.

5. On the links between student recruitment and college finance and function, see Allmendinger 1975.
6. *Substance of the Speech of Sir Charles Wetherell before the Lords of the Privy Council on the Subject of Incorporating the London University* (London, 1834), 23.
7. See Hans 1951 and Bryant 1986. An ethic of consumption had long since spread to the colonies. According to one historian, consumerism helped draw the colonies together by helping to create a distinct American national mentality. See Breen 1988.
8. Information on London is taken from Harte 1986 and from the sources cited in Rothblatt 1988.
9. For similar reasons, the founders of Hackney College in London, a late eighteenth-century foundation of Baptist origin, preferred the word 'college' to the appellation 'academy', not 'for the sake of imitating the Establishment, but because the word academy (applied of late to every common school) does not convey a proper idea of our plan of education' (Bryant 1986: 109, 168).
10. The state's interest in maintaining a uniform standard of achievement at the top of the educational system was also provided for in the Scottish Universities Act of 1858 which required innovation in any one of the four universities to be approved by the others (Anderson 1983*a*: 257).
11. Unless otherwise noted, sources for the University of Durham are taken from Fowler 1904; Heesom 1982; Whiting 1932; 1937.
12. Malden (1835: 143): 'I wish merely to show that the English universities in their present state are very different from their original form . . . and hence to refute the argument . . . that the University of London is not composed of the essential elements of a university, and is not of the form of a legitimate university, merely because it differs from the present form of Oxford and Cambridge.'
13. On the matter of an 'open' university at Durham, see the debates on the second reading of the University of Durham Bill in the House of Lords for 22 May 1832, cols. 1209–18.
14. For details about Scotland, unless otherwise stated, see Anderson 1983*a*; 1983*b*.
15. Indeed, the curriculum of the pre-university college in America, especially in the nineteenth century, was modelled on this Scottish curriculum 'characterized by a concern for breadth' and still resembles it more closely than it does the single-subject English honours degree.
16. For professionalism and the service society culture, see Perkin 1969; 1989.

17. The Land-grant endowments in the US embodied exactly this principle of a one-time subvention to then-independent institutions. In both cases, additional regular sources of income were later required, though the sources differed in the two countries. The Morrill Act of 1862 and its successors were specifically designed 'to force the states to significant increases in their efforts on behalf of higher education. The Federal government, having promoted the establishment of new colleges, made it incumbent upon the states to supply the means of future development and expansion' (G. C. Lee 1963).
18. This was very similar to the attitudes of state governments to state universities in the US all through the nineteenth century, despite the provisions of the Morrill Act.
19. An absolutely crucial difference between funding patterns of British and American higher education is that in the former support for both teaching and research eventually came from central government. By contrast, in the US, state governments, student fees, alumni gifts, and endowments came to support the basic teaching function, while foundations, the Federal government, and industry have come to support most university-based research. Efforts are currently being made in Britain to shift the funding of British higher education toward American models.
20. For a summary of such activity and secondary source references, see Rothblatt 1983.
21. The two contrasting cultures of Victorian Britain are analogous to distinctions appearing in America in the early nineteenth century. For 'aristocratic' read 'colonial/Federalist', and for 'liberal' read 'Jacksonian'. The cultural/political substance of these distinctions, however, differed sharply in the two societies.
22. Cremin (1980: 487) writes that irrespective of their source of support or funding, all American institutions of the last century saw themselves as in some sense community institutions because they were 'educative'. He concludes that such a self-conception inevitably embroiled them in all kinds of distinct public controversies. Once again, the observer is struck by the remarkable parallels between Scotland and the United States up to about the 1830s or the 1850s.

8

Towards Meritocracy? Recent Evidence on an Old Problem[1]

ANTHONY HEATH, COLIN MILLS, and JANE ROBERTS

Equality of opportunity, particularly equality of opportunity for children from different social classes, has been one of the central topics of educational debate. It has been one of the key issues in the pre-war debates over access to grammar schools, in the post-war debates over comprehensive reorganization, and in current debates about student grants for higher education. It has also been one of the classic topics of research in British education, and is one of the areas where there has been a clear link between research and reform. Notable contributions included Lindsay 1926, Gray and Moshinsky 1938, and Floud, Halsey, and Martin 1956. More recently, concerns with gender and ethnicity have been added to those with social class.

This concern with equality of opportunity stems partly from the fact that education is a desirable consumption good but even more from the fact that education is an investment good; the more you have, the better your chances in the labour market tend to be—whether it is in avoiding unemployment or in obtaining secure and well-paid professional and managerial jobs. In the modern world education is one of the primary determinants, perhaps *the* primary determinant, of one's life chances.

It is, moreover, quite widely assumed that the link between education and occupation has been strengthening. This is clearest in American writings on the 'logic of industrialism'. Blau and Duncan, for example, have argued that industrial society is characterized by:

> a fundamental trend towards expanding universalism which has profound implications for the stratification system. The achieved

status of a man, what he has accomplished in terms of some objective criteria, becomes more important than his ascribed status, who he is in the sense of what family he comes from. This does not mean that family background no longer influences careers. What it does imply is that superior status cannot any more be directly inherited but must be legitimated by actual achievements that are socially acknowledged. Education assumes increasing significance for social status in general and for the transmission of social standing from fathers to sons in particular. (Blau and Duncan 1967: 430)

These American writers have tended to assume that it is employers' recruitment and promotion practices that have changed. They assume that the modern, efficient business cannot afford to recruit inferior quality applicants who simply happen to wear the right school tie and belong to the right gender or ethnic group. 'Ascriptive' characteristics of this kind are seen as sources of inefficiency which are destined to wither away under the competitive pressures of modern business. Instead, employers must recruit on merit, and educational achievements are taken to be a prime indicator of merit. These writers thus anticipate that the influence of education on occupational attainment will strengthen while the influence of ascribed characteristics such as social origin, gender, and ethnicity will weaken.

British research and reform on the other hand has concentrated not on recruitment to occupations but on recruitment to educational institutions. British researchers have largely taken the link between education and occupation for granted and have focused more on the selection processes that take place to and within schools rather than the recruitment practices of firms. They have also focused on the impact of externally imposed government-sponsored reforms rather than on the internal changes that businesses have introduced to strengthen their competitive position.

The paradigmatic British social reform was the 1944 Education Act, which in effect replaced selection on financial criteria by selection on intellectual ability. In his classic study of social mobility David Glass expressed the hope that the Act would 'greatly increase the amount of social mobility in Britain' (1954: 22). 'Given the diminishing importance of economic and social background as a determinant of the type of secondary education a child receives, social mobility will increase, and probably increase greatly' (ibid.: 24). Similar hopes have been expressed about comprehensive reorganization.

These British writers have thus tended to assume, or hope, that deliberate social reform could weaken the link between social origin and educational attainment. Assuming there are no compensating changes in the labour market, this would then tend to weaken the overall connection between origin and destination.

We can put this in the form of a path diagram. Thus the British educational reformers have hoped that link 'a' (the path from origin to education) would decline in importance; the Americans have assumed that link 'b' would also decline while 'c' would increase. There would thus be a shift towards meritocracy and an open, mobile society. Of course, it might not be quite this simple. Professor Halsey in his important paper 'Towards Meritocracy?' found that, comparing men educated before and after the 1944 Act, link 'b' did appear to have weakened and 'c' to have strengthened, just as predicted by the Americans, but link 'a' had rather spoilt the fun by moving in the opposite direction to that predicted by the Britons. Greater meritocracy in the labour market had been met by reduced meritocracy in the educational market, leaving the overall openness of the society unchanged. As Halsey concluded:

> what has happened is the weighting of the dice of social opportunity according to class, and 'the game' is increasingly played through strategies of child-rearing refereed by schools through their certifying arrangements . . . Economic and technical changes since 1945 have enlarged occupational opportunities, but social and education policy

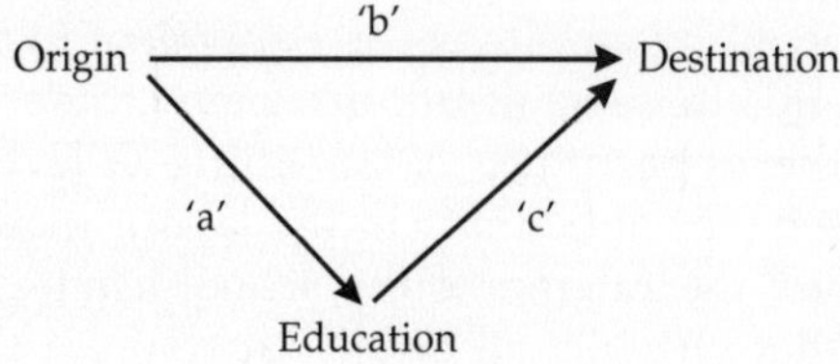

FIG. 8.1. Path Diagram of Occupational Attainment

have not successfully seized on these circumstances in such a way as to realize either an egalitarian or a meritocratic society. (Halsey 1977: 184)

One interpretation of Halsey's results is that, as schools, universities, and employers have changed their recruitment practices, so privileged families have increasingly realized that they have to play the educational game successfully if their children are to succeed. In other words, the changes in recruitment practices in the labour market have led to compensating adjustments in families' child-rearing practices and educational strategies so that the net effect on equality of opportunity and social mobility becomes zero. In this way the advantaged social classes have been able to outmanœuvre the social reformers.

The aim of this paper is to update Professor Halsey's work, but also to extend it by taking more explicit account of two phenomena to which he alludes, but which are not formally included in his analysis, namely the changing availability of educational and occupational opportunities. The selection and recruitment practices to available openings are clearly of importance. But the actual numbers of openings have also changed substantially, and indeed these may be more directly under government influence than are recruitment practices *per se*.

Most obviously, successive governments have controlled the school-leaving age and the number of openings in higher education. Reforms such as the introduction of the CSE have also affected the number of qualified school-leavers entering the labour market. The CSE examination was designed for less able children than British public examinations (such as the School Certificate and its successor, GCE) had traditionally catered for. Particularly important was the fact that a CSE grade 1 was recognized by employers as equivalent to a pass at GCE O-level, and this in effect meant that many more children were now given the opportunity of obtaining O-level equivalents and the consequential benefits in the labour market.

Furthermore, the raising of the school-leaving age to 16 in 1974 meant that virtually all pupils (apart from Easter leavers) were brought within sight of the public examinations of CSE and GCE. This almost certainly contributed to a great increase in the numbers taking these examinations (now of course merged in the GCSE).

Even in the absence of any changes in schools' or firms' procedures for selecting pupils or recruiting employees, these changes will have had considerable impact on the educational experience of the social classes, on the occupational chances of people with varying educational level, and perhaps on the numbers of mobile people in the population as well.

DATA

The data that we use come from the General Household Survey. the GHS is a continuous survey based on a sample of the general population resident in private (that is, non-institutional) households in Great Britain and has been running since 1971. It aims to provide a means of examining relationships between the most significant variables with which social policy is concerned and, in particular, of monitoring changes in these relationships over time. The GHS therefore covers a wide range of social and economic topics, including the respondents' educational qualifications and their own and their fathers' occupations. The surveys can thus be used to give us a series of cross-sectional snapshots of the social origins, the educational attainments, and the occupational achievements of the adult population with which we can explore the changes over time. (For further details see the annual GHS reports.)

For our analysis of change over time we have chosen the 1973 and 1985 surveys.[2] We restrict our analysis to respondents aged 25 and over as many of the younger respondents would still be in full-time education at the time of the survey. Since father's occupation was asked only of respondents aged under 50, we therefore restrict our analysis to those aged 25–49. Our respondents to the 1973 survey will thus have been leaving school and entering the labour market from 1938 up till the 1960s, while the respondents to the 1985 survey will have been entering the labour market from 1951 onwards.

In the GHS father's occupation is coded into 17 socio-economic groups. We have excluded SEGs 16 and 17 (members of armed forces and occupations inadequately described or not stated respectively) and have grouped the others into three broad social classes which effectively correspond to John Goldthorpe's model of social class (1980):

The Service Class

This is 'the class of those exercising power and expertise on behalf of corporate bodies' and is largely composed of salaried professional, semi-professional, managerial and administrative employees in secure employment within the bureaucracies of modern corporations, both public and private. Goldthorpe distinguishes between the higher and lower level of the service class, the former consisting of full professionals, higher administrative staff, and managers in large enterprises. We make use of this distinction later in this chapter.

The Intermediate Classes

Here, because of the small numbers involved, we combine three classes: routine non-manual workers, the petty bourgeoisie, and foremen and technicians. The petty bourgeoisie consists of own-account workers and small employers. The routine non-manual workers are a kind of white-collar labour-force, 'functionally associated with, but marginal to, the service class'. The foremen and technicians on the other hand are functionally associated with, but marginal to, the working class, having rather greater autonomy and authority within the work-place than the working class proper.

The Working Class

This consists of rank and file employees in industry and agriculture. The defining feature of this group is that they are 'wage labourers' who are directly subject to the employer's authority.

We should also note that father's occupation is his 'usual' one. This is not the ideal measure in the analysis of social origins since some fathers' usual occupation will be rather different from the one they had when their children were young.

We have followed the same procedure for allocating the respondents' current occupations into social classes as we have done with fathers' occupations. In our analyses of the respondents' occupations, however, we restrict our attention to people who were economically active at the time of the survey (that is to say, who were in paid work, waiting to take up paid work, temporarily absent, or unemployed but seeking paid work).

Compared to many European and North American educational systems, the British system is particularly complicated. For the sake of simplicity we have chosen to index educational level by the highest level of educational qualification held by the respondent at the time of the relevant survey. We use the following four categories.

Degree or Equivalent

This includes Higher degree (Census Level A), First degree, and other qualifications obtained from universities, colleges of further education, or from professional institutions of degree standard (Census Level B).

A-Level Standard but below Degree

This includes GCE A-level; SLC/SCE/Supe at Higher Grade or Certificate of Sixth Year Studies; City and Guilds Full Technological, Advanced, or Final; HNC/HND; ONC/OND; BEC/TEC; Nursing Qualifications (Census Level C); Non-graduate teaching qualifications (Census Level C); and qualifications obtained from universities, colleges of further education, or from professional institutions below degree but above GCE A-level standard (Census Level C).

O-Level Standard but below A-Level

This includes one or more subjects at GCE O-level obtained before 1975, or in grades A–C if obtained later; one or more subjects at SCE Ordinary obtained before 1973 or in bands A–C if obtained later; one or more subjects at CSE grade 1 or at School Certificate/SLC lower/SUPE Lower; City and Guilds Craft or Ordinary.

Below O-Level

This group largely consists of people with no formal academic qualification at all, but also includes people with apprenticeships; some clerical and commercial qualifications, CSE grades 2–5 or ungraded, GCE O-level obtained 1975 or later in grades

D or E; SCE Ordinary obtained 1973 or later in bands D or E, and 'other' qualifications.

This is a collapsed version of the variable 'highest educational qualification' used in the GHS. The ordering used in the GHS has been preserved, but some adjacent categories have been combined. As can be seen, the categories include many technical and vocational qualifications, but as a convenient shorthand we shall term the four levels: degree, advanced, ordinary, and low respectively. Respondents with foreign qualifications are excluded from the analysis as there are insufficient details about the level of these qualifications to assign them to one of our four groups.

EDUCATIONAL AND OCCUPATIONAL EXPANSION

Two of the most notable features of British society in the second half of the twentieth century have been the expansion of the professional, managerial, and administrative jobs of the service class and the increases in the educational qualifications of the population. Thus in the 1973 survey 18 per cent of men came from service-class origins, but by the 1985 survey this had risen to 29 per cent.

TABLE 8.1. Changing Class Origins

Father's Class	Men		Women	
	1973	1985	1973	1985
Service class	18.0	29.1	19.5	27.8
Intermediate classes	21.1	24.2	21.2	23.4
Working class	60.8	46.7	59.2	48.7
TOTALS	99.9	100.0	99.9	99.9
	(4,768)	(3,935)	(5,069)	(4,001)

A similar trend emerges if we look at the respondents' current occupations. In the 1973 survey, 24 per cent of men were in the service class at the time of the survey, but this had increased to 36 per cent by 1985. Women's occupational distribution is of course well known to be different from men's with women heavily concentrated in lower white-collar work (which we have allocated to the intermediate class). But the same trend over time occurs for women's occupations as it does for men's, the proportion of working women with service-class jobs rising from 18 per cent in 1973 to 31 per cent in 1985.

These trends may well be linked to the 'logic of industrialism' described by Blau and Duncan. The expansion of the professional and managerial jobs of the service class appears to be a general feature of advanced industrial or post-industrial societies, and is by no means unique to Britain.

TABLE 8.2. Changing Class Destinations

Respondents' Class	Men		Women	
	1973	1985	1973	1985
Service class	24.2	36.3	17.7	31.0
Intermediate classes	24.1	27.3	41.0	38.6
Working class	51.6	36.4	41.3	30.5
TOTALS	99.9	100.0	100.0	100.1
	(5,237)	(3,982)	(3,332)	(2,865)

The changes in the educational field have been even more dramatic than those with occupation. This is shown in Table 8.3. In the 1973 survey 68 per cent of men had either low or no academic qualifications. By 1985 the corresponding figure had fallen to 44 per cent.

Women are not as likely as men to have higher-level qualifications—largely because they miss out on the higher technical and vocational qualifications rather than because they lag behind at school examinations such as GCE. As we can see from Table 8.3, however, the direction and scale of the change over time is almost identical to that for men. This spread of educational qualifications can in part be explained by the changing shape of the class structure. The higher social classes are more likely to acquire higher-level qualifications (perhaps because they place greater store by educational qualification than do the lower classes or perhaps because they have greater

TABLE 8.3. Changing Qualifications

Highest Qualification	Men		Women	
	1973	1985	1973	1985
Degree	5.6	13.0	1.8	6.6
Advanced	13.4	25.4	8.5	16.8
Ordinary	12.9	17.3	12.5	20.7
Low	68.1	44.3	77.2	55.9
TOTALS	100.0	100.0	100.0	100.0
	(4,768)	(3,766)	(5,393)	(4,129)

resources for acquiring them). We would therefore expect a changing class structure in the parental generation to lead to a changed distribution of qualifications in the filial generation.

But the expansion of educational qualifications has far outstripped what would have been expected from the changing class structure in the parental generation. In other words, there has been a major spread of qualifications *within* origin classes. Thus in 1973 22 per cent of men from working-class origins had qualifications at ordinary level or above, but this had risen to 40 per cent by 1985. Similarly 62 per cent of men from service-class origins had qualifications at ordinary level or above in the 1973 survey, and this had risen to 80 per cent in 1985. All social classes alike, therefore, have increased their acquisition of educational qualifications, and by almost identical amounts.

There are various possible explanations for this increased acquisition. Reforms like the raising of the school-leaving age to 16 in 1974 and comprehensive reorganization from 1965 onwards will probably have affected only small proportions of our respondents, even in the later surveys. On the educational side we would place more weight on the increasing availability of CSE (with its O-level equivalent of grade 1) in the 1960s and 1970s which surely gave many younger people an opportunity to obtain educational qualifications that was not present for their elders.

While the opportunities to obtain qualifications have improved, it is also possible that the motivation to acquire them has changed as well. If people believe that there is a tightening bond between education and occupation—that qualifications are increasingly necessary to obtain the higher-level jobs of the service class or to avoid unemployment—then their incentive to acquire qualifications may increase.

THE LINK BETWEEN ORIGIN AND EDUCATION

Even the most cursory glance at Table 8.4 suggests that the link between origin and education has changed little. All classes alike have taken advantage of the increased opportunities to obtain qualifications (or have been motivated to increase their take-up of the opportunities available). There is little evidence that educational expansion has enabled the working class to catch up.

There are many different possible measures of class inequality in education. Perhaps the simplest is to look at the percentage point difference between the classes. For example, in the 1973

TABLE 8.4. Changing Class Differences in Educational Attainment (Father's Class)

	Service		Intermediate		Working	
	Men	Women	Men	Women	Men	Women
			1973			
Low	37.6	50.0	62.0	70.9	78.0	87.9
Ordinary	21.6	25.3	15.9	15.9	9.7	7.4
Advanced	25.0	19.1	14.9	10.9	9.8	4.2
Degree	15.8	5.6	7.2	2.3	2.6	0.5
TOTALS	100.0	100.0	100.0	100.0	100.1	100.0
	(768)	(930)	(892)	(1,015)	(2,617)	(2,896)
			1985			
Low	20.1	28.6	42.4	54.2	59.5	71.0
Ordinary	19.0	27.8	17.9	21.6	15.8	16.7
Advanced	33.1	28.2	29.0	19.6	19.1	9.7
Degree	27.8	15.4	10.7	4.7	5.5	2.6
TOTALS	100.0	100.0	100.0	100.1	99.9	100.0
	(1,039)	(1,063)	(854)	(899)	(1,695)	(1,896)

survey, 22 per cent of men from working-class origins had obtained qualifications at ordinary level or above compared with 62 per cent of men from service-class origins, a gap of 40 percentage points. In the 1985 survey the gap was still 40 points.

Further up the educational hierarchy the gap has actually widened. Thus in the 1973 survey, 16 per cent of men from service-class origins had obtained degree-level qualifications compared with 3 per cent of men from working-class origins, a gap of 13 percentage points. In the 1985 survey the gap had widened to 22 points.

Broadly speaking, the same story applies to the class differences among women, and to the differences between men and women themselves. The differences have stayed much the same or have actually increased.

The percentage point difference tells us how similar or different the educational experience of the classes or sexes are. The story told by Table 8.4 about these educational experiences is the one that we would indeed expect from previous research (Halsey, Heath, and Ridge 1980; Heath and Clifford 1990). In the early part of the century, the classes were alike in tending to leave school early without qualifications. Educational expansion at secondary level then led to a growing divergence between the classes at mid-century as the service class was first to take advantage of the new opportunities. The gap between the classes then stabilized as the working class began to increase its take-up. And the gap between the classes can finally be expected to decline towards the end of the century as the service class reaches saturation (at ordinary level) while the working class at last begins to catch up. Educational expansion thus tends to follow what is termed a logistic pattern (see Fig. 8.2).

Our two surveys capture the middle stage of this process (between the vertical lines A and B), when the difference between the classes at ordinary level has reached its maximum. We would expect future General Household Surveys to show the gap to be declining as we move to the right of line B. Meanwhile, higher education is still at a much earlier stage of development and we are, in effect, still to the left of line A. The classes (and the sexes) are still broadly similar in that the majority of people from all classes alike do not go on to university or to degree-level courses. The picture of higher

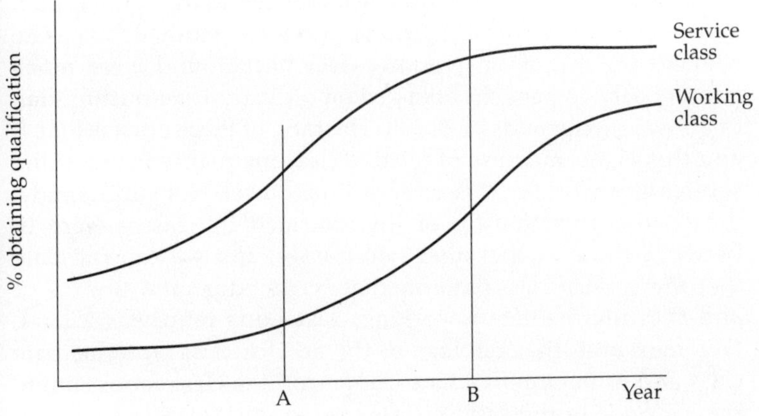

FIG. 8.2. Logistic Model of Educational Expansion

education at the end of the century is much like that of secondary education at the beginning, with the gap between the classes still widening.

While the *absolute* difference in the classes' educational experience is of considerable interest, we would argue that the theories with which we began this paper need to be tested by a somewhat different measure of class inequality. We suggest that odds ratios are the appropriate measure (see Feinberg 1980). These can be thought of as measuring the outcome of a competition between people of different class origins to achieve one rather than another educational qualification. In essence they are concerned with the *relative* chances of the classes.

The mathematical properties of odds ratios are such that they tell us whether the gaps between the classes have grown by more or less than would have been expected on the basis of the logistic pattern shown in Figure 8.2. It follows, therefore, that widening absolute gaps can be consistent with static, or indeed declining, relative differences (as measured by odds ratios), and vice versa.

In some cases, of course, the two measures can tell the same story, and this is what we find at ordinary level. Thus among men from service-class origins in the 1973 survey, 62 per cent obtained an ordinary-level qualification (or above). The odds of obtaining ordinary-level qualifications or above rather than lower-level or no qualifications were therefore 62 : 38. The chances for men from working-class background were much poorer; only 22 per cent obtained an ordinary-level qualification or above, giving odds of 22 : 78. The ratio of these odds is 5.9 : 1, and this is our measure of relative class inequality between the service and working classes at ordinary level. Not surprisingly, the competitive chances of the intermediate classes were in between those of the other two classes, and we can calculate that the service class : intermediate class odds ratio was 2.7 : 1 and the intermediate : working class odds ratio was 2.2 : 1. (We may note that the logs of the service class : intermediate class and of the intermediate class : working class ratios sum to the log odds of the service class : working class ratio.)

While the odds for men from all three classes are substantially better in 1985 than they were in 1973, the odds ratios show little change. Thus the service-class odds improved to 80 : 20 while the working-class odds also improved to 40 : 60. But the service class : working class odds *ratio* remained at 5.9 : 1 in 1985 just as it had been in 1973.[3]

These results are closely in line with Heath and Clifford's cohort analysis (1990) of inequalities in education over the twentieth century. To be sure, McPherson and Willms (1987) have found evidence for some narrowing of class inequalities in Scotland in the period since comprehensive reorganization. Comprehensive reorganization took place rather earlier in Scotland than it did in the rest of Britain, and very few of our respondents will have been to comprehensive schools. Our surveys cannot therefore shed light on the consequences of comprehensive reform.

However, our surveys do show one interesting change, although it cannot be ascribed to comprehensive reform: among women, class inequalities have decline somewhat. In the 1973 survey, class inequalities among women were even greater than they were among men. Whereas the service class : working class odds ratio for men was 5.9 : 1 in 1973, it was 7.3 : 1 for women. By 1985 it had fallen to 6.1 : 1, not significantly different from the male figure. Working-class women remain the group who are least likely to get ordinary-level qualifications or above, but in relative (although not in absolute) terms they have caught up somewhat. They remain doubly disadvantaged as women and as working class, sharing the disadvantages that women in general have and that the working class in general has. But in the 1973 survey working-class women suffered a unique *additional* disadvantage in the competition for educational qualifications, and it is this unique disadvantage that now seems to have disappeared.[4]

EDUCATION AND OCCUPATION: THE DEVALUATION OF QUALIFICATIONS

Our next step is to look at the relation between education and occupational attainment and to test the hypothesis of a tightening bond between the two. Table 8.5 shows the relationship between educational qualifications and occupational attainments for men and women. It reveals expected patterns. Thus men and women with degree-level qualifications are highly likely to enter the service class and to avoid the working class. Conversely, people with low qualifications, or with no qualifications at all, are to be found predominantly in the working class. There are also some marked gender differences. As Table 8.2 showed, women tend to be concentrated in the intermediate classes (and in particular in the lower white-collar work that we have assigned to the intermediate classes), and they are therefore under-represented both in the service class and in the working class.

This pattern is repeated at the lower levels of qualification, where of course the great majority of the respondents are to be found. Thus women with ordinary-level qualifications or lower ones are much more likely to be in the intermediate class than are their male counterparts. At advanced level and above, however, the pattern is more complex. Women with advanced-level qualifications are particularly likely to be found in the service class, largely because of occupationally specific qualifications like nursing and teaching ones which lead directly into service-class jobs. For once, then, women actually have *better* chances than men with qualifications of broadly similar level. However, these nursing and teaching qualifications give access to the lower ranks of the service class. If we look at access to the

TABLE 8.5 Education and Occupation

Highest qualification	Working class	Intermediate classes	Service class		N
		1973			
Degree					
Men	1.2	6.4	92.5	100.1	(266)
Women	1.4	12.2	86.5	100.1	(74)
Advanced					
Men	18.6	22.8	58.6	100.0	(618)
Women	3.1	17.5	79.5	100.1	(292)
Ordinary					
Men	30.9	30.2	38.9	100.0	(592)
Women	12.2	67.3	20.5	100.0	(361)
Low					
Men	65.2	24.6	10.1	99.9	(3,199)
Women	52.0	40.6	7.4	100.0	(2,453)
		1985			
Degree					
Men	1.5	6.9	91.6	100.0	(479)
Women	1.7	13.1	85.2	100.0	(229)
Advanced					
Men	20.6	27.1	52.3	100.0	(919)
Women	9.0	21.6	69.4	100.0	(523)
Ordinary					
Men	32.9	31.4	35.7	100.0	(630)
Women	19.3	58.9	21.9	100.1	(581)
Low					
Men	58.0	30.8	11.2	100.0	(1,596)
Women	47.2	40.8	12.0	100.0	(1,440)

higher ranks, then we find the more familiar pattern of male advantage.

Turning to the trends over time, however, there is a rather more surprising finding. The occupational chances of graduates have remained effectively constant; the occupational chances of people with intermediate-level qualifications (particularly those whose highest qualification was at advanced level) have deteriorated; but paradoxically the occupational chances of people with low or no qualifications have if anything improved.

Thus the percentage of male graduates reaching the service class has fallen one point; in the case of men whose highest qualification was at advanced level, the percentage reaching the service class has fallen six points; in the case of men whose highest qualification was at ordinary level, it has fallen by three points; and in the case of men with low qualifications or with no qualifications at all, it has actually risen by one point. In effect, this means that the occupational benefits associated with qualifications have actually declined, relative to having low qualification or none at all. The overall picture, in other words, is of stable pay-offs at the top and bottom of the educational hierarchy, but declining chances for people with intermediate qualifications. (Rather similar results have been obtained by Mills and Payne (1989) in their analysis of data from the Social Change and Economic Life Initiation.)

The explanation for this devaluation of intermediate qualifications must be in part the relative rates of expansion in the supply and demand for qualified labour, that is the relative rates at which educational qualifications and vacancies in the service class respectively have increased. As we saw at the beginning of this chapter, the size of the service class increased by around 12 percentage points from 24 per cent to 36 per cent while the number of graduates increased by around 7 percentage points from 6 per cent to 13 per cent. (These figures are for men only. The picture is somewhat different if we include women, although to some extent men and women compete within different labour markets within the service class.) The increased size of the service class has therefore been able to soak up these extra graduates without any problems.

The expansion of intermediate-level qualifications has, however, meant problems for the people concerned. In 1973, for example, there would in principle have been room in the service class for everyone with advanced-level qualifications or above. Altogether in 1973 there were 19 per cent of men with such qualifications, rather less than the total 24 per cent of men who were in the service class at that time. But by 1987 38 per cent of men had qualifications of advanced level or above, but there was room only for 36 per cent of men to be in the service class. Some of them simply had to take lower-level occupations, even if men with ordinary-level qualifications or below were wholly excluded.

The fact that the unqualified have managed to preserve their chances of access to the service class despite this squeeze from more qualified people is rather paradoxical. One possible interpretation of this finding is that employers believe that the value of ordinary level qualifications, relative to no qualifications, has been devalued. For example, while educationists may recognize a CSE grade 1 as equivalent to a C grade at O-level, it is by no means clear that employers will accept the equivalence between the two examination results. Or again, employers may simply believe that 'more means worse'; they may believe that the greater numbers of school-leavers possessing ordinary-level qualifications means that standards must have been lowered.

Employers may or may not be correct in these beliefs, but it is important to recognize that the occupational pay-offs of particular qualifications may depend on employers' beliefs about their value rather than on their intrinsic educational worth (whatever that may be).[5]

SOCIAL ORIGIN, EDUCATION, AND OCCUPATIONAL ATTAINMENT: ASCRIBED AND ACHIEVED CHARACTERISTICS

So far, our results give rather equivocal support to the 'logic of industrialism' thesis. As predicted by the thesis, there has been an expansion of higher-level managerial and professional jobs, but the evidence for a tightening bond between education and occupation is missing.

A crucial aspect of the thesis, however, concerns the direct link between origin and destination (link 'b' in Fig. 8.1), a link to which we now turn our attention. This link refers to the direct transmission of occupational standing from father to son or daughter independently of education. Such transmission might, for example, take the form of the direct inheritance of property, such as the family business, or the exploitation of connections and social networks to secure certain kinds of job. It need not of course be deliberate. It may simply be the result of an unconscious preference on the part of employers to recruit 'one of us'. At any rate, a major claim is that these mechanisms will have been declining in importance as competitive pressures make these unmeritocratic procedures an expensive luxury which businesses cannot afford.

To test this thesis we need to investigate the *net* effects of social origin on current occupation controlling for education. (It is also of course logically possible that this analysis will modify our conclusions about the effects of education on occupation, but in practice we shall find that it leaves all our earlier conclusions intact.)

To investigate this we must analyse the five-way table of origin by education by destination by sex by year. Such a large table does not lend itself to easy presentation or comprehension, and we shall therefore make use of the summary device of logistic regression instead. This enables us to summarize the 'direct effects' of origin, gender, and education on current occupation in our two surveys.

In these logistic regressions, our dependent variable is the chance of being in the service class (strictly, the log odds of being either in the service class or in one of the other classes), and our independent variables are social origin, highest qualification, and gender. The analysis therefore looks at the *net* relationship of each independent variable to service-class access. We present the results for 1973 and 1985 separately, so that we can get some idea of whether the net relationships are getting stronger or weaker. (We can then test more rigorously to see whether the changes are statistically significant.)

Table 8.6 shows the net chances of reaching the service group *relative* to the lowest category of the variable in question (lowest purely in the sense of having the poorest chances). Thus we compare the chances of people from service-class or intermediate-class origins relative to those from working-class origins, which are set at zero. (The parameters can be interpreted as fitted log odds ratios.)

As might be expected from previous research in this area, there are highly significant relationships between qualification and membership of the service class, both in 1973 and 1985. These are the strongest relationships in the analysis. Even after controlling for qualifications, however, we still find significant relationships with social origin. In other words, even among people with similar educational levels, those from service-class origins are more likely to be found in the service class

TABLE 8.6. Access to the Service Class

	logit parameters			
	1973		1985	
Constant	0.01	(0.03)	−0.06	(0.02)
Highest qualification				
Degree	2.21	(0.11)	2.00	(0.07)
Advanced	1.39	(0.05)	1.12	(0.04)
Ordinary	0.68	(0.05)	0.51	(0.04)
Low	0.00		0.00	
Father's class				
Service	0.37	(0.04)	0.28	(0.04)
Intermediate	0.21	(0.04)	−0.01	(0.04)
Working	0.00		0.00	
Gender				
Male	0.13	(0.04)	−0.01	(0.03)
Female	0.00		0.00	
Chi^2	89.30		76.80	
df	17.00		17.00	
P	0.00		0.00	
N	6,987		6058	

Note: Figures in brackets give standard errors.

themselves than are those from working-class origins. Britain is by no means a pure meritocracy.

Net of the other relationships in the model, the gender effect is rather weak (only just reaching statistical significance in 1973 and disappearing altogether in 1985). This is partly because women (particularly those with the relevant qualifications) have rather good chances of reaching occupations such as teaching and nursing (which make up SEG 5.1 and have been allocated to the service class).

However, if we look at access to the *higher* level of the service class, the gender difference is very much larger. It proves to be much larger than those associated with social origin, and indeed comes to rival education itself. This is shown in table 8.7.[6]

It is also perhaps of some interest that the qualification parameters are rather smaller in the case of access to the higher service class than they were for access to the service class as a whole, suggesting that access to these higher-level jobs is rather less meritocratic than is access to the lower-level ones. It may be that *recruitment* to the service class is based on educational credentials while *promotion* to higher posts depends more on on-the-job expertise or other qualities that become more visible once people have joined the staff. Alternatively, perhaps additionally, there may be some sectoral differences at work. Many of the lower-level service-class jobs are in the public sector organizations such as schools, the NHS, and local authorities. These organizations appear to be somewhat more meritocratic (strictly speaking, more credential-oriented) than are the private-sector business enterprises.

TABLE 8.7. Access to the Higher Service Class

	logit parameters			
	1973		1985	
Constant	−1.08	(0.04)	−1.04	(0.03)
Highest qualification				
Degree	1.77	(0.08)	1.66	(0.07)
Advanced	1.06	(0.06)	0.98	(0.07)
Ordinary	0.81	(0.07)	0.58	(0.08)
Low	0.00		0.00	
Father's class				
Service class	0.38	(0.06)	0.29	(0.05)
Intermediate	0.19	(0.06)	0.10	(0.06)
Working	0.00		0.00	
Gender				
Male	1.12	(0.08)	0.74	(0.05)
Female	0.00		0.00	
Chi^2	12.90		18.42	
df	17.00		17.00	
P	0.74		0.36	
N	6,987		6,058	

Note: Figures in brackets give standard errors.

Turning to the changes over time between 1973 and 1985, we see the devaluation of qualifications which we described in the previous section. Both in access to the service class as a whole (Table 8.6) and to the upper echelons of the service class (Table 8.7) we see marked declines in the qualification parameters, particularly those for ordinary-level qualifications.

Social origins also tend to decline in importance somewhat, although the only change that reaches statistical significance is that for people from intermediate origins in gaining access to the service class as a whole. We would wish to see this finding replicated in further surveys before placing much weight on it.

Gender declines in importance too.[7] Both Table 8.6 on access to the service class as a whole and Table 8.7 on access to the higher levels tell much the same story about change over time. In Table 8.7 the change is particularly marked, and indeed the decline of gender inequalities is the only change in Table 8.7 that reaches statistical significance.

The logic of industrialism thesis had expected that 'achieved' characteristics such as education would become more important while ascribed characteristics such as social origin and gender would reduce in importance. This is not quite the story told by Tables 8.6 and 8.7. Rather we find that *all* characteristics have tended to become less important over our period. In other words, membership of the service class has become somewhat more random with respect to the variables included in our model.[8]

One possible interpretation of this finding is that luck rather than meritocracy increasingly determines access to the service class, and this is by no means an implausible interpretation.[9] In a period of rapid growth and keen competition for the people who come on to the labour market, employers with vacancies to fill may have to be less choosy. It may be better to fill the vacancy with somebody, even if they are less qualified, from the wrong background, or have the unfortunate handicap of being a woman, rather than wait for the ideal meritocrat to turn up.

If such an interpretation were correct, the decline in the size of the various parameters might prove to be temporary: as rates of growth slow, employers could become more choosy once again and all the parameters in our models might once again increase. Alternatively, the changes might reflect rather more permanent developments on the side of either the supply or the demand for labour. For example, our period is one which includes some major legislation on equal opportunities for women, and this may have led some employers to change their recruitment or promotion practices.

Women's attitudes to work and promotion may also have changed over this period. As is well known, married women's participation in the labour market has increased, and there is clear evidence of a concomitant change in attitudes too (Hunt 1968; Martin and Roberts 1984; Witherspoon 1988). It would hardly be surprising if these changes in attitudes to work were not also accompanied by some changes in attitudes to promotion. Women's improved chances of access to the higher service class, relative to men's, might therefore be due in part to changes in their orientations to work.

IMPLICATIONS FOR SOCIAL POLICY

Our major findings are that the numbers of people holding higher-level jobs and holding higher-level qualifications have both expanded. But the expansion of higher education has led to a widening of the absolute gap between the classes. And since middle-level qualifications have shown a greater expansion than the number of service-class jobs, there has been some deterioration in the occupational pay-offs accruing to these

TABLE 8.8. Logit Models of Access to the Service Class

Model		Chi^2	df	p
1	All 2-way interactions	215.19	40	0.000
2	plus CES	87.47	37	0.000
3	plus CES, CEO	70.13	31	0.000
4	plus CES, CEO, CEY	42.71	28	0.037
5	plus CES, CEO, CEY, COY	31.00	26	0.228
6	plus CES, CEO, CEY, COY, CSY	27.31	25	0.341

Note: C represents respondents' current class; O represents father's class; E represents respondent's highest qualification; S represents respondent's sex; Y represents year of survey.

TABLE 8.9. Logit Models of Access to the Higher Service Class

Model		Chi^2	df	p
1	All 2-way interactions	53.94	40	0.069
2	plus CES	51.39	37	0.058
3	plus CES, CEO	42.46	31	0.082
4	plus CES, CEO, CEY	37.30	28	0.112
5	plus CES, CEO, CEY, COY	36.76	26	0.079
6	plus CES, CEO, CEY, COY, CSY	22.72	25	0.594
7	plus CSY	39.03	39	0.469

Note: C represents respondents' current class; O represents father's class; E represents respondent's highest qualification; S represents respondent's sex; Y represents year of survey.

qualifications. This is the primary story, and it is essenially one about the dynamics of the supply and demand for qualified labour.

Once we take account of these changes in supply and demand we find that there are rather small changes in the class relativities. There is some evidence that the overall relation between education and occupation has weakened, although this may well be due to the nature of the career process, which is not well captured by our snapshots. The biggest change in relativities has occurred with men's and women's relative chances of access to the higher levels of the service class.

These results suggest that social reform may be rather better at changing *totals* than at changing *relativities*. Thus the total number of children obtaining ordinary-level qualifications has increased very substantially, and reforms such as the introduction of the CSE must surely have played some part in this. What is clear, however, is that people from all social origins alike have been able to take advantage of these new opportunities.

It should be said, however, that the period to which our surveys refer was not one in which very great efforts were made to change class relativities in education. All that we should perhaps conclude is that, left to themselves, social origin differences in educational attainment will not conveniently wither away. Whether vigorous attempts to reduce them would be successful remains a moot point and one which the research reported here cannot answer. (But compare Halsey, Heath, and Ridge 1980 on the effects of the 1944 Education Act with McPherson and Willms 1987 on comprehensive reorganization.)

Nor is the evidence very strong that social origin differences in occupational attainment will wither away as a result of the competitive pressures on business to be efficient. While the direct effects of social origin on occupational attainment have tended to decline, the changes are small and do not in general reach statistical significance. It remains to be seen, too, whether the changes are permanent or simply reflect the problems of recruitment in a period of rapid expansion.

Most encouraging and perhaps most instructive for the social reformer are the changes in gender inequality. The 1970s saw legislative reform here, but they also saw the development of the women's movement and of changing attitudes to women's work. What the causal relations, if any, between these phenomena are it is impossible to say. But one certainly ought to entertain the hypothesis that legislative reform on its own would not have been successful in reducing relativities.

It is typically the hope of social reformers that legislation can be used to tilt the balance of power from one group towards another. But the history of educational reforms suggests that legislation on its own is rarely sufficient (and perhaps not even necessary). Legislation may change the rules of the game, but the players who are most motivated to succeed may be able to adapt their strategies so that they succeed at the new game just as they did at the old. In the case of gender, what may have happened is that one of the groups has become more motivated to succeed at a game where they had previously taken defeat for granted.

NOTES

1. We are grateful to OPCS for permission to use the General Household Survey and to the ESRC Data Archive for providing the data tapes. The analyses and interpretations in this paper are entirely the responsibility of the three authors, not of OPCS.
2. The 1973 survey is the first available in the 'Surrey' SPSSX files

while the 1985 survey is the most recent one currently available to us.

3. These figures relate to the chances of getting low or no qualifications versus qualifications at ordinary level or above. If we look at all four levels of qualification simultaneously, we also find no evidence of change in relative class chances. For men the loglinear model OE,OY,YE (where O represents class origin, E represents education, and Y represents year of survey) gives an acceptable fit to the data: $Chi^2 = 9.78$ with 6 degrees of freedom; $p = 0.134$.

   We should note that these results are rather different from Halsey's. This is not, we suggest, because of a real change in the periods covered by the two studies but because of differences in the statistical techniques used. Halsey used path analysis and therefore employed standardized regression coefficients. These are more akin to measures of absolute differences between the classes rather than to measures of relative differences, such as odds ratios and loglinear parameters. If we regress highest qualification (treating it as a four-point scale) on father's class (a three-point scale), we find that, for men, the standard regression coefficient was 0.328 in 1973 and 0.374 in 1985 (the unstandardized coefficients being 0.394 and 0.483 respectively). The increase in these coefficients captures the fact that the absolute differences between the classes in acquisition, for example, of degree-level qualifications has actually widened.
4. If we look at all four levels of qualification simultaneously, we find that, for women, the loglinear model OE,OY,YE does not give an acceptable fit to the data: $Chi^2 = 15.44$ with 6 degrees of freedom; $p = 0.17$. Inspection of the adjusted residuals shows that the biggest discrepancies between the predictions of the model and the observed frequencies concern working-class women with low or no qualifications. If we restrict ourselves to the three higher levels of qualification we find that, for women, none of the adjusted residuals is greater than 2 and the OE,OY,YE model now gives an acceptable fit: $Chi^2 = 4.68$ with 4 degrees of freedom; $p = 0.322$.
5. Another possibility is that qualifications are simply a proxy for other qualities which job applicants have, such as their drive or ability and that, with the expanded number of people possessing qualifications, the marginal holder of a qualification is now of lower drive or ability than was hitherto the case. As far as we know, however, there is no way of testing this hypothesis.
6. The models shown in Tables 8.6 do not give good fits to the data. This is because of interactions between, for example, gender, qualifications, and occupation. These interactions are of considerable interest in their own right, although they are not the major focus of

the current chapter. Since they are necessary for modelling access to the service class as a whole (Table 8.8), but not for modelling access to the higher service class (Table 8.9), this suggests that there are some rather special features about access to the lower service class, and probably to the ancillary occupations in particular.

7. We should remember that women with advanced-level qualifications actually had superior chances to men in gaining access to the service class, and what we find is that their advantage over men declines. In this particular case, then, a decline in the size of the gender parameter does not necessarily imply that women have improved their position relative to men.
8. In logistic regression the index of concentration is in some respects analogous to the concept of variance explained in ordinary least squares regression. For the models of Table 8.6, the index of concentration falls from 0.343 in 1973 to 0.331 in 1985, and for the models of Table 8.7 the index falls from 0.264 to 0.249.
9. Another possibility is that procedural changes in the conduct of the surveys is responsible. For example, if there had been a reduction in the reliability with which current occupation was coded, this would in effect introduce more 'noise' and reduce the associations of other variables with current occupation. Another possibility is that the 1980 classification of occupations (and/or their allocation to SEGs) produces a classification that is more heterogeneous with respect to our independent variables than was the 1970 classification. We can check this to some extent by comparing the results of the 1979 and 1980 surveys. When we do so, we obtain very similar results for the two years, suggesting that the change in classification is not a serious problem.

9

From Social Research to Educational Policy

10/65 to the Education Reform Act 1988

George Smith and Teresa Smith

> Without a foundation of near consensus no general social welfare policy would be possible.
>
> T. H. Marshall, 'Value Problems of Welfare-Capitalism', *Journal of Social Policy*, 1 (1972), 20.

Future historians, reviewing the influence of social research on educational policy in England and Wales over the past twenty-five years (1965–90), may well conclude that the first few years—from circular 10/65 on the reorganization of secondary schooling, to circular 11/72 on pre-school expansion—marked the high point. They would note the widespread consensus that research on selection at 11+, particularly that of Halsey and Floud on social class and educational opportunity, had made a key contribution to the policy shift in the 1960s from selective to comprehensive secondary education. They would note, too, the active networks linking researchers, administrators, and politicians, not least in the appointment in 1965 of Halsey as research adviser to Crosland, then secretary of state for education at the Department of Education and Science (DES), as circular 10/65 marking the first stage in this policy change was in preparation. And in confirmation they would be able to quote the views of participants, both politicians and civil servants, that they had been influenced by research, had taken it into account, though the exact nature of this influence would, no doubt, remain subject to continuing controversy. Throughout the period they would find this change in secondary schooling and the later Educational Priority Areas programme (EPA 1968–72) cited almost as textbook examples of the way that social research really could—and did—influence policy (Banting 1979; Abrams 1985; Thomas 1985; Finch 1986).

At the other end of their twenty-five-year span, our historians will no doubt be impressed by the scope of the 1988 Education Reform Act (ERA), ranging—to mention only major school-level changes—from the introduction of a national curriculum and national assessment to the control, financing, and management of schools—hailed by its principal architect as 'the greatest reform of education since the war'. They will be impressed, too, by the speed of implementation. Yet we suspect that any account of the direct influence of social or educational research on the origins of this reform might be slight. True, comparative research on educational performance, for example the widely quoted studies by Prais and Wagner (1985; Prais 1986), suggesting that pupils in England were falling substantially behind their peers in competitor nations, reinforced the belief that education, particularly at secondary level, had somehow failed. On the curriculum side, surveys by HMI of primary and secondary education (HMI 1978; 1979) underlined the diversity of coverage in different schools. These and other findings contributed to a climate where radical change was seen to be needed. Yet even so it would be difficult to argue that ERA grew strongly from a research root.

From one angle such a contrast is hardly surprising. The standing of social research had declined dramatically from a peak of high expectation and promise to a point in the early 1980s where the very title 'social science' was under challenge. And the spread of 'conviction politics' left little room and less need for the uncertainties on which a more sceptical research stance thrives. Political change, too, meant that some of the networks linking researchers with policy setting were at least temporarily in abeyance.

Yet from another angle there is something to explain. First, by the late 1980s, despite cutbacks along the way, far greater resources were devoted to social and educational research. Second, these resources were increasingly bent to policy-related research. Thus the DES, the largest single source of educational research funds for much of this period, explicitly shifted from the role of research 'patron' to commissioning projects directly related to DES policy interests (Kay 1979). Other sources of research funds tended down the same track, emphasizing the practical and applied. And third, the public impact of social and educational research had almost certainly increased. Using the crude yardstick of media coverage, research findings, sometimes even technical research controversies, have received greater public prominence in the last few years. But why, then, did it all apparently make so little impact on major educational policy?

This is the question we set out to explore in this chapter—not as a history of recent educational policy—this will have to wait the passage of time—nor as a general analysis of the relationship between research and policy. Rather we present a commentary on the changing links between research and educational policy over this twenty-five-year period. Inevitably we will draw heavily on the outstanding contributions that Halsey has made to this field, as academic, researcher, policy adviser, and powerful advocate of the role that research can play in social policy and social reform. This is not simply because of their significance and the nature of this volume, but because they have directly shaped and influenced our own work over the past twenty years of operating—often in Halsey's tracks—across many of the intersections of research, policy, and practice.

We begin by sketching four different stances on the relationship between research and policy. These provide an outline on which we then map some of the changes that have occurred over this twenty-five-year period. Finally we draw out some interim conclusions and pointers for the future.

SOCIAL RESEARCH AND SOCIAL POLICY: FOUR POSITIONS

If we ever believed that the relationship between research and policy was straightforward, just a question of posting robust research findings through the right letterbox on time, then the weight of analysis, the growing number of studies on the way research is used in policy-making, and personal experience would quickly have taught otherwise. There is no simple linear process, luckily so, we might add. Thus while the encouraging research findings on the positive effects of pre-schooling in the

1960s disappointingly did not lead to universal provision, neither did we close down nurseries in response to the dismal follow-up results of 'wash-out' in the Westinghouse report (Cicirelli *et al.* 1969), nor need to reopen them again with the brighter news from the longitudinal studies of long-term impact a decade later (Lazar and Darlington 1982). And yet most social researchers strongly assert that research should influence policy. The key question is 'how?' and perhaps more difficult, 'how best?'.

We have selected four of many possible positions on these questions and structured our comments around four main issues. The first is how the problem of values is handled; the second whether research findings are seen to be cumulative. The third concerns the sometimes neglected means by which research findings become recommendations for policy and practice; and the fourth, the way that such recommendations are implemented as policy. A further theme is the conception of social research, social reform, and change that underlies each position.

The Engineering Model

Bulmer (1982) uses the term 'engineering model', somewhat dismissively, to cover that part of the empirical research tradition where 'facts are held to speak for themselves' and the transition from research findings to policy is a straightforward process. Rather surprisingly he includes Coleman's 'policy research' (Coleman 1972) under this heading. We would prefer a more restricted coverage. Basically social research here is seen as a technical process, investigating solutions to specified problems, and the researchers primarily technicians. In the clipped words of the first Rothschild report (1971: para. 6) on applied R and D: 'the customer says what he wants; the contractor does it (if he can); and the customer pays.'

Here most of the questions we have posed either do not apply or appear unproblematic. The question of values in problem selection is removed from the research to the commissioning process or agency. Researchers have no or very limited choice. If the question of cumulation applies and it is not merely a case of unrelated studies or 'abstracted empiricism' then findings would be expected to cumulate. The conversion of research findings into recommendations and their adoption is either straightforward or again no business of the research or researchers. After all, as a distinguished lawyer advised one of us in a case of ownership of a social policy research study: if a carpenter had made you a table, you would hardly expect him to enter your home and dispute its location or use—still less to attempt to recover it and give it to somebody else, if you had stopped using it and consigned it to the attic; and even less, it might be added, supply you with a chair instead, on the grounds that it better met your needs.

As often presented, the engineering model is a straw man set up to knock down. We doubt that many social researchers have ever believed it valid, or if valid, wholly legitimate. Though some may accept their role should be restricted to 'fact-gathering', this does not necessarily imply that they also believe that this is sufficient by itself to determine policy. Even the Heyworth Report which laid the basis for a substantial increase in public funding of applied social research in 1965, while it refers to the 'engineering' function of applied social research, recognizes the complexity of the research-policy process; 'in all kinds of social science research the application of results is not likely to be simple and straightforward; it is often a matter of sophisticated judgment' (Heyworth 1965: para. 124). However, the engineering model has had a powerful impact on administrators' conceptions of policy-related research, within which researchers have increasingly had to operate.

The Political Arithmetic Tradition: Experimental Social Administration

Halsey places his own research firmly in the 'political arithmetic' tradition which he traces through the work of Hogben and David Glass. Political arithmetic, he argues,

> has a double intent; on the one hand it engages in the primary sociological task of describing and documenting the 'state of society'; on the other hand it addresses itself to central social and political issues. It has never, therefore, been a 'value-free' academic discipline, if such were in any event possible. Instead it has been an attempt to

marry a value-laden choice of issue with objective methods of data collection. (Halsey, Heath, and Ridge 1980: 1)

For Halsey 'political arithmetic' is centrally concerned with social stratification—in education 'calculating the chances of reaching various stages in the educational process for children of different class origins' (Karabel and Halsey 1977: 11). We would extend this to include a wider range of studies using the same methods and a similar perspective.

Here the starting-point for the researcher is a contemporary social issue or problem; the target, social reform. The tradition very consciously draws on its own roots and is explicitly committed to cumulation or progress, particularly in policy (Halsey 1985), where the goal is incremental improvement through the interplay of social research, policy and evaluation. Yet there remains some unease at the way research findings are translated into policy recommendations. Here values come back in; they are not just the starting-point for the enquiry. Social research findings rarely, if ever, point unerringly to a single policy outcome. Thus in introducing the conclusions of the three-year EPA programme Halsey accepted that these were based not only on the research, but also 'on the wider experience of ourselves and others and on the general priorities which we have not tried to disguise . . . [they have] . . . neither the conclusive authority of social science nor [are] beyond challenge on political or social grounds' (1972: 179).

With the final question of implementation we are back on firmer ground. It was certainly not accepted that 'good research travels on its own legs', a response attributed to Pile, permanent secretary at the DES at the time the EPA team was pressing for more active dissemination of research results. Possession of research findings was confidently seen as an entry ticket to the policy debate, if not a trump card. The campaign at the conclusion of the EPA programme in 1972 to get Whitehall to take up its recommendations is well charted by Banting (1979) and Thomas (1965). Neither side saw this as an illegitimate extension of research. Indeed Mrs Thatcher, then secretary of state for education, was at the same moment pressing for a meeting with 'Dr Halsey', in part to gain a research ally for the pre-school initiative to be launched in the

'Framework for Expansion' white paper later in the same year (Banting 1979).

The EPA programme (Halsey 1972) marked an important step forward at the point where the political arithmetic tradition was at its weakest. Empirical social research, almost by definition, has to deal with what is, rather than with what might be. There are, of course, ways of looking forward by projecting trends, prediction, modelling techniques, or theory. But social research is better at pointing out weaknesses in present policies. Thus the research contribution to the policy shift from selective to comprehensive secondary education in fact underlined the social and educational implications of the existing 11+ system. If there had been any studies of the few comprehensive schools then in existence, they would reasonably have been dismissed as a poor guide to future national policy. Ironically recent attempts to use research evidence to argue for a return to selective education (Marks, Cox, and Pomian-Srzedniski 1983) by comparing examination results from different types of secondary school have run into the same difficulty in reverse, as the few remaining selective schools are no longer likely to be typical of a national system, though there are other serious flaws in the research design of these studies (Gray, Jesson, and Jones 1984; Clifford and Heath 1984).

'Action research' or 'experimental social administration' (Halsey 1970) represented a way of reducing the gap between research findings and future policy. In contrast to the traditional mode of reform where 'a nostrum . . . held to be certain in its cure' is announced and implemented on a national scale (Halsey 1970), experimental social administration would instead subject these claims to firm standards of proof through pilot projects. 'Action research' in the EPA project was the device for testing out some of the Plowden Report's recommendations in real world settings. Amid the trials of turning this idea into practice in the EPA and later much larger Community Development Projects (CDP), it was easy to deride the notion of such rational policy development and its limitations in settings of conflict (G. A. N. Smith 1975). Nevertheless, with hindsight, action-research brought clear progress in certain fields. Firm knowledge of the long-term effects of pre-schooling, based mainly on research in the United States but also in Britain, could not have been achieved without some form of intervention study (Smith and James 1975; Sylva and Smith 1989).

'Political arithmetic' and its extension into action research gave a prominent role to the researcher, both in determining starting-points and promoting policy or practice conclusions. It was definitely 'engaged' and strongly empirical. Its preferred research method was primarily quantitative and its model of success, centrally driven policy change. Indeed it might be seen as the institutional extension of the role of individual research advisers within government, described by Banting (1979)—as Halsey put it for the physical sciences, 'the trend has been away from advisory virtuosos like Professor Lindemann towards councils and committees' (1970: 249)—the routinization of charisma. The political arithmetic tradition allowed for the possibility that there would be other groups of researchers with different starting-points, values and goals. And in the EPA programme with its locally based projects there was always a strong element of local diagnosis and control, which grew to dominate the later CDP programme.

Research as Enlightenment

'Research as enlightenment' came to prominence in the 1970s with the work of Janowitz (1972) and Weiss (1979), but the idea that research operates by subtle permeation of the way that policy-makers address problems is at least as old as Keynes (1936: 383): 'practical men, who believe themselves to be quite exempt from any intellectual influences, are usually the slaves of some defunct economist'. As Weiss notes

> rarely does research supply an 'answer' that policy actors employ to solve a policy problem. Rather, research provides a background of data, empirical generalizations and ideas that affect the way that policy makers think about problems. It influences their conceptualization of the issues with which they deal; it affects the facets of the issue that they consider inevitable and unchangeable or amenable to policy action; it widens the range of options that they consider . . . by altering the terms of policy discussion. (Weiss 1982: 289)

This style of 'research utilization' seems to 'fit' the pattern of 'diffuse decision-making' Weiss detects in many agencies. That is, decisions tend to 'emerge' rather than be clear-cut outcomes at a specific time and place. Yet research can also be a source of 'endarkenment'; the influence is not all positive, to better decision-making. We should be clear that Weiss is not advocating 'enlightenment' as her preferred method. It is just the way that research *does* influence policy and practice (Weiss and Bucuvalas 1980). But it is not sufficient: 'diffuse enlightenment is no substitute for careful, directed analysis of the policy implications of research. Ways have to be found to improve targeted applications of targeted research' (Weiss 1982: 303).

On values Weiss is clear. They permeate social research, not just in issue or problem selection. Indeed she sees the tendency for social researchers to be predominantly 'liberal, reformist, egalitarian' (ibid.: 307) as one of the reasons why their findings and recommendations have often been ignored by governments of a different persuasion. Cumulation of research findings is not ruled out, but is a weak feature—'the results of a series of studies in the same substantive area do not necessarily converge and cumulate. Often they provide divergent and even contradictory conclusions' (Weiss and Bucuvalas 1980: 19). The transition from research findings to policy recommendations 'usually requires an extensive leap' (Weiss 1982: 292). This, it seems, 'may be guided by the researchers' ideological predelictions, practical lore, assessment of political feasibilities, judgments of clients' preferences and biases, or ignorance' (Weiss and Bucuvalas 1980: 18). Anything goes, it would seem.

'Research as enlightenment' thus cuts the Gordian knot of values by absolving researchers from any charge of improperly peddling value-laden conclusions. Any impact on policy is indirect, through a free market of ideas, from which the products somehow seep through into policy-makers' consciousness. It is a case of *caveat emptor*.

In the 'enlightenment model' research and decision-making fit together. However, we should remember that Weiss often focuses on relatively low-level and routine agency processes that with hindsight may turn out to have set a policy. But it is possible to exaggerate the extent to which all policy-making follows this diffuse mode, particularly at the level of major national policy change (Donnison 1972*a*).

'Value Critical' Research

The final position 'value critical' research, is most clearly represented in the work of Rein. Like Weiss, Rein does not rule out other forms of research-policy relationship, though the way he characterizes this gives some primacy to the 'value critical' method. He challenges the linear notion underlying much research-policy debate, where theoretical ideas lead to empirical studies which in turn lead on to policy reform. This formulation, Rein argues, gives rise to a false dichotomy between thought and action, knowledge and use. For Rein the whole is more of a piece. Indeed in some strong sense practice and policy considerations are the driving-force. Thus he quotes with approval Park: 'theory follows practice and serves to generalize, justify and rationalize it' (Rein 1983: 222). 'Concepts, ideas and knowledge have no meaning independent of their use. Hence, the task of research is to uncover the uses and interests that are served by knowledge, rather than the other way round . . . Theory itself cannot be divorced from practice or policy and is simply another expression of it . . . The challenge is not linking research to policy, but uncovering the latent policies that organize the empirical research carried out by social science' (ibid.: 243–5).

While value-critical research may extend understanding by exposing the policy stance underlying apparently independent research, Rein derides researchers who 'yearn[ed] for an adjudication role by means of which research could rise above particular claiming perspectives and become the instrument of discovering some general interest within which competing claims could be assimilated . . .' (ibid.: 232). These views link with his earlier conception of a 'policy paradigm' (Rein 1976) within which both researchers and policy-makers operate. Rein uses the term paradigm 'to suggest a working model of why things are as they are, a problem solving framework, which implies values and benefits but also procedures, habits of thought, and a view of how society functions . . . a guiding metaphor of how the world works which implies a general direction for intervention' (ibid.: 103). The role of value-critical research is to reveal and test these sets of assumptions and thereby lead to amendment of the paradigm.

Cumulation of findings is possible, at least within a particular paradigm or value set. This all-embracing framework also provides the route by which research findings are turned into policy recommendations and implemented. Thus to take a Rein example, the 'cycle of poverty' paradigm tended both to shape the type of research undertaken and the policy conclusions, where the life-styles or family patterns of the poor were the main targets for research and change, rather than the opportunity structure of society. Value-critical research is thus catholic in form and may draw on many different methods 'to make an assault on older, widely held paradigms' (ibid.: 123).

With the value-critical approach we have come almost full circle from the engineering model. Here the whole process is shot through with values, and the role of research is to break free from a given perspective, though the conception of society as potentially little more than an aggregate of competing interest groups sets limits to any truly independent stance.

These four positions provide a rough map for a brief exploration of the changing patterns in the relationship between social research and educational policy since the mid-1960s.

RESEARCH AND EDUCATIONAL POLICY: CHANGING RELATIONSHIPS, 1965–1988

Promise and Performance, 1965–1972

In 1965 the government's National Plan reaffirmed the central role of education as 'both an important social service and an investment for the future' (Cmnd. 2764: 192). By then the series of major reports on education (Crowther; Robbins; Newsom; soon to be joined by Plowden) had set a broad framework for educational development, drawing on these twin themes and supported by widespread consensus that education should be at the centre of social policy.

Turning to research, the first point to underline was the still very limited number of policy-related studies. The exception was research specially commissioned for the major educational reports. The importance these gave to research can be judged by the increasingly extensive and often at the time technically advanced studies that resulted. The research volumes of the

Robbins and Plowden Reports remain even now formidably impressive documents. These reports had thus established a pattern where policy recommendations were made against a background of detailed research. But even here research coverage was limited. Thus the Plowden Committee was able to draw on its own national surveys to establish the incidence of pre-schooling, but concluded that the research evidence on its impact was 'too sparse and too heavily weighted by studies of special groups of children to be decisively in favour of nursery education for all' (Plowden 1967: para. 303). Michael Young, a member of the Plowden Committee and first chairman of the Social Science Research Council, in a plea for more policy-related research, particularly on educational innovation, lamented the lack of studies in this field: 'of all the qualities for which British education is notable, innovation and research are not prominent among them' (M. Young 1965: 1).

Two reasons for this lack of research stand out. First, policy research had much lower status than more theoretical 'discipline' and largely university-based studies. It also lacked security. It was therefore difficult to recruit suitably qualified staff (a major theme of the Heyworth Report in 1965), particularly with the more attractive opportunities offered by the expansion of higher education. And second, funding sources gave no particular priority to such work. The DES was still essentially a patron of research, responding to proposals from a mainly academic research community (Kay 1979).

Pressure for change and expansion in policy research came not from the research community at large, but from a minority committed to such development, often closely involved in research for the major commissions. There was also explicit political commitment to more 'rational' policy development and planned intervention. The influx of policy advisers with social research backgrounds under the new administration was both a reflection of this trend and gave it further impetus. Banting's (1979) account of their influence on government policy attributes this in part to the fact that the civil service defences against this new culture were not yet in place. But this may underestimate the extent of support, at least in key positions. It was after all the time of the National Plan, and the spread of in-house social research capacity within government departments (Blume

1982). The idea of field-testing policies, pioneered by Plowden and the EPA project, spread to other departments, first to the Home Office, where Morrell realized the potential for national innovation and reform in this mix of pilot action and research with the interdepartmental Community Development Project. But CDP is another story.

If there was a dominant approach to research and policy at this time it was not so much the engineering model, more the 'political arithmetic' tradition, where research involvement in setting the critical questions was high. This was the tradition within which many of the research advisers studied by Banting consciously worked, where they expected to have—and often got—considerable access to policy setting. Donnison (1972*b*: quoted in Rein 1976: 115) makes a plea for this crucial intermediary role—the 'insider-outsider' with an independent base: 'we must develop social networks of creative, well trained scholars with a policy oriented turn of mind, capable of moving in and between the worlds of practice, politics and technology'. One characteristic they may have brought to a machine not always characterized by rapid decision-making, was just this capacity to crystallize a decision rapidly. Several, after all, held, at one time or another, major administrative positions in and around government—evidence perhaps of Rein's claim 'that it is often social scientists acting as reformers, rather than social science per se, who contribute to the development of policy' (Rein 1983: 210).

We should be careful not to exaggerate the impact of social research in this period. It remained of marginal if growing influence, perhaps more on the tone than substance of policy. To have got this far required first, a climate where planned policy intervention at a national level was seen as the key to greater effectiveness; second, at least some commitment from enough members of the research community to develop policy-related research and become more closely involved with government; and third, an administrative and policy context in which such a contribution could be developed. In the next sections we summarize how this picture has changed.

Second Phase: 1972 And After

Changing Research Perspectives: Illumination and Critique

If the 'political arithmetic' tradition dominated the first phase, there were predictably reactions in the following decade. The apparent failure of such research to make the expected impact on policy and practice reinforced this reaction.

First, previous policy research was criticized for ignoring educational content and process—'how knowledge is selected, organized and assessed' (M. F. D. Young quoted in Finch 1986: 33)—and focusing excessively on large-scale educational organization. Instead, it was argued, the emphasis should be on micro-processes in classroom, curriculum, and teacher–pupil relationships. Large-scale quantitative surveys were also attacked as part of the 'positivist' number-crunching tradition that neglected the way these processes were understood by actors in the situation. In their review of educational research, Karabel and Halsey (1977), while querying the methods and contribution of this 'new' sociology of education, in part accepted this charge of neglect through 'selective inattention' to what went on within the 'black box' of education.

But it was not just a question of different research methods or a 'new' or 'old' sociology, but differences in the way the research-policy relationship was perceived. Thus part of the critique was an attack on the assumption that educational progress was best promoted by centrally directed policy change. Rather the key lay in changing practice in the classroom—by disseminating research more widely, involving practitioners more closely, and targeting teachers and teacher trainers rather than policy-makers as the prime audience for research. 'Action-research' now came to mean teachers and researchers working together on curriculum development in the classroom (Carr and Kemmis 1986). In Parlett and Hamilton's work (1972) on 'evaluation as illumination' the researcher appears as natural historian or social anthropologist whose task is to 'unravel . . . a complex scene'. And the skills of researcher 'as novelist' were cited by supporters of the case-study method. It was also the time of the Oxford Pre-school/Education Research Groups (OPRG and OERG) with their blend of formal research methods but strong emphasis on local studies, local dissemination, and involvement.

Second, political polarization in the 1970s undercut the working assumption that close relationships between social research and central government were proper and desirable. Thus in CDP, the successor to the EPA project, research and evaluation for central government came to be viewed with suspicion—at its extreme a form of 'intelligence gathering' on the poor by the powerful. Instead research in CDP was increasingly put at the service of local groups, for example exposing local housing conditions or local and national power structures. The results were then channelled to those who could put pressure for change on central or local government. In the United States, Coleman (1984: 132) suggests, 'social policy research is most widely used where there is extensive conflict over policy, and is most used by those without direct control over policy, who challenge the policies of those in positions of authority . . .' While such 'oppositional' research in Britain was always restricted by the limited sources of funding other than central government, there is little doubt that this form of research spread at both local and national level.

While these developments, particularly the clash over methods, generated much sound and fury at the time—and the controversies still echo in current debate at least in the United States (Gage 1989)—their influence on national policy was much less marked. Indeed Finch's study (1986) is primarily an attempt to explain the lack of impact on national policy made by such qualitative studies. Nor in the longer term was it these groups who made the greatest impact in changing the dominant 'policy paradigm', despite their explicit intentions in this direction. For this we must rather look to other parts of the political spectrum. It was the groups which had hammered away since the late 1960s at issues such as educational standards, parental choice, and the assumption that improvements necessarily required additional resources, which successfully set the parameters for the policy debate in the 1980s (Cox and Dyson 1969; Jones 1989; Flude and Hammer 1990). However, though their agenda-setting and political skills have been of impressively high order, these groups have never really developed a detailed and credible base of empirical research to underpin their position.

A third strand was the gradual build up of research studies. Paradoxically this increase in volume meant that the route from research to policy for any single study was far more cluttered. There was rarely the clear run given to researchers in the 1960s. Thus by the early 1980s the DES lists some ninety separate research projects in operation at any one time. It is difficult to see how each on its own could influence policy, except at a very low level.

If we had to select which of our four models dominated research thinking at this period, the answer would have to be Weiss's 'enlightenment' or for a minority Rein's 'value-critical' stance. At an international conference of educational researchers at the Hague in the early 1980s 'enlightenment' was the one position that all researchers endorsed (Kallen *et al.* 1982). This model had made a successful transition from an analysis of how research influences policy to an explicit strategy. Thus in his 1988 presidential address to the American Education Research Association (AERA), Shavelson made clear that enlightenment was his preferred model; the way that policy-makers had wilfully ignored consistent research findings on 'educational vouchers' had convinced him that direct engagement was doomed to failure; rather 'the contribution of research most often lies in constructing, challenging, and changing how policymakers and practitioners think' (Shavelson 1988: 6).

The Administrative Context: Customers and Contractors

As the amount of policy-related research grew, it was to be expected that governments would seek to organize and control its development. Thus Mrs Thatcher in 1970, foreshadowing the first Rothschild Report in the following year, very reasonably argued that DES research policy should

> move from a basis of patronage—the rather passive support of ideas which were essentially other people's, related to problems which were often of other people's choosing—to a basis of commission . . . the active initiation of work by the Department on problems of its own choosing, within a procedure and timetable . . . relevant to its needs. (Quoted in Nisbet and Broadfoot 1980: 2)

The Rothschild Report (1971), with its call for applied research to be funded on a customer-contractor basis, supplied the language and framework, which spread even to areas not specifically covered by its remit. Changes in the DES research programme over the next ten years represented a gradual evolution in this direction, though the research working groups and *ad hoc* research consultancies periodically set up during this period never reached the elaborate forms for identifying needs, setting priorities, and commissioning research developed within the DHSS, nor the same degree of incorporation or permanence (*Review of the Framework for Government Research and Development* 1979; Kogan and Henkel 1983; Blume 1982). However, broad research priorities were established and by the end of the decade Kay could claim 'instead of a series of isolated research projects spread thinly across the whole range of Departmental interests, there is a growing tendency to focus at least part of the research effort on a limited number of areas of agreed importance and to form working groups to draw up the broad specifications for programmes of interrelated research' (Kay 1979: 25).

Two further developments occurred in the 1980s. First, the criteria for 'policy relevance' were progressively tightened. The objective of focusing DES research 'in those areas where there is greatest public concern' in the government's 1979 review of research and development (*Review of the Framework for Government Research and Development* 1979: 46), later became 'areas of policy concern' (DES 1981). An objective in the Review (1979: 46) to 'enlarge the foundation of knowledge on which [national educational policies] are based' was no longer listed among the criteria for policy-related research in the 1980s (DES 1981). Second, by the mid-1980s it was clear that individual policy branches within the DES had increased responsibility for commissioning research, with greater emphasis on the direct contribution the results would make to the branch programme. In line with these changes arrangements for steering and monitoring research were more tightly drawn.

In combination these changes have brought a substantial shift from a position in the early 1970s where the impetus for research came largely from outside the DES and the potential audience was similarly dispersed, to one where in principle commissioned research was largely an extension of the DES, or even individual branch, programme. One result was that research projects tended to be shorter in duration and increasingly addressed to issues immediately at hand (DES 1981–9). Commentators (Blume 1982) have pointed out that the DES never developed a formal in-house research capacity—the 1979 government review indicates that just 3 per cent of its research expenditure went on in-house studies, compared with 64 per cent at the Home Office (*Review* 1979: 54). Nevertheless, perhaps in part as a product of this close contact with commissioned research, research sophistication has spread widely within government. There was a growing capacity to subject research findings to independent technical criticism. Thus the licence and access to policy setting sometimes granted in the early days to anyone with a 'research finding', would now be subject to detailed technical scrutiny of the small print. The guard that Banting (1979) detected was down in the 1960s was firmly in place.

A further development that may have affected the contribution of research was a change in policy-making style. This method perhaps first emerged clearly with MSC programmes for the young unemployed from the mid-1970s onwards, though it has some similarity with the earlier Urban Programme and through that to the 'categorical' Federal programmes of the American 'War on Poverty' (G. A. N. Smith 1983). Typically a detailed policy is drawn up by a small 'task group' often working to a very tight timetable. Consultation is similarly very tightly scheduled and more or less restricted to an already detailed policy specification. Implementation follows the same rapid pattern. In this setting the opportunity for a direct research contribution to policy formation may be very limited. The role for research here is rather for evaluation of policy once implemented. Interestingly, Rein (1983) contrasts the American emphasis on 'post eventum' policy evaluation with the more subtle incorporation of research ideas in policy formation he sees as characteristic of some European settings. Perhaps times have changed. Certainly the pattern and pace of ERA 1988 was very different from educational policy-making twenty years before, with its heavy emphasis on 'partnership' (McPherson and Raab 1988). Decision-making, we might also note, was concentrated and explicit, not diffuse.

If there is a model of the research-policy relationship

underpinning the administrative position it is the engineering approach. Here the relationship is straightforward, the contribution of research technical and controlled, and the problems sometimes mundane. A form of research that flourishes under these conditions is policy evaluation. However, even here the tendency is for far more tightly controlled studies than in the 1960s and 70s, where evaluation often ended in a fundamental challenge to basic policy assumptions.

Changes in the Policy Climate

Changes in the policy climate are a third ingredient. Research, of course, contributes to this climate by demonstrating what can be done or underlining weaknesses in existing policies. Thus in the 1960s, research on early child development (Hunt 1961; Bloom 1964) contributed to a climate where pre-school intervention came to be seen as 'the outstandingly economical and effective device in the general approach to raising educational standards . . .' (Halsey 1972: 180). Yet policy research requires an active policy agenda to work off. Research alone did not produce the change in climate that led to pre-school expansion. There were changes in employment, in family size, and an emphasis on the child—in Halsey's phrase—as a 'quality product', as well as concern to raise educational performance, particularly among the most disadvantaged.

In the 1960s education was at the centre of the government's social programme. The method employed by the major commissions (Newsom; Robbins; Crowther; Plowden) of carefully testing the educational consensus and then, like a skilled fly-half, punting their recommendations just ahead of the pack, helped sustain some momentum for both policy and research. There was widespread expectation that these recommendations would form the basis for future developments; the disagreement was rather over the speed and scale of change, not the general direction.

The pessimistic conclusions of Jencks and colleagues (1972) on the impact of schooling crystallized opinion that education had somehow failed, despite steadily rising resources. Growing youth unemployment from the mid-1970s reinforced this conclusion. And under pressure to control expenditure governments were naturally anxious to break the pattern of rising educational expectations and budgets, that were now seen to come increasingly from a sectional interest group. Education dropped back in the mainstream of policy development. Though we might want to contest Morris and Griggs's (1988) title *Education: The Wasted Years? 1973–1986*, it would be difficult not to agree something of a policy vacuum for this period. It was hardly surprising that envious eyes should be cast on the rapidly expanding role of the MSC (later the Training Agency) from the mid-1970s, as the growth of special provision for the young unemployed began to threaten staying-on rates in formal education by the mid-1980s.

A major preoccupation for research throughout this period was the basic challenge raised by Jencks—does schooling make any difference? This was the key theme running through *Origins and Destinations* (Halsey, Heath, and Ridge 1980), and the focus of the school effectiveness movement which has flourished since Rutter's pioneering work (Rutter *et al.* 1979). It is the combination of encouraging results from these studies (Mortimore *et al.* 1988; Smith and Tomlinson 1989) with the growing body of comparative research, reaffirming the association between successful educational systems and economic growth in West Germany, Japan, and now South Korea (Postlethwaite 1988; Lapointe *et al.* 1989) that has again brought education to the centre of the policy stage. In turn this change in policy climate leads to an increased confidence and emphasis on research. Symbolically, perhaps, it was President Reagan who officially reaffirmed the power of education and educational research in his preface to *What Works* (US Department of Education 1986), a national source book for parents and teachers of forty-one tried and tested educational 'research findings'.

SOCIAL RESEARCH AND EDUCATIONAL POLICY: SOME CONCLUSIONS

Researchers who have spent even limited time associated with government cannot fail to notice how far social research now pervades the government machine. Research, or the language of research, helps shape the dimensions of the educational policy debate, and detailed research findings provide some of the currency of exchange in those debates. Research, too, frequently demands a critical or technical response from government to assess its quality and significance for policy and practice. At a more mundane level commissioned studies have to be steered and managed. At times 'research' may conveniently serve as a surrogate for some underlying policy debate. An example in Britain might be the sometimes heated discussion in the early 1980s on research into the relative effectiveness of selective and non-selective secondary schooling, as this issue returned to the fringes of the policy agenda.

The question is no longer whether research influences policy, but how. Our sketch of the changing pattern of relationships suggests that the research and administrative communities came to endorse radically different answers to this question. For the administrator the 'engineering model' offered a tidy and rational solution, a way perhaps of disciplining the potentially 'awkward' research squad. For the research community, 'research as enlightenment' conveniently justified some distance from government. There was no need for direct engagement or to push and shove, if it was through permeation that ideas or findings made most impact. If researchers were denied the ear of the prince, there was some consolation in knowing that they might, indirectly, have the last word.

Historians will judge whether this mismatch merits any more than a footnote to the changing relationship between research and educational policy over this twenty-five-year period: political changes will rightly receive much greater prominence. However, in the mean time we can draw some conclusions.

First, no single model is now likely to encompass the complex relationship between research and policy. Each of the four models, and others besides, contributes some part to the overall picture. The engineering model may fit administrative requirements for information and fact-gathering, but it has two major weaknesses. It may waste a scarce resource—social research skills—on day-to-day administrative problems. And, as Glennerster and Hoyle (1972: 208) argued more than twenty years ago, the administrator 'is unlikely to think in terms of long-term foundation building projects . . . many of these areas are politically sensitive. Merely to initiate a major project may of itself be a political act.' The engineering model in practice seldom provides the longer-term perspective required for major policy development. When this need arises, the research cupboard may be bare.

'Research as enlightenment' frees the researcher from any obligation to develop close links with government or policy. Such a position is clearly attractive to researchers who wish to keep their distance. But what began as an analysis of how research influences policy, has turned into a strategy. While 'enlightenment' may well be the most important route, this does not mean it is sufficient or adequate in itself. As Weiss herself has pointed out, 'research that policy actors hear about and come to accept is not necessarily the best, most comprehensive, or most up to date' (1982: 309). It would seem cynical to rely on the vagaries of this approach, if there were indeed better answers or better research available. Further, Weiss's 'diffuse decision-making' hardly fits some of the policy developments we have covered.

The 'value critical' position has also made an impact on the policy climate, and on the type of policies considered. But again the impact of such studies is unpredictable and highly dependent on the wider political climate. At times what is often labelled 'research' in this context may be strong in ideas and general propositions, but weak in empirical evidence to substantiate its claims and turn them into detailed policy specification. Such research may thus temporarily win the day at the level of ideas, but lack the empirical base to carry these through into longer term policy and practice.

Finally, with the 'political arithmetic' tradition we conclude that attempts to link research more closely to policy development were not misplaced. The independence given to the researcher in defining problems and putting forward solutions increased the contribution of research to major policy areas. The key element provided by empirical research here stems from a close and critical study of linkages in practice between ends and means, particularly so in an action-research setting where specific interventions may be field tested. This provides a different perspective from the practitioners' concern with the particular case and the policy-makers' interest in the overall picture. However, the political arithmetic tradition worked best when there was sufficient consensus to hold researchers and policy-makers together in a programme of reform—or at least sufficient consensus about ends for a dialogue. These conditions existed in the 1960s and early 1970s, but perhaps only intermittently since then. Without this such research tends to become oppositional, with little or no direct influence on current policy.

Values and Research

A fundamental issue running through this chapter is the relationship between values and research. To conclude we should make our own position clear. First, few researchers involved in policy research are themselves simply disinterested observers. Effective social policy research requires both technical skill and substantive knowledge of the field—most unlikely to be acquired without some degree of practical engagement. This is a further reason why it is appropriately part of the researcher's role to put forward policy or practice recommendations based on this experience. If researchers do not, others—sometimes much less qualified—will.

There may be no clear rules governing the transition between research findings and policy recommendations, but that does not mean that the process is without principle, a question of 'anything goes' as some have come close to arguing. The final chapter of a research report is no longer a licence for a free shot at a favourite policy target. The criteria have rightly been tightened; it is a question of judgement whether the 'leap' from research findings to recommendations can be justified. Critical here is the way that empirical data lead to modification of starting-positions. Results must always be open to further test. Policy recommendations stemming from research are in effect hypotheses to be validated or modified by further study. Such a stance provides a narrow bridge across the prescriptive divide.

Second, research values have sometimes been interpreted in simple 'left/right' political terms, as if there were '"right-wing" facts [to be] refuted by "left-wing" facts and vice versa' (Rex 1961 quoted in Bulmer 1982: 157). In practice, researchers' value positions are much more varied than this simple dichotomy would suggest. And while value relativism remains intellectually seductive, in practice researchers from very different starting-points rarely collect or use radically different data. When they do, rational dialogue and exchange with other researchers normally remains possible, despite differences in preferred social means and ends. For the canons of good research apply equally to all. One problem here is that researchers are prone to exaggerate their differences to establish the unique and special nature of their own contribution. Reviews of research often have much less difficulty in welding together such findings. Rather the difference lies in the interpretation and significance given to patterns across the data; or through researchers being 'selectively inattentive to problems that are nonetheless real' (Karabel and Halsey 1977: 8). Further, the position of some policies on the political spectrum is potentially quite fluid. An example might be a 'national curriculum', introduced in Sweden primarily for social egalitarian reasons by a left of centre government, and in England and Wales under a government of very different persuasion.

Third, in settings where there are conflicts of interest and strong opinions, the failure of governments to respond to clear research findings, for example in the case of educational vouchers (Shavelson 1988), has been used as a powerful argument against directed policy research. Research here may well be difficult and unrewarding, but the fact that results might be ignored cannot be a sufficient reason for abandoning the attempt. If researchers in the physical sciences had conducted their work on the basis of such public or political approval, we might have made much less progress.

Finally, to highlight a major change over the twenty-five-year period we have reviewed, the sheer amount of social research now requires a different stance. Kogan (1984) refers to the 'middle men' between researchers and policy-makers who digest and interpret research findings. This role has increasingly been matched by a technology to synthesize different research studies. Examples are Glass's 'meta-analysis' (Glass, McGaw, and Smith 1981), where the results of all known research studies on a particular topic are combined in quantitative form, or the refinement of this catch-all in 'best evidence' synthesis (Slavin 1984; 1986), where some assessment of research quality must be included.

Some of the research studies that have had most influence on educational policy in recent years have been based on a synthesis of results. Thus the LEAP review of long-term pre-school impact (Lazar and Darlington 1982) was based on the quantitative synthesis of results from twelve different intervention projects. *What Works*, with its summary of forty-one established educational research findings, is a qualitative example. Such studies are not themselves beyond criticism, either for their selection of studies or topics (Richardson-Koehler 1988) or for their methods of synthesis. But they reduce dependence on a single research project. They also avoid the difficult problem of timing, where research findings only by chance coincide with a policy initiative. Such synthesis methods can be linked directly to specific policy initiatives, though this still requires research to be taken seriously in policy-setting.

In his 1970s essay on social science and government, with its powerful plea for the wider use of 'experimental social administration', Halsey argued that 'the challenge . . . for the social scientist to become involved in the development of social policy, its definition of ends, its planning and allocation and its measurement of results' (1970: 251) was irresistible—though he was careful to note that such an approach 'takes it for granted that there is an agreement about social ends just as there is consensus about the nature and desirability of good health'. Since then the preferred move by researchers, if they could afford it, has been to distance themselves from government, and illumine and enlighten—or oppose—from afar. Administrators in their turn have emphasized the technical and dependent position of research they commission. But neither maximizes the contribution that social research could make to policy development. Perhaps in the present decade it is time to return to the challenge for closer involvement laid down by Halsey more than twenty years ago.

10

Women's Studies: Theory or Practice?

ANN OAKLEY

This chapter begins with a brief case-study which signals several of its key themes, most importantly the rupture between personal and socially organized experience out of which the impetus to feminism (both in and outside sociology) is born (D. E. Smith 1979). The reasons for including the case-study are twofold. First, the subject-matter of women's studies draws attention to fundamental flaws in conventional ways of building, and presenting, knowledge about the world, and suggests alternative ways of proceeding. Secondly, this volume itself has a dual purpose, being intended both as a contribution to discourse around the theme of relations between academia and social policy, and as a personal tribute to A. H. Halsey, whose own work has been very much occupied with this question.

Once upon a time there was a young woman, brought up in a left-wing academic household, who found it very difficult to make up her mind what to do with her life. Through a childhood and adolescence peopled by such personages as R. H. Tawney, Richard Crossman, Harold Wilson, John Vaizey, Peter Townsend, Barbara Wootton, and others of their (and different) ilk, she had imbibed (though would probably then have been unable to articulate) the notion that the only proper aim of knowledge is, or should be, the reform of society through democratic political means. On the other hand, the young woman's formal education in a single-sex school with a conservative political orientation, suggested that, if women were socially important (a large question mark hung over this assumption at the time), then their vocation and contribution to the politics of social reform might be somewhat more complex than that of men. It even, perhaps, would call into question central notions such as that of 'democracy' itself.

With all these ideas churning around in an inchoate mass

inside her, the young woman went to Oxford in 1962 to study Politics, Philosophy, and Economics. She hoped to find some answers. However, after grappling for two years with economic theory, symbolic logic, and a philosophy of philosophy that seemed entirely language- and therefore culture-bound, as it appeared to rest its scientific foundations exclusively on the anatomy of concepts used by the British upper classes, she was none the wiser. Then she learnt that two papers in sociology were to be introduced on to the politics syllabus part of the PPE degree. The paper on Modern Social Institutions was to be taught by A. H. Halsey. At her first tutorial, the young woman was set a critique of Ralf Dahrendorf's *Class and Class Conflict in Industrial Society*, a book which, though limited by its time, none the less contained ideas and questions that she recognized. From then on, and under the continuing tutelage of A. H. Halsey, she determined that sociology probably offered her three things which she had not been able to find elsewhere.

First, it promised her an understanding of the 'real' world as lived in, and struggled with, by ordinary people. Second, and because of this, there was some chance that it would provide her with an understanding of her own place in it. Thirdly, the relevance of sociological analysis to political issues and ideas was immediate and obvious, although, and fortunately, healthy argument might attend the working out of the exact political implications of any particular exercise of the sociological imagination.

The young woman became a sociologist in the sense that she subsequently earned her living from engaging in, and writing about, sociological research. In important ways, sociology for her lived up to its promise, and in equally important ways it did not. The success and the failure are intimately linked; and the observations that follow are an attempt to provide some commentary on this schism—one which has constituted the subject-matter of what are euphemistically termed 'women's studies'. The central question concerning women's studies in sociology is both one about the social formation and action of a movement for social and political reform, and one about the extent to which sociology as theory and practice is capable of being reformed.

In 1945 the Swedish social scientist Alva Myrdal published a book entitled *Nation and Family*, which was an attempt to unravel some of the complex questions concerning the social position of women, population policy, and democratic planning. In Chapter 1, Myrdal outlines the view of the relations between social science and social reform on which her book is based, and which highlights both the potential and the weakness of traditional sociological work on the intersections of gender, sociology, and social reform:

> The principal difficulty in constructive social engineering is . . . the need of value premises to supplement knowledge of facts. One of the chief reasons for the underdeveloped state of the allied social science field today is the approach towards dealing with values. An established tendency to drive values underground, to make the analysis appear scientific by omitting certain basic assumptions from the discussion, has too often emasculated the social sciences as agencies for rationality in social and political life. To be truly rational, it is necessary to accept the obvious principle that a social program, like a practical judgement, is a conclusion based upon premises of values as well as upon facts.
>
> We can then proceed by selecting and stating explicitly our values relating to means as well as to goals. By applying this system of relevant value premises to the system of ascertainable facts, we can construct social programs which per se are just as rational as any social theory. (Myrdal 1945: 1–2)

Myrdal describes sociology as 'emasculated' by the refusal to confront underground value assumptions, but the assumptions concerning gender contained in that word are of course themselves interesting, especially in the light of the feminist epistemological critique developed in the 1970s which has settled on the embeddedness of values within the masculine model of rationality as one of the core problems to be faced in liberating the reformist potential of social science (Sherman and Beck 1979). Myrdal's description of the problem identifies three distinct areas of difficulty which have all been taken up and pursued under the heading of women's studies. These are (1) the nature of social 'facts' as indisputable scientific knowledge; (2) the practical fusion between, but ideal separation of, facts and values; and (3) the notion of a 'rational' social policy based on discoverable social facts.

WAYS OF KNOWING

The idea of a social world 'out there' separate from individual consciousness and waiting to be mapped by sociologists, was grafted on to models of the physical or natural world as constituting the territory of scientific inquiry in the early claims of sociology to be a legitimate professional activity in its own right (Wootton 1950). Social facts derive their importance from sociology's imitation of 'science proper'—the 'Is sociology a science?' question of undergraduate essays.

The analogy between 'natural' and 'social' science bred an assumption of methodological equivalence between the two. In this, the collection of discrete facts about separate, quantifiable units forms the basic technique of building knowledge and theory. As Hilary Graham (1983*a*) has outlined the principles of the survey method, these not only follow the precepts of methods in the natural sciences, but were also importantly modelled on the form of labour relations prescribed for capitalist production. Similarly, basic social scientific theories concerning the division of labour between individuals and groups are rooted in the distinction between public and private labour. Theory proceeds on the assumption that most key social phenomena can be explained by reference to what happens in the world of labour processes and relations outside the home, but an understanding both of the gender division of labour and of women's particular social experiences can only be obtained from studying the private domain (Stacey 1981). The most outstanding example of this dichotomized approach on both theoretical and methodological levels, is the mapping of social experience in the form of 'class' consciousness, behaviours, conflict, and so forth, where the principal denominator of class is taken to be economic occupational title. Those who lack such a title, or any stable relationships over time to the occupational hierarchy, can only be deemed anomalous within the frame of reference of the analysis. More seriously, however, the fact that one social group—women—exhibits a characteristically different distribution of occupational positions even within this narrow frame of reference, is still taken as evidence of deviation from a previously designated standard which relates to the behaviour of men. (Crompton and Mann 1986; Dex 1987).

The sociological study of social class exemplifies the alliance of a methodology and a theory of knowledge derived from the natural sciences which is, in important ways, limited and limiting when applied to the study of social phenomena. Thus, as Abbott (1987) has observed in relation to the whole debate about 'women and class' that has taken place over the past fifteen to twenty years, much less prominence has been given to questions of class orientation or class action than to other facets of class such as skill level or property ownership. If 'class' is about the links between social position and the social relations of labour over a lifetime, then *all* experiences of labour—productive, reproductive, and consumptive—must be taken on board in the analysis, as also must the question of the meaning to individuals of their experiences.

Walby's (1988) dissection of the various stages of the feminist critique of social science exposes reasons both for the responsiveness of sociology to reform and of its failure to be so. The central problem has to do with the constitution of knowledge itself. According to Walby, when sociology's treatment of women (or gender, see Oakley 1989) is first criticized by those who wish it to become a less sexist discipline, the criticism is along the lines of pointing out omissions, or flaws, and fallacies and underlying assumptions, and the reconstruction of some strands of sociological 'knowledge' as research questions. The next stage is primarily an additive one: women are 'added' to the analysis. In the final stage there is the 'full theoretical integration of the analysis of gender into the central questions of the discipline itself' (Walby 1988: 215).

There are few who would query the historical reality within British sociology of the first two of Walby's stages of the feminist critique. Since the early 1970s a large amount of sociological work has been carried on under the general heading of exploring the nature of gender as a social signifier. This has entailed sensitivity to gender as an axis of potential difference in different social contexts and areas of sociological work; a great deal of data gathering, much of it in the form of 'qualitative' material; and some development of theoretical perspectives which take more account of women's self-defined social position than the dominant theoretical traditions of sociology have done in the past. In general it would probably be fair to say that the exploration of themes concerning the household and both social and biological reproduction have received more thorough attention than have those to do with the public sphere, and in terms of the need to develop new theoretical approaches (see, for example, Delphy 1980). In part this is because sociological analysis of the public domain has suffered from the strait-jacket of taking male experience as the standard with which women's is compared, whereas the study of the household and maternity has had to centre on an exposition, previously muted, of women's own, and this has inevitably proved more fertile in generating new approaches. Equally, however, and despite these endeavours, no one could argue that the final stage of the full integration of women's studies in sociology has been reached. It would seem, then, that whatever has been accomplished in the way of 'feminizing' (not the same thing as the 'emasculation' of Myrdal's language) sociology has been at the same time held back by an insufficiently radical vision. The model has primarily been one of a collection of social facts and of theories as facts, from which women have been omitted; rather than one of a system and an epistemology of knowledge which has been unable to accommodate the lived realities of women's experiences precisely because it mirrors both capitalist and patriarchal structures of relations.

This point has become clearer as the debate, not about social science as knowledge, but about the methods and assumptions of science in general, has laid bare the essence of the scientific enterprise as knowledge construction. The claim of science to be an objective, value-neutral enterprise for fact-gathering and theory-testing hides the premisses critical to its operation. These include the notion that scientific inquiry is not only able to yield abstract and absolute truths about nature but that it must do so, as science is the chief instrument for 'man's' domination of the world (Witt *et al.* 1989). As Sandra Harding has pointed out, a further critical characterization of the scientific enterprise in modern society that follows from this is that science (scientific knowledge) is sacred. Thus:

> We are told that human understanding is decreased rather than increased by attempting to account for the nature and structure of scientific activity . . . The project that science's sacredness makes taboo is the examination of science in just the ways any other institution or set of social practices can be examined. (Harding 1986: 38–9)

In whatever guise it appears, or discipline within which it shelters, 'knowledge' in modern industrialized societies is constituted and seen in ways which effectively make it the intellectual property of the dominant social group. Epistemology and methodology are connected, moreover, so that legitimated ways of acquiring knowledge reflect what knowledge 'is' rather than what it might be. To put it another way: the stages of the feminist attempt to reform sociology would have been better run in reverse; the aim of full integration being the primary and initial goal and thus requiring at the outset that reformers systematically dismantle the entire sociological edifice as a way of knowing about the world in order to replace it with a set of practices capable of knowing differently.

One increasingly important way this unresolved hiatus is being expressed within sociology is in the form of a dispute between quantitative and qualitative methods. Traditionally, the former have been preferred as being more likely to produce valid, generalizable knowledge. Qualitative methods have particularly come to the fore in relation to the representation of the social experiences of the (relatively) powerless. The main distinction between the two types of method lies in the relationship between the specification of research issues and variables on the one hand, and the process of doing the research on the other. In the quantitative tradition, hypotheses concerning relationships between variables, and the isolation and definition of variables themselves, are specified before data-collection begins. Qualitative researchers, on the other hand, carry out these tasks at the same time as they gather data. Thus a second important difference concerns influence and generalizability. Qualitative work is not oriented to the discovery of the incidence and frequency of a characteristic within a population, but rather to exploring the nature of the characteristic and its meaning for individuals located in particular social contexts. Thirdly, quantitative methods allow the researcher no subjectivity and therefore do not prescribe reflexivity: the researcher is an instrument or technique, not part of the studied social world. Sensitivity to the researcher's own cultural assumptions and social position is, on the other hand, a requirement of the qualitative approach. It is important to note that quantitative and qualitative methods do not differ in their dependence on induction as part of their logic of inquiry. But whereas quantitative methods rely on the principle of enumerative induction as used in natural science, qualitative methods employ analytic induction. As Julia Brannen, who has recently systematically explored these issues, comments: 'enumerative induction abstracts by generalising whereas analytic induction generalises by abstracting' (1989: 6).

It is easy to see why a qualitative methodology should have become the pre-eminent and preferred technique of feminist researchers (Finch 1984; Oakley 1981; Stanley and Wise 1979). Given that the values and beliefs of minority groups are likely to be rendered 'unknowable' by the very social structures and processes that define 'their' position, the task of researchers wishing to reform this situation must be centrally to provide a situation in which such values and beliefs and attitudes can not only be expressed but be recognized to have been expressed. This is not the problem, however. The problem is the nature of the disjunction between the two methodologies: qualitative methods are not simply different from quantitative methods; they are, rather, perceived as less valued, less prestigious, less 'scientific' and therefore inherently less capable of producing or enhancing 'knowledge'. To suggest that this opposition is not unlike former characterizations of the relative social and biological positions of men and women themselves may be ingenuous; none the less it points to a central and significant difficulty in the attempt to reform the sexist stance of sociology 'as a science'—the fact that the tools of reform (concepts, languages, methods) themselves carry ideological baggage which it is difficult to shed. At its most simple, this can be stated thus: the emancipation of sociology from its sexist shackles requires the invention of a new language within which a new epistemology of both theory and methods can be stated. And/or: the fact that significant reform has not occurred is, at least in part, due to the use by reformers of the old language concerning both what knowledge 'is' and the means by which it may be added to, reshaped, or altered in any way.

UNDERGROUND VALUES?

Myrdal's 1945 text speaks of 'An established tendency to drive values underground', which gives sociological analyses the guise of *appearing* scientific because 'certain basic assumptions' are omitted from the discourse. The enforced articulation of value premisses has been a central plank in the feminist critique. From revelations about sociology's 'founding fathers' (Oakley 1974) to the unpacking of the assumption that the household is necessarily a unit in which resource-sharing flourishes (Brannen and Wilson 1987); from the dominance of labour-market position in stratification theory (Marshall *et al.* 1988) to the implicit characterization of child-rearing as socialization rather than health-care work (Graham 1984), the contention has been successfully put that sociology's capacity to increase our understanding of the social world is weakened by its incorporation of conventional ideologies of gender. The response, after two decades or so of this work, is, however (to some extent), what then? Beyond the specific very valuable individual contribution, what kind of impact has there been on sociology in general? What are the most prestigious areas of sociological work? What kinds of papers fill the pages of the sociology journals? Which are the research projects that get funded? And so on. Within the quantitative paradigm one would rephrase these as research questions and set about answering them quantitatively by defining variables (of prestige, for example), and carrying out numerical counts over time to test the hypothesis that the feminist attention to values has, or has not, made a difference to the evaluation of different types of sociological work. A qualitative researcher would set about the task somewhat differently—perhaps initially by carrying out a small number of in-depth interviews with the practitioners (teachers, researchers, writers) of sociology. Both quantitative and qualitative research would, however, as previously noted, affirm the notion that there is only one way to assess the progress of sociology, and that is within the accepted language (politics) of difference.

A further question stemming from the elucidation of value premisses embedded in sociological work is the extent to which this has affected the status of sociology as 'knowledge'. Following Harding's (1986) observation that it is improper to evaluate science as social practice, it is taboo to suggest that a thoroughgoing and scientific appreciation of science requires descriptions and explanations of the regulations and underlying causal tendencies of science's own social practices and beliefs. Flowing from this is the implication that a science which carries out such introspection is not science; or that a sociology which expresses a concern to articulate the values brought to academic study from personal experience is somehow 'less good' than one that does not do so. Commonly used words are 'polemical' and 'biased'. The term 'feminist' is also often used in this context with a pejorative intention. It is perhaps redundant to note that there is no equivalent term which offers itself for pejorative use in the case of men who identify with the interests of men as a group: both 'sexist' and 'chauvinist' have somewhat different meanings. Nor is it perhaps either necessary or appropriate to quote again the works of one male sociologist: 'My biases are of course no more or less biases than those I am going to examine; let those who do not care for mine use their rejections of them to make their own . . . explicit and . . . acknowledged . . .' (C. W. Mills 1959: 21).

FROM FACTS TO POLICY?

Janet Finch has argued that methods of generating knowledge favoured by those who practice 'women's studies' are precisely those deemed least relevant to the study of social policy. This relates to Graham's observations about the origins of the survey method as an instrument developed by men to study the fractures of the social world induced by urbanization and industrialization. The early poverty inquiries of the nineteenth century surveyed population or community samples for the incidence of material deprivation: social research was seen as essential to social reform. Values determined the topic on which research should be done, but the model of research as a way of knowing was firmly in the enumerative tradition. Social analysts such as Beatrice Webb, whilst understanding the importance of obtaining 'qualitative material by means of the personal interview' none the less took social facts as established by quantitative means as the material on which reforming strategies should be based (see Finch 1986). Because this was the dominant emphasis, research which made any real attempt to combine different approaches is likely to have received little attention. One example is Ethel Alderton's *Report on the English Birth Rate* (1914) which is an elegant exercise carried out by a member of the Galton Eugenics Laboratory staff to produce statistical profiles of regional fertility patterns in relation to various social indices, but at the same time to elucidate through interviewing in different localities the meanings attributed by men and women to reproduction and its prevention (see Oakley 1991).

The tradition of using quantitative research to inform social policy is a long one, and has often entailed researchers being frank about their own political positions. Hence, indeed, as Finch points out, the term 'political arithmetic'. Chief amongst the policy concerns treated in this way have been inequalities in both education and health fields. 'Poverty' surveys of particular social groups, for example pregnant women, are also re-emerging in the 1980s as a direct response to the policies of the Thatcher government. But the question arises—and it is of course highly germane to the argument of this chapter—as to why qualitative research has not been used to feed in to the process of policy-making in the same way as quantitative research. Finch's answer is twofold. First of all, the use made of survey research by Victorian reformers and policy-makers was importantly geared to the conservative goal of classifying the population as a means of enabling central government to exercise more control over it. Social research provided government housekeeping statistics. Statistical surveys of poverty also served to keep the phenomenon itself at a distance. The tradition of intellectual positivism combined with the reluctance of policy-makers personally to engage with the distressing experiences of those surveyed ensured that the point of the research was not to give the researched a voice, but to collect facts on them whose role in determining policy would then be judged by others. Secondly, but related to this, the fact that the policy-research link had already been shackled to the positivist tradition carried the implication that in the twentieth century researchers whose work is less positivist have had difficulty achieving credibility with policy-makers. A third factor identified by Finch concerns the separation between sociology and social administration, which left the former without a significant policy focus. Overt policy concerns came to be disdained by sociologists who saw their work as 'pure' in the pseudo sense that natural science has claimed a lack of 'contamination' by personal and social meaning. Policy-relevance may only enter the research process at the point at which dissemination of the research findings is necessary. Once the question becomes 'dissemination to whom' then policy interests can and do appear on the horizon.

All these considerations help to explain why research which falls under the general heading of women's studies is least likely of all types of research to have a place in the rational social programmes advanced by Myrdal as a necessary part of social-scientific work in the postwar period. Feminist researchers do not engage in political arithmetic, nor do they elevate the objectivity of social facts above the personal meaning of these. In desiring to supply a voice for the researched, they are in direct conflict with policy goals which conceive of research data as designed to serve the housekeeping interests of government. There are, of course, a whole set of further factors ensuring that women's studies research does not inform social policy initiatives, including, most importantly, the structural position of women researchers, who are least likely to be in permanent, high-status positions, the curriculum place of women's studies which is most likely to be marginalized, the difficulty of funding this kind of research, and now, at the close of the 1980s and the start of the 1990s, the fact that social ideology marks this distinctively as the (or a) 'post-feminist' era. Feminism (again) has had its day. It is interesting to speculate on the reasons for the historical periodicity of feminism as a political movement; such speculations would include the possibility that the emergence of feminism as a political movement has little to do with the parameters ('social facts') of women's position, but a great deal to do with the wider political climate. Feminism flourishes in the soil of other 'isms'. Paradoxically, women's consciousness of themselves as a distinct and disadvantaged social group appears most likely to emerge when other groups are making the same claim (Mitchell 1971; Rowbotham 1972).

REFORMING SOCIOLOGY: THE DISCOURSE OF FEMINISM

Sociology has been changed by women's studies, but the two have not achieved integration, largely because sociology's resistance to central precepts of women's studies work has been, and remains, too great to allow this to happen. It is rather like what has happened in the domain of the family. Changes in the role and social position of women in the family over the last twenty years have affected family functioning but not its essential form. As represented within the gender division of labour, men's domesticity reflects this: small changes at the last minute (to rework a more revolutionary phrase) have allowed the underlying denominator of female responsibility to continue to press its uneven logic on family relations (Lewis and O'Brien 1987).

This chapter has argued that the lack of integration of women's studies within sociology has many explanations, but that one of the most important of these is a basic incompatibility between the two areas of intellectual work. Sociology remains in an important sense the study of social facts and the invention of theories rooted in these, aimed at providing overarching systems of understanding social life. Women's studies begins from a point of scepticism about the very existence of social facts, and sees the unification of these in theory as inherently less likely to generate useful overall understandings than to misrepresent the plurality of these—the 'fact' that different social groups see the world differently, that these visions make up the whole, which is a patchwork and not a single neatly homogenized idea. Crucial here is Lukacs's (1971) argument that men's social domination results in more partial and blinkered understandings than is the case for women, whose subjection forces them to see the world more clearly from diverse points of view. But this reformist potential exists within the context of sociology's male-domination (both quantitative and qualitative). Even if sociology has no impulse of its own in the direction of feminist liberation, the institutional structures of the university and higher education would impose their own restrictive pattern.

Women in the first feminist movement of the twentieth century, in desiring citizenship, gave little thought to whether it was indeed citizenship in the male sense (which was the only format available) that they wanted. In precisely the same way nursing—one of women's chief paid occupations—emulates the medical model of professionalization, without appearing to ponder much on the many implications for health work that a model relying so heavily on social distance between client and care-provider (amongst other things) would entail (Oakley 1986). And, also similarly, feminist sociologists in the early 1970s wished to influence sociology—to 'feminize' it rather than to set up an alternative discourse of their own. The problems in the latter case are most clearly illustrated in the area of methodology, where feminists' preferences for qualitative methods have not, by and large, succeeded in raising the status of these. As noted earlier, the use of the terms 'quantitative' and 'qualitative' as a form of opposition has not helped, and may often be inaccurate anyway. Bryman (1984) observed that this opposition confuses epistemology and technique. Whilst the two overlap they are not the same. Furthermore, qualitative researchers use quantitative concepts ('most', 'more', 'some', etc.) and the quality of numerative data may seem much 'softer' in reality than it does in the ideal model of research. One striking example of the inappropriateness of the term 'quantitative' is the work of scientist Barbara McClintock, whose discoveries concerning the cytogenetics of maize stemmed from methods of detailed knowledge of and sensitivity to individual differences between plants—a 'feeling for the organism' rather than more conventional methods of obtaining scientific knowledge (Keller 1983).

A critical distinction developed by Dorothy Smith between a sociology of, and a sociology for, women must be mentioned here. Smith says:

> In attempting to develop a sociology from the standpoint of women, we find a persistent difficulty that does not yield to the critique of

standard themes and topics. In any of the many ways we might do a sociology of women, women remain the objects of study. Sociologies of sex roles, of gender relations, of women, constitute women as the object of inquiry. It never quite makes sense to do a sociology of men, nor is it clear how that would differ from the sociology we do. By insisting that women be entered into sociology as its subjects, we find that we cannot escape how its practices transform us into objects. As women we become objects to ourselves as subjects.

In a sense it would, then, seem as though it is the politics of feminism specifically that are incompatible with the doing of sociological work. For sociology taking the social world as its domain of study, as the territory in which its theories are (albeit only partially) grounded, must inevitably view human beings as packages of facts moving around that world. To allow them (us) their (our) subjectivity is to lose that objectivity which is sociology's own claim to credibility, and certainly to a place in the struggle to make social policies which are something other than the selective social engineering of an élite group. Smith's own proposal of a sociology which takes as problematic the operation of the everyday world (equivalent to a Copernican shift in ideology) would seem only to meet the problem half way. If the everyday world is the problematic then some conceptual revolutions become possible: micro and macro levels of analysis may unite, for example, giving concepts such as power a meaning which would lead to the abandonment of the practice of studying power only in relation to certain types of organization and areas of social life. People may state their own point of view, and all points of view become valid data. What is not clear, however, (and again) is what would happen next. Who would put the analyses together, bringing together the multifarious interpretations in some sort of communicable whole? Would there be such things as 'research findings' even? Whatever the particular problematic chosen for analysis, sociologists study people, women study women (though men as well), and people are either objects or subjects of study, even though they may slip more easily between the two than they did before.

The question as to whether studying women is unethical for feminists doing women's studies has been raised elsewhere (see Oakley forthcoming *b*). I do not know the answer to this question. The teaching of women's studies in sociology may be somewhat different from researching these: at least the issue of women as sources of data on themselves is historical, of retrospective rather than prospective interest. But the general question is, I think, only just beginning to be asked. Indeed, it has only recently emerged from the substantially misleading morass of other questions to do with the qualitative/quantitative methods distinction, and concerning the 'women and' definition of areas of study, none of which has really been about integrating women's studies and sociology, but rather about making it into what it can only pretend to be—a study of social facts.

11

Beyond the 'Mixed Model': Social Research and the Case for Reform of 16–18 Education in Britain

DAVID RAFFE

> The demand for qualified manpower is an economic phenomenon, but its satisfaction is more than that . . . In short, the problem of the role of education in relation to the supply of manpower is a sociological one which can be analysed for the most part in terms of the reciprocal relations of educational institutions and the system of stratification.
>
> J. Floud and A. H. Halsey, 'The Sociology of Education: A Trend Report and Bibliography', *Current Sociology*, 7 (1958), 177.

> In both the sociology of economic life and of education there is a discernible disciplinary convergence of sociology and economics onto a revived interest in political economy . . . [E]ducation can be seen as a positional good either in the economist's sense of a screening, sifting or queuing device for selecting and allocating recruits to the labour market or in the sociologist's sense of a collective negative sum game with its associated inflationary credentialism and intensified status competition. This . . . concept is socially of great importance if only because it is part of the unintended consequences of public policy, not the deliberate result of purposive planning.
>
> A. H. Halsey, 'A Turning of the Tide? The Prospects for Sociology in Britain', *British Journal of Sociology*, 40 (1989), 369–70.

INTRODUCTION: THE AGENDA FOR THE 1990S[1]

Post-compulsory education and training in Britain are in need of reform. This at least is the view of a wide range of participants in current policy debates. There is also substantial agreement on the objectives of this reform. Opportunities for education and training should be increased, and should be equal for individuals of different gender, race, or class. Unnecessary forms of selection, or barriers to access to education, should be removed. Opportunities for educational and occupational mobility should be increased. A common curriculum should be developed, or at least a common core, with increased emphasis on general education. Parity of esteem for different courses and qualifications should be promoted. The divisions created by the bi- or tripartite organization of education and training should be overcome. Levels of participation, and levels of attainment, should be substantially increased.

I shall refer to the programme of reforms summarized in the previous paragraph as the 'agenda for the 1990s'. Certainly, if a substantial part of it is implemented, the 1990s promise to be a busy decade. But this seems possible. One of the striking features of this agenda is the extent to which, by the beginning of the decade, it has come to represent something approaching a consensus among those engaged in policy debates on education and training for 16–18s. One should not exaggerate this; several areas of disagreement remain, notably regarding selection and differentiation. But many items of this agenda have been included in speeches and statements of government ministers and opposition leaders, and in reports by the Confederation of British Industry (1989) and the Trades Union Congress (1989). Similar ideas have been frequently expressed in policy, political, and academic debates.[2]

What makes this degree of consensus the more remarkable is that the reformist agenda for the 1990s has much in common with the earlier agenda for the 1960s which ushered in the reforms of that decade. These reforms included the comprehensive reorganization of secondary education, the decision (belatedly implemented) to raise the school leaving age to 16, the reform of industrial training, and the expansion of higher education. Yet many of these reforms, most notably comprehensive education, are now widely perceived by left and right alike as having been misconceived, and as having 'failed'. It is therefore surprising to find similar ideas reappearing on current agendas.

Perhaps the strongest element of continuity between the agendas for the 1960s and the 1990s respectively is that both are essentially about systems. Both seek to improve the coherence and effectiveness of education as a system, and its consequent capacity to achieve social and economic as well as educational goals. This aim is reflected in such terms as coherence, rationalization, integration, and articulation, which permeate the debate. In part this is a reaction to the *ad hoc* nature of policy-making in the 1970s and the early 1980s, and the piecemeal and short-term innovations of that period. (See, for example, Watts 1985.) The 1990s agenda demands a more 'systemic' approach. It seeks coherence and a degree of commonality of the curriculum. It requires consistent criteria to regulate access to different types of education and training, and subsequent movements within and between them.[3] It requires that the scale of the system, its composition, and its content are responsive to changing educational, social, and economic demands. This systemic focus may explain why, political differences apart, the 1990s agenda is remarkably similar to the earlier movement for comprehensive education.

True, there are differences of presentation and emphasis between the respective agendas for the 1960s and for the 1990s. In listing the 1990s agenda at the beginning of this chapter I have translated out of the VETspeak in which it is more usually expressed. In recent policy documents you may find relatively few references to mobility, common curriculum, general education, or parity of esteem, but you will find progression, common learning outcomes, core skills, generic competencies, articulation, and integration. I may have taken some liberties with the translation, but the similarities seem inescapable.

The agenda for the 1990s has been prompted more by 'economic' than by 'social' concerns. It has developed from a growing awareness that the Thatcher governments of the 1980s failed to remove the fundamental weakness of the British economy, and from fears that the Single European Market might further expose this competitive weakness. International comparisons suggest that average levels of attainment in education and training have been lower in Britain than in other developed countries, and that this has contributed to poor British economic performance.[4] Changes in technology and economic organization are perceived to require higher levels and more complex types of skill.

But while the underlying concerns of the 1990s agenda may be mainly economic, this does not make it very different from the earlier 1960s agenda. One of the main contributions of the sociology of education of that period was to point out that an education system organized along the lines of social class was not only unjust, it was also inefficient. As Bernstein noted in his 1974 review of the discipline, '(i)t is important to realise that Floud and Halsey used a manpower and equality argument as a double-barrelled weapon to bring about change in the procedures of selection and the organisational structure of schools' (Bernstein 1974: 152–3). Conversely, the reformist agenda for the 1990s can be glossed in social as well as economic terms. Perhaps it partly reflects a renewed awareness, forgotten in the early 1980s, that a healthy society and a healthy economy are complementary not conflicting objectives. There may be a wide range of possible objectives for societal and other reforms to pursue, but there can be no simple distinction between social and economic—or any other—types of reform.

This discussion draws attention to a further parallel between the 1960s and 1990s agendas—the contribution of social researchers. Social research—and sociology in particular—is widely perceived to lack influence over current policy debates. This perception may be exaggerated; sociologists may not have the direct and powerful influence that they enjoyed in the earlier period (Kogan 1970), but one should not underestimate the dependence of government and the policy community not only on the data generated by social researchers, but also on their analytical insights. In this chapter I seek to demonstrate the continued relevance of social research to social reform. In particular, I suggest that one of the traditions within the sociology of education which influenced the agenda for the 1960s is still pertinent. This is the tradition which emphasizes the importance of the selective function of education, and its relationship to social stratification, for the economy and for other social institutions. I take as my starting-point the goals of the reformist agenda for the 1990s; my argument primarily concerns the necessary means to achieve these goals. Many of the specific policy measures that are proposed in order to achieve the goals of the 1990s agenda may not in fact do so. Often this is because the proposals are based, albeit implicitly, on two questionable assumptions.

The first of these assumptions is that *labour-market structures and processes can be treated as 'given'*. Education may be reformed in order to solve the problems of the labour market, but very rarely is the labour market reformed in order to solve the problems of education. Typically, this approach is justified in either of two ways. One is by assuming that the causal links run in only one direction, from education to the labour market. Educational reformers must therefore be mindful of the knock-on effects of their reforms on the labour market, but they need not worry about labour-market factors constraining or distorting their reforms of education. The other justification is more subtle: the causal links are recognized as running in both directions, but the influence of the labour market on education is assumed to be benign. Typically this latter position incorporates a market-led perspective on education: not only are the demands of employment assumed to be consistent with social and educational objectives, they are also assumed to be effectively mediated by the market.

The second assumption is that *the particular institutional structures through which education and training are provided do not matter*. This assumption represents a break from the reformist agendas for the 1960s. The earlier reforms were centrally concerned with the institutions in which education was delivered, and specifically with the need to reform them on comprehensive lines. Indeed these reforms were subsequently criticized for focusing on institutional change and ignoring other considerations such as curriculum and certification (Hargreaves 1982; Reynolds, Sullivan, and Murgatroyd 1987). Now the position is the other way round. There is wide agreement on the need for reform of curriculum and certification, and for increased participation among 16–18-year-olds, but much less agreement on whether this expansion should be based on school, college, work-based training and/or other institutional structures. The prevailing view seems to be that it does not matter: that the aims of reform could be equally well served by a number of different institutional arrangements. What matters, in this view, is the 'output' of the system, the knowledge and competences acquired and the standards reached—not the particular institutional structures by which this output is delivered. Reforms should therefore concentrate on getting curricula and certification structures right, and on securing coherence among them. This is the logic behind the Training Agency's Standards Programme and the work of the National Council for Vocational Qualifications in England and Wales (Kendall 1989; Thompson 1989). In Scotland the educational rationalization process has been taken a step further with the modular National Certificate, introduced by the 1983 Action Plan (Scottish Education Department 1983; Raffe 1988*a*). In neither system have serious steps yet been taken to incorporate all 'academic' education within the new structures.

These two assumptions are closely related. Tacitly, at least, the belief in the unimportance of institutions rests on a faith in the benign influence of markets, and in their ability to secure the best pattern of supply, that is, the best institutional mix.[5] More explicitly, it is justified by reference to international comparisons. If such countries as Germany, Japan, France, and the US can succeed with such very different systems, then surely this is evidence of the unimportance of institutions? What matters is the superior 'output' of these systems, both quantitatively and qualitatively in terms of standards and their emphasis on such notions as 'competence'? (Institute of Manpower Studies 1984). However, an alternative reading of these international comparisons supports a very different practical conclusion. This is that there may indeed be no absolute superiority for any one institutional form; what matters is rather the relationship between the institutions of education and training and other social, cultural, and economic structures of society, in particular the labour market (Maurice *et al.* 1986; Finegold and Soskice 1990). A conservative implication of this 'societal' approach is that education and training institutions should be reformed in a way that 'goes with the grain' of existing labour-market structures and processes (Raffe

1988*b*). An alternative and more radical implication is that the only way to achieve a satisfactory relationship between education and training on the one hand and the labour market on the other is to reform both simultaneously.

It is probably fanciful to treat the two assumptions discussed above as purely intellectual failings. There are other reasons why reformers have tended to shy away from the necessary reforms of the labour market or of education and training institutions: in particular, they have been unable or unwilling to offend vested interests in industry, education, and training. Radical reforms which conflict with powerful interests can only succeed if they are given high political priority; this has not been the fortune of education and training reform in Britain. Moreover, the British government has lacked the tools to influence employers' behaviour in the labour market. Nevertheless in this chapter I seek to engage the intellectual argument and to suggest that both assumptions are false. In the next section I describe structural features of the British labour market which influence the education system in ways that are not benign on economic, let alone educational or social, criteria. In the following section I argue that institutional structures do matter, by describing the sociological differences between different 'modes' of post-compulsory education in Britain. In the final section I suggest that the weakness of the British system may be related to its retention of a 'mixed' model in which no single mode is dominant. I use the term 'education' broadly, to refer to all post-compulsory education and training for 16–18-year-olds. The ends of education and training may differ, but their means intersect, and overlap. They require to cohere as a system if the goals of the 1990s agenda are to be achieved.

THE BRITISH LABOUR MARKET

In this section I discuss four features of the British labour market which have implications for the education system, and which help to account for its relatively underdeveloped character.

The first is the relatively low use of, and consequently demand for, skills in the British economy. This is the problem diagnosed by Finegold and Soskice as the 'low-skills equilibrium, in which the majority of enterprises staffed by poorly trained managers and workers produce low-quality goods and services'. A 'self-reinforcing network of societal and state institutions', including 'the organisation of industry, firms and the work process, the industrial relations system, financial markets, the state and political structure' together with the education and training system, 'interact to stifle the demand for improvements in skill levels' (Finegold and Soskice 1990; see also Campbell and Warner forthcoming). The essence of the equilibrium is that although improvements in education are a necessary condition of economic advance, they will have little effect without accompanying reforms of the other institutions involved. Consequently no demand-led regime will ever produce the desired educational advances since it will merely express the demands of an unreformed economy and labour market. The vicious circle is aggravated by the short-term orientation of the British economy. Investment in education and training tends to pay off over the long term, and cannot be justified by the short-term calculations of British managers and policy makers (Finegold forthcoming).

Second, the youth labour market in Britain encourages early leaving from full-time education. Early leavers are as much influenced by 'pull' factors associated with the labour market as by 'push' factors associated with school (Gordon 1981). They do not simply reject school: they reject it in favour of something else, and nearly all early leavers from British schools enter the labour market. There are three reasons why the encouragement to early leaving is particularly strong in Britain. The first is the scale and composition of the British youth labour market. Not only are there more jobs for teenagers in Britain than in most developed nations (recession apart); these jobs tend to be better paid and more of them are full time and in relatively attractive, 'primary-sector' occupations and industries. Although young people tend to be concentrated in particular sectors this is less true of Britain than of other developed nations, particularly for males (Marsden and Ryan 1986; 1990*b*; Ryan 1983). Consequently the labour market in Britain is able to attract even relatively well-qualified 16- and 17-year-olds away from school. Second, British employers often favour 16- and 17-year-olds over older recruits, for reasons which include the lower wages payable to under-18s, the belief that young people are more easily socialized into company practices, and the relatively low 'technical' demands of many jobs. Recruitment to many occupations is patterned in terms of age: often this takes the form of maximum age-limits for entry, notably to apprenticeships and training schemes (Jolly *et al.* 1990; Ashton *et al.* 1982; Ashton and Maguire 1986; Furlong 1990). The 'historical specificity of the British training system', as Ashton has termed it, contributes to this. It is notoriously front-end loaded and allows limited opportunities for adults (Ashton 1988). Finally the legal and institutional boundaries between apprenticeship and employment are weak in Britain. This has important consequences. Many relatively well qualified young people leave school at 16 to become apprentices, but because apprenticeship is not clearly distinguished from ordinary employment they help to reinforce perceptions that early leaving for employment is 'normal' for all but the most academically successful 16-year-olds.[6]

The result of all this is a long tradition of young people leaving school at an early age, and a powerful incentive for them to do so. There is the short-term incentive of a job, a wage, and the material and cultural rewards they may provide (Brown 1987); and a long-term incentive, since opportunities that are not taken up by a certain age may not be available again later. Both incentives are particularly powerful for young people with near-average attainments, who are likely to be on the margins of the decision to stay on at school. Staying-on may be a gamble for all except those most confident of success in further examinations; those who do not increase their qualifications substantially may harm their employment prospects as a result of staying on (Raffe 1984*a*; Roberts *et al.* 1989). An ironical consequence is that many young people who do stay on at school do so for the negative reason that there are no jobs available locally, rather than to prepare themselves for expected future employment (Raffe and Willms 1989).

Third, employers tend to use conservative criteria for selecting young workers and they thereby reinforce existing educational status hierarchies. Employers prefer to recruit from 'high-status' courses in the belief that these courses attracted the best students in the first place; conversely low-status courses are stigmatized. The process is self-reinforcing because the best students seek to enter the courses with the best employment prospects. The result is to discourage innovation in the education system. It is extremely difficult to innovate from the bottom up, starting with low-status students, because the innovations themselves acquire low status; conversely, high-status sectors of the education system tend to be more resistant to change in the first place, as their vested interests are not only strong but also fearful of losing their high status through innovation. Examples of this conservatism include the comprehensive school curriculum, which has tended to imitate that of the high-status grammar school, and the relative failure of vocational initiatives, usually introduced for low-attaining or unemployed young people, to influence higher-status areas of the curriculum.

'Conservative credentialism' of this kind is not unique to Britain; there is an extensive American literature on screening and signalling, and credentialism and the 'diploma disease' have been identified as world-wide phenomena (Arrow 1973; Spence 1973; Dore 1976).[7] The problem may affect Britain differently, however, because of the agism of the British labour market (making 'level' rather than 'length' of education the more important criterion), because of the relative weakness of occupational labour markets in Britain (inhibiting the pluralism which more occupationally specific education might encourage), and because of the particular cultural traditions of British education. The content of high-status courses is largely irrelevant to the process, described above, which reinforces their high status. It is more likely to reflect contingent historical factors and the influence of dominant social groups, than the intrinsic demands of the labour market. In some countries these factors have helped to give high status to engineering and technology; in Britain, or more specifically England, a less utilitarian, more aristocratic culture is still influential (Halsey and Trow 1971).

These three features of the British labour market—low skill demands, agism, and conservative credentialism—all illustrate the influence of the labour-market 'context' upon the nature and development of education (Raffe 1984*b*; 1985; 1987). As these examples indicate, the influence of the market is not always benign, even on economic criteria. The market signals are distorted (see also Lee *et al.* 1990; Finegold forthcoming). However, although the three features discussed above are in varying degrees distinctive of the British labour market, none is uniform across it. Some sectors of the British economy do not appear to be trapped in the 'low-skills equilibrium', and demand educated and skilled labour. The labour-market 'pull' on 16-year-olds is substantially stronger for males than for females, being associated especially with craft-level 'male' occupations; as a result, female participation in full-time education beyond 16 is substantially higher (Raffe 1984*a*). Employers' selection criteria for young workers also vary, not only across levels of employment, but also to some extent across sectors. Some (mainly female) occupations recruit young workers on the basis of vocational qualifications gained in full-time education. Moreover in addition to the 'academic' status hierarchy that pervades much of full-time education one can identify a different hierarchy within vocational education—in which occupationally specific courses tend to have highest status, and broadly based courses the lowest (Gleeson 1983; Spours 1988).

All this may reflect a fourth feature of the British labour market—its institutional diversity. Some aspects of this diversity have been discussed elsewhere in terms of the segmentation of the youth labour market (Ashton *et al.* 1982; 1987).[8] This diversity is closely linked with the relative weakness of state regulation of the labour market, and with the strong but highly variable influence of trades unions and industrial relations practices (Rubery 1988; Lane 1989). An important feature of this diversity is the concentration of apprenticeship training systems in particular sectors of employment, and their virtual absence from other sectors. Diversity is sometimes experienced as an obstacle by comparative researchers, making it difficult to paint a general picture of the British labour market.[9] But it is itself an important feature of this picture.

This labour-market diversity is reflected in diverse structural links between the labour market and education, and consequently in diversity within the education system itself. The post-compulsory stage of British education is internationally distinctive as a 'mixed model', in contrast with the 'dual model' of the German-speaking countries and the 'schooling model' of most other developed nations (OECD 1985). Other countries have a mixture of different institutional forms of education and training for 16–18s, but they are usually more successful in achieving coherence among them. They do this, partly by applying consistent principles of access and selection to the different institutional forms (sometimes, as in the German case, linked to earlier educational selection), but more importantly by making one of these forms dominant. That is, other sectors of education and training, and other social institutions such as the labour market, are oriented towards this dominant form, and may be planned coherently in relation to it. In Britain, by contrast, principles of access and selection are inconsistent (see below), and no single form is dominant. In the following section I identify four modes of education and training for 16–19s in Britain, and suggest that at least two of these are dominant in the sense described above. The influence of labour-market structures and processes varies across these four modes.

THE BRITISH MIXED MODEL: ANALYSING THE MIXTURE

Selection, sponsorship, and leadership are three different ways by which labour-market interests (in particular those of employers) are communicated to the education system and influence it, intentionally or otherwise.

Selection refers to the backwash effect of anticipated selection in the labour market. Employers' recruitment practices and selection criteria, for example their relative preferences for young people with different qualifications or educational backgrounds, generate 'market signals' which influence the decisions of individual students and of the system as a whole. I have already discussed this kind of influence, and suggested that in Britain 'conservative credentialism' tends to reinforce traditional status hierarchies within education and to stigmatize curricular innovations.[10] The unintended consequences of selection processes can be as important as the intended ones. Often they arise from the scarcity (and cost) of information in the labour market and the ways in which recruitment practices and selection criteria respond to this scarcity.

Sponsorship refers to the role of an employer (or, more rarely, a professional body or trade union) in mediating individuals' access to education—for example, through direct provision of a training course or through sponsoring attendance at college in the firm's own time. Sponsors can thus influence the quantity, content, and distribution of education. In calling this 'sponsorship' I have reversed the principle of Turner's celebrated typology: sponsorship is here identified with the labour market rather than with education. Turner's analysis of education systems, while deservedly influential, is weakened by his neglect of labour-market processes and his consequent readiness to attribute success in a system of contest mobility to the individual's 'own efforts'.[11] (There is a similar lacuna in much other work in the area, notably the influential *Inequality* by Jencks and his colleagues (1972). Had they paid attention to the structures and processes which mediated the link between education and labour-market outcomes, their findings might have been received, not as a critique of the inefficacy of education, but as an indictment of the malfunctioning of the American labour market.) Many of the characteristic problems of sponsorship relate to conflicts between the individual and collective interests of employers, for example with respect to the supply of education or training that is not employer-specific.

Selection and sponsorship influences are the aggregate products of disaggregated decisions concerning individual students. The third type of influence, leadership, is exercised through institutional structures designed to communicate labour-market interests to schools or colleges or to the education system. These structures include governing bodies, arrangements for education-industry liaison, and 'industry-led' organizations which determine policy for curriculum, standards, and qualifications. Training and Enterprise Councils (TECs), and Local Enterprise Companies (LECs) in Scotland, are important innovations of this kind. If the characteristic problems of selection arise from labour-market information costs, and those of sponsorship arise from the conflict between individual and collective interests, those of leadership may relate to the aggregation and representation of interests. Leadership is an increasingly important phenomenon in education, and deserves further study, not least because its influence is often at odds with the influence communicated through selection or sponsorship. However, leadership is at least relatively constant across different parts of the system. The following analysis focuses on differentiation within the system and presents a typology of modes of 16–18s education in Britain. It takes as its starting-points the concepts of selection and sponsorship.

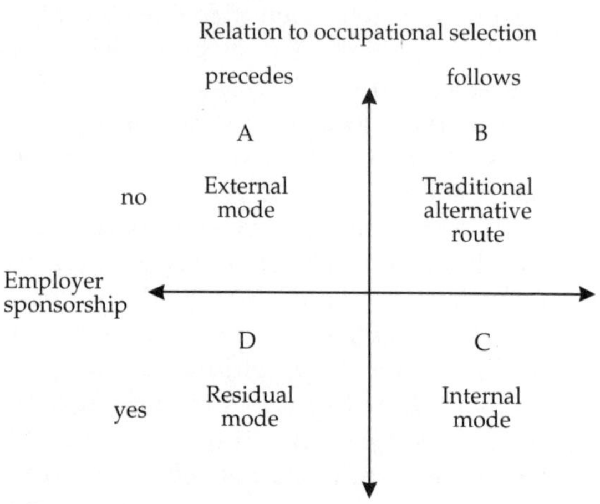

FIG. 11.1. A Typology of Modes of Post-Compulsory Education and Training

Figure 11.1 summarizes this typology. The strength of selection influences is represented by the horizontal axis, which distinguishes whether education precedes or follows selection to the student's first occupation. This assumes that education which precedes initial selection is subject to selection influences, while education which follows it is not. In practice this operationalization is imperfect; education which follows initial selection may still be influenced by the backwash effects of anticipated future selection. For example, young workers may enter courses of education or training in order to get a different and better job. Sponsorship is defined by the vertical axis in Figure 11.1, which distinguishes whether or not access to a course is mediated by an employer. In practice sponsorship influences, like selection influences, may be a matter of degree;

there may be varying levels or types of employer mediation of access. However, to simplify the following discussion I shall treat both dimensions as simple dichotomies.

The two dichotomies give rise to the four 'modes' shown in Figure 11.1. Mode A, or what I shall call the *external mode*, includes most full-time education or training that is not directly sponsored by an employer. It includes virtually all courses at school and most full-time college courses. It accounts for about one-half of British 16-year-olds, a proportion which declines to nearer a third by the age of 18. It is oriented to two principal destinations, to continued full-time (higher) education, and to employment in the external labour market: hence its label, the 'external' mode. Mode B is what I shall call the *traditional alternative route*. It mainly comprises part-time courses and most of its students are in full-time jobs. However, they have entered and chosen the courses on their own initiative and they attend in their own time. Although it follows initial selection the traditional alternative route tends in practice to be oriented mainly to employment in the external labour market (typically at a higher level than the current job), or to further full-time education, but it may be used as a means of advancement in the internal labour market in sectors where employers are not prepared to sponsor the necessary training themselves. I call this the traditional alternative route because earlier in this century it included most part-time education in Britain; but it now accounts for relatively few 16–18-year-olds. It has been progressively replaced by mode C in Figure 11.1, or what I shall call the *internal mode*. This includes apprenticeships, traineeships, and full- or part-time courses sponsored by the student's employer. It includes state-subsidized training schemes for young people who are either employed by, or expect to be kept on by, the sponsoring employer. It is therefore oriented towards the internal labour market, hence its label the internal mode. I define 'internal labour markets' to include occupational as well as firm (internal) labour markets; most apprenticeships in Britain give access to one or other of these (Doeringer and Piore 1971; Althauser and Kalleberg 1981). The scale of the internal mode is smaller than the external mode, but is difficult to quantify precisely. This is partly because it includes a number of relatively short training experiences, as well as longer apprenticeships and training schemes; partly because the boundary with the residual mode, which it dominates, is not clearly drawn. The *residual mode* (D in Figure 11.1) mainly comprises training schemes that are sponsored by employers but do not guarantee future employment in their internal labour markets. Such schemes have often been provided for unemployed young people, and have accounted for up to a quarter of the age group in recent years. Although the state may guarantee a place for all who want one, most schemes are run by employers or private providers who may select the individuals on their schemes. Since the residual mode caters for trainees who have not been selected for jobs it is potentially oriented towards the external labour market. However, in practice the internal market tends also to be influential, since many training schemes offer no certainty but varying probabilities of employment with the sponsoring firm or work-experience provider. The residual mode thus overlaps substantially with the internal mode. There is also overlap between the internal mode and the traditional alternative route, as there may be varying degrees of employer mediation of access to part-time courses.

The sociological character of education, and in particular the pressures and influences of the labour market, vary across the four modes. I shall discuss this variation mainly in relation to the internal and external modes. Not only are these the two dominant modes, in the sense described earlier, they are also polar opposites. The external mode represents the presence of selection influences and the absence of sponsorship influences; the internal mode, vice versa. Some of my argument is summarized in Table 11.1.

Access to the external mode is not, by definition, mediated by employers. It tends to be formally open, although access to particular courses may well be restricted on the criterion of prior attainment. Any such criterion, however, must be publicly legitimate. The opportunity to progress to later stages within the external mode is similarly open or subject to 'meritocratic' criteria. The exception to this is the private sector, which is particularly significant at the 16–18 stage (Halsey 1988). Students in the external mode tend to have relatively high social and educational status, reflecting the mode's near-monopoly of access to higher education. They are also disproportionately

TABLE 11.1. Characteristics of the Two Dominant Modes

	External mode	Internal mode
Examples	Most full-time education	Apprenticeship, training schemes for firm's employees
Access	Formally open/meritocratic	Sponsored by employer
Bias in recruitment	Female, socially and educationally advantaged	Male, average attainment 'acceptable'; geographical variation
Scale	Varies over longer term	Affected by short-term labour-market changes
Main use of certification (and other credentials)	To indicate potential; used in selection to job/higher education	To indicate competence; used as quality guarantee, or to confirm/promote in present job
Pressures for differentiation	'Vertical'; based on potential; normative and structural uniformity	'Horizontal'; based on competence; normative and structural diversity
Bias in content	To reproduce educational status rankings	Towards specific and short term rather than general and long term

female, because the sectors of employment associated with the internal mode tend to be male.

Young people educated in the internal mode have, in a sense, been doubly selected. They have been selected for employment, and they have been sponsored for education (or training) by their employers. The internal mode tends to be sectorally concentrated, particularly in 'male' craft occupations in construction and engineering. Employer regulation of access to the internal mode has a number of other implications. First, inequalities in labour-market selection—for example, in relation to gender, race, or social class—come to be directly reflected in educational selection.[12] The effects may or may not be less 'egalitarian' than those associated with educational selection for the external mode, but it means that education in the internal mode cannot be used as a lever to encourage change in the labour market, except by restricting the discretion of sponsoring employers. Second, universalistic principles governing access to education are effectively undermined, since employers may use particularistic criteria for selection.[13] Third, geographical inequalities in access to employment are reflected in, and perhaps indirectly legitimated by, inequalities in access to education and training. Finally, continuation within the internal mode—in other words educational progression or mobility—tends to depend on the current opportunities for occupational mobility; in many of the sectors concerned these opportunities are characteristically scarce.

Of the other modes, students on the traditional alternative route tend to be disproportionately female, reflecting female exclusion from the internal mode; and the residual mode caters primarily for socially and educationally disadvantaged young people. There is a rough status ranking among the four modes, but with very substantial overlap. There is no consistent overarching principle that regulates access to the different modes and thus gives the system coherence. Similarly, the relative sizes of the different modes respond to changing local circumstances and to social and economic changes. The scale of the residual mode, in particular, varies widely across local labour markets. The scale of the external mode tends to vary over the longer term, while the two employer-sponsored modes tend to be subject to short-term changes in labour-market conditions.[14]

Certification performs different functions within the external and internal modes. (This is also true of other types of credentials, including educational differentiation by curriculum or institution.) The main function of certificates in the external mode is to serve as criteria for selection to employment or higher education. In the internal mode, by contrast, their main function is to guarantee quality to the sponsoring employer; they may also be a condition either for confirming or for promoting students/trainees in their current jobs, but the extent of this is likely to vary across sectors. Credentials in the external mode are primarily required to differentiate vertically in terms of potential; credentials in the internal mode are primarily required to differentiate horizontally in terms of competence.

In the case of the external mode this reflects the backwash effect of selection to employment and to higher education.

There is little demand from British employers for occupationally specific education for 16–18s in the external mode.[15] (The main exceptions concern 'female' occupational areas such as catering and clerical and secretarial work.) When young people leave the external mode to look for jobs, they tend to be selected on the basis of potential rather than competence, and of personal and social, as well as intellectual qualities. Job-selectors use qualifications, in effect, as indicators of an individual's ranking on a continuum measuring desired personal, social, and intellectual qualities (Raffe 1984*a*). The fact that these different qualities are perceived to lie on a single dimension reflects the continuing close relationship between social and educational stratification in Britain. There are consequent strong pressures for vertical differentiation within the external mode; certification is graded and norm-referenced, and different courses and qualifications form a recognizable status hierarchy. Courses or qualifications which try to dodge these pressures, and fail to grade their students, are assumed to have low status.

The external mode is therefore the most directly affected by the 'conservative credentialism' discussed earlier. Courses which recruit and reward the 'best' students therefore have the highest market value, and therefore continue to recruit the 'best' students, and so on. Since higher education is the preferred destination of many of the 'best' students in the external mode, this confirms the dominant influence of higher education on the curriculum. But to the extent that employers rate the quality of students on the same dimension, they will rely on the same educational criteria to identify the 'best' students available to them; they will consequently tend to reinforce traditional educational status hierarchies, and to penalize innovations. An ironical consequence of this is that the 'market signals' generated by employers' recruitment practices often discourage the very educational innovations which employers claim to favour, because these innovations are stigmatized as low status (Central Policy Review Staff 1980; Bell and Howieson 1988).[16]

The internal mode, by contrast, is more directly shaped by the demands of the occupation or industry concerned. It consequently varies across sectors. The length, level, and mode of delivery of education may vary widely across sectors; modular provision, which facilitates such flexibility, is favoured.

Certification tends to be criterion-referenced, and to emphasize the competences relevant to an occupation rather than more general notions of potential. In general, the internal mode tends to be characterized by normative and structural diversity, and horizontal differences matter more than vertical differences (Raffe and Tomes 1987). There is therefore less pressure for certificates to show grades of pass or to be grouped into general levels.

Because of the direct control by the students' own employers, the characteristic bias in the content of the internal mode is towards employer- or occupation-specific training that meets short-term demands. This is a long-standing problem that has been diagnosed over a long period, but it appears still to be present (Lee *et al.* 1990; Finegold forthcoming; Roberts *et al.* 1987).

The modes, as I have described them, are ideal types. The specific details of my account are somewhat speculative, although it draws upon a substantial body of evidence from social research. My analysis raises a number of questions, notably how each mode reacts to an overlay of 'leadership', the third kind of labour-market influence discussed earlier. However, I hope my account has sufficed to establish the general case that labour-market influences and constraints vary substantially across different parts of the post-compulsory education system.

I have focused on the external and internal modes because these two share dominance in the British system, in a way that is less characteristic of most other systems. Whereas both the 'traditional alternative route' and the 'residual mode' can be represented as marginal sources of flexibility, the same is not true of either the external or the internal mode. Some examples of the kinds of mutual influence exerted by the two dominant modes are given in the following section. Underlying the failure of any single mode to dominate the British system is the diverse nature of its labour market and, in particular, the fact that each mode provides the main means of access to distinct sectors of the labour market. These sectors, moreover, are not merely vertically ordered 'strata', but relate to other dimensions of differentiation, such as gender and area. In this sense, at least, the youth labour market is segmented, and a segmented labour market gives rise to a segmented education and training system.

BEYOND THE MIXED MODEL

There are three main conclusions from this analysis. The first is that the labour market should not be treated as a 'given' by educational reformers. Many of the distinctive features of post-compulsory education and training in Britain, including many of its weaknesses, are created and sustained by the distinctive structures and operations of the British labour market. The causal arrow runs from education to the labour market, as well as in the opposite direction. The influence of the labour market on education is not always benign, even when judged on economic criteria, as the more simplistic notions of market-leadership would have us believe. Labour-market influences on education are in many respects distorted; and many of the distortions can be diagnosed using the same principles of market analysis that advocates of market-leadership themselves espouse.[17] A programme for educational reform must be based on a recognition that the organization and content of education are not only causes, but also consequences, of what goes on in the labour market. The policy rhetoric of the 1970s and 1980s typically blamed education for many of the problems of the economy and the labour market. The 1990s agenda must recognize the labour market itself as being at least as responsible for many of the problems of education, and must be prepared to reform it accordingly.

The second and related conclusion is that delivery systems—that is, the institutional structures and arrangements for providing education and training—matter. This is evident from the analysis of modes in the previous section. The principles regulating access and progression, the influences on the scale of provision, the demands on certification, the pressures for differentiation and the biases in the curriculum all vary systematically across the different modes of education. This variation has usually been discussed in terms of the different resources, social environments, and opportunities for learning available under different institutional arrangements (full-time versus part-time, work-based versus school-based, and so on). I have suggested that an equally important reason why modes of education matter is that labour-market constraints and pressures vary across them. An effective programme of reform needs to be aware of these constraints and pressures. It cannot simply specify its aims in terms of required 'outcomes' and leave the means of delivering them to look after themselves.

The third and more speculative conclusion from this analysis is that not only do institutional arrangements matter, but so too does their combination within an educational system. In the first part of this paper I suggested that one way in which the reformist agenda for the 1990s resembled earlier programmes for comprehensive reform was that it sought to make post-compulsory education and training cohere *as a system* to serve educational, social, and economic goals. This coherence is harder to achieve in the British mixed model, which tries to share the dominant role between two different modes: the external mode, drive by selection influences and emphasizing vertical differentiation and structural uniformity, and the internal mode, driven by sponsorship influences and emphasizing horizontal differentiation and structural diversity.

Principles concerning access, choice, and equal opportunity are difficult to implement in this system. The criteria for access differ radically between the modes. The system is differentiated by gender, geographical, and other factors, and there are no consistent overarching principles regulating access to different modes. A mixed model similarly constrains mobility within the system. Both horizontal and vertical movements are inhibited by the different principles which regulate progression within each mode, and by the barriers to movement between modes.

The rationalization of certification is inhibited by the very different uses of, and demands on, certification in different modes. In the external mode, the competitive pressures of occupational selection call for norm-referenced graded assessment for grouped certificates classed into general levels; in the internal mode, the pressures are more likely to favour certification that is criterion-referenced, competence-based, and modular. The difficulty of reconciling these different pressures within a single coherent framework is demonstrated by the modular Scottish National Certificate. This has been broadly successful in catering for the internal mode, but has consequently found it harder to gain status within the external mode (Raffe and Tomes 1987; Raffe 1988*a*; Spours 1988). The NCVQ and other bodies responsible for rationalizing qualifications and standards in England and Wales face the same conflicting pressures, as their remit also straddles different modes.

Attempts to increase curricular coherence, and to promote common elements of the curriculum across modes, must confront the very different pressures on the curriculum within each mode. To offset these centrifugal forces requires much tighter regulation than has been characteristic of recent British policy (Spours 1988; Marsden and Ryan 1989; Lee *et al.* 1990).

The apportionment of education and training costs among the state, employers, and individuals varies widely across different parts of the system. It is hard to find economic justification of this apportionment, or of the processes and principles which create it. The suggestion that a mixed system 'fosters greater diversity and flexibility of provision, and introduces a moderate degree of competition', is not easily supported in the British case (OECD 1985). The competition, as we have seen, is distorted, and there is little reason to expect that the winner of the competition will necessarily be the mode which best meets educational, social, or economic needs. The balance among modes tends to vary geographically, and over time, in response to fluctuations in the state of the labour market and in particular in the level of unemployment. Again it is hard to accept that this variation reflects educational, social, or economic needs. Instead it reflects the very different pressures which affect the scale and composition of different modes.

A further factor inhibiting co-ordination is the division of state responsibilities, at both central and local level, between education and manpower authorities. But this in turn is a reflection of the different sources and character of pressures on the different modes. Merely to create a combined ministry of education and training, and to integrate TECs and LECs with local authorities, would be to tackle the symptom more than the cause.

Not only is it difficult to weld the modes into a coherent system; each mode tends to subvert the effectiveness of the other. To the extent that the external mode succeeds in monopolizing access to higher education and attracts the higher-attaining 16-year-olds, then it hinders recruitment to the internal mode. Complaints by employers about poor or declining standards of entrants to craft occupations can largely be explained in terms of the way that recruitment pegged to 16-year-old leavers involves moving 'down market' as rates of staying-on increase (Roberts *et al.* 1987). Conversely, the internal mode subverts the external mode, by attracting 16- and 17-year-olds into employment, and maintaining the tradition of early leaving (Ashton 1988*b*). This problem is aggravated by the lack of any clear status distinction between apprenticeship and employment. In the eyes of their peers relatively well-qualified 16-year-olds who leave school to enter apprenticeships have left education for employment; it is difficult to create the expectation that other 16-year-olds with similar or lower qualifications should remain in full-time education instead.

The experience of the Youth Training Scheme in Britain provides a further example of the subversive effect of the internal mode. YTS helped young people to find jobs, but it did so largely by giving them privileged access to jobs in the internal labour market, with the employers who sponsored YTS schemes or provided work experience. YTS trainees who were not kept on by their YTS employers were not greatly helped by their training to find jobs in the external market (Main and Shelly forthcoming; Whitfield and Bourlakis 1989; Roberts and Parsell 1988; Raffe 1988*b*; 1990). They were disadvantaged in two ways. They were stigmatized by the fact that they had either been rejected by their scheme employers or had failed to get on a scheme from which sponsoring employers recruited; and their training was often narrow, the result of internal mode pressures of the kind discussed above. In this way, although YTS straddled the internal and external modes, it was dominated by the internal mode. It failed to develop into a work-based variant of the external mode. The strength of the internal mode in Britain has meant that work-based education tends to have status only if it is also employment-based. This has made it very hard for the external mode to diversify its provision (for example, to include more work-based or 'prevocational' courses) to cater for a larger number and wider range of stayers-on.

Finally, the British mixed model of education for 16–18-year-olds has harmful effects on other parts of the education system. There is no single mode in relation to which other sectors of education can be planned. Education for 14–16-year-olds, while notionally providing a common, comprehensive course, must cater for students many of whom will enter the labour market at 16 (and possibly continue further education in the internal mode), while others will continue full-time education. Conversely, planning in the labour market—and especially for training—is handicapped by the diversity of routes by which young workers, even at a similar occupational level, have entered it. A further disadvantage of the mixed model is that it produces wide variation in the ages at which students leave full-time education. It therefore prolongs the period of education which is significantly affected by the 'backwash' effects of occupational selection.

Many of these disadvantages of a mixed model—such as the restrictions on flexibility and mobility, the encouragement to early leaving, and the effects on compulsory education—either do not apply, or are less serious, in respect of later stages of education. My argument concerns the 16–18 stage. Institutional diversity may be much more acceptable, perhaps necessary, at later stages of education such as 18- or 19-plus.

What are the practical implications of this analysis? One possible approach is to accept the institutional framework of the present British system, but to pursue reforms of curriculum, pedagogy, and certification which seek to reduce as far as possible the problems of incoherence implicit in the mixed model. The most promising British attempt at reform of this kind is the Scottish 16-plus Action Plan which introduced a single, coherent modular framework to replace all non-advanced vocational courses in schools and colleges (Scottish Education Department 1983; Raffe 1988*a*). While there are limits to its scope—it excludes the main 'academic' qualification which leads to higher education—the Scottish reform has introduced a framework which is more coherent and flexible, and offers better opportunities for mobility, than anything yet contemplated in England and Wales.

If it fails, however—or even if its success is less than total—reformers may need to contemplate a more radical restructuring of post-compulsory education and training in Britain. The precise form taken by this reform may be less important than the fact that the resulting system should cohere. It might be possible, in other words, to construct a reformed system around *either* the external mode *or* the internal mode: the important point is not to give both a leading role as at present. In practice, a reform based on the internal mode might be harder to achieve. It would amount to a revival and extension of apprenticeship in Britain. The conditions for this would include a clear legally and socially recognized difference between education in the internal mode and employment; more stringent standards and the machinery to police these; regulation of occupational labour markets; better opportunities for subsequent educational and occupational mobility; greatly increased employer commitment to, and competence in, training; and the extension of the internal mode to the many sectors of employment which have no apprenticeship tradition (Marsden and Ryan 1989). Mere tinkering with existing institutions will not produce a German-style apprenticeship system in Britain.

This suggests that the external mode would provide the better basis for reform. A similar conclusion is reached by analyses which suggest that social and economic objectives are better served by the kind of 'general education' which is more likely to be encouraged by the external mode, given the pressures described earlier. A possible goal might be the replacement of apprenticeships and other internal-mode provision for under-18s by shorter, more focused apprenticeships for adults (aged 18-plus), with expanded external-mode provision for under-18s to fill the gap. The external mode, as I have defined it, could include work-based provision, or it could be complemented by other forms of provision, perhaps in the residual mode, to provide marginal flexibility. The important point is that the external mode should be dominant, and other sectors of education and the labour market planned in relation to it.[18] To achieve such a goal would require major intervention in the labour market, not only to restructure apprenticeship but also to influence selection procedures and to outlaw, or severely to restrict, the full-time youth labour-market for 16- and 17-year-olds. It would also require an abandonment of 'the profound British dislike of coherent organisation, especially if centrally administered, especially if under the aegis of the state, and especially if a charge on public funds' (C. Barnett 1986: 209).

NOTES

1. Earlier versions of this chapter were presented to seminars at the Universities of Edinburgh, Essex, and Stirling. I am grateful to participants on those occasions, and to John Bynner, David Finegold, Anthony Heath, Phil Hodkinson, David Lee, Paul Ryan, and Hilary Steedman for helpful comments and suggestions. The support of the Economic and Social Research Council (XC00 280004) is gratefully acknowledged.
2. Other examples of the debate include 'Education Training and Economic Policy', special issue of the *Oxford Review of Economic Policy* (1988), 'Comprehensive Education and Training from 16 plus', special issue of *Comprehensive Education* (1989) and Cassels 1990.
3. 'In general, those calling for co-ordination have articulated the central purposes which must be served by the resulting framework as being: that it must present a comprehensive and understandable set of choices to young people; that it must afford pathways which enable young people to progress to opportunities in further, higher and adult education, training, and employment, and to transfer between routes according to need and circumstance, and that it must secure recognition and status for vocational and pre-vocational studies, and widen access for young people to credible and recognized certification' (Evans 1990: 41–59).
4. See, for example, reports by Valerie Jarvis, S. J. Prais, Hilary Steedman, and Karin Wagner, published in several issues of the *National Institute Economic Review* from 1981 onwards; *Oxford Review of Economic Policy* 1989; and Ryan forthcoming.
5. Thus, in the two documents cited earlier, the CBI explicitly endorses market leadership, while the TUC puts more emphasis on individual choice, which amounts to much the same thing.
6. More generally, the influence of apprenticeship on the recruitment and remuneration of young workers has, in varying degrees, permeated non-apprenticed sectors. See Marsden and Ryan 1990*b*.
7. I am grateful to Paul Ryan for suggesting the term 'conservative credentialism'.
8. See also Marsden and Ryan 1989 on the 'uneven manner' in which occupational labour markets have decayed in Britain.

9. The fruitful line of comparative analysis pursued by Marsden and Ryan may perhaps be limited by their focus on male, and especially apprenticed, employment. See, for example, Marsden and Ryan 1990*a*.
10. Selection may also mediate the influence of professional associations or trades unions on education, where these determine or influence criteria for selection to occupations.
11. 'Contest mobility is a system in which élite status is the prize in an open contest and is taken by the aspirants' own efforts . . . Since the "prize" of successful upward mobility is not in the hands of the established élite to give out, the latter are not in a position to determine who shall attain it and who shall not' (Turner 1961).
12. For a summary of some of the massive literature on this topic see Roberts 1984.
13. In Jenkins's terms, 'acceptability' matters as well as 'suitability': see, for example, Jenkins 1983.
14. For example the decline of apprenticeship in the later 1970s and early 1980s, and the pressures on YTS in south-east England in the late 1980s. See also Lee *et al.* 1990.
15. This reflects the weakness of occupational labour markets in Britain, and the fact that those that exist look either to higher education or to the internal mode (that is, apprenticeships) for their training. See Marsden and Ryan 1990*b*.
16. Employers often use their 'leadership' influence to promote such innovations; this is an example of conflict between selection and leadership influences.
17. In particular, in terms of information costs and the distinction between 'specific' and 'general' training. See Marsden 1986 and Rubery 1988.
18. For more detailed proposals along these lines, see Finegold *et al.* 1990.

12

Active Labour-Market Policy: Its Content, Effectiveness, and Odd Relation to Evaluation Research[1]

HAROLD L. WILENSKY

It is no news that the desire to work is everywhere exceeding the supply of jobs. Whatever the cyclical fluctuations, rich democracies have since the early 1970s experienced the unhappy combination of accelerated rates of general labour-force participation and rising unemployment insurance and welfare costs for selected groups: displaced workers in their prime, as well as the hard-to-employ young, minorities, handicapped, single mothers, displaced home-makers, and older men. Although national strategies for coping with these problems are diverse, there is increasing recognition that a major trade-off can be made between expensive, passive policies that make no contribution to human resource use and what has come to be known as 'active labour-market policy'.

By *active labour-market policy* (ALMP) I mean direct government action to shape the *demand* for labour by maintaining or creating jobs; to increase the *supply* and *quality* of labour via training and rehabilitation; and to encourage *labour mobility* via placement, counselling, and mobility incentives. ALMP is counter-posed to such passive policies as unemployment insurance and public (or social) assistance. Excluded by most experts are policies that aim merely to redistribute existing work rather than increase it, such as affirmative action or coercion and bribes to eliminate older workers or immigrants from the labour market. Always excluded are measures that may affect the labour market indirectly: fiscal and monetary policy, regulation or deregulation, incomes policies, or trade and industrial policies. Programmes marginal to the definition include work-sharing and regional redevelopment, which may or may not increase job or training opportunities. Of the twenty-one different programmes that one can roughly fit into this definition of ALMP, sixteen comprise the core, with five others somewhat marginal (see Fig. 12.1).

FIG. 12.1. 21 Types of Programmes Labelled 'Active Labour Market Policy'[a]

Government policies to create or maintain jobs
(shape demand for labour)

A. Direct provision of work via:
  1. sheltered workshops and other job-creation measures for handicapped workers;
  2. employment in regular public service;
  3. public works projects—e.g. building and highway construction, conservation (e.g. Civilian Conservation Corps). Proposals for National Youth Service Corps fit items 2 and 3.

B. Subsidies to private business to:
  4. hire new employees;
  5. extend seasonal work year round—e.g. winter construction subsidies;
  ?6. locate or relocate work-places in areas of high unemployment and create new jobs (e.g. area redevelopment).

C. Laws or subsidies to maintain demand for labour via:
  7. short-time work (e.g. pay workers some of the difference between part-time pay and full-time pay to prevent lay-offs);
  8. redundancy payment laws that increase the cost to the employer of work-force reductions (assumes employers will be shocked into better human resource planning).

Government policies to increase the labour-supply and/or improve its quality by promoting or regulating:
  9. apprenticeship training;
  10. on-the-job training and retraining;
  11. work-study programmes to ease transition from school to work (e.g. part-time jobs while in school so student gains orientation to work, good work habits, job experience);
  12. job transition training for workers threatened with lay-offs—training while still working for the same employer on the threatened job;
  13. employability training—remedial programmes to increase basic literacy and improve work habits and attitudes.

Government policies to decrease the labour-supply by:

?14. lowering the retirement age;

?15. raising the age for compulsory schooling;

?16. shortening the working week or reducing overtime;

?17. reducing immigration of guest workers or encouraging their return (through subsidies or coercion.

Government policies to encourage labour mobility via:

18. placement services—labour exchanges providing job information to increase efficiency in matching job-seekers and job vacancies (can include compulsory notification of job vacancies or lay-offs);
19. vocational counselling in school and during the work-life;
20. mobility allowances and relocation advice for displaced workers; 'starting allowance' if search is necessary;
21. relocation assistance via housing allowances or rent supplements tied to item 20 (includes government regulation of rules for apartment waiting lists).

---

[a] From Wilensky 1985: 2. Based on Janoski 1986; Reubens 1970; and Lester 1966; question mark indicates a programme marginal to the definition but included by some students.

Countries vary greatly in their balance between active and passive policies. For instance, as a percentage of GNP in the mid- to late 1970s, Sweden was spending roughly four or five times as much on active labour-market programmes as it was on unemployment insurance; the ratio was about 2:1 for Norway. In contrast, Canada and the UK reversed the ratio: Canada about 2.5:1 and the UK about 1.2:1 in favour of unemployment insurance. (Based on Johannesson and Schmid 1980: 401; OECD 1978: 118–19). The US has fluctuated between these extremes: in 1970 it spent about three times as much on unemployment compensation as it did on ALMP; by 1978, with the expansion of the Comprehensive Employment and Training Act (CETA and its job-creation and youth programmes), the US was spending only about three-quarters as much on unemployment compensation as it did on ALMP; since then the government reversed the ratio again. (Based on the *Manpower Report of the President* 1971; the *Budget of the United States* 1973; and the *Employment and Training Report of the President* 1980; and subsequent reports.)

In this chapter I shall sift out a few themes from the literature evaluating the effectiveness of particular kinds of programmes and from my analysis of the effectiveness of active labour-market policy in eight countries; I shall then offer reflections on the uses and limits of evaluation research, which some scholars view as a distinctive strength of American government effort. While a few countries, notably Sweden, West Germany, and Japan, have concentrated on programme development, the US has become a specialist in evaluation research.[2] In fact, there may be an inverse relationship between such research and the financing and implementation of programmes. In order to highlight the limits and possibilities of this uniquely American evaluation-research industry, I shall briefly describe an unusual cost-benefit analysis of the most expensive federally run social programme in the US, the Job Corps. The Job Corps is among several programmes whose budgets declined while evidence of their success piled up. The final section suggests that ALMP is increasingly important as rich countries facing global competition restructure their industries; and that in most countries demographic and political forces are more favourable for the expansion of ALMP in the coming years than they have recently been. The cross-national transferability of policy in this area, I argue, is easier than in most policy areas; we can all learn from the policy leaders.

A SUMMARY OF THEMES FROM EVALUATION RESEARCH: EVALUATING PARTICULAR PROGRAMMES

Although the researchers listed in this chapter come to their conclusions on the basis of informed judgement and rather uneven evidence, and although they differ in their policy preferences, doubts, and enthusiasms, there is some consensus on programme effectiveness measured by efficiency and equality: they are most impressed with various training programmes, although the obstacles to cost-effectiveness are numerous; they seem to view job creation as a close second; all authors emphasize the need for stable funding and strong administrative structures with tight links to secondary schools; and they are unimpressed with negative strategies such as work-sharing, the export of guest workers in hard times, and the forced retirement of the aged.

Is training best?

There are plenty of success stories for every alternative—job creation, mobility incentives, training, and placement. And, of course, they are all interdependent. But if we had to choose the one policy cluster that is most cost-effective it would be training and placement. Evaluating changes in policy-mixes in Europe and America since the Arab oil shock of 1973–4, Casey and Bruche (1985) conclude that job training comes closest to simultaneously achieving equality (improving the situation of the most disadvantaged, which they call 'equity') and efficiency (increasing or maintaining employment at least cost). Looking back at Swedish experience and assessing the strengths and weaknesses of the Swedish model, Gosta Rehn, a pioneer in the development of ALMP, reports that about 70 per cent of Swedish participants in vocational training courses are employed six months after leaving, most in jobs for which they were trained (1985: 75). In 1989 many employers in Stockholm were stealing National Employment Training Board trainees before they graduated.

Even mediocre training programmes may be better than medium- or long-term unemployment. First, there is solid sociological evidence showing that unemployment leads to loss of self-respect and initiative, social isolation, political apathy, and an increase in crime and in mental and physical illness. Second, by purely economic criteria, unemployment is very costly. Using the National Longitudinal Surveys of Labor Market Experience, Parnes (1982) shows that unemployment in the United States not only reduces earnings for the time of enforced idleness but leads to long-term reductions in earning capacity, especially among younger men and women. Thus, even if training programmes do not fit immediately available jobs, they may reduce long-term unemployment and increase adaptability and thereby be economically cost-effective. Consistent findings for eight countries are reported below.

The record suggests three major obstacles to the short-run success of training. First, except for Sweden, we see a perverse decline of funding for training when it is needed most (Casey and Bruche 1985). Second, there is the inevitable difficulty that wage or training subsidies paid to employers without tight control may result in displacements and windfalls—for example, youth employment programmes that displace traditional jobs for adults or payments to employers who would have hired and trained workers anyway. If controls are too tight, however, employers, especially large firms, will avoid training or wage subsidies.

A related obstacle is 'creaming'—a general tendency to concentrate on the most promising, least-needy recruits. 'Despite growing . . . long-term unemployment and the heavy concentration of joblessness among unskilled and older persons,' Casey and Bruche observe (ibid.: 46), 'it was the younger, better-qualified job-seekers who tended to predominate' in the training programmes of most countries. The motives are plain: the programme managers want to look good; employers are risk averse; and, where earnings are a function of average group performance, workers resist hiring disadvantaged workers who might bring performance down.

In short, there is a great temptation to save the already saved. Haveman and Saks (1985) note that the demise of the Comprehensive Employment and Training Act (CETA) and its job-creation and youth programmes was hastened by its reorientation towards more targeting of the employment handicapped (for example, women on welfare). When CETA concentrated on the already saved, it could report good results; when it turned toward the hardcore poor, not only did the research evaluations sometimes look bad, but CETA became politically unpopular.

The political costs of targeting training to the poor are matched by the cost of employer avoidance of the products of such programmes—an effect of stigma. If job training programmes are seen as part of the 'welfare' system for the hard-to-employ—as is the case for most American programmes including those emphasizing 'workfare'—they share the stigma of the poor (Osterman 1988: 30). A clever experiment recently demonstrated the negative effects of American employers' stereotype that trainees in highly targeted programmes are part of the unreliable poor. The experimenters (Burtless 1985) randomly assigned 808 economically disadvantaged job seekers to three equal groups and sent them to potential employers: the first group carried cash vouchers—a government subsidy to the employer worth up to one-half of the applicant's first-year wage and one-quarter of the second-year wage; the second carried Targeted Jobs Tax Credit vouchers of the same value; the third (control) group did not identify themselves as clients of the employment and training system and offered the employer no such subsidy. Matched in disadvantages, the groups were randomly drawn from the welfare system in Dayton, Ohio, about half on AFDC (typically single mothers in their twenties) and half on general assistance (typically young and members of one- or two-member families). The results were remarkable: during an eight-week training and job-search period the two vouchered groups had a significantly *lower* placement rate than the group that carried neither a cash subsidy nor a tax subsidy; tax credit vouchers and rebate vouchers were equally damaging to the employment chances of the job seekers. Employers viewed the products of targeted training programmes with such suspicion that they refused a substantial cash incentive; they went for the unstigmatized applicants who in every other way were alike. (Reviewing additional evidence, including a 1982 survey of 3,000 employers concerning their attitudes toward the Targeted Jobs Tax Credit (TJTC) programme as well as their hiring practices and wage offers, Bishop (1989) confirms that stigma reduces both hiring rates and earnings of the disadvantaged TJTC applicants who were so labelled.) As we shall see in our eight-country comparison, the ALMP leaders avoid stigma by making training and placement part of an all-encompassing labour-market policy cross-cutting social strata.

Despite these political and economic constraints, most studies report evidence that training and placement programmes have considerably reduced unemployment, achieved some rehabilitation of tough cases, and probably facilitated industrial restructuring. All authors who analyse the Swedish case conclude that it is an impressive success story.

Funding and administration

Evaluation researchers emphasize that *strong, stable funding and a tripartite administrative structure* using well-trained professionals in placement, counselling, and training are critical for the success of active labour-market policies. If a single national labour-market board with regional and local offices co-ordinates a wide array of policies; if unions and employers participate fully in policy, implementation, and outreach at every level, providing realistic feedback to government administrators as well as political support for programmes, then active market policies are likely to be cost-effective.

If these structures can be linked closely to secondary schools to smooth the transition from education to work, so much the better. In Germany, almost half of youths leaving compulsory school at age 16 enter apprenticeships lasting two to three years. This famous 'dual system' combines practical training on the job and more general occupational training at a vocational school. The accent is on 'polyvalent' (multiple) skills and good work habits. During apprenticeships, training allowances begin low and gradually increase to about half of what skilled workers earn. Retention rates are very high. Because of this tight relation between school and work, unemployment rates among German youths are usually lower than the average for adults (Schmid 1985; Glover 1981). That pattern persisted through most of the 1980s (Auer 1988). Austria and Switzerland, with similar apprenticeship systems, also evidence youth unemployment rates close to (also low) adult rates.

In contrast, the US sharply separates education and work. It has a weak, understaffed employment service, whose operations are only loosely related to school counselling, testing, tracking, and vocational guidance and training; occupational information in American schools is sparse; apprenticeship, mainly financed by private industry, is a minor and unstable part of the picture.[3] Youth unemployment remains far above adult rates, as it does in the UK, Italy, and France.

American neglect of basic education in schools and the radical separation of school from work explain why the US has been uniquely driven to experiment with intensive residential training centres such as the Job Corps, essentially a remedial effort. If Sweden, Germany, and Japan neglected their public schools and routine job-training systems as much as the US does, they, too, would be forced into heroic remedial action.

Work-sharing

Although increasingly debated and adopted, *work-sharing is less effective than other measures to reduce unemployment.* In general, all authors are sceptical about the claims made for work-sharing. Most forms of it—short-time compensation, elimination of overtime, reduction of the working week with no cut in pay—impose direct costs on employers and delay the necessary restructuring of industry; at the same time it creates few new jobs.[4] Work-sharing does nothing for the hard-to-employ or long-term unemployed.

However, the creation of part-time jobs and flexible schedules in industries where these make sense (banks, shops, estate agents, extended opening service industries), *has* met a demand, principally from working mothers, for part-time jobs that fit family responsibilities. Such rescheduling and life-cycle phasing of work and leisure would be useful for coping with the needs of older workers through flexible retirement schemes.

Eliminating Guest Workers

Exporting unemployment in bad times by getting rid of guest workers is one of those obvious strategies that does not work too well. Like the Man Who Came to Dinner and stayed for several months, the guest workers of Europe and undocumented workers in the United States settle down in the host countries for long periods, even their whole working lives. Both the countries supplying foreign workers and the workers themselves have pressed for equity in housing, schools, jobs, and welfare benefits—which implies the special attention and funding needed by culturally handicapped minority groups everywhere. And economic slumps, instead of inspiring guest workers with an acquiescent willingness to go home, have made most of them hold still more tenaciously to their jobs. During the crises since 1973–4, as Casey and Bruche (1985) show, the size of the foreign work-force in some countries remained steady or actually increased. It took strong coercive measures in Germany and Switzerland to make significant reductions and the potential for further cut-backs may now be exhausted.

Eliminating the Aged

A final negative strategy to reduce the labour supply in all rich democracies consists of *attempts to remove the aged from the labour-force* through a combination of coercion and bribes. There is no doubt that for many decades increasing numbers of talented older people have been forced to retire before they choose to. Since 1890, in almost all industrial countries there has been a steady decrease in the labour-force participation rates of older men. The main causes: employer preferences for younger married workers and middle-aged women; government attempts to increase job opportunities for the unemployed young, minorities, and women—both reflected in the rise of compulsory retirement rules in legislation and in collective-bargaining contracts; and, finally, the growing occupational obsolescence of the aged (Long 1958; Riley and Foner 1968; Fisher 1978; Wilensky 1981*a*.) At the same time, increased longevity and improved health have prolonged the years of productive life. The inevitable results of the intersection of these trends is a growing number of able older workers who are excluded from the labour market completely or are chronically unemployed or under-employed. Thus, discrimination against older workers, especially the 'young-old' (55–70 and healthy), accelerated as rich countries got richer—perhaps the only major social category for which job discrimination did not decline in this century (Wilensky and Lawrence 1979).

Whatever the legislation or philosophy, recent practice continues this long-term trend. Although it does not exactly signify a 'new class war', we do see intensified competition among three populations competing for more work: (1) unemployed and under-employed young together with most working women; (2) middle-aged men and women who have established themselves in stable careers or secure jobs; and (3) older workers who want to stay on.

Because of the growing political importance of the aged, this widespread effort to shift the burden of unemployment to older workers is both costly and of dubious social value. If they are going to be tossed on the scrap heap, older workers demand very generous pensions, preferential unemployment benefits and tax treatment, and more liberal disability benefits. There is some evidence that in several countries medical disability pension costs are rising swiftly because they are being used as a kind of permanent unemployment insurance for discouraged older workers. The only country that has begun to reduce the decline in older persons participation rates is Sweden, which has not only led in expenditures on active labour-market policy, but has also given close attention to partial retirement schemes.

Of course some of the trend toward early retirement in several European countries is rooted in the generosity of pension and related benefits (described by Myles 1989: 66–71), combined with a taste for leisure, especially among people who have unpleasant jobs. But over the past century coercion, both subtle and crude, has increasingly played a role in the 'choice' for retirement.

EVALUATING THE GENERAL EFFECTS OF ALMP: AN EIGHT-COUNTRY COMPARISON[5]

The literature on labour-market policy I was able to review up to 1987 justifies an impressionistic rank-order of eight countries in the degree of success in implementation of ALMP—inferences for each country regarding the political and administrative resources it devotes to this policy area, persistence of élite commitment, and achievement of the main goal all of the countries appear to share—reduction of unemployment. We generated a qualitative judgement first and then compared relevant quantitative data on unemployment. Where authors disagreed about success, we made judgements of the relative merits of data and arguments. To validate the qualitative rankings, we compared them with the average unemployment rate of each country for long periods to smooth out short-term fluctuations and to capture cumulative effects; most of these policies are designed to deal with long-run problems of adjustment anyway.

Although the goals of ALMP include equality (improving the situation of the most disadvantaged), the reduction of skill shortages and production bottlenecks, the improvements of working life productivity, and even the control of inflation (Rehn 1985; Wilensky 1985), the dominant goal, with strongest

TABLE 12.1. Active Labour-Market Policy (ALMP) and Unemployment Rates

Summary ranking of successful implementation of ALMP inferred from literature	Unemployment Rates (unemployed as annual percentage of labour force averaged by period)				
	1950–73	1965–73	1974–9	1980–4	1985–8
1. Sweden	1.8 L	2.0 LM	1.9 L	2.9 L	2.3 L
2. West Germany	2.2 ML	0.7 L	3.2 ML	5.7 M	6.5 M
3. Japan	1.6 L	1.3 L	1.9 L	2.4 L	2.7 L
4. Austria	2.1 L	1.4 L	1.8 L	3.2 L	3.5 L
5. Netherlands	1.7 L	1.8 LM	4.9 MH	9.9 H	9.9 H
6. France	2.3 ML	2.3 M	4.5 M	8.0 MH	10.3 H
7. United States	4.9 H	4.9 H	6.7 H	8.2 MH	6.4 M
8. UK	2.7 M	3.1 H	5.0 MH	10.3 H	10.2 H
Average for 19 rich democracies	2.8 (N = 19)	2.3 (N = 19)	4.2 (N = 18)	6.8 (N = 18)	7.1 (N = 18)

Sources: *OECD Manpower Statistics* (Paris: OECD), various years; *OECD Labour Force Statistics* (Paris: OECD), various years.
Note: For all 8 countries except Austria for the early 1950s, the figures are adjusted to conform as closely as possible to the US definition of unemployment. Early Austrian figures from *ILO Yearbook of Labour Force Statistics* (Geneva: ILO) various years.
H = high; M = medium; L = low.

mass support, is to reduce unemployment. Table 12.1 therefore aligns average unemployment rates next to our qualitative ranks.

We averaged annual unemployment rates from 1950 to 1973. The post-1973 period is divided to capture adaptation to massive external shocks. Unemployment during 1974–9 should capture the speed and strength of readjustment after the Arab oil embargo of late 1973; unemployment during 1980–4 should capture adjustment to the oil shock of 1979 and the concurrent interest-rate shock generated by Paul Volcker of the US Federal Reserve Board—which was self-administered for the United States but external for other countries—and a deep world-wide recession and recovery.

Except for West Germany in all periods (save 1965–73) and

the UK in the first period, the qualitative rankings of success essentially match the unemployment rates; countries highest in resource commitment and most successful in implementation show the lowest long-term unemployment rates and vice versa. In sophistication, resource commitment, and policy continuity, as well as success in reducing unemployment, *Sweden* is unrivalled. Its combination of job training, job creation, placement services, and mobility incentives has clearly helped keep unemployment low even as industry adjusts and even when economic growth has been slow and inflation high (as in the 1970s). During the second half of the 1970s the estimated net effect on unemployment (that is, point reduction of potential unemployment) averaged 3.2 per cent in Sweden compared to 1.3 per cent in West Germany (Scharpf 1981: 29; Haveman 1982; Rehn 1985; Johannesson and Schmid 1980; Schmidt 1982). The difference parallels the expenditures in the two countries for ALMP in 1978, a year of West German cutbacks: 2.4 per cent of GNP for Sweden, 0.5 per cent for West Germany (Wilensky 1985: 6). That West Germany has a somewhat higher unemployment rate for three periods than its summary rank warrants may be partly explained by fluctuation in resource commitment (Sengenberger 1984: 339) and partly by its policy mix: in the 1970s and early 1980s it relied more on short-time work to keep, and wage subsidies to hire, redundant workers and less on training and job creation (Johannesson and Schmid 1980: 400–1); arguably the former are less effective in the long run. Still, West Germany ranks high because of its consistently successful placement service, extensive apprenticeship programmes, and (until recently) training programmes, as well as its successful job-creation effort in the 1970s (Janoski 1986: chap. 3). However, ALMP was further cut back in the 1980s, at a time of greatest need, and the government has failed to combine ALMP with other policies to prevent persistent unemployment at medium levels from 1980 to 1988. A policy reversal was apparent in the late 1980s with training becoming more important in the German policy mix—two-thirds of it for the unemployed (Auer 1988).

That Sweden and West Germany lead the eight countries in the summary rank confirms the picture derived from specific programme evaluations: in large measure they both meet all the structural conditions for cost-effectiveness—heavy resource commitment, a strong labour-market, tripartite administration, and tight links between school and work.

Like Sweden and West Germany, third-ranked Japan has a strong labour-market board. By the early 1960s Japan had reached its goal of full employment. By 1965 the Public Employment Security Offices, with an extensive network of offices throughout the country, accounted for 70 per cent of all placements. By 1970 Japan was spending 0.4 per cent of GNP on ALMP—less effort than Sweden, the UK, and West Germany, but more than the US (OECD 1974: 53). The accent was on training, retraining, and mobility incentives. In the mid-1970s a major expansion began, embracing subsidies for employment adjustment for industrial restructuring, vocational training (including training allowances, job-search and moving expenses, and targeted subsidies for employers who hire and/or train hard-to-employ groups and workers displaced by industrial restructuring), and an employment stabilization fund—counter-cyclical subsidies to deal with temporary lay-offs and training—as well as public works (Japan Institute of Labor 1979*a*: 14, 18–20 and 1979*b*). Government policies serve as backup for continual enterprise training.

After the 1973–4 oil shock Japan made a remarkably quick employment adjustment; full employment with low inflation was maintained through the 1970s. Although job training is mainly internal to the large firms, and government expenditures have declined since 1975, ALMP supplements the enterprise-based employment system (Shimada 1980: 21), and there is good co-ordination among employers, unions, workers, and the government bureaucracy (ibid.: 27; Levine 1983: 43). Among other sources of success were the following: employers' willingness to invest in human resources in the one-fourth to one-third of the economy dominated by large and growing companies with low inter-company mobility; a strong basic education system on which job training can build; extreme labour-market segmentation; and pressure on women and older workers to leave jobs in hard times (Cole 1979; Rohlen 1979; Shimada 1977; Inoue 1985). Both women's subordination to the job needs of men and the willingness of older workers to retire early are now diminishing.

Austria too has been highly successful in holding down

unemployment, even in the post-shock periods, but its main instruments have been fiscal, incomes, and social policies, not ALMP. It was also committed to employment stability in its nationalized industries and to early retirement as a general policy. Austria gets good returns on the ALMP money it spends, however (see Katzenstein 1984: 42; OECD 1967*a*). Social partnership sets the context for all policies.

Because our qualitative rankings are based both on resource commitment and successful implementation, we have placed Austria in the middle of the pack to balance low effort against high success for the limited effort sustained. Much of Austria's success on the labour-supply side comes from its commitment to vocational training in the educational system. Like Germany and Switzerland, Austria integrates school and work through an extensive apprenticeship system. Apprenticeship is a grey area in the measurement of ALMP that has yet to be sorted out by analysts of labour-market policy.

Medium-ranking Netherlands had an outstanding performance during 1950–73, almost matching the low average unemployment of Sweden and Japan. Its rank of five reflects the decreasing success of all its policies since the early 1970s. Established just after the Second World War, its ALMP has been run by a strong General Directorate for Manpower, advised by tripartite local commissions. Success was apparent in placement, regional job creation, apprenticeship programmes, and a modest vocational training effort, with some job creation in public service. Concepts, programmes, and expenditures expanded greatly after 1969. But ALMP grew increasingly expensive because of the extensive use of government employment as a last resort for the handicapped and unemployed, with full public-employee status and good pay in industrial production centres and the public services. ALMP proved unable to combine effectively with other public policies to prevent unemployment from rising to 12 per cent in 1983; unemployment from 1985 to 1988 averaged a high 9.9 per cent—close to the United Kingdom's 10.2 per cent. Increasing tension and rigidity marked the relationship of the social partners (business and labour).

The bottom three—France, the US, and the UK—made no major commitment to ALMP until the 1960s and either vacillated in their budgets and policies or saw ALMP as incidental. The early *French* focus on industrial policy, modernization, and restructuring for the most part did not include ALMP. It can be argued that the French planners have hardly distinguished between industrial and labour-market policies. For instance, when they anticipate a plant shutdown in one area, they often try to locate new enterprises in the area through selective credit allocations and other financial instruments (Cohen 1977). In any case while ALMP was very weak before the events of 1968, it expanded in the early 1970s, emphasizing job placement and training, with some success. The labour-market board expanded rapidly both as a placement service and a coordinator of ALMP.

In the years of 'liberal' austerity (1976–81) aimed at industrial redeployment, unemployment was viewed as a secondary problem; ALMP was cut back as unemployment rose. Training programmes continued (apprenticeships and on-the-job training as well as subsidies to firms to hire youth). Some studies showed that unemployment was not thereby reduced; instead employers benefited from cheap temporary labour and deferred permanent hiring (Mouriaux and Mouriaux 1984: 157). The larger the firm, the greater the windfall—a pattern common to several countries (Haveman 1982; Casey and Bruche 1985: 47). In 1981, the new Socialist government, responding to rising unemployment, began substantial expansion of ALMP: it strengthened the labour-market board (1,500 new staff jobs), created a new ministry for occupational training, set up local job-creation programmes run by tripartite local committees (250 by 1982), and expanded subsidies to firms for hiring the hard-to-employ. The Mitterrand/Mauroy government also pushed for work-sharing and for early retirement with a requirement that the employer hire replacements. Although there have been scattered successes (Mouriaux and Mouriaux 1984), the net effect is in doubt. Clearly, ALMP was not able to counter other Socialist policies in 1981 and 1982 that increased the unemployment rate—reflationary measures in the face of austerity measures adopted by France's trading partners, increased minimum wages and social spending, nationalizations that increased managerial uncertainty and alienated business and banking circles. Reversals in these policies came too late to repair either the economic or political damage. Although France fits our hypotheses before Mitterrand, it was an exception in the early 1980s.

The US had no ALMP during 1946–64 except for a meagre job-placement operation; in fact, a rather active employment service was gutted after the Second World War and became a passive agency for employer and veteran needs, by the 1980s accounting for less than 10 per cent of new hires. From 1962 to 1982 the US adopted a moderate range of job-training and job-creation policies, with some success. From a very limited base, funding climbed through the Johnson, Nixon, Ford, and Carter administrations. With minor fluctuations, annual federal outlays in employment and training programmes moved from less than one-tenth of 1 per cent of GNP in 1950–64 to a peak of 0.52 per cent in 1978 and 1979. Under President Reagan's assault on civilian public spending for the non-aged, outlays had dropped to 0.18 per cent by 1983 (Wilensky 1985: 17). For any one type of programme, however, funding tended to be unsteady, co-ordination among programmes weak, and political contention intense. With some exceptions and in contrast to European practice, the accent was more on short-term formal evaluation and experimentation than on programme implementation, administration, intensity, and outreach (Haveman and Saks 1985: 26; Wilensky 1983, 1985; Aaron 1978). Performance reflects the lack of consensus on the importance of unemployment reduction and the lack of structures for linking ALMP to other policies.

The UK shows a stop-and-go pattern as erratic as that of the United States. ALMP started in the mid-1960s, expanded in the mid-1970s—under Labour governments—and were cut back in 1979–80 by the Thatcher government. The 1973 Education and Training Act strengthened industrial training grants and exemptions and created a tripartite Manpower Services Commission (MSC) to run public employment and training and plan a long-term manpower policy. Funding expanded for a wide range of programmes. Despite initial cut-backs in ALMP by the Conservatives (adult employment subsidies, for example, were cut 50–75 per cent), the role of the MSC continued to grow in response to dramatic increases in unemployment (Moon 1984: 32). However, when the Conservatives tried to double the number of employer representatives, labour (the TUC) objected and withdrew; the MSC was abolished in 1988 (Grant 1989: 16; Longstreth 1988: 417). Nevertheless, since 1980 the Thatcher government expanded ALMP to a level which by the decade's end exceeded that of the last Labour government; the main policy instrument has been the Youth Training Scheme (Casey and Bruche 1985: 56; McArthur and McGregor 1986).

The big problem for the UK has been disjunction between ALMP and other policies such as fiscal and monetary measures to fight inflation and defend sterling (Moon 1984: 34). Unemployment rose from 2.6 per cent in 1970 to 12.2 per cent in 1982. ALMP has doubtless created some jobs and trained workers, but unemployment remains very high. Despite the recent ALMP expansion, the success of ongoing industrial and employment-adjustment efforts remains very much in doubt.[6]

In a recent study reviewing comparative evidence, Finegold and Soskice (1990) conclude that Britain is stuck at a 'low-skill equilibrium' because it combines poor performance during compulsory school years (measured by international mathematics and science tests) and a high percentage of students leaving full-time education or training at the age of 16 (Britain was the only member of the OECD to experience a decline in the participation rate of the 16–19 age grade from 1975–9 and still ranks at the bottom despite some reversal of that trend); and because it ranks much lower in quality and quantity of employer-based training than its competitors (for example, Germany, France, Japan). They conclude that education/training deficits are a major explanation for Britain's lower productivity, higher unemployment, and lack of flexibility in production strategies. This study independently confirms my earlier ranking of the UK at the bottom of the eight countries in ALMP effectiveness.

THE USES AND LIMITS OF EVALUATION RESEARCH

Because American policy debates are typically framed in cost-benefit terms, increasingly guided by a burgeoning evaluation research industry (whose products I necessarily draw upon), I shall now attempt an evaluation of the evaluations and speculate about their policy impact. The American experience has broad relevance because researchers in a few countries in Europe have used it as a model for their own recent policy-research efforts.

In their concise and valuable overview of ALMP Haveman and Saks (1985) are struck with the contrast between the American penchant for careful evaluation research and the European habit of acting on many fronts without much systematic assessment of outcomes. Although they recognize that cost-benefit analyses are sometimes based on narrow criteria, they reject the notion that American programme evaluation is an obstacle to appropriate funding and action: 'Good evaluation research can save good programs as well as destroy bad ones,' they say (1985: 22). Agreed. But that formulation is a bit over-rationalistic. In my view, the character of evaluation research and its effect on labour-market policy (or public policy generally) depend upon the context in which it is financed and used: fragmented and decentralized political economies such as the US foster isolated, single-issue research, typically focused on short-run effects and used for political ammunition rather than policy planning; more 'corporatist' systems such as those of Sweden, Norway, Austria, and perhaps Germany foster dialogue between researchers, bureaucrats, and politicians in which a wider range of issues are connected, longer-range effects are more often considered, and research findings are more often used for policy planning and implementation as well as budget justification. Larger contexts for bargaining—especially among labour, management, and government—mean larger contexts for policy analysis, with or without rigorous evaluation research (Wilensky 1983: 61–8).

American evaluation of programmes for job training and job creation is a dramatic illustration of Wilensky's law: the more evaluation, the less programme development; the more demonstration projects, the less follow-through. In no other policy area in the United States—not even in the Pentagon—has the demand for rigorous evaluation research loomed so large. And nowhere among the rich democracies has such research been so politicized. Three problems are apparent: (1) the research itself is usually quite narrow, politically naïve, and in design and execution often seriously flawed; (2) research focused on a single programme obscures the interaction and interdependence of many programmes (for example, education in schools, job-training programmes, and job creation); and (3) evaluated success has had little to do with programme funding.

Consider earnings gains as an evaluation criterion for job training, a typically narrow efficiency measure. Reflecting on extensive evaluation research in the war on poverty, Aaron observes that research was guided by the 'impulse to isolate individual influences; to make complex social and economic processes statistically and mathematically manageable through abstraction' (1978: 156). The interdependence of policies is thereby obscured. Thus, in Aaron's words:

> improved education and training may be ineffective in increasing earning capacity unless steps are also taken to change the mix of available jobs, and efforts to change the mix of available jobs may fail if low-wage workers lack training and education. Either taken alone might fail, when both together might succeed. Research and experimentation would detect the failures but have no way to indicate the hypothetical potential success. A rather vague assumption of such an interrelatedness marked early political rhetoric about the War on Poverty but was wholly absent from the precise, but partial, analyses of its effectiveness performed by social scientists. (Aaron 1978: 156–7)

Similarly, Haveman and Saks (1985) report mixed results of evaluation and exerimentation involving CETA: using post-programme wage gains as the benefit and a much more comprehensive account of taxpayer costs, researchers found that CETA had a poor benefit-cost ratio for direct job creation measures but better ratios for targeted training measures. Such research suffers not only from the single-issue, short-duration disease but also from the natural distortion resulting from political combat about redistribution of income and power. The more CETA accented its presumably more effective but less popular targeting of the 'employment handicapped', the more vulnerable it became; it was eliminated in 1981.

In the same vein, did the Job Corps, which tried to train and place hardcore unemployed youth, raise the subsequent earnings of Corps members? According to Aaron (1978), the Job Corps received mixed marks by this and similarly limited criteria, and by such criteria probably yielded benefits greater than its costs. Yet its critics, noting the costs, called press conferences and delivered such lines as, 'For the huge sums wasted on one Job Corps member we could send a student to Harvard', selectively adding a non-completion or non-placement rate from one of the reports (50 per cent, 43 per cent, 62 per cent, or whatever); the programme was sharply cut back. Conversely, Head Start, a programme to provide pre-school education and health care to young children of the poor, was pronounced a failure by the limited criteria of evaluation research yet it remained politically popular.[7] In fact, after sharp cuts in funding of both social and labour-market policies, more recent, more sophisticated evaluation research—taking account of long-term effects and a wider range of gains and costs—has shown that *both* the Job Corps and Head Start were impressively cost effective.

There may be a corollary to Wilensky's law: not only does single-issue, short-term evaluation research subvert programme development but evaluation research breeds more evaluation research. Once a culture of evaluation research is established with its supporting think tanks, training programmes (for example, schools of public administration or public policy), and agency research units, then the legislative committee, government agency, or interest group that does not have its own cost-benefit analysis will be defenceless in pursuit of its goals. Whether all this research functions only to legitimize established policy positions or actually adds an increment of rationality in policy-making depends, again, on the political context in which the research is done and used—the weight of adversarial *vis à vis* consensual structures for bargaining (Wilensky 1983; Aberbach and Rockman 1989).

A Model for Social Accounting

In order to highlight the limits of much past research, especially econometric research, and to illustrate potential contributions which the uniquely American policy-evaluation industry might well make, I shall briefly describe an unusual evaluation study. If we really wish to develop this industry fully and take its products seriously, a recent evaluation study of the Job Corps, described in Long *et al.* (1981) and Mallar *et al.* (1980), approximates the standard we must reach. It is one of the most careful and comprehensive cost-benefit analyses ever done on a social programme.

The Job Corps provides a wide range of services to disadvantaged youth—vocational skills training, basic education, and health care—typically in residential centres. It is the most expensive federally run social programme. It pursues several goals: not only increased output from Corpsmembers (and related earnings increases), but also reduced dependence on public assistance and less antisocial behaviour. Long after its budget declined, Long *et al.* (1981) published their estimates of programme effects. They collected data in periodic interviews with Corpsmembers and with a comparison group of similar youths who were never enrolled—a baseline survey of the two groups in May 1977 followed by two additional interviews. Baseline and follow-up data were available for about 5,100 youths. By the time of the second follow-up in April 1979, the Corpsmembers had been out of the Job Corps for an average of 18 months and for as long as two years. Their average training period was 5.9 months. To estimate the Job Corps impact for the period covered by the interviews, researchers used multiple regression techniques, controlling for both observed and unobserved differences between the Corpsmembers and comparison youths.

What is most useful about this study is its social accounting framework. This appears in their summary table (see Table 12.2) showing estimated total annual costs of the programme to society, including Corpsmembers ($5,070 in 1977 dollars) and the total benefits to society ($7,343)—for a net gain to society of $2,271 per Corpsmember.

If we concentrate only on the increased post-programme output and earnings, as is typically done, we would miss almost half the societal benefits shown for the Job Corps. For instance, the net social value of reductions in arrests—reductions in criminal justice system costs, personal injury and property damage, and the value of stolen property—amounts to about $2,000 per Corpsmember during the observation period. Apparently, while many matched non-Corps youth were vigorously engaged in robbery, burglary, theft, bar-room brawls, mugging old men in back alleys, peddling drugs, and an occasional murder—all the while collecting an average of $1,357 more on AFDC, General Assistance, Medicaid, Food Stamps, Unemployment Insurance, and Workers Compensation than Job Corpsmembers collected—the Corpsmembers were off the street during training and often worked in conventional jobs afterward. Some minor savings came from reduced drug/alcohol use; but the big savings were in the reduced criminal activity accompanying their use.[8]

Incidentally, the researchers used rather conservative assumptions regarding the fading effect of the benefits: 'As long as the benefits do not decay extremely rapidly, that is, greater than 50 per cent per year after the two-year postprogram observation period, the program is economically efficient' (Long *et al.* 1981: 69).

Finally, if we consider unmeasured variables, it is plain that this study, as comprehensive as it is, none the less shares a common limitation of all such studies: the unmeasured costs incurred when we put people through these programmes (for example, the value of trainees' foregone leisure) are seldom as numerous and important as the unmeasured benefits over the long run. For instance, if trainees come to prefer work over welfare and increase their self-esteem from holding regular jobs; if society prefers employment and training over welfare; if everyone prefers a reduction of poverty and wider sense of well-being, how do we measure *those* benefits?[9]

Many labour-market policies in the US are funded for a short period and at such a meagre level that the fuss about their alleged failure to solve some huge problem is absurd. Some of these programmes were hardly launched before they were shot down in a cloud of complaints about great costs and limited benefits, often reinforced by short-term, single-issue, evaluation research. In the rare case where careful evaluations were made and evidence was found of some modest success, the results were pronounced as benedictions at the graveside. Political success may have been inversely related to evaluated success. In the absence of effective coalitions of politicians, bureaucrats, and experts, in the absence of a system for aggregating interests, achieving consensus, and integrating social and economic planning, each interest group can interpret research results according to its preconceptions with no accommodation

TABLE 12.2. Estimated Net Present Value per Corpsmember under the Benchmark Assumptions (1977 dollars)[a]

	Society	Corpsmembers	Rest of society
Benefits			
A. Output produced by Corpsmembers			
In-programme output	757	83	673
Increased post-programme output	3,896	3,896	0
Increased tax payments on post-programme income	0	−582	582
Increased utility due to preferences for work over welfare	+	+	+
B. Reduced dependence on transfer programmes			
Reduced transfer payments	0	−1,357	1,357
Reduced administrative costs	158	0	158
C. Reduced criminal activity			
Reduced criminal justice systems costs	1,152	0	1,152
Reduced personal injury and property damage	645	0	645
Reduced value of stolen property	315	−169	484
Reduced psychological costs	+	+	+
D. Reduced drug/alcohol use			
Reduced treatment costs	30	0	30
Increased utility from reduced drug/alcohol dependence	+	+	+
E. Utilization of alternative services			
Reduced costs of training, educational, and PSE programmes	390	0	390
Reduced training allowances	0	−49	49

TABLE 12.2. cont.

	Society	Corpsmembers	Rest of society
F. Other benefits			
Increased utility from redistribution	+	+	+
Increased utility from improved well-being of Corpsmembers	+	+	+
Total benefits	$7,343[b]	$1,823	$5,520
Costs			
A. Programme operating expenditures			
Centre operating expenditures, excluding transfers to Corpsmembers	2,796	0	2,796
Transfers to Corpsmembers	0	−1,208	1,208
Central administrative costs	−1,347	0	1,347
B. Opportunity cost of Corpsmember labour			
Foregone output	881	881	0
Foregone tax payments	0	−153	153
C. Unbudgeted expenditures other than Corpsmember labour			
Resource costs	46	0	46
Transfers to Corpsmembers	0	−185	185
Total costs	$5,070	−$665	$5,736
Net present value (benefits less costs)	$2,271	$2,485	−$214
Benefit–cost ratio[c]	1.45	1.82	0.96

a See the text for a review of the assumptions, estimation procedures, and their implications for the values presented in this table. Reprinted with permission from Long *et al.* 1981.

b Details may not sum to totals because of rounding.

c The numerators for the benefit–cost ratios include all of the benefits listed in this table as either positive benefits or negative costs, and the denominator includes all of the costs listed in this table as either positive costs or negative benefits.

to opposing preconceptions. The voice of research, even scholarly analysis, is drowned out by the noise.

It is small wonder that the pioneers of active labour-market policies who have embraced training and placement as a religion—Sweden, Japan, and Germany—are reluctant to divert their energies to this new industry of evaluation research. As an early head of the Swedish Labor Market Board said when confronted with the suggestion that he undertake extensive programme evaluation, 'No, let's get something done instead' (personal interview). Some practitioners of the art see the real trade-off as investment in human resources and active labour-market policies versus soaring welfare and unemployment insurance costs plus an abundance of misleading evaluation research.[10]

THE SWEDISH CASE: A LESSON IN POLICY LINKAGES

For students of labour-market policies, Sweden holds special fascination. Not including unemployment compensation, its National Labor Market Board spends about 2.4 per cent of GNP per year (1982–3), the equivalent of about $80 billion in 1983 dollars for an economy of US size. Its unemployment rate for the past 20 years (since data comparable to US labour-force surveys have been available) has remained below 4 per cent; the average is much lower. Further, as Rehn (1985) persuasively argues, the commitment of resources and the low unemployment rate are tightly connected.

Finally, if we average annual inflation rates and do the same for real annual GDP growth per capita per year from 1950 to 1974 and compare the performance of the 19 rich democracies with a population of a million or more, Sweden comes out above average in inflation and only slightly below average in growth (the US was tops in controlling inflation, but among the worst four in both growth and unemployment). After the oil shock, despite its much greater oil dependence and negligible domestic supply of energy, Sweden's job-creation record in the late 1970s put it near the top of OECD countries: Sweden's labour-force participation rate grew faster even than that of the

US; its female labour-force participation rate climbed to 75 per cent.

This excellent performance in utilization of human resources and average economic performance by other measures was accompanied by the development of a civilized welfare state (Sweden is a welfare state leader—or if you prefer, a profligate spender and a confiscatory taxer—and is the world-beater in social and economic quality); all this with very little tax-welfare backlash. (Wilensky 1976; 1978; 1981*b*; Wiles 1974.) In short, Sweden has *not* been spending itself into the grave, either economically or politically.

The Swedes have given much thought to the question, 'How can a rich democracy continue to control inflation and still have full employment, good growth, and remain competitive in world markets?' Swedish labour-market policy was devised as one component of a general strategy for dealing with universal dilemmas of market-oriented democracies since the Second World War. Wildly over-simplified: under modern conditions if we rely exclusively on Keynesian demand management to maintain full employment we risk too much inflation. If we rely exclusively on monetary policy to fight inflation, as many governments do today, we risk high unemployment and low growth; if we rely on subsidies and trade restrictions for depressed regions, industries, or firms, we end up with 'lemon socialism' ('capitalism'?) and a decline in international competitiveness. And if we rely too much on taxes on corporations and capital gains to finance the welfare state, we not only depress private investment but we quickly discover that only a small portion of welfare-state costs can be so financed. The Swedish response to these dilemmas was the 'Rehn/Meidner' model, which was discussed and adopted by the labour movement and the social democratic party in the early 1950s. It consisted of three main themes (cf. Scharpf 1983; Martin 1979; and Rehn 1985):

1. The labour movement should adopt a policy of 'wage solidarity' that (*a*) reduces differentials between skilled and unskilled, (*b*) provides equal pay for equal work regardless of differences in ability-to-pay by region and sector. Less-profitable firms would thereby be forced to become more efficient or shut down and workers would be displaced.

2. The government should not try to eliminate all unemployment through Keynesian management of aggregate demand (too inflationary).

3. The unemployment resulting from (1) and (2) should be countered by an active labour-market policy—commitment to placement and counselling services linked to mobility incentives (to encourage mobility from weak to strong regions and sectors) and an expansion of training and retraining opportunities.

In the more difficult times of the seventies and eighties, when world-wide recessions reduced private-sector employment and resistance to labour mobility increased, Sweden added regional employment subsidies and greatly expanded other labour-market policies. Second, it expanded public-sector employment (by 1980, about 29 per cent of all employment). Third, it expanded part-time jobs to about one-quarter of the labour-force—the highest in Europe. Throughout the three decades, in order to protect its competitiveness and limit unemployment, Sweden avoided heavy taxes on private-sector profits and investments and frequently made the necessary trade-offs to encourage wage constraint; it financed the welfare state by mass taxes, as other big social spenders have done.

Rehn (1985) shows how these ideas and policies worked out in practice; he accents the central role of active labour-market policy as a source of social consensus, reducing worker hostility to industrial readjustment. He shows that ALMP can at once reduce unemployment *and*, what is seldom recognized, help control inflation by improving lifetime productivity and meeting skill shortages. He offers a fascinating account of the way Swedish labour moved away from various money illusions and concentrated on labour and industrial policies that were fair to workers and yet enhanced national economic performance.

Sweden illustrates the point that you cannot expect labour to behave 'responsibly'—to take account of the impact of labour costs on inflation and growth—unless government and industry collaborate in a total strategy for sharing the burdens and benefits of readjustment equitably. And you cannot treat labour-market policy in a separate compartment; its success depends on simultaneous and reinforcing action in macroeconomic policy, industrial policy, and educational policy. Such policy linkages are a necessary condition for successful industrial readjustment. In fact, without the prior or simultaneous development and expansion of active labour-market and/or social policics, no rich democracy has successfully implemented either industrial policies or incomes policies (Wilensky and Turner 1987). For instance, the Austrians and West Germans could not have implemented their relatively successful incomes policies unless they had in placed expansive social and labour-market policies that made wage restraint tolerable to union leaders and workers. And the Japanese could not have instituted a successful industrial policy without strong structures for national collaboration among industry, commerce, and government; local collaboration between management and labour, including bargaining about job security; and, as we have seen, a quite active labour-market policy—in other words, structures and policies to cushion the shocks of industrial readjustment.

TRANSFERABILITY: CAN THE LAGGARDS LEARN FROM THE LEADERS?

Obviously, neither the UK nor the US will move quickly toward the Swedish model. As yet they lack the centralized structures of bargaining that permit labour, management, and the government to create sufficient consensus for the integration of social, labour, and industrial policies. The scope of American and British bargaining on these issues is narrow; policy segmentation is extreme. However, even if no major shifts in the structure and interplay of government, labour, and industry occur, even if no new channels for big-bloc bargaining are cut, we might still see an expansion of active labour-market policy.

Beyond the economic and political shocks of the years ahead there are three reasons to suppose that more action in this area is politically feasible and may even come to pass in the next decade or so: ALMP does not require Left or social democratic power; a pool of relevant administrative talent is already in place; and demographic trends are favourable.

Labour-Market Policy is not Confined to the Left Agenda

Conservatives from Margaret Thatcher in Britain to the Centre-Right coalition in West Germany, after some initial cut-backs, have in recent years supported the expansion of ALMP. Both social democrats and 'bourgeois' parties have found it necessary to deal with unacceptable levels of unemployment; party competition between them has sometimes escalated spending on training and job creation. Even if they are not worried about the electoral consequences of unemployment of the hard-to-employ (in Germany the Kohl administration and the labour movement alike have been quiet about the underclass), they do worry about displaced workers who are more active politically.

In the US, the Reagan Administration has been the only exception; with only minor fluctuations, annual Federal outlays in employment and training programmes moved from less than one-tenth of 1 per cent in the period 1950–64 up to a peak of 0.52 per cent of GNP in 1978 and 1979, then steadily down to 0.18 per cent in 1983. They increased through Johnson, Nixon, Ford, and Carter, then dropped under Reagan in an indiscriminate assault on public civilian spending (Gottschalk 1983; Janoski 1986).

The Pool of Relevant Talent has Increased

A study of the process of implementation of youth employment programmes in the US, varying in success, found that recently developed policy infrastructures in metropolitan areas have contributed to effective implementation (Levin and Ferman 1981: 59–60). The key is a new generation of activist bureaucrats who combine commitment to training and employment programmes, years of practical experience, and skills in the politics of community development and fund-raising, as well as good contacts with local and federal officials. Many are alumni of President Johnson's Great Society programmes, including CETA, MDTA, and the Neighborhood Youth Corps. Many, perhaps most, know the limits and possibilities of these programmes. These seasoned 'programme professionals' provide a base for action whenever the political will develops.

It is not too much to suppose that there is now a British counterpart: the veterans of nearly a decade of expansion of

ALMP provide a pool of experienced trainers, planners, and administrators. They are a product of the New Training Initiative (NTI) of 1981 whose centrepiece was the Youth Training Scheme (YTS), with its successive reforms; the Technical and Vocational Education Initiative of 1982 (TVEI), an attempt to increase the industrial relevance of secondary-school curricula through teacher training and curriculum assessment; which led to the establishment in 1986 of the National Council for Vocational Qualifications (NCVQ) with the mission of rationalizing all training into five levels, ranging from YTS to engineering professionals; and the Training Opportunities Scheme (TOPS), the Job Training Scheme (JTS and new-JTS), providing short-duration training and work experience for the long-term unemployed. However uncoordinated and inefficient all these acts and agencies may be, they must have provided practical experience upon which a seriously committed government can build.

Demographic Trends are Favourable

There is a demography of public policy that creates both constraints and opportunities. The smaller cohorts entering the labour market from 1980 until the late 1990s create a favourable situation for modest improvement in job programmes. Fewer youths are now competing for entry jobs, so any programme expenditure will be modest compared to the cost of comparable action in the seventies. The number of young workers is actually declining in both the US and the UK. The sharp increase in women heading families is both a political pressure to which governments are likely to respond and a favourable opportunity. Women, evaluation research suggests, have done better in training than men. Finally, the cost explosion for pensions and health insurance, rooted mainly in the ageing of the population, creates another political pressure for part-time jobs and inspires hard thought about phased retirement, alternative work schedules, and job creation for the 'young-old'.

SUMMARY AND CONCLUSION

My analysis suggests that ALMP, especially training, placement, and job-creation efforts—well and stably funded, lodged in tripartite administrative structures, and linked closely to secondary schools—has been effective in increasing productivity, reducing unemployment, and facilitating flexible adaptation to industrial readjustment. Successes are evident in countries of very different political structure and culture—Sweden, Germany, Japan. For three reasons, their policy experience is more transferable than experience in other policy areas and other times: ALMP finds support from parties of both Left and Right; a fund of talent and experience is now widely diffused; and the baby boom has turned into a baby bust, thereby opening a window of opportunity in the 1990s as smaller cohorts enter the labour-force, reducing programme costs.

If policies are transferable to the policy laggards, is American-style evaluation research also transferable? Although I am sceptical about the benefits to Europe of the American evaluation-research industry, it appears to be spreading at least in small measure. In the past fifteen or twenty years, policy researchers in Germany, the UK, and Canada have shown interest in American-style cost-benefit analysis of particular programmes (Levine *et al.* 1981: 27–60; Fitzsimmons 1981: 107–30; and my interviews). However, like the quick spread of the Planning-Programming Budgetary System (PPBS) from the US (Wilensky 1967: 183–91) to Britain, France, Germany, Canada, and Belgium and its quicker demise (Levine *et al.* 1981), this scattered enthusiasm may pass. Receptivity to such evaluation research is likely to be greatest in least-corporatist, most-fragmented and decentralized democracies. The United States is at one extreme: its decentralized federalism, its diffuse decision-making process, and its increasingly polarized politics, with the mass media, single-issue groups, and the courts filling the policy vacuum—all foster research that is short-term, narrow, and ideological, used mainly for partisan ammunition rather than policy-making, programme development, and implementation (Wilensky 1983). The voice of research, although loud, is cast to the winds. At the other extreme are more centralized, more 'corporatist' political economies with more consensual politics, and tighter integration of knowledge and policy—Norway, Sweden, Austria, and, to a lesser extent, Belgium and the Netherlands. In these countries, either American-style evaluation research is not done at all or, if done, it is more closely tied to policy deliberations and is used to foster consensus and implement policy (Wilensky 1983: 57–68; Levine *et al.* 1981: 36–57; Richardson 1982: 169–77). Larger contexts for bargaining among economic interest groups, political parties, and the state mean larger contexts for policy analysis in which a wider range of issues is connected and longer-range effects are more often considered—an advantage in successful implementation of ALMP. Sweden and Norway epitomize the extreme of policy linkages; the US, the extreme of policy segmentation.

In its politics and in the structure of its bargaining arrangements linking labour, management, and the state, Germany is somewhere in the middle of these extremes, which may explain why its policy-makers are both attracted and repelled by one-issue, short-term, forensic research and why much German evaluation research in contrast to that in the US is 'softer', less rigorous, and more oriented toward improving consensus or facilitating political bargains (cf. Hellstern and Wollman 1981: 68–72, 80–6; Fitzsimmons 1981). Until the 1980s, little evaluation was done on job training in Germany; hence there was little criticism and substantial action (Janoski 1986: 185).

With or without evaluation research and its sometimes perverse effects, the rich democracies can learn much from one another, from the scores of policies and programmes that have been adopted to minimize the waste of human resources and to develop the talents and skills of the entire labour force. It is not the lack of proof of the success or failure of ALMP that blocks progress among the ALMP laggards; nor is it solely the absence of centralized structures for bargaining among labour, management, and the state; it is the failure of political will.

NOTES

1. This chapter is a much revised and elaborated version of Wilensky 1985. It is part of my forthcoming book, *Tax and Spend: The Political Economy and Performance of Rich Democracies.* I am grateful to Thomas Janoski, Susan Reed Hahn, and Fred Schaffer for research assistance and to the Institute of Industrial Relations, University of California at Berkeley for support.
2. In the month of February 1981 alone the General Accounting Office of the USA—which accounts for only a small share of the evaluation research industry—issued 41 evaluation reports. The 1975 Congressional sourcebook on federal programme evaluations cites 1,700 evaluation reports issued by 18 executive branch agencies and the GAO during 1973–5 (Nachmias 1980: 1164).
3. Beyond the weakness in ALMP, one reason that both British and American employers do not employ apprentices is that they receive up to three-quarters of the adult wage compared to 20–30% in Germany.
4. The case for subsidies for short-term work is in dispute: some firms misuse it to subsidize regular fluctuations in demand or production processes. But German studies suggest that during recessions the employment impact of short-time compensation linked to training can be substantial. If the downswing is brief, the employer keeps his experienced work-force and avoids the costs of dismissals and new hires. Workers receive more than they would under unemployment compensation. (See Schmid 1985; Sengenberger 1982: 82–3). Short-time work is now being used to ease the path of industrial readjustment in East Germany. Regarding the dispute over the employment effects of a shorter working week, German studies suggest that reduced hours in metal-working industries beginning in 1985 increased net jobs, with some small benefit to the unemployed (Auer 1989). Metal-working hours are scheduled to drop to 35 in 1995.
5. The data on which this section is based—a chronology of policies and sources for estimating their initiation, expansion, continuity, and effectiveness—are reported in detail in Wilensky and Turner 1987: 55–79.
6. Critics of 'European' labour-market policies argue that comparisons of the unemployment rates of the US and, say, those of Sweden, Austria, or Germany are misleading because they ignore the superior job-creation record of the US, at least since 1976. For a discussion of the ambiguity of growth in rates of employment

(versus unemployment) as a measure of economic performance, see Wilensky and Turner 1987: app. B and Wilensky 1992. It shows why there is no consensus on this issue, while there *is* general agreement that the combination of low unemployment, low inflation, and high persistent real growth in GDP per capita is desirable. My analysis of employment growth in 18 countries shows that it is unrelated to economic performance by the usual measures; that, at the extremes, the star job-creation machines from 1968 to 1987 (US, UK, and Australia) are often the great unemployment machines (except for 1980–4); and that the major cause of job creation is the relative rate of increase in the supply of cheap labour—especially migrants, young people, and women, particularly divorced women, in low-wage jobs. There is a trade-off between job creation and increased productivity and rising standards of living.

7. The research pronouncing failure was seriously flawed. For instance, research concluded that a brief stint in a special school, as one might expect, brought only a small, temporary improvement in reading readiness, which faded after the first grade. A Rand Corporation evaluation of the evaluations, however, noted that research on Head Start and on similar programmes for older children did not assign treatment and non-treatment children on a random basis, evaluated unrepresentative projects, were contaminated by 'radiation effects' spilling over from project to non-project children, or had other defects (Aaron 1978: 84). In the case of tests of reading achievement of older children, the fading effect after a year (losing ground during the summer) ignored the differences between students in summer school and those whose only compensatory education was administered by street gangs (Heyns 1978). Thus, although Head Start was at first an evaluated failure, follow-up studies, better designed, suggest more success (Lazar *et al.* 1979; Schweinhart and Weikert 1980). But whether evaluation research found failure or success, Head Start remained popular in Congress; the Bush administration has joined Congress in support of increased funding in 1990.
8. President Reagan proposed to wipe out the Job Corps (*Wall Street Journal*, 6 Dec. 1984). At the logical and ludicrous extreme, a 'neo-conservative' cost-benefit analyst could defend its elimination by costing out a number of potential savings: society would benefit from the greater number of murders (lower medical and pension costs for the deceased); then there is the gain to free enterprise (self-employed fences would profit from the increase in stealing).

9. It is revealing that Sweden, which spends the most on implementing labour-market policies and avoids single-issue evaluation, undertakes 'general level of living' surveys that emphasize the effect of all social and economic policies. Such surveys attempt to assess the typically unmeasured aspects of the standard of living. (cf. Erikson and Uusitalo 1987.)
10. When Swedish planners do undertake specific programme evaluation—the two main agencies are the National Audit Bureau (RRV) and the Swedish Agency for Administration Development (SAFAD) —they seek co-operative relationships between researchers and programme managers and emphasize the evaluation of *effectiveness* (achievement of major goals). In contrast, evaluation researchers in the American and British governments tend toward adversarial '*efficiency audits*' (where the evaluations expose waste and fraud and try to force change on the target agency). For a comparison of Swedish and British evaluation research, see Richardson 1982.

REFERENCES

AARON, H. J. (1978), *Politics and the Professors: The Great Society in Perspective* (Washington, DC: The Brookings Institution).

ABBOTT, P. (1987), 'Women's Social Class Identification: Does Husband's Occupation Make a Difference?' *Sociology*, 21: 91–103.

ABEL, E. K. (1969), 'Canon Barnett and the First Thirty Years of Toynbee Hall', unpub. Ph.D. thesis, University of London.

ABERBACH, J. D., and ROCKMAN, B. A. (1989), 'On the Rise, Transformation and Decline of Analysis in the US Government', *Governance*, 2: 293–314.

ABRAMS, P. (1977), 'Community Care: Some Research Problems and Priorities', in J. Barnes and N. Connelly (eds.), *Social Care Research* (London: Policy Studies Institute).

—— (1985), 'The Uses of British Sociology 1831–1981', in Bulmer (1985), 181–205.

AITKEN, M., and LONGFORD, N. T. (1986), 'Statistical Modelling Issues in School Effectiveness Studies', *Journal of the Royal Statistical Society*, 149: 1–26.

AITKEN, R. (1986), 'MSC, TVEI and Education in Perspective', *Political Quarterly*, 57: 231–5.

AITKEN, W. F. (1902), *Canon Barnett Warden of Toynbee Hall* (London: Partridge).

ALESZEWSKI, A. and MATHORPE, J. (1988), 'Decentralizing Social Services', *British Journal of Social Work*, 18: 63–74.

ALDGATE, J., MALUCCIO, A., and REEVES, C. (1989), *Adolescents in Foster Families* (London: Batsford).

ALLMENDINGER, D. F. Jr. (1975), *Paupers and Scholars: The Transformation of Student Life in Nineteenth-Century New England* (New York: St Martin's Press).

ALTER, P. (1987), *The Reluctant Patron, Science and the State in Britain, 1850–1920* (Oxford: Berg).

ALTHAUSER, R. P., and KALLEBERG, A. L. (1981), 'Firms, Occupations and the Structure of Labor Markets: A Conceptual Analysis', in Ivar Berg (ed.), *Sociological Perspectives on Labor Markets* (New York: Academic Press).

ALWIN, D. F. (1976), 'Assessing School Effects: Some Identities', *Sociology of Education*, 49: 294–303.

—— and OTTO, L. B. (1977), 'High School Context Effects on Aspirations', *Sociology of Education*, 50: 259–73.

Anderson, R. D. (1983*a*), *Education and Opportunity in Victorian Scotland: Schools and Universities* (Oxford: Clarendon Press).

—— (1983*b*), 'Education and the State in Nineteenth-Century Scotland', in *Economic History Review*, 36: 518–34.

Annan, N. (1955), 'The Intellectual Aristocracy', in J. H. Plumb (ed.), *Studies in Social History* (London: Longmans Green), 241–87.

Apple, M. W. (1979), *Ideology and Curriculum* (London: Routledge and Kegan Paul).

Archer, M. S. (1979), *The Social Origin of Educational Systems* (Beverly Hills, Calif., and London: Sage).

—— (1982), 'The Theoretical Problem of Educational Expansion', in id. (ed.), *The Sociology of Educational Expansion: Take-off, Growth and Inflation in Educational Systems* (Beverly Hills, Calif., and London: Sage), 3–64.

Armytage, W. H. G. (1955), *Civic Universities: Aspects of a British Tradition* (London: Ernest Benn).

Armstrong, D. (1983), *The Political Anatomy of the Body* (Cambridge: Cambridge University Press).

—— (1987), 'Silence and Truth in Death and Dying', *Social Science and Medicine*, 24: 651–7.

Arrow, K. (1973), 'Higher Education as a Filter', *Journal of Public Economics*, 2: 193–216.

Ashbee, C. R. (1910), *The Building of Thelema* (London: Dent).

Ashton, D. (1988*a*), 'Educational Institutions, Youth and the Labour Market', in D. Gallie (ed.), *Employment in Britain* (Oxford: Blackwell).

—— (1988*b*), 'Sources of Variation in Labour-Market Segmentation: Youth Labour Markets in Canada and Britain', *Work, Employment and Society*, 2: 1–24.

—— and Maguire, M. (1986), *Young Adults in the Labour Market*, Research Paper No. 55, London, Department of Employment.

—— —— and Spilsbury, M. (1987), 'Labour Market Segmentation and the Structure of the Youth Labour Market', in P. Brown and D. Ashton (eds.), *Education, Unemployment and Labour Markets* (Lewes: Falmer).

—— —— and Garland, V. (1982), *Youth in the Labour Market*, Research Paper No. 34, London, Department of Employment.

Audit Commission (1985), *Managing Social Services for the Elderly more Effectively* (London: HMSO).

—— (1986), *Making a Reality of Community Care* (London: HMSO).

Auer, P. (1988), 'Labour, Market and Labour Market Policy: Trends in Selected Industrialized Countries 1980 to 1985', Discussion Paper FSI 88–2, Wissenschaftszentrum Berlin für Sozialforschung.

—— (1989), 'Trends in Employment and Labour Market Policy: An International Overview', in E. Matzink (ed.), *No Way to Full Employment* (Berlin: Wissenschaftszentrum).

AYDELOTTE, W. O. (1962), 'The Business Interests of the Gentry in the Parliament of 1841–47', the Appendix to G. K. Clark, *The Making of Victorian England* (London: Methuen), 290–305.

BAILEY, R. and BRAKE, M. (1975) (eds.), *Radical Social Work* (London: Arnold).

BAILYN, B. (1960), *Education in the Forming of American Society* (Chapel Hill, NC: University of North Carolina Press).

BANKS, J. A. (1954), *Prosperity and Parenthood* (London: Routledge).

—— (1972), *The Sociology of Social Movements* (London: Macmillan).

—— (1981), *Victorian Values: Secularism and the Size of Families* (London: Routledge).

—— and BANKS, O. (1964), *Feminism and Family Planning in Victorian England* (Liverpool: Liverpool University Press).

—— —— (1976), 'Feminism and Social Change: A Case Study of a Social Movement', in G. K. Zollschan and W. Hirsh (eds.), *Social Change: Explorations, Diagnoses and Conjectures* (New York: Wiley).

BANKS, O. (1986), *Becoming a Feminist: The Social Origins of 'First Wave' Feminism* (Brighton: Wheatsheaf Books).

BANTING, K. G. (1979), *Poverty, Politics, and Policy* (London: Macmillan).

BARCLAY, P. M. (1982), *Social Workers: Their Role and Tasks* (London: Bedford Square Press).

BARNETT, C. (1986), *The Audit of War: The Illusion and Reality of Britain as a Great Nation* (London: Macmillan).

BARNETT, H. O. (1918), *Canon Barnett: His Life, Work and Friends* (London: John Murray).

BARNETT, S. A. (1888), *Universities' Settlement in East London*, 26 November 1888.

—— (1897), *The Service of God* (London: Longmans Green).

—— (1907), *Religion and Progress* (London: Adam and Charles Black).

—— (1911), *Religion and Politics* (London: Wells Gardner, Darton and Company).

—— (1913), *Worship and Work* (Letchworth: Letchworth Garden City Press).

—— and BARNETT, S. A. Mrs (1909), *Towards Social Reform* (London: Fisher Unwin).

BAUMAN, Z. (1988), 'Britain's Exodus from Politics', *New Statesman and Society*, 29 July 1988.

BEER, S. (1982), *Britain against Itself* (London: Faber).

BELL, C., and HOWIESON, C. (1988), 'The View from the Hutch: Educational Guinea Pigs Speak about TVEI', in D. Raffe (ed.),

Education and the Youth Labour Market: Schooling and Scheming (Lewes: Falmer).

BENINGTON, J. (1975), 'The Flaw in the Pluralistic Heaven: Changing Strategies in the Coventry CDP', in Lees and Smith (1975).

BERESFORD, P., and CROFT, S. (1986), *Whose Welfare?* (Brighton: Lewis Cohen Urban Studies Centre).

BERNSTEIN, B. (1974), 'Sociology and the Sociology of Education: A Brief Account', in J. Rex (ed.), *Approaches to Sociology* (London: Routledge and Kegan Paul).

BEVERIDGE, Lord (1953), *Power and Influence* (London: Hodder and Stoughton).

BISHOP, J. H. (1989), 'Toward more Valid Evaluations of Training Programs Serving the Disadvantaged', *Journal of Policy Analysis and Management*, 8: 209–28.

BLACK, A. (1984), *Guilds and Civil Society in European Political Thought from the 12th Century to the Present* (London: Methuen).

BLAGG, H., and SMITH, D. (1989), *Crime, Penal Policy and Social Work* (Harlow: Longman).

BLAND, R., BLAND, R. E. B., CHEETHAM, J., LAPSLEY, I., and LLEWELLYN, S. (forthcoming), *The Efficiency, Effectiveness and Quality of Care in Scottish Old People's Homes*, Social Work Research Centre, University of Stirling.

BLAU, P. M., and DUNCAN, O. D. (1967), *The American Occupational Structure* (New York: Wiley).

BLOOM, B. S. (1964), *Stability and Change in Human Characteristics* (New York: Wiley).

BLUME, S. S. (1982), *The Commissioning of Social Research by Central Government* (London: SSRC).

BLUNKETT, D., and GREEN, G. (1983), *Building from the Bottom: The Sheffield Experience*, Tract 491 (London: Fabian Society).

—— and JACKSON, K. (1987), *Democracy in Crisis: The Town Halls Respond* (London: Hogarth).

BOLI, J. F., RAMIREZ, O., and MEYER, J. W. (1985), 'Explaining the Origins and Expansion of Mass Education', *Comparative Education Review*, 29: 145–70.

BOOTH, T. (1985), *Home Truths: Old People's Homes and the Outcomes of Care* (Aldershot: Gower).

BOTTOMORE, T. (1979), *Political Sociology* (London: Hutchinson).

BOTTOMS, A. E., and MCWILLIAMS, W. (1979), 'A Non-treatment Paradigm for Probation Practice', *British Journal of Social Work*, 9: 159–202.

BOUCHIER, D. (1983), *The Feminist Challenge* (London: Macmillan).

Boulay, S. du (1984), *Cicely Saunders: The Founder of the Modern Hospice Movement* (London: Hodder and Stoughton).

Bourdieu, P., and Passeron, J. C. (1970), *La Reproduction* (Paris: Les Éditions de Minuit).

Bowles, S., and Gintis, H. (1976), *Schooling in Capitalist America: Educational Reform and the Contradictions of Economic Life* (New York: Basic Books).

Branca, P. (1975), *Silent Sisterhood: Middle-Class Women in the Victorian Home* (London: Croom Helm).

Brannen, J. (1989), 'Combining Qualitative and Quantitative Approaches', background paper for training seminar, London.

—— and Wilson, G. (1987) (eds.), *Give and Take in Families: Studies in Resource Distribution* (London: Allen and Unwin).

Breen, T. H. (1988), '"Baubles of Britain": The American and Consumer Revolutions of the Eighteenth Century', *Past and Present*, 119: 73–104.

Brewer, C., and Lait, J. (1980), *Can Social Work Survive?* (London: Temple Smith).

Briant, K. (1962), *Marie Stopes: A Biography* (London: Hogarth Press).

Brittan, S., and Lilley, P. (1977), *Economic Consequences of Democracy* (London: Temple Smith).

Brookover, W. B., Schweitzer, J. H., Schneider, J. M., Beady, C. H., Hood, P. K., and Wisenbaker, J. M. (1978), 'Elementary School Social Climate and School Achievement', *American Educational Research Journal*, 15: 301–18.

Brown, G. (1987), 'Social Factors and the Development and Course of Depressive Disorders in Women: A Review of a Research Programme', *British Journal of Social Work*, 17: 615–34.

Brown, P. (1987), *Schooling Ordinary Kids: Inequality, Unemployment and the New Vocationalism* (London: Tavistock).

Bryant, M. (1986), *The London Experience of Secondary Education* (London: Athlone).

Bryman, A. (1984), 'The Debate about Quantitative and Qualitative Research', *British Journal of Sociology*, 35: 75–92.

Bulmer, M. (1982), *The Uses of Social Research: Social Investigation in Public Policy-making* (London: Allen and Unwin).

—— (1985) (ed.), *Essays on the History of British Sociological Research* (Cambridge: Cambridge University Press).

—— (1986), *Neighbours: The Work of Philip Abrams* (Cambridge: Cambridge University Press).

—— (1987), *The Social Basis of Community Care* (London: Unwin Hyman).

BULMER, M., LEWIS, J., and PIACHAUD, D. (1989) (eds.), *The Goals of Social Policy* (London: Unwin Hyman).

BURNHAM, W. D. (1974), 'The United States: The Politics of Heterogeneity', in R. Rose (ed.), *Electoral Behavior: A Comparative Handbook* (New York: Free Press).

BURNHILL, P. M. (1984), 'The 1981 Scottish School Leavers Survey', in D. Raffe (ed.), *Fourteen to Eighteen: The Changing Pattern of Schooling in Scotland* (Aberdeen: Aberdeen University Press).

BURSTEIN, L. (1980), 'Issues in the Aggregation of Data', in D. C. Berliner (ed.), *Review of Research in Education* (Washington, DC: American Educational Research Association).

BURTLESS, G. (1985), 'Are Targeted Wage Subsidies Harmful? Evidence from a Voucher Experiment', *Journal of Industrial and Labor Relations Review*, 39: 105–14.

BYRNE, D., WILLIAMSON, W., and FLETCHER, B. (1975), *The Poverty of Education: A Study in the Politics of Opportunity* (London: Martin Robertson).

CAMPBELL, A., and WARNER, B. (forthcoming), 'Training Strategies and Microelectronics in the Engineering Industries of the UK and West Germany', in P. Ryan (ed.), *International Comparisons of Vocational Education and Training* (Lewes: Falmer).

CARLILE, R. (1826), *Every Woman's Book, or, What is Love?* 4th edn. (London: R. Carlile).

CARR, W., and KEMMIS, S. (1986), *Becoming Critical: Education, Knowledge and Action-Research* (Lewes: Falmer).

CASEY, B., and BRUCHE, G. (1985), 'Active Labor Market Policy: An International Overview', *Industrial Relations*, 24: 156–73.

CASSELS, J. (1990), *Britain's Real Skill Shortage and What to Do about it* (London: Policy Studies Institute).

CECCHINI, P. (1988), *The European Challenge* (Aldershot: Wildwood House).

Central Council for Education and Training in Social Work (1989), *Requirements and Regulations for the Diploma in Social Work*, CCETSW, Paper No. 30.

Central Policy Review Staff (1980), *Education, Training and Industrial Performance* (London: HMSO).

Charity Trends (1990), 12th edn., Charities Aid Foundation.

CHALLIS, D., and DAVIES, B. (1986), *Case Management in Community Care* (Aldershot: Gower).

CHEETHAM, J. (1985), *The Attitudes of Magistrates, Social Workers and Probation Officers to the Punishment of Juveniles* (unpublished).

Church of England (1985), Archbishop of Canterbury's Commission on Urban Priority Areas, *Faith in the City* (London: Church House Publishing).

Cicirelli, V. G. (1969), *The Impact of Head Start on Children's Cognitive and Affective Development* (Washington, DC: Westinghouse Learning Corporation).

Clark, G. K. (1973), 'Statesmen in Disguise: Reflections on the History of the Neutrality of the Civil Service', reprinted in P. Stansky, *The Victorian Revolution: Government and Society in Victorian Britain* (New York: New Viewpoints).

Clayson, C. (Chairman) (1973), *Report of the Departmental Committee on Scottish Licensing Law*, Cmnd. 5354 (Edinburgh: HMSO).

Clifford, P., and Heath, A. (1984), 'Selection Does Make a Difference', *Oxford Review of Education*, 10: 85–8.

Cohen, S. (1975), 'It's Alright for You to Talk: Political and Sociological Manifestos for Action', in Bailey and Brake (1975).

Cohen, S. S. (1977), *Modern Capitalist Planning: The French Model* (Berkeley, Calif.: University of California Press).

Cole, R. E. (1979), *Work, Mobility and Participation: A Comparative Study of American and Japanese Industry* (Berkeley, Calif.: University of California Press).

Colebrook, L. (1961), 'Euthanasia', *Lancet*, 2: 485.

Coleman, J. S. (1972), *Policy Research in the Social Sciences*, (New Jersey: General Learning Systems).

—— (1984), 'Issues in the Institutionalization of Social Policy', in Husen and Kogan (1984), 131–41.

Collins, R. (1979), *The Credential Society: An Historical Sociology of Education and Stratification* (New York: Academic Press).

Comprehensive Education (1989), 2/1, special issue on 'Comprehensive Education and Training from 16 Plus'.

Confederation of British Industry (1989), *Towards a Skills Revolution: A Youth Charter* (London: CBI).

Corless, I. B. (1983), 'The Hospice Movement in North America', in C. A. Corr and D. M. Corr (eds.), *Hospice Care: Principles and Practice* (London: Faber).

Cormack, R. J., and Osborne, R. D. (1983), *Religion, Education and Employment: Aspects of Equal Opportunity in Northern Ireland* (Belfast: Appletree Press).

Cox, C. B., and Dyson, A. E. (1969) (eds.), *Fight for Education*, Critical Quarterly Society.

Craig, G., Dericourt, N., and Loney, M. (1982) (eds.), *Community Work and the State: Towards a Radical Practice* (London: Routledge and Kegan Paul).

Cremin, L. (1980), *American Education: The National Experience, 1783–1876* (New York: Harper and Row).

Crompton, R., and Mann, M. (1986) (eds.), *Gender and Stratification* (Cambridge: Polity Press).

Crowther, G. (Chairman) (1959), *15 to 18: A Report of the Central Advisory Council for Education* (London: HMSO).

Crozier, M., Huntingdon, S. P., and Watanuki, J. (1975), *The Crisis of Democracy* (New York: New York University Press).

Dahrendorf, R. (1987), 'The Erosion of Citizenship and its Consequences for Us All', *New Statesman and Society*, 12 June 1987.

—— (1988), *The Modern Social Conflict* (London: Weidenfeld and Nicolson).

Davie, G. E. (1961), *The Democratic Intellect, Scotland and her Universities in the Nineteenth Century* (Edinburgh: The University Press).

—— (1986), *The Crisis of the Democratic Intellect* (Edinburgh: Polygon).

Davies, B., and Knapp, M. (1988) (eds.), 'The Production of Welfare Approach: Evidence and Argument from the Personal Social Services Research Unit', *British Journal of Social Work*, 18, Special Supplement.

Davies, M. (1981), *The Essential Social Worker* (London: Routledge and Kegan Paul).

—— and Wright, A. (1989), *The Changing Face of Probation*, Social Work Monographs (Norwich: University of East Anglia).

Davies, P. (1983), 'The Relation between Taxation, Price and Alcohol Consumption in the Countries of Europe', in M. Grant, M. Plant, and A. Williams (eds.), *Economics and Alcohol* (London: Croom Helm).

Dealy, M. B. (1945), *Catholic Schools in Scotland* (Washington, DC: University of America Press).

Degler, C. N. (1980), *At Odds: Women and the Family in America from the Revolution to the Present* (Oxford: Oxford University Press).

De Leeuw, J., and Kreft, I. (1968), 'Random Coefficient Models for Multilevel Analysis', *Journal of Educational Statistics*, 1: 57–85.

Delphy, C. (1980), 'A Materialist Feminism is Possible', *Feminist Review*, 4: 79–105.

Dennett, J., James, E., Room, G., and Watson, P. (1982), *Europe Against Poverty: The European Poverty Programme 1975–1980* (London: Bedford Square Press).

Dennis, N., and Halsey, A. H. (1988), *English Ethical Socialism: Thomas More to R. H. Tawney* (Oxford: Clarendon Press).

DES (1972), *Education: A Framework for Expansion*, Cmnd 5174 (London: HMSO).

—— (1981–9), *Current Educational Research Projects supported by the Department of Education and Science*, Annual List 1 (London: DES)

DEX, S. (1987), *Women's Occupational Mobility* (London: Macmillan).

DOERINGER, P. B., and PIORE, M. J. (1971), *Internal Labor Markets and Manpower Analysis* (Lexington, Mass.: Heath).

DOMINELLI, L., and MCLEOD, E. (1989), *Feminist Social Work* (London: Macmillan).

DONNISON, D. (1972*a*), 'Ideologies and Policies', *Journal of Social Policy*, 1: 97–117.

—— (1972*b*), 'Research for Policy', *Minerva*, 10: 519–36, reprinted in M. Bulmer (ed.) (1978), *Social Policy Research* (London: Macmillan), 44–66.

—— (1983), *Urban Policies: A New Approach*, Tract 487 (London: Fabian Society).

DORE, R. (1976), *The Diploma Disease* (London: George Allen and Unwin).

—— (1987), 'Citizenship and Employment in an Age of High Technology', *British Journal of Industrial Relations*, 25: 201–25.

DRYSDALE, G. (1869), *The Elements of Social Science: Or Physical, Sexual and Natural Religion*, 8th edn. (London: Truelove).

DUFFY, J. C., and PLANT, M. (1986), 'Scotland's Liquor Licensing Changes: An Assessment', *British Medical Journal*, 292: 36–9.

ECHOLS, F., MCPHERSON, A. F., and WILLMS, J. D. (1990), 'Choice among State and Private Schools in Scotland', *Journal of Educational Policy*, 5: 207–22.

EDITORIAL (1961), 'Euthanasia', *Lancet*, 2: 351.

EDITORIAL (1981), *Guardian* (15 Nov. 1981).

EHRENREICH, B., and ENGLISH, D. (1973), *Witches, Midwives and Nurses: A History of Women Healers* (New York: Feminist Press).

ELDERTON, E. (1914), *Report on the English Birthrate*, Part I: *England, North of the Humber* (London: Dulau and Co.).

ELKINS, S., and MCKITRICK, E. (1968), 'A Meaning for Turner's Frontier: Democracy in the Old Northwest', in R. Hofstadter and S. M. Lipset (eds.), *Turner and the Sociology of the Frontier* (New York: Basic Books).

ERBRING, L., and YOUNG, A. A. (1979), 'Individuals and Social Structure: Contextual Effects and Endogeneous Feedback', *Sociological Methods and Research*, 7: 396–430.

ERIKSON, R., and UUSITALO, H. (1987), 'The Scandinavian Approach to Welfare Research', in R. Erikson, E. J. Hanson, S. Ringen, and H. Uusitalo, *The Scandinavian Model: Welfare States and Welfare Research* (New York: M. E. Sharpe).

European Commission (1981), *Final Report from the Commission to the Council on the First Programme of Pilot Schemes and Studies to Combat Poverty* (COM(81)769), Dec.

European Commission (1988*a*), *Social Dimension of the Internal Market* (SEC(88)1148) Brussels.

—— (1988*b*), *Interim Report on a Specific Community Action Programme to Combat Poverty* (COM(88)621 final), Brussels.

—— (1989), *Community Charter of Fundamental Social Rights* (Preliminary Draft), COM(89)248, Brussels.

EVANS, K. (1990), 'Post-16 Education, Training and Employment: Provision and Outcomes in Two Contrasting Areas', *British Journal of Education and Work*, 3: 41–59.

FARR, W. (1842*a*), 'Population', in Appendix to the Fourth Annual Report of the Registrar-General of Births, Deaths and Marriages in England (London: HMSO), 85–90.

—— (1842*b*), 'Public Health in the Year 1840', in Appendix to the Fourth Annual Report of the Registrar-General of Births, Deaths and Marriages in England (London: HMSO) 128–31.

—— (1844), 'Public Health—1842', in Appendix to the Sixth Annual Report of the Registrar-General of Births, Deaths and Marriages in England (London: HMSO), 284.

—— (1856), 'Mortality of Women in Childbearing', in Appendix to the Seventeenth Annual Report of the Registrar-General of Births, Deaths and Marriages in England (London: HMSO), 72–4.

FEINBERG, S. E. (1980), *The Analysis of Cross-Classified Categorical Data*, 2nd edn. (Cambridge, Mass.: MIT Press).

FERLIE, E., CHALLIS, D., and DAVIES, B. (1989), *Efficiency—Improving Innovations in Social Care of the Elderly* (Aldershot: Gower).

FINCH, J. (1984), '"It's Great to Have Someone to Talk to": The Ethics and Politics of Interviewing Women', in C. Bell and H. Roberts (eds.), *Social Researching: Politics, Problems, Practice* (London: Routledge).

—— (1986), *Research and Policy: The Uses of Qualitative Methods in Social and Educational Research* (Lewes: Falmer).

—— (1989), *Duty Bound? Family Relations and Social Change* (Cambridge: Polity Press).

FINEGOLD, D. (forthcoming), 'Institutional Incentives and Skill Creation: Understanding the Decisions that Lead to a High-Skill Equilibrium', in Ryan (forthcoming).

—— and SOSKICE, D. (1990), 'The Failure of Training in Britain: Analysis and Prescription', *Oxford Review of Economic Policy*, 4: 21–53.

—— KEEP, E., MILIBAND, D., RAFFE, D., SPOURS, K. and YOUNG, M. (1990), *A British Baccalauréat? Ending Divisions in Education and Training* (London: Institute for Public Policy Research).

FISCHER, J. (1976), *The Effectiveness of Social Casework* (Springfield, Ill.: Charles C. Thomas).

FISHER, P. (1978), 'The Social Security Crisis: An International Dilemma', *Aging and Work: Journal on Age, Work and Retirement*, 24: 1—14.

FITZPATRICK, T. A. (1986), *Catholic Secondary Education in South-West Scotland before 1972* (Aberdeen: Aberdeen University Press).

FITZSIMMONS, S. J. (1981), 'The Transfer of Public Policy Research from the United States to the Federal Republic of Germany', in R. A. Levine, M. A. Solomon, G.-M. Hellstern, and H. Wollman (1981).

FLOUD, J. E., HALSEY, A. H., and MARTIN, F. M. (1956), *Social Class and Educational Opportunity* (London: Heinemann).

—— —— (1958), 'The Sociology of Education: A Trend Report and Bibliography', *Current Sociology*, 7: 165–235.

—— —— (1961), 'Introduction', Halsey, Floud, and Anderson (1961).

FLUDE, M., and HAMMER, M. (1990), *The Education Reform Act 1988: Its Origins and Implications* (Lewes: Falmer).

FOLKARD, M. S., SMITH, D.E., and SMITH, D. D. (1976), *IMPACT (Intensive Matched Probation and After Care Treatment)*, ii, The Results of the Experiment, Home Office Research Study, No. 36 (London: HMSO).

FOUCAULT, M. (1976), *Histoire de la sexualité*, i, *La Volonté de savoir* (Paris: Gallimard).

FOWLER, J. T. (1904), *Durham University, Earlier Foundations and Present Colleges* (London: F. E. Robinson & Co.)

FULTON, Lord, with HALSEY, A. H., and CREWE, I. (1968), *The Civil Service*, Cmnd 3638 (London: HMSO).

FURLONG, A. (1990), 'Labour Market Segmentation and the Age Structuring of Employment Opportunities for Young People', *Work Employment and Society*, 4: 253–69.

CAGE, N. L. (1989), 'The Paradigm Wars and their Aftermath: A "Historical" Sketch of Research on Teaching since 1989', *Educational Researcher*, Oct. 1989: 4–10.

GARLAND, D. (1985), *Punishment and Welfare* (Aldershot: Gower).

GARNER, C. L., and RAUDENBUSH, S. W. (forthcoming), 'Neighbourhood Effects on Educational Attainment: A Multilevel Analysis', *Sociology of Education*.

GASCOIGNE, J. (1989), 'Church and State Allied: The Failure of Parliamentary Reform of the Universities, 1688–1800', in A. L. Beier *et al.* (eds.), *The First Modern Society* (Cambridge: Cambridge University Press).

GELL, P. L. (1884), *Work for University Men in East London* (Cambridge: The Universities' Settlement Association, Fabb and Tyler).

GILHOOLY, M. L. M., BERKELEY, J. S., MCCANN, K., GIBLING, F., and MURRAY, K. (1988), 'Truth Telling with Dying Cancer Patients', *Palliative Medicine*, 2: 64–71.

GLASS, D. V. (1954) (ed.), *Social Mobility in Britain* (London: Routledge and Kegan Paul).

GLASS, G. V., MCGAW, B., and SMITH, M. L. (1981), *Meta-analysis in Social Research* (Beverly Hills, Calif.: Sage).

GLEESON, D. (1983), 'Further Education, Tripartism and the Labour Market', in id. (ed.), *Youth Training and the Search for Work* (London: Routledge and Kegan Paul).

GLEICK, J. (1987), *Chaos: Making a New Science* (London: Heinemann).

GLENNESTER, H. (1989), 'Swimming against the Tide: The Prospects for Social Policy', in Bulmer *et al.* (1989).

—— and HOYLE, E. (1972), 'Educational Research and Educational Policy', *Journal of Social Policy*, 1: 193–212.

GLOVER, R. W. (1981), 'Apprenticeship: A Solution to Youth Unemployment?' *Transatlantic Perspectives*, 5: 21–4.

GODDARD, E. (1986), *Drinking and Attitudes to Licensing in Scotland* (London: HMSO)

GOLDBERG, E. M., WARBURTON, R. W., MCGUINESS, B., and ROWLANDS, J. H., 'Towards Accountability in Social Work: A Year's Intake in an Area Office', *British Journal of Social Work*, 8, 257–84.

—— —— LYONS, J. L., and WILLMOTT, R. R. (1978), 'Towards Accountability in Social Work in an Area Office', *British Journal of Social Work*, 8/3: 253–88.

—— —— (1979), *Ends and Means in Social Work* (London: Allen and Unwin).

GOLDSTEIN, H. (1987), *Multilevel Models in Educational and Social Research* (London: Griffin).

—— (forthcoming), 'Multilevel Mixed Linear Model Analysis using Iterative Generalized Least Squares', *Biometrika*.

GOLDTHORPE, J. H. (1978), 'The Current Inflation: Towards a Sociological Account', in F. Hirsch and J. H. Goldthorpe (eds.), *The Political Economy of Inflation* (London: Martin Robertson).

—— (1980), *Social Mobility and Class Structure in Modern Britain* (Oxford: Clarendon Press).

—— and HOPE, K. (1974), *The Social Grading of Occupations: A New Approach and Scale* (Oxford: Clarendon Press).

GOODY, J. (1983), *The Development of the Family and Marriage in Europe* (Cambridge: Cambridge University Press).

GORDON, A. (1981), 'The Educational Choices of Young People', in O. Fulton (ed.), *Access to Higher Education* (Guildford: Society for Research into Higher Education).

Gordon, L. (1976), *Woman's Body, Woman's Right* (New York: Grossman).

Gottschalk, P. (1983), 'U.S. Labor Market Policies since the 1960s', University of Wisconsin Institute for Research on Poverty Discussion Paper # 730–83.

Graham, C., and Prosser, T. (1988), *Waiving the Rules: The Constitution under Thatcherism* (Milton Keynes: Open University Press).

Graham, H. (1983*a*), 'Do her Answers Fit his Questions? Women and the Survey Method', in E. Gamarnikow, D. Morgan, J. Purvis, and D. Taylorsen (eds.), *The Public and the Private* (London: Heinemann).

—— (1983*b*), 'Caring: A Labour of Love', in J. Finch and D. Groves (eds.), *A Labour of Love: Women, Work and Caring* (London: Routledge and Kegan Paul).

—— (1984), *Women, Health and the Family* (Brighton, Sussex: Harvester).

Grant, W. (1989), 'The Erosion of Intermediary Institutions', *Political Quarterly*, 60: 10–21.

Gray, J., McPherson, A. F., and Raffe, D. (1983), *Reconstructions of Secondary Education: Theory, Myth and Practice since the War* (London: Routledge and Kegan Paul).

—— Jesson, D., and Jones, B. (1984), 'Predicting Differences in Examination Results between Local Education Authorities; Does School Organization Matter?' *Oxford Review of Education*, 10: 45–68.

Gray, J. L., and Moshinsky, P. (1938), 'Ability and Opportunity in English Education', in L. Hogben (ed.), *Political Arithmetic* (London: Allen and Unwin).

Griffiths, R. (1988), *Community Care: Agenda for Action* (London: HMSO).

Guttsman, W. L. (1963), *The British Political Elite* (London: MacGibbon and Kee).

Hadley, R., and McGrath, M. (1980) (eds.), *Going Local: Neighbourhood Social Services* (London: National Council for Voluntary Organisations/ Bedford Square Press).

Halsey, A. H. (1970), 'Social Science and Government', *Times Literary Supplement*, 5 Mar. 1970.

—— (1972) (ed.), *Educational Priority* (London: HMSO).

—— (1974), 'Government Against Poverty in School and Community', in D. Wedderburn (ed.), *Poverty, Inequality and Class Structure* (Cambridge: Cambridge University Press).

—— (1977*a*), 'Towards Meritocracy? The Case of Britain', in J. Karabel and A. H. Halsey (eds.), *Power and Ideology in Education* (New York: Oxford University Press).

—— (1977*b*), *Heredity and Environment* (London: Methuen).

—— (1978), *Change in British Society* (Oxford: Oxford University Press).

HALSEY, A. H. (1985), 'Provincials and Professionals: The British Post-war Sociologists', in Bulmer (1985), 151–64.

—— (1986), *Change in British Society*, 3rd edn. (Oxford: Oxford University Press).

—— (1988), 'Schools', in id. (ed.), *British Social Trends since 1900* (Basingstoke: Macmillan).

—— (1989*a*), 'Only Disconnect: Law, Order, Social Policy and the Community', in Bulmer *et al.* (1989).

—— (1989*b*), 'A Turning of the Tide? The Prospects for Sociology in Britain', *British Journal of Sociology* 40: 369–70.

—— (forthcoming), *British Higher Education: The Decline of Donnish Dominion* (Oxford: Clarendon Press).

—— and TROW, M. (1971), *The British Academics* (London: Faber and Faber).

—— FLOUD, J., and ANDERSON, C. A. (1961), *Education, Economy and Society* (New York: Free Press).

—— HEATH, A. F., and RIDGE, J. M. (1980), *Origins and Destinations: Family, Class and Education in Modern Britain* (Oxford: Clarendon Press)

HANS, N. (1951), *New Trends in Education in the Eighteenth Century* (London: Routledge).

HARDING, S. (1986), *The Science Question in Feminism* (Milton Keynes: Open University Press).

HARGREAVES, D. (1982), *The Challenge for the Comprehensive School: Culture, Curriculum and Community* (London: Routledge and Kegan Paul).

HARMAN, H. H. (1976), *Modern Factor Analysis* (Chicago: University of Chicago Press).

HARRISON, B. (1971), *Drink and the Victorians* (London: Faber).

—— (1978), *Separate Spheres: The Opposition to Women's Suffrage in Britain* (London: Croom Helm).

HARTE, N. (1986), *The University of London 1836–1986* (London: Athlone Press).

HAUSER, R. M. (1970), 'Context and Consex: A Cautionary Tale', *American Journal of Sociology*, 75: 645–54.

HAVEMAN, R. H. (1982), in *Technical Report Series*, T-82.1. US National Commission for Employment Policy, Jan.

—— and SAKS, D. H. (1985), 'Transatlantic Lessons for Employment and Training Policy', *Industrial Relations*, 24: 20–36.

HAYEK, F. A. (1960), *The Constitution of Liberty* (London: Routledge and Kegan Paul), 29.

HEATH, A. F., and CLIFFORD, P. (1990), 'Class Inequalities in Education in the Twentieth Century', *Journal of the Royal Statistical Society*, ser. A, 153: 1–16.

HEATH, D. B. (1989), 'The New Temperance Movement: Through the Looking Glass', *Drugs and Society*, 3: 143–68.

HEESOM, A. (1982), *The Founding of the University of Durham* (Durham: Durham University Press).

HELLSTERN, G.-M., and WOLLMAN, H. (1981), 'The Contribution of Evaluation to Administration', in Levine, Solomon, Hellstern, and Wollman (1981), *Evaluation Research and Practice: Comparative and International Perspectives* (Beverly Hills, Calif. and London: Sage).

HENDERSON, V., MIESZKOWSKI, P., and SAUVAGEAU, Y. (1978), 'Peer Group Effects and Educational Production Functions', *Journal of Public Economics*, 10: 97–106.

HENNING, R. (1984), 'Industrial Policy or Employment Policy? Sweden's Response to Unemployment', in J. J. Richardson, and R. Henning (eds.), *Unemployment: Policy Responses of Western Democracies* (London: Sage).

HERBST, J. (1982), *From Crisis to Crisis: American College Government, 1636–1819* (Cambridge, Mass.: Harvard University Press).

HEYNS, B. L. (1978), *Summer Learning and the Effects of Schooling* (New York: Academic Press).

HEYWORTH, G. (Chairman) (1965), *Report of the Committee on Social Studies*, Cmnd. 2660 (London: HMSO).

HILL, M., and LAING, P. (1978), *Social Work and Money* (London: Allen and Unwin).

HILLIER, E. R. (1983), 'Terminal Care in the United Kingdom', in C. A. Corr and D. M. Corr (eds.), *Hospice Care: Principles and Practice* (London: Faber).

HINTON, J. (1974), 'Talking with People about to Die', *British Medical Journal*, 3: 25–7.

HIRSCHMAN, A. (1970), *Exit, Voice and Loyalty* (Cambridge, Mass.: Harvard University Press).

HMI (1978), *Primary Education in England: A Survey by HMI* (London: HMSO).

—— (1979), *Aspects of Secondary Schools* (London: HMSO).

HMSO (1968), *Children in Trouble* (London).

—— (1971), *Better Services for the Mentally Handicapped* (London).

—— (1975), *Better Services for the Mentally Ill* (London).

—— (1989), *Caring for People* (London).

—— (1990), *Crime, Justice and Protecting the Public* (London).

—— (1990), *Supervision and Punishment in the Community* (London).

HOFSTADTER, R., and METZGER, W. P. (1955), *The Development of*

Academic Freedom in the United States (New York: Columbia University Press).

—— and SMITH, W. (1961), *American Higher Education: A Documentary History*, i (Chicago: Chicago University Press).

HOLLINGSWORTH, T. H. (1969), *Historical Demography* (London: Hodder and Stoughton).

HOPE, K. (1984), *As Others See Us: Schooling and Social Mobility in Scotland and the United States* (Cambridge: Cambridge University Press).

House of Lords, 2nd reading of the University of Durham Bill, 22 May 1832, cols. 1209–18.

HUGHES, H. L. G. (1960), *Peace at Last: A Survey of Terminal Care in the United Kingdom* (London: Calouste Gulbenkian Foundation).

HUNT, A. (1968), *A Survey of Women's Employment* (London: Government Social Survey).

HUNT, J. M. (1961), *Intelligence and Experience* (New York: Ronald Press).

HUSEN, T., and KOGAN, M. (1984), *Educational Research and Policy: How Do They Relate?* (Oxford: Pergamon).

IGNATIEFF, M. (1989), 'Citizenship and Moral Narcissism', *Political Quarterly*, 60: 63–74.

INOUE, K. (1985), *The Education and Training of Industrial Manpower*, World Bank Staff Working Papers No. 729 (Washington, DC: World Bank).

Institute of Manpower Studies (1984), *Competence and Competition: Training and Education in the Federal Republic of Germany, the United States and Japan* (London: NEDO and MSC).

International Labour Organization (various years), *Yearbook of Labour Force Statistics* (Geneva).

JACKSON, M. P., and VALENCIA, B. M. (1978), *Financial Aid through Social Work* (London: Routledge and Kegan Paul).

JANOSKI, T. (1986), 'The Political Economy of Unemployment: The Formation of Active Labor Market Policy in the United States and West Germany', unpub. Ph.D. thesis, University of California, Berkeley. Published as *The Political Economy of Unemployment: Active Labor Market Policy in West Germany and the United States* (Berkeley: University of California Press, 1990).

JANOWITZ, M. (1972), *Sociological Models and Social Policy* (New Jersey: General Learning Systems).

Japan Institute of Labor (1979*a*), *Employment and Employment Policy*, Japanese Industrial Relations Series (Tokyo).

—— (1979*b*), *Labor Unions and Labor-Management Relations*, Tokyo: Japanese Industrial Relations Series (Tokyo).

JENCKS, C., SMITH, M., ACLAND, H., BANE, M. J., COHEN, D., GINTIS, H., HEYNES, B., and MICHELSON, S. (1972), *Inequality: A Reassessment of the Effect of Family and Schooling in America* (New York: Basic Books).

JENKINS, R. (1983), *Lads, Citizens and Ordinary Kids* (London: Routledge and Kegan Paul).

JESSOP, B. (1974), *Traditionalism, Conservatism and British Political Culture* (London: Allen and Unwin).

JOHANNESON, J., and SCHMID, G. (1980), 'The Development of Labour Market Policy in Sweden and in Germany: Competing or Convergent Models to Combat Unemployment?' *European Journal of Political Research*, 8: 387–406.

Joint National Cancer Survey Committee (1952), *Report on a National Survey Concerning Patients with Cancer Nursed at Home* (London: Marie Curie Memorial Foundation).

JOLLY, J., CREIGH, S., and MINGAY, A. (1990), *Age as a Factor in Employment*, Research Paper, 11 (London: Department of Employment).

JONES, K. (1989), *Right Turn: The Conservative Revolution in Education* (London: Hutchinson Radius).

JORDAN, B. (1974), *Poor Parents* (London: Routledge and Kegan Paul).

—— (1987), *Rethinking Welfare* (Oxford: Basil Blackwell).

KALLEN, D. P. B., KOSSE, G. B., WAGENAAR, H. C., KLOPROGGE, J. J. J., and VORBRECK, M. (1982) (eds.), *Social Science Research and Public Policy Making: A Reappraisal* (Windsor: NFER-Nelson).

KARABEL, J., and HALSEY, A. H. (1977), 'Educational Research: A Review and an Interpretation', in eid. (eds.), *Power and Ideology in Education* (New York: Oxford University Press), 1–85.

KATZENSTEIN, P. J. (1984), *Corporatism and Change: Austria, Switzerland and the Politics of Industry* (Ithaca, NY: Cornell University Press).

KAY, B. (1979), 'The DES and Educational Research', *Trends in Education*, 3: 22–6.

KELLER, E. F. (1983), *A Feeling for the Organism: The Life and Work of Barbara McClintock* (New York: W. H. Freeman).

KENDALL, G. (1989), 'Effective Learning', *Employment Gazette* 97: 521–5.

KERCKHOFF, A. C. (1974), 'Stratification Processes and Outcomes in England and the US', *American Sociological Review*, 39: 789–801.

KEYNES, J. M. (1936), *The General Theory of Employment, Interest and Money* (London: Macmillan).

KINNIE, N. (1985), 'Changing Managerial Strategies in Industrial Relations', *Industrial Relations Journal*, 16: 17–24.

KOGAN, M. (1970) (ed.), *The Politics of Education: Edward Boyle and Anthony Crosland in Conversation with Maurice Kogan* (Harmondsworth: Penguin).

KOGAN, M. (1978), *The Politics of Educational Change* (Manchester, Manchester University Press).

—— and HENKEL, M. (1983), *Government and Research: The Rothschild Experiment in a Government Department* (London: Heinemann Education).

KÜBLER-ROSS, E. (1970), *On Death and Dying* (London: Tavistock).

LANE, C. (1989), 'From "Welfare Capitalism" to "Market Capitalism": A Comparative Review of Trends towards Employment Flexibility in the Labour Markets of Three Major European Societies', *Sociology*, 23: 583–610.

LANSBURY, G. (1928), *My Life* (London: Constable).

LAPOINTE, A. E., and MEAD, N. A. (1989), *A World of Differences: An International Assessment of Mathematics and Science* (Princeton, NJ: ETS).

LASCH, C. (1977), *Haven in a Heartless World: The Family Beseiged* (New York: Brac Books).

LAURIE, A. P. (1934), *Pictures and Politics* (London: International Publishing Company).

LAZAR, I., *et al.* (1979), *Lasting Effects after Pre-school: A Summary Report* (Washington, DC: DHEW Publications).

—— and DARLINGTON, R. (1982), *Lasting Effects of Early Education: A Report from the Consortium for Longitudinal Studies*, Monographs of the Society for Research in Child Development, 47.

LEATHARD, A. (1980), *The Fight for Family Planning* (London: Macmillan).

LEE, D., MARSDEN, D., RICKMAN, P., and DUNCOMBE, J. (1990), *Scheming for Youth: A Study of YTS in the Enterprise Culture* (Milton Keynes: Open University Press).

LEE, G. C. (1963), 'The Morrill Act and Education', *British Journal of Educational Studies*, 12: 19–40.

LEES, R., and SMITH, G. (1975) (eds.), *Action-Research in Community Development* (London: Routledge and Kegan Paul).

LEONARD, P. (1968), *Sociology and Social Work* (London: Routledge and Kegan Paul).

—— *Personality and Ideology: Towards a Materialist Understanding of the Individual* (London: Macmillan).

LESTER, R. A. (1966), *Manpower Planning in a Free Society* (Princeton, NJ: Princeton University Press).

LEVIN, E., SINCLAIR, I., and GORBACH, P. (1989), *Families, Services and Confusion in Old Age* (Aldershot: Avebury).

LEVIN, M.A., and FERMAN, B. (1981), 'Youth Employment Program Successes: A Cautionary Tale', *Journal of Contemporary Studies*, 4: 53–69.

LEVINE, R. A., SOLOMON, M. A., HELLSTERN, G.-M., and WOLLMAN, H.

(1981) (eds.), *Evaluation Research and Practice: Comparative and International Perspectives* (Beverly Hills, Calif. and London: Sage).

Levine, S. B. (1983), 'Japanese Industrial Relations: What Can We Import?' (Madison, Wis.: University of Wisconsin), Industrial Relations Research Institute, reprint No. 250, from *Thirty-Sixth Annual National Conference on Labor* (New York: Matthew Bender & Co.), chap. 2.

Lewis, G., and O'Brien, M. (1987) (eds.), *Reassessing Fatherhood: New Observations of Fathers and the Modern Family* (London: Sage).

Light, R., and Pillemer, D. (1984), *Summing up: The Science of Reviewing Research* (Cambridge, Mass.: Harvard University Press).

Lindsay, K. (1926), *Social Progress and Educational Waste: Being a Study of the 'Free Place' and Scholarship Systems* (London: Routledge).

Lipset, S. M. (1983), 'Radicalism or Reformism: The Sources of Working-class Politics', *American Political Science Review*, 77: 1–18.

Lipsey, D. (1988), *Grassroots Initiatives* (London: New Society).

Llewellyn Davies, M. (1915), *Maternity: Letters of Working Women* (London: Bell).

Loch, C. S. (1895), *Charity Organization Review*, Aug. 1895.

Lofland, L. H. (1978), *The Craft of Dying* (London: Sage).

London Borough of Brent (1985), *A Child in Trust: The Report of the Panel of Inquiry into the Circumstances Surrounding the Death of Jasmine Beckford.*

London Borough of Greenwich (1987), *A Child in Mind: The Report of the Commission of Inquiry into the Circumstances Surrounding the Death of Kimberley Carlisle.*

Long, C. D. (1958), *The Labor Force under Changing Income and Employment* (Princeton, NJ: Princeton University Press).

Long, D. A., Mallar, C. D., and Thompson, C. V. D. (1981), 'Evaluating the Benefits and Costs of the Job Corps', *Journal of Policy Analysis and Management*, 1: 55–76.

Longstreth F. H. (1988), 'From Corporatism to Dualism? Thatcherism and the Climacteric of British Trade Unions in the 1980s', *Political Studies*, 36: 413–32.

Lukacs, G. (1971), *History and Class-Consciousness* (Cambridge, Mass.: MIT Press).

Lunceford, J. (1981), 'Hospice in America', in C. Saunders, D. H. Summers, and N. Teller (eds.), *Hospice: The Living Idea* (London: Arnold).

McAnear, B. (1955), 'College Founding in the American Colonies, 1745–75', *The Mississippi Valley Historical Review*, 42: 44.

McArthur, A. A., and McGregor, A. (1986), 'Training and Economic

Development; National versus Local Perspectives', *Political Quarterly*, 57: 246–55.

McIntosh, J. (1977), *Communication and Awareness in a Cancer Ward* (London: Croom Helm).

McIvor, G. (1989), *An Evaluative Study of Community Service by Offenders in Scotland* (Stirling: Social Work Research Centre, Stirling University).

—— (1990), *Sanctions for Persistent or Serious Offenders: A Review of the Research* (Stirling: Social Work Research Centre, Stirling University).

McKenzie, R. T., and Silver, A. (1968), *Angels in Marble* (London: Heinemann).

Mackintosh, M., and Wainwright, H. (1987) (eds.), *A Taste of Power: The Politics of Local Economics* (London: Verso).

MacLaren, A. (1978), *Birth Control in Nineteenth-Century England* (London: Croom Helm).

McPherson, A. F. (1973), 'Selections and Survivals: A Sociology of the Ancient Scottish Universities', in R. Brown (ed.), *Knowledge, Education and Cultural Change* (London, Tavistock), 163–201.

—— and Willms, J. D. (1987), 'Equalisation and Improvement: Some Effects of Comprehensive Reorganisation in Scotland', *Sociology*, 21: 509–39.

—— and Raab, C. D. (1988), *Governing Education: A Sociology of Policy since 1945* (Edinburgh: Edinburgh University Press).

Macrae, N. (1983), 'Future Life Styles', in E. Goodman (ed.), *Non-Conforming Radicals of Europe* (London: Acton Society Trust), 195–206.

Madsen, D. (1966), *The National University* (Detroit).

Main, B. G. M., and Shelly, M. A. (forthcoming), 'The Effectiveness of YTS as a Manpower Policy', *Economica*.

Malden, H. (1835), *On the Origin of Universities and Academical Degrees* (London), 146–7.

—— (1838), *On the Introduction of the Natural Sciences into General Education* (London: University College).

Mallar, Charles, *et al.* (1980), *An Evaluation of the Economic Impact of the Job Corps Program*, Project Report 80–06 (Princeton, NJ: Mathematica Policy Research).

Mann, M. (1985), *Socialism Can Survive* (London: Fabian Society).

Manning, M. (1984), *The Hospice Alternative* (London: Souvenir Press).

Mansbridge, A. (1948), *Fellow Men: A Gallery of England, 1871–1946* (London: Dent).

Marks, J., Cox, C., and Pomian-Srzedniski, M. (1983), *Standards in English Schools*, NCES Report No. 1.

MARQUAND, D. (1988), 'Richesse Oblige: The New Tory Wave', *New Statesman and Society*, 3 June 1988.

MARRIS, P., and REIN, M. (1974), *Dilemmas of Social Reform* (Harmondsworth: Penguin).

MARSDEN, D. (1986), *The End of Economic Man? Custom and Competition in Labour Markets* (Brighton: Wheatsheaf).

—— and RYAN, P. (1986), 'Where do Young Workers Work? Youth Employment by Industry in Various European Economies', *British Journal of Industrial Relations*, 24: 83–102.

—— —— (1989), 'Employment and Training of Young People: Have the Government Misunderstood the Labour Market?' in A. Harrison and J. Gretton (eds.), *Education and Training UK 1989* (Newbury: Policy Journals).

—— (1990*a*), 'The Structuring of Youth Pay and Employment in Six European Economies, in P. Ryan, P. Garonna, and R. C. Edwards (eds.), *The Problem of Youth: The Regulation of Youth Employment and Training in Advanced Economies* (London: Macmillan).

—— —— (1990*b*), 'Youth Employment and Modes of Regulation of the Youth Market', in P. Ryan, P. Garonna, and R. C. Edwards (eds.), *The Problem of Youth* (London: Macmillan).

MARSHALL, G., NEWBY, H., ROSE, D., and VOGLER, C. (1988), *Social Class in Modern Britain* (London: Hutchinson).

MARSHALL, T. H. (1950), *Citizenship and Social Class* (Cambridge: Cambridge University Press).

—— (1963), *Sociology at the Crossroads and Other Essays* (London: Heinemann).

—— (1972), 'Value Problems of Welfare-Capitalism', *Journal of Social Policy*, 1: 15–32.

—— (1981), 'Afterthought on "Value Problems of Welfare Capitalism"', in *The Right to Welfare* (London: Heinemann).

MARTIN, A. (1979), 'The Dynamics of Change in a Keynesian Political Economy: The Swedish Case and its Implications', in C. Crouch (ed.), *State and Economy in Contemporary Capitalism* (New York: St Martin's Press).

MARTIN, J., and ROBERTS, C. (1984), *Women and Employment: A Lifetime Perspective* (London: HMSO).

MASON, W. M., WONG, G. Y., and ENTWISLE, B. (1984), 'Contextual Analysis through the Multilevel Linear Model', in S. Leinhardt (ed.), *Sociological Methodology 1983–1984* (San Francisco: Jossey Bass).

MATRAS, J. (1966), 'Social Strategies of Family Formation: Data for British Female Cohorts Born 1831–1906', *Population Studies*, 19: 167–81.

MAURICE, M., SELLIER, F., and SILVESTRE, J. (1986), *The Social Foundations of Industrial Power* (London: MIT Press).

MAY, H. (1978), *The Enlightenment in America* (New York: Oxford University Press).

MAYER, J., and TIMMS, N. (1970), *The Client Speaks* (London: Routledge and Kegan Paul).

MEACHAM, S. (1987), *Toynbee Hall and Social Reform 1880–1914: The Search for Community* (New Haven, Conn.: Yale University Press).

MEYER, J. W. (1970), 'The Charter: Conditions of Diffuse Socialization in Schools', in W. R. Scott (ed.), *Social Processes and Social Structures: An Introduction to Sociology* (New York: Holt, Rinehart and Winston).

—— (1977), 'The Effects of Education as an Institution', *American Journal of Education*, 83: 55–77.

MILLS, C., and PAYNE, C. (1989), 'Service Class Entry in Worklife Perspective', SCELI working paper, 10, Nuffield College, Oxford.

MILLS, C. W. (1959), *The Sociological Imagination* (Oxford: Oxford University Press).

MITCHELL, J. (1971), *Women's Estate* (Harmondsworth: Penguin).

MOODY, T. W. (1958), 'The Irish University Question in the Nineteenth Century', *History*, 43: 90–109.

MOON, J. (1984), 'The Responses of British Governments to Unemployment', in J. J. Richardson and R. Henning (eds.), *Unemployment: Policy Responses of Western Democracies* (London: Sage Publications).

MORRIS, M., and GRIGGS, S. (1988), *Education: The Wasted Years? 1973–1986* (Lewes: Falmer).

MORTIMORE, P., SAMMONS, P., STOLL, L., LEWIS, D., and ECOB, R. (1988), *School Matters: The Junior Years* (London: Open Books).

MOSTELLER, F., and TUKEY, J. W. (1977), *Data Analysis and Regression* (Reading, Pa.: Addison-Wesley).

MOUNT, F. (1983), *The Subversive Family: An Alternative History of Love and Marriage* (London: Unwin).

MOURIAUX, M.-F. and MOURIAUX, R. (1984), 'Unemployment Policy in France, 1976–82', in J. J. Richardson and R. Henning (eds.), *Unemployment: Policy Responses of Western Democracies* (London: Sage Publications).

MYLES, J. (1989), *Old Age Pensions in the Welfare State: The Political Economy of Public Pensions*, rev. edn. (Lawrence, Kan.: University Press of Kansas).

MYRDAL, A. (1945), *Nation and Family* (London: Kegan Paul, Trench, Trubner & Co.).

NACHMIAS, D. (1980), 'The Role of Evaluation in Public Policy', *Policy Studies Journal*, 8: 1163–9.

The National Plan (1965), Cmnd. 2764 (London: HMSO).

NEVINSON, H. W. (1923), *Changes and Chances* (London: Nisbet).

NEWSOM, F. (Chairman) (1963), *Half our Future*, Report of the Central Advisory Council for Education (London: HMSO).

NIGHTINGALE, F. (1952) (originally 1859), *Notes on Nursing* (London: Duckworth).

NISBET, J., and BROADFOOT, P. (1980), *The Impact of Research on Policy and Practice in Education* (Aberdeen: Aberdeen University Press).

NORDLINGER, E. A. (1967), *The Working-Class Tories* (London: MacGibbon and Kee).

NORMAN, E. (1987), *The Victorian Christian Socialists* (Cambridge: Cambridge University Press).

OAKLEY, A. (1974), *The Sociology of Housework* (London: Martin Robertson).

—— (1981), 'Interviewing Women: A Contradiction in Terms', in H. Roberts, *Doing Feminist Research* (London: Routledge).

—— (1986), 'On the Importance of being a Nurse', in *Telling the Truth about Jerusalem* (Oxford: Blackwell).

—— (1989*a*), 'Who's Afraid of the Randomized Controlled Trial?' *Women and Health*, 15/2: 25–59.

—— (1989*b*), 'Women's Studies in British Sociology: To End at our Beginning?' *British Journal of Sociology*, 40: 442–70.

—— (1991), 'Eugenics, Social Medicine and the Career of Richard Titmuss in Britain 1935–1950', *British Journal of Sociology*, 42/2: 165–94.

OECD Labour Force Statistics (various years) (Paris: OECD).

OECD Manpower Statistics (various years) (Paris: OECD).

OECD Observer (1982), Paris: OECD Publications, 115 (Mar.).

OECD (1967*a*), *Manpower Policies and Problems in Austria*, Paris: OECD Reviews of Manpower and Social Policies, 5.

—— (1967*b*), *Manpower and Social Policy in the Netherlands*, Paris: OECD Reviews of Manpower and Social Policies, 6.

—— (1973*a*), *Manpower Policy in France*, Paris: OECD Reviews of Manpower and Social Policies, 12.

—— (1973*b*), *Manpower Policy in Japan*, Paris: OECD Reviews of Manpower and Social Policies, 11.

—— (1974), *Manpower Policy in Denmark*, Paris: OECD Reviews of Manpower and Social Policies, 14.

—— (1975), *OECD Labour Force Statistics 1962–73* (Paris: OECD).

—— (1978), *Youth Employment* Paris: OECD).

—— (1979), *Policies for Apprenticeship* (Paris: OECD).

—— (1985), *Education and Training after Basic Schooling* (Paris: OECD).

—— (1986), *National Accounts 1960–1984*, i. *Main Aggregates* (Paris: OECD).

O'Higgins, M., and Jenkins, S. (1989), *Poverty in Europe: Estimates of the Numbers in Poverty in 1975, 1980, 1985* (paper presented to a seminar on Poverty Statistics in the European Community, organised under the sponsorship of the European Commission in Noordwijkerhout, Netherlands, October).

Oldfield, A. (1990), 'An Unnatural Practice?: A Citizen's Guide', *Political Quarterly*, 61: 177–87.

—— (1990), *Citizenship and Community* (London: Routledge).

Olson, M. (1965), *The Logic of Collective Action* (New Haven, Conn.: Yale University Press).

OPCS (1970), *Classification of Occupations 1970* (London: HMSO).

—— (1988*a*), *The Prevalence of Disability Among Adults*, Report 1 (London: HMSO).

—— (1988*b*), *The Financial Circumstances of Disabled Adults*, Report 2 (London: HMSO).

Osborne, G. S. (1966), *Scottish and English Schools: A Comparative Survey of the Past Fifty Years* (London: Longmans).

—— (1985), *Religion and Education Qualifications in Northern Ireland* (Belfast: Fair Employment Agency).

Osborne, R. D. (1985), *Religion and Educational Qualifications in Northern Ireland* (Belfast: Fair Employment Agency).

Osterman, P. (1988), 'Rethinking the American Training System', *Social Policy*, 19: 28–35.

Oxford Review of Economic Policy (1988), 4/3: Special Issue on 'Education Training and Economic Policy'.

Parker, J., and Mirrlees, C. (1988), 'Welfare', in A. H. Halsey (ed.), *British Social Trends since 1900* (Basingstoke: Macmillan).

Parker, R. (1989), 'Social Work and Social Policy in the Twentieth Century: Retrospect and Prospect', in M. Bulmer, J. Lewis, D. Piachaud (eds.) (1989), *The Goals of Social Policy* (London: Unwin Hyman).

—— (1990), *Safeguarding Standards* (London: National Institute for Social Work).

Parkin, F. (1967), 'Working-class Conservatives: A Theory of Political Deviance', *British Journal of Sociology*, 18: 78–90.

Parlett, M., and Hamilton, D. (1972), *Evaluation as Illumination: A New Approach to the Study of Innovative Programmes*, Centre for Research in the Educational Sciences, University of Edinburgh, Occasional Paper No. 9. Reprinted in D. Hamilton *et al.* (1977) (eds.), *Beyond the Numbers Game* (Basingstoke: Macmillan).

Parnes, H. S. (1982), *Unemployment Experience of Individuals Over a*

Decade: Variations by Sex, Race and Age (Kalamazoo, Mich.: Upjohn Institute for Employment Research).

PATERSON, L. (1991), 'Trends in Attainment in Scottish Secondary Schools', in Raudenbush and Willms (1991).

PATERSON, R. and AITKEN-SWAN, J. (1954), 'Public Opinion on Cancer', *Lancet*, 857–61.

PATTEN, J. (1989), Published Letter to the Chief Probation Officer in Inner London, *NAPO Views*, Feb. No. 17.

PAYNE, G., and FORD, G. (1977), 'Religion, Class and Education Policy', *Scottish Educational Studies*, 9: 83–99.

PERKIN, H. (1969), *The Origins of Modern English Society, 1780–1880* (London: Routledge and Kegan Paul).

—— (1989), *The Rise of Professional Society: England since 1880* (London: Routledge).

PETCH, A. (1990), *Heaven Compared to a Hospital Ward* (Stirling: Social Work Research Centre, University of Stirling).

—— (forthcoming), *At Home in the Community* (Aldershot: Avebury Press).

PINKER, R. (1982), 'An Alternative View', in Barclay (1982).

—— (1989), 'Social Work: Retrospect and Prospect', in Bulmer, Lewis, and Piachaud (1989).

PLANT, M. A. (1982), 'Trends in Alcohol Consumption and Alcohol-related Problems in Britain', in A. Turner, *Nutrition and Health: A Perspective* (Lancaster: MTP Press).

PLANT, R. (1988), *Citizenship, Rights and Socialism* (London: Fabian Society).

PLOWDEN, B. (1967) (Chairman), *Children and Their Primary Schools*, A report of the Central Advisory Council for Education (London: HMSO).

PORTER, D., and PORTER, R. (1989), *Patient's Progress: Doctors and Doctoring in Eighteenth-Century England* (Cambridge: Polity Press).

POSTLETHWAITE, N. (1988), *Science Achievement in 17 Countries: A Preliminary Report* (Oxford: Pergamon).

PRAIS, S. (1986), 'Educating for Productivity: Comparisons of Japanese and English Schooling and Vocational Preparation', *Compare*, 16: 121–47.

—— and WAGNER, K. (1985), 'Schooling Standards in England and Germany: Some Summary Comparisons Bearing on Economic Performance', *NIESR Economic Review*, 112: 53–76.

PURCELL, J. (1987), 'Mapping Management Styles in Employee Relations', *Journal of Management Studies*, 24: 533–48.

PURKEY, S. C., and SMITH, M. S. (1983), 'Effective Schools: A Review', *Elementary School Journal*, 83: 427–52.

RACHMAN-MOORE, D., and WOLFE, R. (1984), 'Robust Analysis of a Non-linear model for Multilevel Educational Survey Data', *Journal of Educational Statistics*, 9: 277–93.

RAFFE, D. (1983), 'The End of the "Alternative Route"? The Changing Relation of Part-Time Education to Work-Life Mobility among Young Male Workers', in D. Gleeson (ed.), *Youth Training and the Search for Work* (London: Routledge and Kegan Paul).

—— (1984*a*), 'School Attainment and the Labour Market', in D. Raffe (ed.), *Fourteen to Eighteen* (Aberdeen: Aberdeen University Press).

—— (1984*b*), 'The Content and Context of Educational Reform', in id. (ed.), *Fourteen to Eighteen* (Aberdeen: Aberdeen University Press).

—— (1984*c*), 'The Transition from School to Work and the Recession: Evidence from the Scottish School Leavers Surveys, 1977–1983', *British Journal of Sociology of Education*, 5: 247–65.

—— (1985), 'Education and Training Initiatives for 14–18s: Content and Context', in Watts (1985).

—— (1987), 'The Context of the Youth Training Scheme: An Analysis of its Strategy and Development', *British Journal of Education and Work*, 1: 1–31.

—— (1988*a*), 'Modules and the Strategy of Institutional Versatility: The First Two Years of the 16-plus Action Plan in Scotland', in D. Raffe (ed.), *Education and the Youth Labour Market: Schooling and Scheming* (Lewes: Falmer).

—— (1988*b*), 'Going with the Grain: Youth Training in Transition', in S. Brown and R. Wake (eds.), *Education in Transition* (Edinburgh: Scottish Council for Research in Education).

—— (1990), 'The Transition from YTS to Work: Content, Context and the External Labour Market', in C. Wallace and M. Cross (eds.), *Youth in Transition* (Lewes: Falmer).

—— and TOMES, N. (1987), *The Organisation and Content of Schooling at the Post-Compulsory level: Country Study: Scotland*, Educational Monograph (Paris; OECD).

—— and WILLMS, J. D. (1989), 'Schooling the Discouraged Worker: Local-Labour-Market Effects on Educational Participation', *Sociology*, 23: 559–81.

RAUDENBUSH, S. W. (1988), 'Educational Applications of Hierarchical Linear Models: A Review', *Journal of Educational Statistics*, 13: 85–116.

—— and Bryk, A. S. (1986), 'A Hierarchical Model for Studying School Effects', *Sociology of Education*, 59: 1–17.

—— and WILLMS, J. D. (1991) (eds.), *Schools, Classrooms and Pupils:*

International Studies of Schooling from a Multilevel Perspective (New York and London: Academic Press).

Registrar-General (1944), *Statistical Review of England and Wales 1940* (London: HSMO).

—— (1972), *Statistical Review of England and Wales 1970* (London: HMSO).

REHN, G. (1985), 'Swedish Active Labor Market Policy: Retrospect and Prospect', *Industrial Relations*, 24: 62–89.

REID, W. J. and EPSTEIN, L. (1972), *Task Centred Casework* (New York: Columbia University Press).

—— —— (1977), *Task Centred Practice* (New York: Columbia University Press).

—— and HANRAHAN, P. (1982), 'Recent Evaluations of Social Work: Grounds for Optimism', *Social Work*, 27/4.

REIN, M. (1976), *Social Science and Public Policy* (Harmondsworth: Penguin).

—— (1983), *From Policy to Practice* (London: Macmillan).

REUBENS, B. (1970), *The Hard to Employ: European Programs* (New York: Columbia University Press).

Review of the Framework for Government Research and Development (1979), Cmnd. 7499 (London: HMSO).

REYNOLDS, D., SULLIVAN, M., and MURGATROYD, S. (1987), *The Comprehensive Experiment* (Lewes: Falmer).

RICHARDSON, J. J. (1982), 'Programme Evaluation in Britain and Sweden', *Parliamentary Affairs*, 35: 160–80.

RICHARDSON-KOEHLER, V. (1988), '"What Works" Does and Doesn't', *Curriculum Studies*, 20: 71–9.

RILEY, M., and FONER, A. (1968), *Aging and Society*, i. *An Inventory of Research Findings* (New York: Russell Sage Foundation).

ROBBINS, L. (Chairman) (1963), *Higher Education*, Cmnd. 2154 (London: HMSO).

ROBERTS, K. (1984), *School Leavers and their Prospects* (Milton Keynes: Open University Press).

—— and PARSELL, G. (1989), 'The Stratification of Youth Training', ESRC 16–19 Initiative, Occasional Paper, 11, City University.

—— DENCH, S., and RICHARDSON, D. (1987), *The Changing Structure of Youth Labour Markets*, Research Paper, 59 (London: Department of Employment).

—— SIWEK, M., and PARSELL, G. (1989), 'What are Britain's 16–19 Year Olds Learning?' Occasional Paper, 10, ESRC 16–19 Initiative, Social Statistics Research Unit, City University.

ROBSON, D. W. (1983), 'College Founding in the New Republic, 1776–1800', *History of Education Quarterly*, 23; 323–41.

Robson, D. W. (1985), *Educating Republicans: The College in the Era of the American Revolution, 1750–1800* (Westport, Conn.: Greenwood).

Rogers, F. (1913), *Labour, Life and Literature: Some Memoirs of Sixty Years* (London: Smith Elder).

Rohlen, T. P. (1979), 'Permanent Employment Faces Recession, Slow Growth, Aging Labor Force', *Journal of Japanese Studies*, 5: 235–72.

Room, G. (1986), *Cross-National Innovation in Social Policy* (London: Macmillan).

—— (1990), *'New Poverty' in the European Community* (London: Macmillan).

—— Lawson, R., and Laczko, F (1989), 'New Poverty in the European Community', *Policy and Politics*, 17: 165–76.

Rothblatt, S. (1983), 'The Diversification of Higher Education in England', in K. H. Jarausch (ed.), *The Transformation of Higher Learning, 1860–1930* (Chicago: University of Chicago Press).

—— (1974), 'The Student Sub-culture and the Examination System in Early 19th-Century Oxford', in L. Stone (ed.), *The University in Society*, i (Princeton, NJ: Princeton University Press).

—— (1982), 'Failure in Early 19th-Century Oxford and Cambridge', *History of Education*, 11: 1–22.

—— (1983), 'The Diversification of Higher Education in England', in K. H. Jarausch (ed.), *The Transformation of Higher Learning, 1860–1930* (Chicago: University of Chicago Press).

—— (1987), 'Historical and Comparative Remarks on the Federal Principle in Higher Education', *History of Education*, 16: 151–80.

—— (1988), 'London: A Metropolitan University?' in T. Bender (ed.), *The University and the City* (Oxford: Oxford University Press).

—— (1989*a*), 'The Idea of the Idea of a University and its Antithesis', *Conversazione* (Seminar on the Sociology of Culture, La Trobe University, Australia).

—— (1989*b*), 'Merits and Defects of the American Educational System', *Liberal Learning* 75: 22–5.

Rothschild, V. (Chairman) (1971), *A Framework for Government Research and Development*, Cmnd. 4184 (London: HMSO).

Rowbotham, S. (1972), *Women, Resistance and Revolution* (London: Allen Lane).

Royal Commission on Law Relating to Mental Illness and Mental Deficiency (1957) (London: HMSO).

Rubery, J. (1988), 'Employers and the Labour Market', in D. Gallie (ed.), *Employment in Britain* (Oxford: Blackwell).

Ruggles, P., and Marton, W. P. (1986), *Measuring the Size of the Underclass: How Much do we Know?* (Washington, DC: Urban Institute).

RUTTER, M., MAUGHAN, B., MORTIMORE, P., and OUSTON, J. (1979), *Fifteen Thousand Hours: Secondary Schools and their Effects on Children* (London: Open Books).

RYAN, P. (1983), 'Youth Labour, Trade Unionism and State Policy in Contemporary Britain', Faculty of Economics and Politics, University of Cambridge (mimeo.).

—— (forthcoming) (ed.), *International Comparisons of Vocational Education and Training* (Lewes: Falmer).

SABEL, C. F. (1984), 'Industrial Reorganization and Social Democracy in Austria', *Industrial Relations*, 23: 334–61.

SAINSBURY, E., NIXON, S., and PHILLIPS, D. (1982), *Social Work in Focus: Clients' and Social Workers' Perceptions in Long Term Social Work* (London: Routledge and Kegan Paul).

SAUNDERS, C. (1959), 'The Care of the Dying', reprint from *Nursing Times* (London: Macmillan).

—— (1961), 'Euthanasia', *Lancet*, 2: 548–9.

—— (1984), 'Evolution in Terminal Care', in C. Saunders (ed.), *The Management of Terminal Malignant Disease* (London: Arnold).

SCHARPF, F. (1981), 'The Political Economy of Inflation and Unemployment in Western Europe: An Outline', Wissenschaftszentrum Berlin: International Institute of Management, Discussion paper, IIM/LMP.

—— (1983), 'Economic and Institutional Constraints of Full-Employment Strategies: Sweden, Austria and West Germany (1973–1982)', Wissenschaftszentrum Berlin: International Institute of Management, Discussion paper, IIM/LMP 83–20.

SCHMID, G. (1985), 'Labour Market Policy under the Social Liberal Coalition', in K. von Beyme and M. G. Schmidt (eds.), *Policy and Politics in the Federal Republic of Germany* (Aldershot: Gower).

SCHMIDT, M. G. (1982), 'Does Corporatism Matter? Economic Crisis, Politics and Rates of Unemployment in Capitalist Democracies in the 1970s', in G. Lehmbruch and P. Schmitter (eds.), *Patterns of Corporatist Policy-Making* (Beverly Hills, Calif.: Sage).

SCHWEINHART, L. J., and WEIKART, D. P. (1980), *Young Children Grow Up: The Effects of the Perry Preschool Program on Youths Through Age 15* (Ypsilanti, Mich.: The High/Scope Press).

SCOTLAND, J. (1969), *The History of Scottish Education*, ii. *From 1872 to the Present Day* (London: University of London Press).

SCOTT SMITH, D. (1973), 'Family Limitation, Sexual Control and Domestic Feminism in Victorian America', *Feminist Studies*, 1: 40–57.

Scottish Education Department (1961), *Transfer from Primary to Secondary Education* (London, HMSO).

—— (1965), *Reorganization of Secondary School Education on Comprehensive Lines*, Circular No. 600 (Edinburgh: HMSO).

Scottish Education Department (1983), *16–18s in Scotland: An Action Plan* (Edinburgh: SED).

Sengenberger, W. (1982), 'Federal Republic of Germany', in E. Yemin (ed.), *Workforce Reductions in Undertakings: Policies and Measures for the Protection of Redundant Workers in Seven Industrialized Market Economy Countries* (Geneva: International Labour Office), 79–105.

—— (1984), 'West German Employment Policy: Restoring Worker Competition', *Industrial Relations*, 23: 323–43.

Sewell, D. H., and Hauser, R. M. (1975), *Education, Occupation and Earnings* (New York: Academic Press).

Shavelson, R. J. (1988), 'Contributions of Educational Research to Policy and Practice: Constructing, Challenging, Changing Cognition', *Educational Researcher*, 17: 4–22.

Shearer, M. H. (1989), 'Maternity Patients' Movements in the United States 1820–1985', in I. Chalmers, M. Enkin, and M. J. N. C. Keirse (eds.), *Effective Care in Pregnancy and Childbirth* (Oxford: Oxford University Press).

Sheldon, B. (1978), 'Theory and Practice in Social Work', *British Journal of Social Work*, 8: 1–22.

—— (1986), 'Social Work Effectiveness Experiments: Review and Implications', *British Journal of Social Work*, 16: 223–42.

—— (1987), 'Implementing Findings from Social Work Effectiveness Research', *British Journal of Social Work*, 17: 573–86.

Sherman, J. A., and Beck, E. T. (1979) (eds.), *The Prism of Sex: Essays in the Sociology of Knowledge* (Madison, Wis.: University of Wisconsin Press).

Shimada, H. (1977), 'The Japanese Labor Market after the Oil Crisis: A Factual Report (II)', *Keio Economic Studies*, 14: 37–59.

—— (1980), *Japanese Employment System*, Japanese Industrial Relations Series (Tokyo: Japan Institute of Labor).

Shinn, C. H. (1986), *Paying the Piper, the Development of the University Grants Committee, 1919–1946* (Lewes: Falmer Press).

Shorter, E. (1973), 'Female Emancipation, Birth Control and Fertility in European History', *American History Review*, 78: 605–40.

—— (1975), *The Making of the Modern Family* (New York: Basic Books).

—— (1984), *A History of Women's Bodies* (London: Pelican).

Sinfield, A. (1969), *Which Way for Social Work?*, Fabian Society tract, no. 393 (London: Fabian Society).

Slavin, R. (1984), 'Meta-analysis in Education: How Long has it been Used?' *Educational Researcher*, 13: 6–27.

—— (1986), 'Best Evidence Synthesis: An Alternative to Meta-analytic and Traditional Reviews', *Educational Researcher*, 15: 5–11.

Smith, B. (1986) (ed.), *Truth, Liberty, Religion, Essays Celebrating Two Hundred Years of Manchester College* (Oxford: Manchester College).

SMITH, D. E. (1979), 'A Sociology for Women', in Sherman and Beck (1979).

SMITH, D. J., and TOMLINSON, S. (1989), *The School Effect: A Study of Multi-racial Comprehensives* (London: Policy Studies Institute).

SMITH, E. A. (1916), *Allegheny—A Century of Education, 1815–1915* (Meadville, Pa.: Allegheny College History Company).

SMITH, G. A. N. (1975), 'Action-Research: Experimental Social Administration?' in Lees and Smith (175: 188–9).

—— (1983), 'Innovation, Experiment and Research in the Social Services', unpublished Sidney Ball lecture, Department of Social and Administrative Studies, Oxford.

SMITH, G., and JAMES, T. (1975), 'The Effects of Preschool Education: Some British and American Evidence', *Oxford Review of Education*, 1: 223–40.

SMITH, T. (1989), 'Decentralization and Community', *British Journal of Social Work*, 19: 137–48.

SMOUT, T. C. (1987), *A Century of the Scottish People* (London: Fontana).

SOLTWEDEL, R. (1984), *Mehr Markt am Arbeitsmarkt* (Munich: Philosophia Verlag).

SPENCE, M. (1973), 'Job Market Signalling', *Quarterly Journal of Economics*, 87: 355–74.

SPENDER, H. (1926), *The Fire of Life* (London: Hodder and Stoughton).

SPOURS, K. (1988), *The Politics of Progression*, Working Paper, 2, Post-16 Education Centre, University of London Institute of Education.

STACEY, M. (1981), 'The Division of Labour Revisited or Overcoming the Two Adams', in P. Abrams, R. Deem, J. Finch, and P. Rock, *Practice and Progress: British Sociology 1950–1980* (London: Allen and Unwin).

STANLEY, L., and WISE, S. (1979), 'Feminist Research, Feminist Consciousness and Experiences of Sexism', *Women's Studies International Quarterly*, 2: 359–74.

State Policy in Contemporary Britain, Faculty of Economics and Politics, University of Cambridge.

STEVENSON, O., and PARSLOE, P. (1978), *Social Services Teams: The Practitioners' View* (London: HMSO).

STONE, L. (1979), *The Family, Sex and Marriage in England 1500–1800* (Harmondsworth: Penguin).

SUMMERS, A. A., and WOLFE, B. L. (1977), 'Do Schools Make a Difference?' *American Economic Review*, 67: 639–52.

SUTHERLAND, Dame LUCY (1973), *The University of Oxford in the Eighteenth Century: A Reconsideration* (Oxford: Blackwell).

SYLVA, K., and SMITH, T. (1989), Evidence to the House of Commons

Education, Science and Arts Committee Report, *Educational Provision for the Under Fives* (London: HMSO).

TEMPEST, N. R. (1960), 'An Early Scheme for an Undenominational University', *Universities Review*, 32: 45–9.

THOMAS, P. (1985), *The Aims and Outcomes of Social Policy Research* (London: Croom Helm).

THOMPSON, P. (1989), 'NVQs—What they Mean', *Employment Gazette*, 97: 14–16.

THORPE, D. (1978), 'Intermediate Treatment', in N. Tutt (ed.), *Alternative Strategies for Coping with Crime* (Oxford: Blackwell).

TIBBITT, J., and CONNOR, A. (1988), *Social Workers and Health Care in Hospitals* (Edinburgh: HMSO).

TITMUSS, R. (1958), *Essays on the Welfare State* (London: Allen and Unwin).

—— (1971), *The Gift Relationship: from Human Blood to Social Policy* (London: Allen and Unwin).

TONRY, M. (1990), 'Stated and Latent Features of ISP', *Crime and Delinquency*, 36: 174–91.

TOQUEVILLE, A. DE (1832), *Démocratie en Amérique* (London: Saunders and Otley).

TORRENS, P. (1981), 'Achievement, Failure and the Future: Hospice Analysed', in C. Saunders, D. H. Summers, and N. Teller (eds.), *Hospice: The Living Idea* (London: Arnold).

TOWN, S. (1973), 'Action-Research and Social Policy: Some Recent British Experience', *Sociological Review*, 21: 573–98.

TOWNSEND, P. (1962), *The Last Refuge: A Survey of Residential Institutions for the Aged in England and Wales* (London: Routledge and Kegan Paul).

—— *et al.* (1970), *The Fifth Social Service* (London: Fabian Society).

Trades Union Congress (1989), *Skills 2000* (London: TUC).

TREBLE, J. H. (1979), 'The Development of Roman Catholic Education in Scotland, 1878–1978', in D. McRoberts (ed.), *Modern Scottish Catholicism 1878–1978* (Glasgow: Burns).

TROW, M. (1979), 'Aspects of Diversity in American Higher Education', in H. Gans *et al.* (eds.), *On The Making of Americans* (Philadelphia: University of Pennsylvania Press).

—— (1985), 'Comparative Reflections on Leadership in Higher Education', *European Journal of Education*, 20: 143–59.

TROYAT, H. (1967), *Tolstoy*, trans. N. Amphoux (New York: Doubleday).

TURNER, R. H. (1961), 'Modes of Social Ascent through Education: Sponsored and Contest Mobility', in A. H. Halsey, J. Floud, and A. A. Anderson (eds.), *Education, Economy and Society* (New York: Free Press).

—— and KILLIAN, L. M. (1957), *Collective Behaviour* (Englewood Cliffs, NJ: Prentice Hall).

US Department of Education (1986), *What Works: Research about Teaching and Learning* (Washington, DC).

UTTING, B. (1977), 'The Future of the Personal Social Services', *Social Work Service* (May), 25–30.

VANDENBROUCKE, G. (1987), *Poverty in Belgium* (Antwerp: University of Antwerp).

VELLEMAN, P. F., and HOAGLIN, D. C. (1981), *Applications, Basics and Computing of Exploratory Datas Analysis* (Boston: Duxbury Press).

WADE, N. (1939), *Post-primary Education in the Primary Schools of Scotland 1872–1936* (London: University of London Press).

WAGNER, G. (1988), *Residential Care: A Positive Choice* (London: HMSO).

WALBY, S. (1988), 'Gender, Politics and Social Theory', *Sociology*, 22: 215–32.

WALKER, A. (1982), *Community Care: The Family, the State and Social Policy* (Oxford: Blackwell).

WALKER, H., and BEAUMONT, B. (1981), *Probation Work: Critical Theory and Social Work Practice* (Oxford: Basil Blackwell).

WATTS, A. G. (1985) (ed.), *Education and Training 14–18: Policy and Practice* (Cambridge: CRAC/Hobsons).

WEBB, A., and WISTOW, G. (1987), *Social Work, Social Care and Social Planning: The Personal Social Services since Seebohm* (London: Longman).

WEBB, B. (n.d.), *My Apprenticeship*, 2nd edn. (London: Longmans, Green).

WEINER, R. R. (1981), *Cultural Marxism and Political Sociology* (London: Sage).

WEISS, C. H. (1979), 'The Many Meanings of Research Utilization', *Public Administration Review*, 39: 426–31. Reprinted in Bulmer (1986: 31–40).

—— (1982), 'Policy Research in the Context of Diffuse Decision-making', in Kallen *et al.* (1982: 288–321).

—— and BUCUVALAS, M. J. (1980), *Social Science Research and Decision-making* (New York: Columbia University Press).

WETHERELL, Sir CHARLES (1834), *Substance of the Speech of Sir Charles Wetherell before the Lords of the Privy Council on the Subject of Incorporating the London University.*

WHITE, K. R. (1982), 'The Relation between Socioeconomic Status and Academic Achievement', *Psychological Bulletin*, 91: 461–81.

WHITEHEAD, J. S. (1973), *The Separation of College and State: Columbia, Dartmouth, Harvard and Yale, 1776–1876* (New York: Columbia University Press), 53–89.

WHITEHEAD, J. S. and HERBST, J. (1986), 'How to Think about the Dartmouth College Case', *History of Education Quarterly*, 26: 344.

WHITFIELD, K., and BOURLAKIS, C. (1989), 'An Empirical Analysis of YTS, Employment and Earnings', IER Discussion Paper, 42, University of Warwick.

WHITING, C. E. (1932), *The University of Durham, 1832–1932* (London: privately printed).

—— (1937) (ed.), *The University of Durham 1937* (Durham).

WICKWIRE, F. B. (1965), 'King's Friends, Civil Servants, or Politicians', *The American Historical Review*, 71: 18–42.

WIEBE, R. H. (1984), *The Opening of American Society* (New York: Vintage Books).

WILENSKY, H. L. (1967), *Organizational Intelligence: Knowledge and Policy in Government and Industry* (New York: Basic Books).

—— (1976), *The 'New Corporatism', Centralization, and the Welfare State* (London and Beverly Hills, Calif.: Sage).

—— (1978), 'The Political Economy of Income Distribution: Issues in the Analysis of Government Approaches to the Reduction of Inequality', in J. M. Yinger and S. J. Cutler (eds.), *Major Social Issues: A Multidisciplinary View* (New York: Free Press).

—— (1981*a*), 'Family Life Cycle, Work, and the Quality of Life: Reflecting on the Roots of Happiness, Despair and Indifference in Modern Society', in B. B. Gardell and G. Johansson (eds.), *Working Life: A Social Science Contribution to Work Reform* (London: Wiley).

—— (1981*b*), 'Democratic Corporatism, Consensus, and Social Policy: Reflections on Changing Values and the "Crisis" of the Welfare State', in *The Welfare State in Crisis: An Account of the Conference on Social Policies in the 1980s* (Paris: OECD).

—— (1983), 'Political Legitimacy and Consensus: Missing Variables in the Assessment of Social Policy', in S. E. Spiro and E. Yuchtman-Yaar (eds.), *Evaluating the Welfare State: Social and Political Perspectives* (New York: Academic Press).

—— (1985), 'Nothing Fails like Success: The Evaluation Research Industry and Labor Market Policy', *Industrial Relations*, 24: 1–19.

—— (1992), 'The Great American Job Creation Machine in Comparative Perspective', *Industrial Relations*, 31.

—— and LAWRENCE, A. Y. (1979), 'Job Assignment in Modern Societies: A Re-examination of the Ascription-Achievement Hypothesis', in A. H. Hawley (ed.), *Societal Growth: Process and Implications* (New York: Free Press–Macmillan).

—— and TURNER, L. (1987), *Democratic Corporatism and Policy Linkages: The Interdependence of Industrial, Labor Market, Incomes and Social Policies in Eight Countries*, Research Monograph Series, 9 (Berkeley,

Calif.: Institute of International Relations, University of California, Berkeley).

WILES, P. (1974), *Distribution of Incomes, East and West* (Amsterdam and Oxford: North-Holland).

WILKES, E. (1981), 'The Hospice in Britain', in C. Saunders, D. H. Summers, and N. Teller (eds.), *Hospice: The Living Idea* (London: Arnold).

WILLIAMS, G. (1958), *The Sanctity of Life and the Criminal Law* (London: Faber).

WILLIAMS, G. P., and BRAKE, G. T. (1980), *Drink in Great Britain 1900 to 1979* (London: Edsall).

WILLIAMS, J. (1910), *The Law of the Universities* (London: Butterworth & Co.).

WILLIAMS, R. (1989), 'Awareness and Control of Dying: Some Paradoxical Trends in Public Opinion', *Sociology of Health and Illness*, 11: 201–12.

—— (1990), *A Protestant Legacy: Attitudes to Death and Illness among Older Aberdonians* (Oxford: Oxford University Press).

WILLMS, J. D. (1985), 'The Balance Thesis: Contextual Effects of Ability on Pupils' O-Grade Examination Results', *Oxford Review of Education*, 11: 33–41.

—— (1986), 'Social Class Segregation and its Relationship to Pupils' Examination Results in Scotland', *American Sociological Review*, 51: 224–41.

—— (1990), 'Pride or Prejudice? Opportunity Structure and the Effects of Catholic Schools in Scotland', in A. Yogev (ed.), *International Perspectives on Education and Society: A Research and Policy Annual*, ii. (Greenwich, Conn. and London: JAI Press).

—— and RAUDENBUSH, S. W. (1989), 'A Longitudinal Hierarchical Linear Model for Estimating School Effects and their Stability', *Journal of Educational Measurement*, 26: 1–24.

WILSON, E. (1975), 'Feminism and Social Work', in Bailey and Brake (1975).

WILSON, G. B. (1940), *Alcohol and the Nation* (London: Nicholson and Watson).

WILSON, W. J. (1985), 'The Urban Underclass in Advanced Industrial Society', in P. E. Peterson (ed.), *The New Urban Reality* (Washington, DC: Brookings Institute).

WINKLER, D. R. , 'Educational Achievement and School Peer Group Composition', *Journal of Human Resources*, 10: 189–204.

WINTER, J. M., and JOSKIN, D. M. (1972), (eds.), 'R. H. Tawney's Commonplace Book', *Economic History Review*, Supplement 5, Cambridge.

WITHERSPOON, S. (1988), 'A Woman's Work', in R. Jowell, S. Witherspoon, and L. Brook (eds.), *British Social Attitudes: The 5th Report* (Aldershot: Gower).

WITT, P. L., BAUERLE, C., DERONEN, D., KAMEL, F., KELLEHER, P., MCCARTHY, M., NAMENWIRTH, M., SABATINI, L., and VOYTOVICH, M. (1989), The October 29th Group: Defining a Feminist Science, *Women's Studies International Forum*, 12: 253–9.

WOOTTON, B. (1950), *Testament for Social Science* (London: Allen and Unwin).

—— (1958), *Social Science and Social Pathology* (London: Allen and Unwin).

YOUNG, M. (1965), *Innovation and Research in Education* (London: Routledge and Kegan Paul).

YOUNG, M. F. D. (1973), 'Curricula and the Social Organization of Knowledge', in R. Brown (ed.) *Knowledge, Education and Cultural Change* (London: Tavistock).

INDEX